WINGS AT SEA
— A Fleet Air Arm —
Observer's War 1940~45

Frontispiece: Swordfish L9775 with folded wings in *Ark Royal*'s aftermost lift before the war. The 36ft long aircraft fits into the 45ft lift. Folded wing span is a little over 17ft for a 22ft lift width. In this well posed publicity shot the lieutenant pilot and a stoker, who is one of the lift party (responsible for bringing aircraft up safely to the flightdeck to have wings spread, and to be manhandled into position on the deck, known as 'ranging') stand either side of the aircraft while the rest of the flightdeck party wait round the edge of the lift for the Swordfish to reach the deck. The rating looking into pilot's cockpit waits for the wings to be spread so that he can get into the cockpit and operate the brakes. The rating in the rear cockpit is either an air-mechanic or a telegraphist airgunner attending to the batteries, electrics or radio. Above and beside the aircraft's starboard wing are two of the ship's 6 8-barrel 2pdr pompom AA gun mounts with their associated director and rangefinder above.

Popperfoto

WINGS AT SEA
─── A Fleet Air Arm ───
Observer's War 1940~45

Gerard A Woods

CONWAY

MARITIME PRESS

TO COOKIE AND THE BLACK HAND GANG

© Gerard A Woods 1985

First published in Great Britain in 1985 by
Conway Maritime Press, 24 Bride Lane,
Fleet Street, London EC4Y 8DR

ISBN 0 85177 319 2

Designed by Dave Mills

Typesetting and page make-up by Swanston
Graphics, Derby

Printed and bound in Great Britain by R J
Acford, Chichester

Contents

Preface

This autobiography, written mainly in Canada to while away the long winter evenings in that inhospitable climate, is based on my wartime diaries, my flying logbook, neither of which, fortunately, ever got wet, and my memory, which, although considered above average by my friends, is by no means perfect. So, if a few errors in names, times and places have crept in, it is hoped they will be forgiven. Memories, like sundials, record only the sunny hours.

Special thanks are due to my course-mate and friend, John Hoare, author of *Tumult in the clouds* (Michael Joseph, London 1976) for his advice and encouragement. Among other former shipmates, many of whom at various times occupied the front seat, I am greatly indebted to Captain Terence Shaw DSC RN for correspondence, conversation and photographs; to Lieutenant-Commanders Patrick Chambers, Tony Dixon and Leslie Watson DSC; to Lieutenants John Moffat, David James, Peter Grant and Desmond Kelsall. My thanks are due to Commander Dennis White OBE RN and his staff at the Fleet Air Arm Museum, Yeovilton, as well as the Military Gallery in Bath for being able to use Robert Taylor's superb painting as a jacket. For cockpit illustrations of naval aircraft, I am indebted to Mr Ian Huntley of Aerocam. Many others, too numerous to mention, have added helpful information. Above all, my most grateful thanks to Betty Lethaby for her inspiration and unstinted help, advice and support.

Several books were consulted for confirmation and correction, notably *Ark Royal* by Admiral Sir William Jameson (Hart Davis, London 1957); *Pursuit* by Ludovic Kennedy (Collins, London 1974); *Find, Fix and Strike: Fleet Air Arm at War 1939-45* by John Winton (Batsford, London 1980); *Wings of the Navy* by Captain Eric ('Winkle') Brown CBE, DSC, AFC, RN (Pilot Press/Jane's, London 1980) and *Carrier Air Power* by Norman Friedman (Conway Maritime Press, Greenwich 1981). In the area of confirmation and correction, my thanks also to John Palmer, former Firefly observer, ever ready to help in the tiring business of research.

An addicted reader of maritime stories of exploration and adventure since boyhood, my curiosity increased in postwar years at a strange imbalance between the number of books written by pilots, compared with those written by other aircrew members. This seemed illogical, since observers, navigators, bomb-aimers, airgunners, even flight engineers, all went to the same places as pilots, suffering the same discomforts of cold, inclement weather, and occupational hazards such as boredom, flak, getting lost and airsickness. The immortal squadron song 'A 25' begins:

In the Royal Air Force, a landing's OK
If the pilot gets out and can still walk away.
But in the Fleet Air Arm the prospect is grim,
It's bloody hard luck if the pilot can't swim.

Even in a bawdy song, there's total lack of sympathy for any other occupants of what might be a multi-seater.

Fortunately, during initial training, it was impressed on us continually that we were seamen first and aviators second. I say 'fortunately', since in my 6½ years in the Fleet Air Arm, there were many occasions when it was suddenly realised that one was operating with incomplete, little, or no information at all as to what one was REALLY supposed to be doing, how it was to be done, or to whom one turned for information and/or help. The fact was that one had taken a manacled, blindfold pierhead-jump.

In unrehearsed situations, it was best to use one's commonsense, and NEVER to ask for instructions. Radio silence was usually in force, and if not, the chances were high that a fish-head or non-aviator would be encountered, with built-in prejudices against all who refused to believe that battles could only be won by 16in broadsides. The Admiralty was reputed to house a secret section known as 'Japes and Wheezes', whose planners, aspiring to be postwar novelists, conjured up near-impossible situations which they wished to try out before writing their books. Possibly because the Admiralty considered them more expendable, many observers were 'lurked' into complicated operations where flying was only part of the job.

This book attempts to describe some of the unusual situations in which a trusting young observer can find himself through not realising soon enough three of the most important of Murphy's laws:

(1) That almost every situation in life is easier to get into than out of.
(2) In crises which force a choice among alternative sources of action, most people will always choose the worst possible.
(3) No unselfish deed shall ever go unpunished.

An alternative title might well have been a line from the poetess Frances Cornford, in which she refers to Rupert Brooke as '... a young Apollo, magnificently unprepared for the long littleness of life...'. For that is how I remember so many contemporaries, who did not, alas, survive to celebrate their 21st birthdays. For the second time in 30 years the cream of a generation disappeared.

'Magnificently Unprepared' might also apply to those concerned with the defence of the British Empire, as it was then, who sent us off to fight powerful and ruthless enemies that had long been preparing for war. Hindsight is, of course, always 20/20, and it might be remembered that the United States was almost as ill-equipped as ourselves, but at least we gave them a breathing-space and our battle experience to speed up their readiness. Conversely, in this period, we had their unstinted support in the Lease-Lend programme. But much of this came too late to save the lives of experienced naval airmen, such as Eugene Esmonde VC, DSO, Hughie Hunter DFC, David Godfrey-Fausset, Sam Hankey, and so many other dedicated and gallant officers who, had we been given time to prepare, would almost certainly have been leaders in a far better equipped Fleet Air Arm.

For the truth is that the Top Brass of the Royal Navy between-the-wars simply did not understand the potential of the aeroplane as an offensive weapon. But the aeroplane wasn't new, and some Admirals of World War I *did* understand. As far back as 1917, Admiral Sir David Beatty, C-in-C of the Grand Fleet, had put forward a plan to put flightdecks on merchant ships, equip them with most of the 200 Sopwith 'Cuckoos' he had ordered and carry out a massive torpedo attack on the German High Seas Fleet, skulking in harbour since Jutland. Between the wars, naval budgets were strangulation-tight, and so far as is known, no British naval aviator commanded a first-line aircraft carrier in World War II, a fact certainly not true of the US and Imperial Japanese navies. In fairness, the years of indecision wasted between 1920 and 1937 in arguments with the RAF over the control of naval aviation, left only the short time between the handover in May 1937 and September 1939 for Their Lordships to get the Admiralty's aviation act together. In fact, insufficient time remained to recruit, assemble and train enough aircrew and maintenance personnel. Since coincidentally the RAF rightly demanded priority in production of fighters and bombers, it was totally impossible for the neglected British aircraft industry to satisfy both services' needs.

These, then, were the fundamental reasons why 225mph Skuas and 265mph Fulmars were sent to fight 350mph Messerschmitt 109s and 110s over Norway and the Mediterranean during 1940 and 1941. Our torpedo-bombers — Swordfish, Albacores and Barracudas — were all obsolete and overweight before they entered operational service, many gallant sorties notwithstanding. The US Navy, however, seized the 'Time-out' we gave them to invite private firms to submit aircraft specially designed for carrier operations, and at the end of World War II, the Royal Navy was flying American aircraft almost totally — Wildcats, Hellcats, Corsairs and Avengers. If only Esmonde, Hunter, Godfrey-Fausset and Hankey and their contemporaries had been granted time to combine their operational experience with our aircraft manufacturers' design skills, rather than have the Fleet Air Arm endure successive unsuccessful compromises such as the Albacore, Barracuda, Seafire and Sea Hurricane.

Alas, the most tragic words, so often repeated in the Fleet Air Arm during World War II were '... if only ...'.

8

Chapter 1
Blooded!

When I was a naval rating, it seemed that the Lower Deck got more than its share of being pushed around with little or no information as to changes of plan. But newly-commissioned and at the Royal Naval Air Station Donibristle, in Scotland, during October 1940 I had received three appointments to different squadrons in five days, each one cancelling the previous one. Obviously the Upper Deck suffered as well.

There was a war on outside, and with several contemporaries in 'the Pool', we were all anxious to get into operational flying. Our training as pilots or observers, which in the piping days of peace took up to two years, had been condensed into the minimum possible space of ten months. Yet here we waited apparently until someone in the Admiralty picked our names out of a hat. After training since August 1939 at Gosport, Belfast (where my flying instructor decided that his RAF pension would arrive before I went solo), Lee-on-Solent and Arbroath, I had qualified as an observer. Thence we had gone to the Royal Naval College at Greenwich to learn all about naval history, protocol, the duties of junior naval officers, and at mealtimes in the Painted Hall to boggle at the ladies on the ceiling, all of whom seemed to be suffering from acute mammalian abnormalities. This part of the course, normally two months, had to be crammed into two weeks. With all that apparent urgency, we wondered at the present delay.

Arriving at Donibristle, across the Firth of Forth from Edinburgh, on 21 October — coincidentally Trafalgar Day — I had received an appointment to join 830 Squadron in Malta, but with a catch – it was to be done the hard way. Hard-pressed by the Italian Air Force, the island was defending itself with the legendary three Sea Gladiators, and a handful of Hurricanes, the latter having been delivered by sea, flying from the Royal Navy's oldest purpose-built aircraft carrier *Argus*, with Fleet Air Arm Skua fighter/dive-bombers as escorts. My first job was to repeat this exercise, navigating an escorting Skua, an aircraft I had not yet seen, let alone flown in, with a pilot, Lieutenant Al Wright of the Royal Marines, whom I had yet to meet. On arrival in Malta, we would then join 830 Squadron's Swordfish torpedo-bombers, the island's only offensive force at that time. It all began to sound rather like a bad 'B' movie.

Hardly was the ink dry on my appointment to 830 Squadron than two days later, on 23 October, it was superseded by an appointment to 803 Fighter Squadron, at that moment re-equipping at Donibristle with Fairey Fulmars. Previously flying Skuas from *Ark Royal*, they were to join the new aircraft carrier *Formidable* for working-up trials, eventually to be based on Alexandria as part of the Mediterranean Fleet. At that time the Fulmar was the Navy's newest and fastest fighter, but like most naval aircraft built in Britain, was a compromise between two main types of duty. Adapted from the Fairey Battle light bomber, its main role was to be an eight-gun fighter, but a useful secondary function was also as a fast reconnaissance aircraft, to be sent over heavily-defended enemy territory where it would be suicidal to send the slower Swordfish or Albacore. For reconnaissance an observer or airgunner occupied the rear seat, but he had no rear guns. Speed was relied upon to extricate aircraft and crew from sticky situations. The Skua, even the Swordfish and the Walrus amphibian had rear guns. They were good for morale, if not for offence.

Dutifully I reported to Lieutenant Jasper Godden, the senior observer of 803. My first flight was with Petty Officer Gardner, an old hand, far too wise to take risks in a new aircraft until he had the feel of it. So we flew around the Kingdom of Fife, chatting on the R/T, making radio signals, identifying a few landmarks, and finally, after due warning, he performed a couple of cautious slow rolls. This was a new experience and the effect was rather frightening, as every particle of dust and all loose gear in the rear cockpit changed directions by 360 degrees twice. Most of the dust went unerringly into my eyes, all loose equipment striking me smartly around the head. Somewhat chastened, I lashed down everything prior to my next flight with Sub–Lieutenant Griffith.

'Muscle', as Griffith was known, was a physical fitness freak, playing every game better than average, was a weight-lifter, and for encores would walk on his hands. Most unfortunately this was not known to me when we first flew together, otherwise I might have been prepared, or at least not surprised, by his unadvertised loop. With insufficient speed in the downward first half, he stalled and spun, as I sat petrified in the back seat, clutching the hand-holds in terror, silently repeating my prayers and remembering that somewhere someone had told me that more deaths were attributable to flying accidents than in actual combat. Of course, 'Muscle' quickly recovered from the spin, but it was obvious to me that my skills in navigation, radio and gunnery could be put to much better use in the less glamorous but equally important world of torpedo-bomber-spotter-reconnaissance (TBR) aircraft, to identify the numerous duties expected of Swordfish squadrons.

So it was with considerable relief that three days after my appointment to 803, I was again re-appointed, this time to 820 Swordfish Squadron, recently disembarked at Machrihanish, Argyllshire on the west coast of Scotland, and due to re-embark immediately in the aircraft carrier *Ark Royal*. This already famous ship, which seemed to be continuously in the radio and newspaper headlines, was home briefly to collect spares, stores, and also to fly on her new Fairey Fulmars of 808 Squadron before returning to her station at Gibraltar in Force H.

The summer of 1940 was beautiful in Britain, and especially so in Scotland, where the absence of industrial haze makes the whole countryside so enchanting. Two of 820's aircraft had been flown to Donibristle, and I flew back as navigator to Lieutenant Bob Everett, Hughie Hunter flying the other aircraft. I had no idea how old the pilots were, but to me, not yet accepted in an operational squadron, they seemed ageless. Seasoned warriors, veterans of several campaigns (Norway, the South Atlantic, searching for the *Graf Spee*, Dakar, Oran and Malta convoys) these were real naval airmen, the larger-than-life types one saw on the silver screen. I navigated very carefully, checking drifts frequently and taking bearings on any recognisable towns and cities. Only after we had landed on the grass field at Machrihanish did I notice that Bob Everett had a writing pad attached to his knee with courses and times. Perhaps I had a long way to go before being accepted as a fully-fledged member of 820.

The airfield was owned and normally operated by Scottish Airways, who flew passengers in twin-engined De Havilland Dominies and Dragons around the Western Isles. The hangars were of canvas on wooden framework. A small hut was used as a squadron office, and the officers' mess was at the Uquadale Arms Hotel, a mile or so down the road. But inconvenient as it may have been, here I was, for the first time in an operational squadron, with sentries, salutes, fitters, riggers, armourers and all the trappings of war. The Real Thing.

I was helping to unload my tin trunk and cases from the rear cockpit, to find Everett regarding me with faint surprise, obviously not used to RNVR people and their strange ways, 'Leave it, Corporal Croad will have it sent to the wardroom'. Hughie Hunter said little, and later, when I knew him better, realised that he never did. A very taciturn and self-contained person, not given to expressing himself unless with one or other of his very close chums, 'Feather' Godfrey Fausset or Sam Hankey, or, alternatively, about to explode in anger, noticed only once or twice in the year that I knew him. Even flying with him for two to three hours would rarely produce more than a dozen sentences. A long time afterwards, when all of this trio had been killed, I learned that at the time we first met, Hughie was about 27, Robert Everett, who survived, was about 29. I was 21 at the time, but what a difference those few years made!

The Navy had taken over the Uquadale Arms, which was, to all intents and purposes, a wardroom with all the traditions. Several acquaintances reported in during the evening, one being Malcolm Ferguson, a midshipman pilot, who I'd first met at HMS *St Vincent*(Gosport), and later at Arbroath. We found a gramophone in the bar, and played a couple of records, Robert Everett transfixed us with a basilisk stare. 'This' he pronounced, 'is the wardroom'. Suitably abashed we played shove-ha'penny, very quietly.

Next morning at 0900 I stood waiting to report my presence to the Commanding Officer outside his office in the wooden hut. Hughie came along the corridor. ''Fraid you're wasting your time. We await our new Commanding Officer's arrival'. It seemed that the previous incumbent, Lieutenant-Commander Tony Yeoman, had met with a slight accident the previous evening, while paying a courtesy call on an H-class submarine in nearby Campbeltown harbour. On leaving, he had slipped on the gangway, and falling on to the First World War submarine's outer casing, had hit his head quite heavily. He was likely to be out of circulation for some time. Meantime Lieutenant-Commander James Stewart-Moore had been appointed to take us to sea. He was an observer, as was Tony Yeoman, and it was not uncommon to have observers commanding TBR squadrons. I did so eventually myself, and later in the war came across an observer commanding a single-seat fighter squadron (admittedly on very specialised photographic reconnaissance duties, where the initiative and decision-making was on the ground in the interpretation section).

More of the Squadron returned from leave, some with wives, spending their last few valuable days together in whatever local accommodation was available. Campbeltown was 4½ miles away. I know this because on one occasion I missed the last bus which left for the Uquadale at 2230, and in the wartime absence of alternatives, walked backed all the way. Campbeltown was extremely hospitable, and accustomed to the Navy, having been a 1914-18 naval base. It wasn't the West End, but it put up a social life of a sort. Paul Dick, a surgeon lieutenant, was marrying a local lady, and everyone in Argyllshire seemed to have been invited to the wedding, or even if not, were using the occasion as an excuse for a party. The Dick family were there in force, instantly recognisable by fair hair and healthy complexions; hardly surprising since the entire family, male and female, seemed to be, or wanted to be in the medical profession. I never saw Paul Dick again until 1971, when, with his wife, he occupied seats behind us on a flight to New Zealand. First I recognised his voice, then his face, after 31 years. The nuptial celebrations seemed to extend over several weeks, but in fact occupied only three days, ending in a very colourful ball, at which the whole of Argyllshire seemed to be present, and was the cause of my long walk to the Uquadale.

On 31 October we rendezvoused with the carrier off the little island of Ailsa Craig in the Clyde. It was a brisk, sunny morning, just right for decklanding, or so said Robert Everett, sensing the apprehension at my possible baptism. This was it then. This was what our training had all been about, and as we went into line astern preparatory to landing, I took one last look at the mist-shrouded hills on the Mull of Kintyre, wondering when, if ever, I'd see them again. Then, looking for'ard over Robert's shoulder to see the flightdeck loom larger and larger, was astonished to see him donning spectacles for the landing. Admittedly the Swordfish was a bit of an antique, but this was too much....

I had been on board *Ark Royal* before, when she was in Portsmouth harbour in February 1940, and we were in training at the Signal School. It was a working holiday, and guides showed us over the main parts of the ship. Today was different, and the sooner all aircraft were embarked and stowed, the sooner we would be off to Gibraltar, RNC Greenwich had taught us the routine on joining a ship, and I reported immediately to the operations room in the bridge, to find myself saluting Wolf Bentinck, Commander (Operations), previously in charge of the Observer School at Lee-on-Solent. A warm welcome, since he had given me an excellent report on completion of the course. However, the noise of aircraft landing in rapid succession indicated other priorities, and our joining 'pep talk' was postponed until next morning at the traditional 0900. Fortunately, the Executive Commander, R M T Taylor, had laid on guides to show us to our cabins, and my batman, Royal Marine Bandsman Farrow had my gear already down there, and was efficiently unpacking and storing it. A batman between two sub-lieutenants was indeed a luxury, and in Farrow we had a real 'treasure' who not only looked after us very well, especially during the first few weeks in this floating airfield (when getting lost on the innumerable decks was the rule rather than the exception), but was also bar steward in the wardroom. There he revealed another talent – of keeping aside any rare bottled produce for his 'young gentlemen' as he described us.

Ark Royal was a happy ship – that was instantly obvious. The old sailors' tale that 'your first ship is your happiest ship' was certainly true, and today I would say she was the finest ship I ever served in. From Captain C S 'Hooky' Holland down to the lowliest ordinary seaman, everyone seemed anxious to help, with none of the inter-departmental and inter-squadron rivalries, sometimes to the point of pettiness, which were encountered later in other ships. She was, of course, a very successful ship having taken part in almost every one of the naval campaigns so far fought. Her ship's company was experienced, every evolution being carried out with the minimum of noise, the mark of real efficiency and pride in one's ship.

Several course-mates were also joining today – 'Scruffy' Cooper,

13

'Flossie' Willet, Malcolm Ferguson, Bertie Ingham and Bill Urry. We lunched together with that hilarity which arises when young men embark on a new adventure, and also, because it was the last day of the month, with virgin wine-bills. The ship was still belting along at 20 knots, since although all aircraft were now embarked, squadron commanders had elected to give some of their new pilots more decklanding experience while we were still in relatively friendly waters. As we took our coffee in the ante-room on the port side of the ship, and under the round-down of the flightdeck, there was all of a sudden an unearthly metal-on-metal tearing sound, and something very large indeed flashed past the port quarter. Sirens were going, feet running on the flightdeck, and we joined the crush trying to get through the door to the quarterdeck. A Fulmar had gone over the side, and was just sinking nose first as the 'shepherd's dog' (a destroyer which always took station astern during take–offs and landings) rescued the pilot. Bill Urry of 808 Squadron thought it was 'Percy' Guy, and, so the unfortunate pilot turned out to be, restored to us next day with nothing worse than a severe fright, also experienced by Pat Stringer, the flightdeck officer who, batting Percy on, had to run for his life.

That afternoon, squadron commanders interviewed their new aircrews and paired pilots and observers. The custom was to pair 'sprogs' with experienced officers for the first few trips, after which the senior crews stayed as they were. 'Sprogs' played nautical musical chairs until the right chemical and personal balances were achieved. Robert Everett was second senior pilot and flew with Colin Ennever, senior observer. I was a little perturbed at flying with a pilot who wore spectacles in flight, though his record showed a long record free from prangs. In later years he set up and commanded the Decklanding School at Easthaven (Scotland) with great efficiency. So it was with some relief that I was paired initially with Lieutenant Alan Owensmith, a large and hearty extrovert, who, I seem to recall took about size 18 collar. Though himself an excellent all-round games player, he always found himself spending a disproportionate amount of time explaining to enquirers that though he looked the part, he was not the renowned international rugby player Owen-Smith. Alan, a survivor from the aircraft carrier *Courageous*, sunk a year earlier by *U-29*, had married while on leave. Unfortunately, the honeymoon in London had been interrupted by an air raid, with debris showering the marital couch. Some Italian aircraft had taken part in the raid, so that Alan's war in the Mediterranean now became a very personal feud, and on many occassions he was seen to press home his attacks with unusual vigour to atone for this unwarranted disturbance.

So the days as we headed south were spent mainly on preparing our aircraft for anticipated operations in the Mediterranean. Speed appeared to be of the essence in our passage to Gibraltar, with minimum time spent launching and recovering the continuous anti-submarine patrols that began before dawn and lasted until just after dusk. Five days after leaving the Clyde, we entered Gibraltar, my first sight of the Mediterranean. Although the palm trees exuded an exotic air, most of what we could see was limited to HM Dockyard, with no veiled ladies to excite us. No shore leave was granted, but the old hands assured the 'sprogs' that we were missing nothing, there being only three females on the Rock, all of them past it. It was also rumoured that a subaltern from the Black Watch garrison had recently won a jitterbug contest at the Alameda Gardens dance-hall partnered by a rock ape. Female, of course. Nothing strange about wee Hamish.

A few days later came the wonderful news of the Fleet Air Arm Victory at Taranto on 11 November, which crippled the Italian Fleet not only physically, but also morally, since it never ventured out again for the whole of the war, unless against known inferior forces. We must look to our laurels. The Eastern Mediterranean carriers, *Illustrious* and *Eagle*, had done a superb job, and unless we hit the headlines again soon, these minor leaguers would steal the limelight. Our chance, and my first operational attack, was soon to come.

It all started quietly enough on 27 November for myself and Murray Willcocks, (with whom I had now been crewed permanently) as we carried out the dawn Swordfish anti-submarine patrol. Apart from hunting for submarines, other aircraft were making a wide search for enemy surface vessels which might interfere with the passage of the convoy we were escorting from Gibraltar to the Sicilian Narrows, between Sicily and Tunisia, where it would be handed on to ships of the

A Fairey Fulmar fighter (Sub-Lieutenant Peter Guy RN) of 808 Squadron ditches over *Ark Royal's* port side into the Clyde on 31 October 1940. The decklanding control officer Lieutenant-Commander (A) G N P Stringer DFC, RN runs for his life. Ark Royal *photographer*

Mediterranean Fleet for the rest of the voyage to Alexandria. There was unusual anxiety to get us back on board at the end of our three-hour patrol, which had been relatively uneventful. Up in the operations room things were warming up as one of our reconnaissance aircraft had sighted main units of the Italian Fleet, or what was left of it after Taranto. There were thought to be two forces comprising two battleships and six cruisers, accompanied by destroyers. The range was too great for a gunnery action, though at this moment our heavies, with the Force H flagship battlecruiser *Renown* in the van, were closing the range as rapidly as possible, while the Italians surprisingly were doing the same. It seemed probable that the enemy was under the impression that they had a weakly-escorted convoy at their mercy, unaware that an aircraft carrier, a battlecruiser and four cruisers were a mere 40-50 miles away. The battleship *Ramillies*, with cruisers *Berwick* and *Newcastle*, which were approaching from the east en route for Gibraltar had also received the signal and were closing, having passed through the Sicilian Narrows ahead of the convoy we were escorting in the opposite direction.

Admiral Sir James Somerville in *Renown* decided that his best plan was to send off an aerial torpedo strike on the enemy to slow them down and enable our heavies to get in among them with their more effective armament. Eleven 810 Squadron Swordfish armed with torpedoes and led by Mervyn Johnstone went off at 1130. The sea was calm, the skies all but clear of the biplane's best friend – cloud cover – so Johnstone decided on the alternative, to attack out of the sun. To achieve this, he had to work round ahead of the Italians, a tedious job, since the top speed of a torpedo-laden Swordfish was about 80 knots, and to execute a good attack with the best hope of hits and minimum casualties, the first essential is to gain height. This was not only to avoid AA fire, but also gave the Swordfish a chance to work up a reasonable speed in the dive to make a fast run-in, drop and get away. The Italian lookouts did not spot 810, but suddenly altered course to the west, which threw the squadron into some confusion, as the pilots had now to re-select their targets, and having unreliable R/T, had to communicate by Aldis lamp or hand-signal. Nevertheless, despite all these complications and the presence of several inexperienced crews, the attack was pressed home. Italian warships are noted for their speed and manoeuvred desperately to avoid the torpedos, though 810 claimed one hit on the battleship *Vittorio Veneto*. A disappointed squadron returned to the carrier.

But the alarm had been raised and the enemy steamed away at full throttle for the shelter of the Sardinian coast and protection from their aircraft at Cagliari. With the safe passage of his convoy for the Eastern Mediterranean as top priority, Admiral Somerville broke off the action, and we prepared for the retaliatory bombing attacks that would inevitably follow. However, as a parting shot, 820 Squadron was armed with torpedoes and sent off at 1415, primarily to inflict further damage on any of the enemy ships whose speed might have been reduced by the attack from 810.

The memory of my first torpedo attack is a little hazy to this day, but it should be remembered that Murray, Leading Airman Finney and I had been on our feet since 0600 and had made already one three-hour patrol. Visibility was still splendid, and as we climbed to gain advantage from the slight cloud-cover, we could see the battleships tightly screened by nearly a dozen destroyers, with the cruiser force astern. To take advantage of the sun in attacking the battleships would have meant first flying over the cruisers, probably inviting the combined flak of both columns in our final approach to the dropping position, which must be steady, at 100 knots and 100ft, range 1000 yards or less. Not good odds on success, especially with the inevitable confusion that was bound to occur among relatively inexperienced crews. Stewart-Moore, the squadron CO, therefore elected quite rightly to attack the cruisers only.

We dived down from about 6000ft, the nine aircraft attempting a copybook attack, three on each bow and three amidships, so that whichever way the line turned, some ships must turn into our torpedoes. Though the flak was ragged and badly controlled, all cruisers turned in towards the dropping aircraft to 'comb' the tracks. It was rather frightening to be within 800 yards of a very large enemy ship for the first time, with every colour of heavy tracer coming straight at us as we held on to this steady course, our wheels almost skimming the wavetops. What I do remember is that extraordinary surge of relief as the tinfish dropped away and our aircraft, A4H, leapt into the air as we turned aft to open the range, our airgunner, Finney, loosing off a few pans of tracer and armour-piercing bullets (his own prescription) to keep the enemy heads down. Not satisfied with his position on the initial run, Alan Owensmith made a second attack before dropping, following this with a third attack on a cruiser's bridge with his single front gun, wreaking some vengeance for his interrupted nuptials.

As a finale, 800 Skua Squadron were flown off at 1500 to dive-bomb the cruisers, and we saw their attack just as we left the scene. Like 820, they scored no hits, though two near-misses damaged a cruiser. The inquest on our return and the squadron post-mortem emphasised the great need for continued practice in torpedo attacks. The skills were all there, but required a lot of co-ordination. When it is recalled that fully half the pilots in 810 and 820 had never before heard a shot fired in anger, there was no lack of courage, which, as Shakespeare reminds us in *King John* 'mounteth with the occasion'. There was, naturally, a wigging for Alan Owensmith for bringing his personal affairs into the war.

Since all of the action off Cape Spartivento had taken place almost within sight and sound of the *Regia Aeronautica* base at Cagliari, it was not surprising that we spent the rest of the day being bombed, but

Ark Royal alters course in the Western Mediterranean, November 1940, with a safety destroyer in her wake and a solitary Swordfish ranged aft. The cylinder at her masthead is the Type 72 aircraft homing beacon. *Lt R N Everett RN*

fortunately the enemy also seemed to be lacking operational experience. It was now the duty of the fighters and ships to protect us and the convoy. The eight-gun Fulmars had rare sport, breaking up wave after wave of Savoia Marchetti (SM) 79s, that very ugly tri–motored bomber and torpedo–carrier. Some were seen to jettison their bombs and head homewards at high speed, though others pressed on with the utmost determination. One high-level attack was a close call, several salvos straddling us, apparently the main target. Photographs taken from *Renown* show *Ark Royal* completely hidden by huge water splashes. The flightdeck was drenched, the ship rattled from truck to keel, but only minor damage was reported. Sub-Lieutenant Martin of 808 was unfortunately shot down and killed during the afternoon, but the arithmetic was good – 3 Italian aircraft were definitely shot down and several others were damaged.

During the bombing, which was rather frightening and very noisy, I again wondered if it were preferable to fly in fighters or TBRs as an observer. Despite the less violent aerobatics indulged in by Swordfish pilots, we seemed to have spent the whole day either flying or being bombed when not flying, while the fighters were – naturally – airborne during the bombings. This is over-simplification, of course. What, in retrospect, was most impressive was the shiphandling. Amid all the noise and confusion of battle, the babel of signals and messages coming in from aircraft, warships and convoy, the Captain conferred with the Executive Commander, 'Wings', the Gunnery Officer and Engineer

Commander, 'Chiefie' Oliver, as to when the ship should be turned into wind simultaneously to fly off a relief flight of fighters, and land on those who had exhausted fuel, ammunition or both. Sometimes it was prudent, but not always possible, to stop the ships' guns firing during take-offs and landings. Mike Tritton, a Skua pilot, had to land when all our guns were firing, confiding later that it was 'noisy'. Though I shall never have anything but the utmost admiration for the fighter pilots of the Royal Air Force, every day fighting the *Luftwaffe* for mastery of the skies, I have often wondered how many of them would have been able to fly from a moving airfield, fight and return to a completely different position, to land on a pitching deck with the possibility of being either bombed by the enemy or blasted by your own ship's guns when making the final approach. We had no 'Ace' system in the Fleet Air Arm, and the total number of victories scored were far fewer than those of the RAF, it being doubtful if more than a handful of naval fighter pilots could claim to have shot down more than five enemy aircraft in World War II. But the other dangers involved in being both sailor and airman – and there were those among us who found themselves masquerading as soldiers too – added up to an extremely exciting and dangerous life.

So, as the sun set on 27 November 1940, we had driven off the last of the Italian bombers and rejoined the convoy, which had been steaming peacefully, if warily, along. The merchant ships, loaded with tanks, guns and men for Malta and the Western Desert, were passed through the Narrows without loss, to join their new shepherds, the Mediterranean Fleet, next morning. Meantime, Force H, with *Ramillies*, *Berwick* and *Newcastle* in company turned about for Gibraltar.

My first brush with the enemy had made it an exciting day, and a long one, as I was also duty squadron officer. Making the rounds with PO Mortimer, the Squadron Regulating PO through the messdecks, heavy with tobacco smoke and the smell of bodies, as the portholes had been closed for the night, I looked at the seamen, stokers and naval airmen relaxing off watch, with that inner confidence which comes from a day's work well done. 'A rough day, Chief' I commented. 'Rough sir?' replied Mortimer, with all the pride of his 18 years' service, man and boy, 'You ain't seen nothing yet'. How right he was.

Blackburn Skua L fighter/dive-bomber of 800 Squadron aboard *Ark Royal* in harbour at Gibraltar, December 1940. *Author's collection*

Three Fleet Air Arm sub-lieutenants from *Ark Royal* at Gibraltar's North Front airfield, in January 1941. The author is next to L D (Bill) Urry and M T (Mike) Tritton whose Skua is behind. *Author's collection*

Chapter 2
Gibraltar and the
Western Mediterranean

Carriers were essentially functional. There was no gunroom, so that all officers except the Captain shared the wardroom and ante-room. However, certain unwritten laws had to be learned, certain codes of behaviour preserved. Sub-lieutenants and midshipmen kept to the after end of the ante-room, though this did not appear to apply to fighter squadrons. Lieutenants did not normally come down to our end unless it were to talk shop with a crewmate, or to play shove-ha'penny or chess. The forward end of the ante-room, port side, housed the bar, where most of the lieutenants foregathered whether it was open or not. A small annexe forward but midships in the ante-room was by some unwritten law preserved for the rubicund major of Royal Marines, the commanders of the various departments, the padre and the squadron commanders. Even in harbour, and with shore leave given, no junior officer ever, to my recollection, dared set foot or rest backside in that annexe. At sea, the marine major, who was also wine secretary, was always there when his infrequent regimental duties did not cause him to be absent from the wardroom.

There was a plentiful supply of newspapers and magazines, and because we were not too far from home in the Western Mediterranean, reasonably up-to-date. The padre was responsible for the distribution of reading material, and opened his newspapers to a scrupulously observed time-lag from date of publication. Sometimes annoying when one wanted to read the detail of some sporting event of which we had already learned the result on the BBC Overseas news, but in retrospect, probably good training. Mail service was very good both from and to Britain, no opportunity ever being missed of sending letters by any ship passing through, and any RAF long-distance aircraft. Gibraltar could have been a lot worse.

One duty I never liked was the essential censoring of the troops' mail. All officers' mail was similarly treated by the padre' and a duty trio of Commanders. One acquired insight into certain ratings. One, a rather scruffy individual, was capable of some quite moving poetry in praise of his lady-love, and a surprising depth of philosophy about the war and life in general, was revealed. I thought I knew all the love-codes, too, suffixed to letters or on the back of envelopes. One puzzled me – NORWICH – I thought and thought about this one, but couldn't make it out. SWALK meant 'Sealed with a loving kiss'; HOLLAND = 'Hope our love lives and never dies' but 'NORWICH' had me foxed. It might be a code.... One day, chatting with Leading Airman Finney, I asked in what I hoped was a sufficiently casual manner what the word meant. He looked at me with the sort of scorn that sixth formers reserve for new boys – 'Nickers orf ready when I come home'. Of course, how could I be so dim!

Ashore there was not a lot to do. The few hotels in those days, the Bristol, the Rock, and the Grand, were alternative places to drink and chat, usually with the same people we would chat with aboard, but occasionally one met chums from other ships. Most cruisers and larger ships carried a catapult aircraft with a pilot, observer and airgunner, but differed slightly from carrier crews in that, when not flying, they performed ships' duties, usually qualifying for an executive watchkeeping certificate. With a carrier in the force, their flying was of a token nature to ensure continuity of flying pay, which almost doubled the emoluments of junior officers and airgunners.

There were cinemas, the Naval Officers' Pavilion, or NOP, and other sports grounds. The pitches were generally as hard as concrete (what else would one expect on The Rock) and knee pads were mandatory in the soccer, rugger and hockey season, despite the very heavy rain which could fall between October and March, and on which the inhabitants depended for their drinking water. There was a yacht club and a rowing club. Jonny Hedges and I did try to get a clinker four-oared crew together, but were advised not to in case some Spanish rifleman's enthusiasm overcame his discretion as he peered down his sights just a mile or so away across the Bay. The yacht club did put on some splendid food on very limited equipment, the chef's seafood omelettes being quite famous throughout the garrison.

There were shops too, Saccone & Speed (wine merchants), the ubiquitous Gieves (tailors), and a whole host selling silks, jewellery, perfumes and kimonos, all the gee-gaws Jolly Jack buys for his loved ones when abroad. A number of cafes were available, but these were left to the NCOs and ratings, for whom Gibraltar had little to offer in the way of night life, and they didn't feel comfortable in the hotel bars. One of the larger cafes – the 'Granada' I think – sported a ladies' orchestra. From the distance it looked inviting, and Jack has to have someone to whom he can pour out his heart when away from home. Viewed close to, there was scarcely a peroxided hair under 50, the smiles as fixed as the dead expression in their eyes.

In those early days there was a dearth of feminine company, just a few nurses and occasional visitors from the British Embassy in Madrid, who normally stayed at the Rock Hotel. Sir Samuel Hoare was then ambassador to Spain, and kindly lent the Army an attractive and nubile member of his staff to take the female lead in 'French without tears' at the Garrison Theatre, where there was a full house for weeks. As the war progressed, first Women's Royal Naval Service (Wrens), then Women's Auxiliary Air Force (Waafs) and Auxiliary Transport Service (ATS) drivers arrived, partly as the Rock became safer from the threat of siege and bombing; but also because after the new airfield was built in 1942, Gibraltar became a very busy staging post for flights to North Africa, the Middle East and also to South East Asia and beyond.

When carriers came into harbour, aircraft would be flown ashore prior to the ship mooring, to land on the former racecourse at North Front. This did not exactly please the Spanish Government, who apart from claiming Gibraltar, felt that the racecourse was neutral ground. Though not exactly hostile, the Spanish Government had to incline towards the Axis powers who had helped General Franco establish his regime. British officers were allowed into Spain for the day in plain clothes, provided they carried a *carte d'identité*. It was usual to go to the Frontier Post on the Spanish side of the racecourse, and there hire a cab for the day between three or four, and for a modest outlay, the driver would await the pleasure of the hirers. The usual routine was either to go to a bullfight in La Linea or San Rocque, or with an early start spend the day in Algeciras, 25 miles away. It made a break from the war for a day, and there were good sherries, brandies and wines to sample as well as a meal just a little different from wardroom cooking, which, taken over a month, lacked a certain variety. This is not to denigrate naval cooks, who did a magnificent job, often with limited ingredients and tools, but Spanish cooking was something new to be experienced. Like most Englishmen, I have no time for bullfights. I have seen one, and never again want to see a magnificent animal butchered, however brave the toreadors, matadors and picadors appear to be. Give me cricket every time.

Here I must digress slightly, to hark back to training days in HMS *St Vincent*, when one evening, CPO George Oliver was reading the regulations to those about to go ashore. 'Remember', he admonished, 'To pay proper marks of respect, and salute all naval officers, whether in uniform or plain clothes'. At the end of his party piece, which included instructions as to what to do in the event of an air raid, plus sundry other pieces of personal wisdom and advice which will never be found in any official directive, Chiefie asked 'Any questions'. And of course, we had our official twit, as every course has. This one should have kept his mouth shut, because it cost us a few minutes' drinking time. 'Chief', enquired this worthy, 'How am I expected to recognise a naval officer ashore in plain clothes?' CPO Oliver gave him a glance of withering scorn, and placing his nose just a few inches from the questioner, barked 'A naval orficer in plain clothes, me lad, wears a navy-blue blazer, flannel trahsis, suede shoes, club tie, yeller pullover and a pork-pie 'at. Got it? Right any more bloody silly questions?'. And, of course, he was right as usual. That was our civilian clothes uniform, give or take a club tie or two, and this particular afternoon, the four of us so attired, were waiting at the Customs Station, our taxi driver revving his engine the other side in anticipation. We decided to go first to La Linea: Val ('Duke') Norfolk; Tony ('Maxie') Mayes; Mike ('Mullet') Lithgow and myself, being too junior yet to have a nickname. We drove off instructing the driver to halt at the first reasonable bar. 'Duke' and 'Maxie' started straight into their favourite 'horses' necks' – brandy with ginger ale and a twist of lemon or orange peel. In terms of taste innocuous, they slid down like oysters, but had rather a vicious delayed action – at least on me – and after three or four I was inclined to drowsiness, which didn't seem to be the point of the excursion. Sleeping was safer, more comfortable and economical back on board. But lured by promise of exotic delights to come I carried gamely on.

Some three hours later, 'Duke' and 'Maxie' were well away. Like myself, 'Mullet' was fairly abstemious, drinking only to be sociable in those days. Having acquired tickets for the corrida, and after a pleasant lunch, including more horses' necks for the two tosspots, our driver took us to the arena, vowing to make us *aficionados* for life. Our seats were quite good ones, though their situation, in full sun, was a trifle questionable.

The carnival of the parade over, we settled down to watch, but after a few minutes it became obvious that as a lifelong animal lover, I was not going to enjoy the scene at all. Not only was the bull at a permanent disadvantage, but the picadors' horses were also very emaciated, many showing still-unhealed wounds from previous corridas. 'Duke' and 'Maxie' decided that a little British sportsmanship was required and began to cheer for the bull. Our Spanish neighbours were at first amused, but the Iberians take their pleasures very seriously, and soon it became obvious that it would be better for us to make a dignified, if early, exit in one piece, rather than stay to incur the wrath of the crowd.

Cushions soon began to rain on us both from above and below. 'Duke' was misguided enough to start throwing them back, so that salvos began to descend upon us. More sinister was a cry of what sounded like 'bastardo inglesi'. Now my Spanish at that time was non-existent, and only a little better today, but there was no mistaking the fact that there were better causes to die for than this. After considerable pushing and pulling, 'Mullet' and I managed to get our now-aroused compatriots down the backstairs and into the taxi. Fortunately our driver knew his way around the town, and after dodging a few more cushions thrown from above, we decided to spend the rest of the day quietly and travelled on to Algeciras.

There we drank exquisite sherries and dined well, if early, since we had to be back over the border by nightfall. What was most interesting was that we sat in a very elegant restaurant, quite obviously English by our language if not our dress. At the next table were four Germans, of whom two had been imbibing the Teutonic equivalent of horses' necks for an equivalent period to our champions, and were being restrained by their more sober friends. We knew they were Germans and they knew that we knew. But we smiled at each other, and almost conversed at times. Even today I don't like Germans all that much, but there are some situations where you have to laugh, even if it nearly kills you.

The ship was going to sea without embarking the aircraft she had temporarily put ashore. The squadron CO sent for me and informed me that permission had been granted to demolish the grandstand of the racecourse. This was indeed good news, since when we flew from this grass field, with bald hard patches, it was not uncommon for a tyre to puncture, as all manner of foreign bodies lay just under the surface. Over a period of weeks, working parties had cleaned up the visible hazards, but Gibraltar is a rocky promontory, and the racecourse had been made in the last century by laying hundreds of tons of topsoil on the rock and sand underneath. A strong wind blows either east or west, and in the course of time a lot of the topsoil had been removed, showing the bare rock below. Our daily flights, now increasing, had caused more erosion, and it was likely that North Front would shortly have to take more twin-engined RAF aircraft flying to the Western Desert. For all these reasons, much more elbow-room was needed, and the grandstand's demolition was the first step towards widening the airfield landing area.

I was to contact Major Chalk of the Royal Engineers, an expert on demolition, who spent most of his time within the Rock, blasting out the 'galleries', as the tunnels were called. This was part of an ambitious programme to circumvent any attempt by the King's enemies to capture the Rock. In the event of such an expedition by, say, German paratroops flying from Spanish airfields, the entire garrison would move into the galleries where sufficient food, water, arms, radio and other equipment was stored to hold out until relief arrived. At least that was the story. Many are the legends surrounding this very patriotic colony, one of which is that if the Barbary apes are allowed to die out, Britain will lose possession of the Rock, thus the apes were looked after extremely well, encouraged to breed, and money was allocated officially for their welfare. Old wives' tales or not, the War Office was taking no chances. Perhaps the galleries were also part of the legend, though it always seemed to me that if General Franco wished to deny us use of the harbour at any time – which was Gibraltar's main purpose – he could do so simply by lobbing a few shells over each day. Had we replied by invading Spain (and our invasion record at that date was far from inspiring), the Germans would have had all the excuse needed to come to his aid. A sort of Spanish stand-off.

Meeting Major Chalk RE was an experience in itself. When finally discovered in army overalls, he pretended to be a lowly sapper, talking to me in some almost unintelligible West Country dialect. It was all part of his legend, he having been on the Rock since just before war commenced, making himself so invaluable that he was virtually a prisoner. His repertoire of stories and practical jokes was unending. One which will stand repetition was his habit of firing his daily explosions simultaneously so as not to upset the troops and radio installations. One batch were set off at 0800, the second at 1600, except Sunday. Having trained his subordinates well, 'Chalkie' would wander back to the mess just before the appointed hour, and as the charges were detonated, unsuspecting transient officers would nearly jump out of their skins as they imagined the noise to be bombs dropping. 'Chalkie' would, of course, be quite unperturbed, and when the ashen-faced visitor enquired 'Jesus! What was that?', would reply 'What was what? I didn't hear anything'. A variation was on Sundays, when there were no explosions planned normally. 'Chalkie' would sit in the mess among the regulars, and when, at 0800 and 1600 nothing happened, would leap into the air screaming 'Christ! What was that silence?' Some said he was 'Rock Happy', but I am convinced that only this way could he retain his sanity.

'Chalkie' was a great tutor, and apart from a few practical jokes, mainly juggling with sticks of dynamite and tossing a hand-grenade in the air, with the pin between his teeth, taught us all we needed to know to blow up the grandstand. Prior to the landings in North Africa in November 1942, an enormous concrete runway was built, extending on piles several hundred yards into Algeciras Bay, to take the large numbers of fighters and multi-engined bombers required for the invasion. It seemed almost unbelievable that two years earlier we had to blow up the grandstand to make room for a few Blenheims and Wellingtons.

Christmas Day overseas is something special to the Navy. *Ark Royal*, being a happy ship, was busy with preparations, since we were back in harbour on Christmas Eve, with the usual warm-up party commencing, and developing later into a huge wrestling match, juniors versus seniors. Somewhere in the middle of it, we suddenly found Marine Lieutenant Hogg, wearing his beautiful full dress trousers. Obviously these had to be removed. And were. Debagging then became contagious as each squadron debagged its commanding officer. It was always suspected that Gieves, the naval tailors, instigated these annual rites, since a great deal of uniform repairs were necessary afterwards.

On Christmas Day Admiral Somerville visited every ship under his command, saying a few informal and encouraging words to ships' companies. He stopped in our wardroom for a drink, and, as usual, spent more time chatting with junior officers than with seniors, or so it seemed. This, his Flag Lieutenant explained, was because he wanted to know what really happened on the last operation. Above all, Sir James spent much time with those in the less glamorous, but usually vital departments, such as the engineers and deck handling officers, whose unremitting efficiency contributed enormously to our successes. A particular confidant of the Admiral was Midshipman 'Scruffy' Cooper, not yet 19, an observer, and though studiously polite, chatting away easily like a son to his father. Such was the wonderful spirit everywhere in Force H.

A wardroom tradition in *Ark Royal* was the Christmas tree. Each officer drew a name from a hat, and purchased a present for the one named. Being anonymous, the system enabled subtle hints to be dropped or practical jokes to be played. One 'smoothie', much given to admiring himself in the anteroom mirror received a powder puff; another, whose ablutions were observed to be rather cursory, opened a twin pack of Lifebuoy carbolic toilet soap. Nothing was vicious, and with outlay limited to two shillings per present, great inventiveness was called for. At that time I was having great difficulty encouraging my first beard to grow. My present? A small packet of fertiliser. Expecting a speech from the Admiral, we got one, but not the one expected. The German heavy cruiser *Hipper* had emerged from her base at Brest, attacking a southbound convoy some 700 miles west of Cape Finisterre, the northwest tip of Spain. Though engaged and driven off by the escorting cruisers, *Hipper* was fast, heavily armed and still in the area. Force H would have to deal with the problem, so with a sigh, we belayed Christmas and prepared for sea.

At that time, and indeed throughout the war, there was a number of RAF maintenance ranks still serving in the Fleet Air Arm. There was considerable advantage in this, as the Navy was still short of skilled categories, and for the RAF men, their naval time counted as 'time and a half', thus ensuring a longer home posting on relief. For some strange and unknown reason, probably an old Air Council Instruction, RAF men were allowed shore leave if their ship were in harbour on Christmas Day. The RAF trio from 820 Squadron, Corporals Croad, Lemon and Leading Aircraftman Hanson, along with friends from other squadrons were ashore somewhere in Gibraltar. The Regulating PO was sent ashore to round them up, but had not returned by the time we had singled up wires and had been taken in tow by the tug. Before leaving the West Mole they were in sight in rollicking mood and being shepherded aboard a commandeered motor launch by the RPO. A boat boom was lowered on *Ark Royal's* starboard side with Jacobs ladders streaming. The launch's coxswain brought his charges underneath the boom, and up they scrambled, feeling neither pain nor fear.

As usual, by the time we reached the area where the attack had taken place, *Hipper* had disappeared towards Brest, safe under *Luftwaffe* cover. We spent several days searching for German supply ships, known to frequent this area to refuel U-boats, but seeing nothing, returned to Gibraltar. 'Flaps' of this type occurred frequently, as the Atlantic coast of France provided airfields for the giant Focke-Wulf FW 200 'Kondors' – four-engined long-distance maritime reconnaissance aircraft, whose radius easily covered the area between the Equator and the Arctic. They or a U-boat would sight a convoy or other target and the nearest enemy unit would be instructed to attack. With land, sea and air battles hotting up in the Eastern Mediterranean, our supply lines were long, our escort strength insufficiently strong, and our merchant shipping losses correspondingly heavy. Force H would be called upon again and again to perform its fire brigade act.

The year 1941 came in with a full gale throughout the Straits, causing several merchantment to drag their anchors in harbour, and one, *Northern Prince*, ran ashore. Three other ships and a tug grounded also, but were towed clear. My afternoon watch that day was fairly uneventful, but the Middle Watch, midnight to 0400 was in a violent gale, very wet and full of incident. Huge catamarans used for loading and unloading ships, ships' boats, and even submarines were breaking their moorings. Some destroyers, submarines and small ships put out into the bay to ride out the storm and next morning found most ships recovering their boats and lost gear. Although *Northern Prince* could not join the convoy on the next 'club run' through the Narrows, her troops and stores were distributed among the remaining four ships bound for Malta and the Piraeus, delaying the convoy's departure for several days. Several course-mates were in the convoy, Bob Mancus in the old carrier HMS *Argus*, Barney Rowland the irrepressible Liverpudlian philosopher, and my very close friend, Paddy McGrath of the huge head and matching appetite, were both in *Northern Prince* en route to HMS *Eagle* at Alexandria. To complete the reunion, Jock Moffat arrived to join 818 Squadron in *Ark Royal*. That week we dined in a different ship every night.

Mancus, a slim young man of lugubrious mien, had a delightful self-mocking humour. In the original photograph of No 8A Pilots' course as we left *St Vincent*, he had positioned himself next to the tallest man on the course, a huge fellow named Meyer, later killed while at Elementary Flying School. The two central figures on this photograph were ever afterwards referred to as 'Before and After the St Vincent Course'. The quick wit of Barney, Paddy's gamey stories and the highland profundity of Jock kept us talking until very late. It was Bob Mancus' opinion that the hearty appetites of both Paddy and Jock derived from a serpentine ability to unhinge the lower jaw, since he noticed that neither spoke while eating.

Leaving Gibraltar at 0900 on 7 January, we feigned passage into the Atlantic, doubling back through the Straits into the Mediterranean at night. It is not known if this confused the Axis spies in Algeciras and Tarifa, it certainly confused a lot of Spanish fishermen, in the midst of whose night operations we appeared from time to time. Two days followed of anti-submarine patrols and reconnaissance ahead of our precious convoy, sweeping 180 degrees ahead all the way. On deck we had four aircraft for 821 Squadron, long-range Swordfish to fly to Alexandria via Malta, eventually to work with the ground forces in the desert. They flew off at dawn on 8 January.

While a search was covering the area between Sardinia and the Skerki Bank, known for obvious reasons as 'Bomb Alley', one of our Swordfish sighted two *Southampton* class cruisers sent ahead of the Mediterranean Fleet to meet the convoy and to shepherd it through the Narrows. Mistaking them for enemy units, the observer signalled an Enemy Sighting Report, which probably had grave consequences next day. A further delay was occasioned when René Goddard forced-landed in one of 818's Swordfish, returning crews being signalled to look for them. Murray Willcocks and I discovered them in their yellow dinghy, their aircraft having disappeared, and we directed a destroyer to the rescue, extending our flying time by 90 minutes. We landed on after 4½ hours in the air, our gallant Pegasus engine stopping as we taxied on to the for'ard lift. A very close call!

Probably intercepting the inaccurate Enemy Report, the Italian bombers arrived shortly after lunch, but as they were detected at 50 miles' range by the cruiser *Sheffield*'s radar, we had ample time to scramble our Fulmars which broke up the high-level formation of SM 79s without their scoring any direct hits. Successive waves were similarly dealt with, and two CR 42 Fiat biplane fighters were shot down. Again, no hits, though considerable trepidation was caused by some very near misses. Throughout the remainder of the day, shadowers were intercepted and driven off, and no major attacks ensued. At dusk, with the escorted convoy passing through Bomb Alley to meet the strong Mediterranean Fleet next dawn, 10 January, we made a U-turn for Gibraltar.

Admiral Cunningham, C-in-C Mediterranean, had brought a very strong force to meet this important convoy. Unknown to him, a strong force of Junkers 88 and 87 dive-bombers, Heinkel 111 level bombers and Messerschmitt 110 long-range fighters had moved into the Sicilian airfields a few days earlier and had not been detected by Malta's reconnaissance flights. The aim of *Fliegerkorps X* was to eliminate, or at least to limit the effectiveness of Malta and the Mediterranean Fleet, so that their own convoys could deliver men and stores to the Italian troops, at present on the run, with Bardia captured recently by British forces. The *Luftwaffe's* attention would obviously be centred on the carrier *Illustrious*, which, with *Eagle*, had practically snuffed out the Italian Fleet two months earlier at Taranto.

Concentrating on *Illustrious*, 40 Ju88s and 87s struck with skill and determination, scoring six hits with heavy bombs in a few minutes. Her flightdeck wrecked, her lifts blown out and steering gear disabled, on fire and with 200 casualties, she could no longer operate as a carrier, barely as a ship. Steering on engines alone, she managed to evade the coup de grâce, and finally limped into Malta. The merchant ships with their vital cargoes and troops eventually arrived at their destinations unscathed, though *Southampton* was sunk next day by Ju87 Stuka dive-bombers.

Temporary repairs in Malta, effected between intervals of very persistent bombing, enabled *Illustrious* to go to Alexandria, where she was patched up sufficiently to go to the United States for a complete refit. Her absence for the best part of a year threw a spanner into the works for *Ark Royal* which was having severe boiler trouble. It had been planned that *Formidable*, now properly worked up, would relieve *Ark* at Gibraltar, while we went home for repairs. This would now have to be done by our own and Dockyard engineers in Gibraltar, while *Formidable* relieved *Illustrious* in Alexandria. We received the news en route to Gibraltar, and prior to entry, flew off two sub-flights of Swordfish and one of Fulmars to North Front airfield to provide anti-submarine patrols over the Straits and to give some fighter cover to the Rock while the ship was undergoing repairs and out of action.

Probably the ship's longest spell out of operations was spent in Gibraltar – two whole weeks! Every opportunity was taken to dispose of unwanted equipment; charts and confidential books were brought up to date, our aircraft overhauled, with special attention to engines, many of which were close to their time for renewal. Anti-submarine patrols were flown from North Front, and many incoming ships requested dummy attacks to exercise their guns' crews. Airmen and submariners did exchange trips, and almost invariably came to the same decision mutually, that each others' 'trade' was much too dangerous and we would both stay where we were. Thanks, but no thanks.

January 1941 was a strange month, living aboard, but flying from shore, and being driven through the town of Gibraltar each morning. Sometimes, if going out for the dawn patrol, we would see Rock apes studiously going through the garbage bins in the town centre. Such cars as there were in the town were either service vehicles or civilian-owned, but commandeered by the services. Apparently the radar network on the Rock was sensitive to car horns, which could not be used, though I never discovered the reason. Drivers banged loudly on the outside of their car doors to give 'audible warning of approach'.

Several times that month strange aircraft approached Gibraltar, but it was always difficult to ascertain whether it was a Spanish aircraft off course or a genuine Axis reconnaissance aircraft. With the frontier so close to North Front – in fact on the northern boundary of the airfield – our aircraft were vulnerable to a hit-and-run raid, yet it would be very wasteful to keep even one fighter airborne as a standing patrol by day. Instead, we relied upon the guns of the Royal Artillery to give us good warning. Another problem was that we had information that some of the pilots and aircrews of the *Armée de l'Air* based in Vichy French North Africa wanted to come over to join us. Instructions were broadcast by radio that any French personnel feeling so inclined could approach the Rock on a certain course with undercarriage down, when they would be permitted to land and be granted asylum, or whatever the service equivalent of that is. Again this was dangerous, since some British-hating hero was quite capable of coming in on that bearing, with wheels down, dropping a few bombs among our parked aircraft and escaping by risking a flight over Spanish territory. After the melancholy affairs at Oran and Dakar, a great mutual distrust would exist for many years between the British and the French, which was probably not too surprising when the two countries had been almost perpetually at war for the previous 600 years.

Dawn on 26 January was bright and promising. It was a Sunday, and after Divisions on the flight deck, Tony Dixon and I went out to North Front where we were to carry out dummy torpedo attacks against merchant shipping entering the Bay. The attacks were good and after beating them up for close-range AA practice for a further exhilarating half-hour, we landed at North Front. Our second trip that day was at dusk, when we were to carry out the final anti-submarine patrol, getting airborne at 1645 and landing at 1915. Almost as soon as we took off, the aircraft began to vibrate and lose height. Ahead and sometimes above us were the masts of merchant ships in the Bay. Tony managed to struggle above these, and told me to prepare for ditching, as we had little hope of avoiding a forced-landing unless the engine picked up considerably, when he would return to base. 'Cab' Galloway, our bearded Geordie Telegraphist Airgunner (TAG) whacked out an SOS and lashing down everything which might do us a mischief if we struck hard, I began to fire off red Very lights. By superb stretching of his glide, Tony managed to get us beyond the ships. He made a copy-book landing as a shout of 'Ahoy' came from nearby. There was the duty crash boat from the carrier *Furious* almost alongside as we settled slowly with cockpits under water, but the top mainplane keeping the aircraft afloat. Tony stood on the centre portion, extending his hand to pull me up, and I turned to see 'Cab' swimming towards the crash boat with his beard floating around his ears – something which made me laugh because I'd never thought about it before. Assisted aboard by an experienced boathook hand, Tony and I scarcely got our feet wet, but as we jumped from the sinking top mainplane to the tender, she sank swiftly, a buoy being dropped to mark the spot.

The crash boat took us back inside the inner harbour to the mole where *Ark Royal* lay and we walked into the wardroom. It was just after 1800 and the bar was open. We called for brandy. 'Hey, you two' called Lieutenant Hugh de Graaf Hunter, acting as CO, 'you'd better get a move on, you were due to take off an hour ago'. 'No panic, Hughie' said Tony, 'there's plenty of time'. Hughie took considerable convincing that in the past hour we had taken off, had an unexpectedly short flight, a forced landing, a signal for a relief aircraft and a couple of restorative brandies.

Next morning, with awful prophecies of what would happen if we did it again, we borrowed the senior pilot's aircraft, to carry out dive-bombing exercises on a towed target. No problems, nerves unaffected, and Paul Compton's aircraft was returned intact. With the evidence several fathoms deep, the cause of our involuntary ditching was never discovered, but since there had been a high wind the previous night, and the aircraft had been out in the open with only an engine cover, we suspected that North Front sand had fouled the carburettor system.

The Board of Enquiry convened to ascertain the cause of the crash leading to the loss of one of King George's Stringbags did learn from Tony of two interesting electrical malfunctions. Sometimes such twin happenings cancel out each other, but in this case they were both on the debit side. The first was that our life-saving dinghy did not emerge from the fuselage, though it should have been automatic as soon as we hit the water and the electrical immersion switch was actuated. Since it didn't release, it was extremely fortunate that the accident occurred in the calm and friendly Algeciras Bay. Second, and curiously, Tony also reported that as A4H sank slowly beneath the waves, he noticed to his astonishment that the navigation lights, which he had switched on as we took off for the dusk patrol, remained illuminated under water until the aircraft was lost to sight several fathoms down. The Board noted this curious paradox for further investigation. Next day every aircraft in the ship had its electrical circuits and especially the dinghy-release mechanism checked.

Many years later, I met Tony fortuitously in Devon, and he told me something else which I did not know at the time of the crash. It had always seemed to me to be quite remarkable that *Furious'* crash tender had been alongside so smartly – with an alacrity in fact, which would not have shamed either a dummy run or an Earl's Court Tattoo. It appears that the officer of the watch in *Renown* was having a thoroughly boring spell on the flagship's quarterdeck. Nothing, but nothing, was happening. Early in the first dogwatch, libertymen were ashore, and had not yet begun noisily to return. 'Hands to Supper' had yet to be piped, and above all, it was the 26th of the month and few officers had any money left for a run ashore. All in all, there was on this Sunday evening, a sort of invisible mixture of poverty, boredom and reverence hovering over Force H. To ease the boredom, the officer of the watch focussed his telescope on the Swordfish taking off from North Front, when to his astonishment, it began to lose height rather rapidly. Checking that his eyes and telescope were not deceiving him, he ordered the Duty Yeoman of Signals to whack out a precautionary Aldis message to the duty crash-tender which appeared to be oblivious of our impending calamity. All in all, Tony, 'Cab' and I were extremely fortunate.

At that time, the 'bograts' of 820 were going through a 'Dawn Patrol' phase, affecting the mannerisms and dress of Messrs Errol Flynn and David Niven in that famous World War I film. One such affectation was the wearing of polka dot scarves in the air. Mine, which was red with white spots had bled scarlet all over my white shirt. Walter Lamb, our deputy flightdeck officer (or 'Little F' as he was known) took his usually charitable view of the damage to our uniforms and recommended a generous cash settlement so that we could replace the damaged items. What happened in fact, was that most squadrons kept specially for such investigations a rather clapped-out reefer and trousers, which were presented by each claimant in turn, to obtain maximum cash benefit. By the time it was received, after Admiralty approval, and usually several months later, some items were probably due for replacement anyway. When one takes into consideration the wear and tear to which our uniforms were subjected in an aircraft, including oil and hydraulic fluid stains, immersion in salt water for a short time could only improve them.

In return for this minor largesse, 'Little F' was able to write off several pieces of equipment which had somehow gone missing from his inventory since we left Greenock. I understand that when A4H sank under us, she was carrying four Lewis guns, six Oerlikon magazines as well as a spare Pegasus aero-engine. Ah well, it made a change from the pre-war ditchings, when officers consistently asserted that they were wearing cocked hats, full dress and swords when their aircraft went into the sea.

In those early days of the war, there was no naval equivalent of the Army and RAF battledress, which would have made an ideal flying uniform. Indeed, Their Lordships apparently disapproved strongly of the very sensible variant in heavy naval serge introduced at their own expense by the officers of 832 Squadron in *Victorious* in 1941. Since the few naval tailors in Gibraltar had pathetically low stocks of uniform cloth practically all replacement items had to come out from home, and fortunately our lifestyle was such that few of us put on any weight, so that the measurements of a year ago were usually adequate, and one could order replacements by post. Geoffrey Topham had occasion to order a new uniform from one of the Gibraltar tailors and though in the shop the colour appeared to be the standard dark navy shade, when delivered it was clearly a fraction of a shade lighter, and poor Topham stood out at Sunday Divisions like a fish in a tree. As Captain Holland moved down the line, he stopped in front of Geoffrey and said 'Your Masher Suit, I presume?'. Topham's ego was dealt another blow a few days later when a friend from another ship asked for the tailor's name. Brightening, he gave the name and waited for favourable comment at last. 'Not a bit,' replied the visitor, 'I just wanted to know so that I could avoid him!'

I am often asked by today's younger generation what we thought and talked about in those days ('the olden days' as my sons used to say). I suppose much the same subjects that the 20-year-olds discuss today, wine, women and song, but perhaps with a slightly greater degree of urgency. Few of us were serious about anything, and it isn't easy for today's youngsters to imagine a world without mass communication – especially television, so our ideas were largely our own, they had to be. All we knew was that we were caught up in a war not of our own making in which we must defeat the Axis forces who would keep Europe, if not the world, in conditions of near-slavery. Not that our thinking got quite so profound as that. With most of the wartime warriors, idealism didn't rank high in reasoning for doing whatever one did, though it may have been offered as a reason at the initial selection board. More likely was the thought that since fighting could hardly be avoided, the Fleet Air Arm offered a rather better way of doing it. Here was an opportunity to inflict more damage on the enemy with bombs and torpedoes than with a Lee-Enfield, with better pay and a chance to see something of the world. I confess that these were my reasons plus the fact that it was a pretty smart uniform: one the girls liked.

'Weren't you frightened?' some people ask. In those far off days in the 1940s, any flying had a set of built-in risks which need no repetition, but naval flying contained a host of additional hazards that would scare a martyr. I saw the blackened corpses of two of my 19-year-old friends, 'Doc' Burden and Jimmy Hare, killed in a flying accident at Arbroath before they'd finished training. In *Victorious* in 1941 I saw an Albacore pilot get blown by a freak gust of wind into his own propeller and killed as he was walking from the Briefing Room to his aircraft. A few days later Mike Fuller and Leonard Mann ditched in the Atlantic off Iceland. Though rescued in five minutes by a destroyer, they were frozen solid, and survived by a whisker. In *Ark Royal*, Peter Opdall's aircraft broke in two while being catapulted off, the depth-charges exploding under our bows and killing the three-man crew instantly. I was almost shot in error by a naval pilot I had come to rescue at Salerno, and a few days later was machine-gunned in earnest by the official enemy.

Chapter 3
The Original
'Dambusters' and the
Bombardment of Genoa

So, by 28 January, our ship's engineers, having completed the boiler repairs with a great deal of help from the Dockyard staff, we put to sea for a couple of days' trials to test them. Simultaneously we carried out dummy torpedo and bombing attacks on Force H off Alboran Island, returning to harbour on the 30th, our Captain apparently well pleased with the engineers' work.

There is a curious atmosphere just before an operational trip takes place. With the convoy runs to the Eastern Mediterranean, the entry of merchantmen into Algeciras Bay dispensed with any thoughts of secrecy, though convoys could call at Gibraltar en route to the Cape, but in fact rarely did so, which left small doubt in anyone's mind. It was rare, for instance, for Force H to escort a Freetown or Cape-bound convoy, since the surface escorts were well able to deal with menacing submarines, even though our air reconnaissance and patrols would have been welcome.

. This atmosphere was detectable usually by the absence of senior officers in the wardroom, since they were spending their time in conferences with the Captain and the Admiral's staff. At these times they were more taciturn than usual. Often a cover-story would be put out so ridiculous that it might even be true, sometimes certain unconnected happenings tended to lend further credence. For in Gibraltar we knew that every move was watched and reported to Germany from Algeciras, and it was known that there were Axis spies or at least supporters among the scores of Spaniards who worked in the town and especially the Dockyard, entering and leaving each day.

Our own intelligence network in Italy had reported recently that civilian morale was at a very low ebb, which was hardly surprising, since Mussolini's elite troops had received such a thrashing in Libya and his Navy had been mauled everywhere it went, and wasn't even safe in its own harbours such as Taranto. The intercepted Italian radio reports indicated that the only service doing a good job was the Italian Air Force which had sunk *Ark Royal* at least three times, *Renown* twice plus innumerable cruisers and destroyers. Their real success had been extremely limited, more than 50 per cent of their bombers dropping their loads on the horizon, for which we had visual evidence. What must have been galling for the Italian High Command was the influx of German troops and aircraft, sent to do a job which the proud Italians were unable to do themselves. A substantial blow struck at civilian morale might lead to an unseating of that strutting turkey-cock, the Duce, and the Italians seeking a peaceful and early conclusion to a war for which they patently had no enthusiasm. But for such a blow to be effective, it must be struck before the *Wehrmacht* and *Luftwaffe* made themselves too permanent a part of the Italian scenery.

Captain Holland believed in putting everyone into the picture as soon as we were clear of the boom and committed to action. So, on 31 January as we steamed out of the Bay, he came on to the ship's broadcaster. 'D'ye hear there – this is the Captain speaking', and proceeded to tell us that we were going out to attack the Tirso Dam in Sardinia, which supplied one–third of the hydro power to that island. What we didn't know until some weeks later was that a double-header had been planned, including gunnery bombardment, with aerial bombing of Genoa, La Spezia, Pisa and Leghorn. Somehow it was discovered that a leakage might have occurred in Gibraltar, and rather than carry out both attacks, it was decided to aim for the one with best chance of success in the weather conditions obtaining. It so happened that a sudden storm blew up, with icing conditions and thick cloud at low altitudes, all of which would weight the odds heavily against already heavily-laden Swordfish, especially with our parent ship and escorts in Force H some 700 miles from home base. Hence the decision was made to attack the Tirso Dam on a hit-and-run basis, leaving great confusion behind. Later we could come back for the bigger raid on Genoa, when presumably weather conditions would have improved as we moved from winter into spring.

So 810 Squadron, eight Swordfish with torpedoes, led by Mervyn Johnstone, took off at dawn on 2 February, though one had to return with engine trouble. Flying conditions were dreadful. Lake Tirso stands well inland 1200ft above sea-level in mountainous country and with cloud base at 1500ft and icing conditions above, Johnstone ordered his aircraft to adopt the alternative plan, which was to act independently, attacking from the northern end of the dam with first light. The flak defences were unusually alert, confirming our suspicions of slack security in Gibraltar. Nevertheless, the attack was pressed home with vigour, four torpedoes being seen to run, though there were no subsequent and gratifying explosions. Post-mortems suggested that extra defensive nets had been laid down, but it is more likely that a great amount of silt had accumulated on the lake side of the dam, and the torpedoes may have stuck there. Whatever the explanation, six disappointed crews flew back, one crew having been shot down by a machine-gun post they had attacked with greater zeal than discretion. The pilot was 'Spike' O'Sullivan, an experienced officer who had joined 810 only a few days earlier having been an instructor at the Torpedo Training School at Crail, Scotland. 'Spike' and his observer, Knight, were subsequently reported prisoners of war.

Tony Dixon and I had been off on defensive patrols and reconnaissance, but as the weather worsened, subsidiary attacks on targets of opportunity on the Sardinian coast were impracticable, and Force H headed for Gibraltar. Rumour had it that a leakage had occurred, and that courts-martial and executions followed, but whether this was true or not, several days later, the whole ship's company was given a very tough talking to by Captain Holland on the question of security, so maybe there was some truth in the rumour.

On 7 February we were off to sea again, ostensibly to round up some German supply ships in the Atlantic, and certainly proceeded westward until early evening, when our destroyers attacked a U-boat off Cape St Vincent. During the night we turned back through the Straits, and with *Renown*, the battleship *Malaya*, the cruiser *Sheffield* and 10 destroyers, headed for the Gulf of Genoa to complete the double-header. Early next morning an alarm to action stations was caused by a Spanish commercial aircraft flying over the fleet, and a couple of French commercial aircraft were sighted by our fighter patrols when the force was north of the Balearics. Though a 90 degree turn to starboard was made, suggesting that we were possibly going on a convoy run, and a destroyer was dispatched south to make dummy signals, it is doubtful whether these ruses confused as much as they confirmed, so far were we off the normal convoy routes.

At dawn on 9 February, 16 Swordfish took off to bomb the oil refinery at Leghorn and the important railway junction at Pisa, while mines were to be laid at La Spezia in the canal which leads from the naval dockyard to the sea. Only one aircraft was lost; the crew, Midshipmen Attenborough and Foote with Leading Airman Halifax as TAG, apparently struck a balloon barrage cable in their Swordfish while dive-bombing the oil refinery. Apart from losing this very young and popular crew, the attack was a great success, the bombs and incendiaries starting fires in Leghorn and Pisa which caused significant damage, not only to factories and buildings, but also to civilian morale. Sub-Lieutenant Dick Charlier overshot his target slightly at Pisa, emerging from cloud right over the Leaning Tower with all his bombs on board. Fortunately he rejected the idea of trying to straighten the tower, going on to bomb the rail junction.

All aircraft were landed on by 0700 though a heavy sea mist had made finding the carrier extremely difficult, and reconnaissance and spotting aircraft were now flown off. *Renown*, *Malaya*, *Sheffield* and the destroyers had moved into the Gulf, and in slightly over half an hour pumped over 400 tons of HE into the Ansaldo shipyards, the dockyard and the industrial parts of the city. The defenders really didn't know what had hit them, since for the first 10 minutes of the bombardment, all answering fire was skywards from the flak batteries, and only as Force H's withdrawal began did the shore batteries reply to the ships in a manner less than enthusiastic. Whatever our suspicions about security, there was no doubt that the bombardment of Genoa came as a complete and shattering surprise to military and civilian Italians alike.

Our spotters had done a good job in directing the big ship's guns, despite the dawn mist and black smoke from the fires tending to obscure the target area. Destroyers had a field day. Their work in convoy duty gave rare opportunities for their guns to be exercised, but this was different – it was Open Day. Up and down the Gulf they dashed, in and out of inlets, firing at railway installations, harbours, factories, any target of opportunity. One railway train was seen to dash into a tunnel which was promptly sealed at both ends. As one gunnery officer from HMS *Fortune* enthused later, 'It was a real 'Brock's benefit!'

But in our exposed situation, it was clearly time to get out fast. The fleet made a rendezvous with the carrier, and turned southwest, heading at top speed for Gibraltar, 700 miles distant. Retaliation was anticipated, and a constant patrol of Skuas and Fulmars was kept in the air to fight off shadowers and the inevitable bombers and torpedo-carriers.

My own part in the operation was to patrol ahead of *Ark Royal* during the bombardment searching for small craft or submarines that might attack out of the morning mist. Some months earlier, Britain had issued a warning that any enemy ships outside the three-mile limit would be attacked and sunk, making everything a legitimate target. Unfortunately there was nothing stirring at that hour on which to deposit our four 250lb armour-piercing bombs, so Tony Dixon, Finney and I kept one eye on the bombardment and one on the sea below. Suddenly out of the dawn mists came an extraordinary apparition, a three-masted, fully-rigged sailing ship, painted black and white, looking so reminiscent of HMS *Victory* (which we knew to be concreted into Portsmouth Dockyard,) that we wondered at first if she was a mirage. We discussed dive-bombing her, but having spent my youth amongst sailormen in a small East Coast port, I demurred – it just didn't seem quite cricket to bomb a defenceless ship. After some argument, we compromised, deciding to put the salvo across her bows, beginning a somewhat casual dive from 2000ft. Just as we released the bombs, intending to frighten rather than sink her, twin 20mm Oerlikon guns opened up at us from midships. At this, Tony was all for going back to rake her with our own two machine guns, but after considering the possible humiliation of being shot down and taken prisoner by a sailing ship, decided to drop a couple more flame-floats on her and get back to the carrier. At least we caused her to turn back towards Genoa.

There were two surprises in store for us as the day lengthened and the mists disappeared. First, despite being spotted by two consecutive shadowing Cant Z 1007B seaplanes, both shot down by Fulmars, we sustained no bombing attacks all day. Some bombs, dropped on the horizon, were both seen and heard, but nothing approached Force H as we steamed south down the west coast of Corsica before turning to the westward. It was uncanny. Second, and quite unknown to us, a strong Italian force of 3 battleships, several cruisers and 7 destroyers, strong enough to annihilate Force H had formed up south of Ajaccio that morning, and were well aware of our presence, in fact hoping to engage if conditions were favourable. In the thickening mist, our reconnaissance aircraft had been recalled and no sighting was made. The Italians must have had poor intelligence, and their first real clue to our presence was when a cruiser stopped to pick up survivors from one of the shot down Cants. Even in their own backyard, the Italian Navy was either unwilling or unable to take on an enemy inferior in strength.

So, apart from the loss of one aircraft and crew, it was an all–profit operation. Rome Radio claimed that 76 civilians were killed and 226

The cruiser *Sheffield*'s Walrus flying boat (P5664) in August 1940. It is perched on its handling trolley between the catapult trolley (beneath the tail) and the starboard hangar (it could house two aircraft and one of the ship's two quadruple 2pdr pompom AA guns is on top) abaft the bridge. The handling trolley runs along a guide slot in the deck and the Walrus is also held rigid by a strut beneath the nose. The aircraft's wings are folded fully aft with bomb carrier attachments visible underneath. The tail wheel doubled as a rudder and the cabin window has a spray deflector ahead. The propeller is four-bladed. The catapult track extended outboard for a total of 90ft and could launch the amphibian at up to 56 knots (65mph) on either beam. *Conway Picture Library*

injured, while in retaliation they had shot down a Blenheim (presumably our Swordfish) and had scored bomb hits on *Sheffield*. Amazingly for once they hadn't sunk *Ark Royal*. It is not inconceivable that they bombed one of their own ships, or possibly a French merchantman, since a Marseilles-bound convoy passed us late that afternoon.

It was abundantly clear that our Captain's programme of practice, practice, practice was beginning to pay dividends, since very little attributable to aircrew mistakes had gone wrong with either operation. Our apparent ability to strike at will all over Italy was causing great unrest among the civilian population, as well as among their troops serving abroad or at sea, who now became anxious for the safety of their families. But we could not yet begin to feel the tide turning, and in fact, our little cabbage patch in the Mediterranean was just about the only place whence came good news. Every night the BBC spoke of raids on Coventry, Portsmouth, Plymouth and Liverpool, whence came many of our ship's company. We too had our share of anxiety.

Back in harbour, where we received a tremendous ovation from all ships in harbour as well as from soldiers in the garrison, a post-mortem was held on the operations and improvements made in certain drills. It was clear that the papiermache models of both the Tirso Dam and the Genoa area had been of infinite help in locating targets. At the end of the session Commander Bentinck sent for me. I had made a sketch of the sailing ship we had attacked, and he produced a silhouette from *Jane's Fighting Ships*, showing an uncanny similarity. 'Woods', he said, 'that was the *Amerigo Vespucci* you attacked off Genoa'. I blinked, not comprehending. 'She is the Italian Naval Academy's sail training ship, with a complement of 300 officers and men, and usually carries 90 to 100 officer cadets.' He went on. 'If you had sunk her, the Italian Navy would have been very short of junior officers a couple of years from now.' I was confused, and asked if he thought our sparing her was wrong. 'I don't know, Woods. I don't know' he replied, 'I was a cadet myself many years ago.'

When I see that still proud sailing ship at naval reviews and at Tall Ship Meetings all over the world, at Spithead, the Hudson River, the St Lawrence Seaway. – I know now that our compromise was the right one. She is quite magnificent, and I learned only a few years ago, was launched in 1930 as an approximation in steel of Nelson's *Victory* at the express order of Benito Mussolini. Eighteen years after that misty morning in the Gulf of Genoa my own son was a naval cadet. It was the right decision, and the Italian nation have much to thank Charlier, Tony and me for. One day I hope to go aboard *Amerigo Vespucci* and read her log for the morning of 9 February 1941. I'm afraid I can't speak for Charlier and the Leaning Tower, but am sure he's pleased he left it intact.

Chapter 4
Ship and Squadron
Mates

Just as people have differing personalities, so do groups of people, and this applies especially to squadrons. Obviously fighter and TBR pilots are selected during training so that they may specialise on the last leg, before joining their squadrons. Observers, witness my own experience, aren't so fortunate, or maybe this is a tribute to our flexibility. There were many instances where pilots moved from one type of flying to another (fighter to bomber or vice-versa) usually, as in Malta or in the Western Desert, through necessity and shortages of trained personnel. The quickest conversion on record must be that of the great Bobby Bradshaw, an outstanding torpedo-bomber pilot who eventually won the DSC three times. Joining 826 TBR Squadron at Dekheila (Alexandria) as a midshipman, he was, only three years later, its CO at the age of 21, and almost certainly the youngest-ever lieutenant-commander in the Navy. A 'press on regardless' type, he would fly anything with a propeller and wings. On one occasion in the Western Desert, he was sent forcibly on leave from Alexandria, but departed not for Cairo and the fleshpots, but forward to an RAF operational base, where he persuaded the CO to let him fly a Hurricane, after having had instruction and accompanied by another Hurricane flown by an RAF pilot. While enjoying the Hurricane, an enemy aircraft was sighted, engaged and shot down. This was great, but it put the Hurricane CO in a very embarrassing situation, since Bobby was manifestly entitled to half the victory, but as he was supposed to be on leave in Cairo, and wasn't even authorised to fly Hurricanes, what was to be done? In typical Bradshaw fashion he solved the situation by magnanimously giving the whole credit to the RAF pilot. I knew him well, admired him tremendously, and was greatly saddened to hear of his death some years after the war in a car accident with members of his family.

Another surprising oddity was the number of pilots who trained on and flew Walrus amphibians from the catapults of cruisers and battleships and later became fighter pilots. There could be no two 'trades' or temperaments further apart, yet a surprisingly large number crossed this very wide Rubicon.

Even squadrons had different personalities, due probably to the personalities of their senior officers. In *Ark Royal* we had three TBR squadrons. Mervyn 'Johnnie' Johnstone's 810 were generally accepted to be the best by a whisker from James Stewart-Moore's 820, with Tim Coode's 818 bringing up the rear. In retrospect it is probable that 810 had more experienced pilots than the other squadrons and the senior observer, Lieutenant Terence Shaw, had been an instructor at the Observer School at Ford in Sussex. This gave a dual advantage in that he knew the capabilities of many of his junior observers better than the other squadrons' senior observers knew theirs, and so was able to continue to train them more efficiently under operational conditions.

Number 818 Squadron had suffered several casualties already, losing one aircraft and crew in December when two Swordfish collided in mid-air during a dummy torpedo attack off Gibraltar. Later, Malcolm Ferguson and his crew failed to return from a long reconnaissance in the Atlantic. Decklandings by 818 seemed to produce a higher accident rate than the other two TBR squadrons, whereas 820 had a useful number of experienced pilots who nursed their less-experienced observers through the early days of the commission as working-up continued. Apart from Colin Ennever, there was no other lieutenant observer in the squadron, while both 810 and 818 had more than one of this rank and experience.

It was at that time customary for TBR squadrons to have either a pilot or observer in command, which fact also had an effect, if not on the squadron's efficiency, certainly on its personality. Those led by pilots appeared generally to have a certain panache often lacking in those led by observers. This may be pure imagination, but several years later, when my own turn came to lead, the other three squadrons in the group were led by pilots who, in situations requiring instant decisions could take effective action without consultation. An observer CO did not always have this luxury. However, since much of a TBR squadron's work was reconnaissance, involving navigation, ship and aircraft recognition, signals and communication, there were areas where the experience and technical competence of observers were more important. We junior officers spent much of our spare time discussing and arguing over the merits and demerits of pilot and observer COs.

So much of the work we carried out in the early days of the war was new territory and experience, especially as things hotted up in 1940 and 1941. The inability of many senior officers to understand the potential as well as the limitations of aircraft meant that many situations were not foreseen, and hence not practiced. Very few carrier captains throughout the war had any personal flying experience, and I well remember John Longmuir's story when he came to join 818 from a battleship where he had been the observer in a Swordfish floatplane. It appeared that when he reported for duty in October 1940, the Captain of the battleship enquired the significance of the gold 'A' in the RNVR curl on John's single wavy stripe. It was explained that his denoted Air Branch. 'I see,' said the Captain, 'So you have come to operate our flying machine?'. Regrettably, said John, this was not an attempt at humour, but indicative of this gentleman's appreciation of naval aviation. Fortunately, as the war moved on, and the capabilities of our 'flying machines' became more appreciated by friend and foe alike, this Wright Brothers' mentality began to disappear.

There were certainly contrasting personalities within 820. James Stewart-Moore was an apparent introvert, a trait shared with his senior pilot, the bearded Lieutenant Paul Compton. Later as we got to know them better, it became clear that both were rather shy by nature, though Paul – usually on party nights – revealed an unsuspected repertoire of bawdy songs. Robert Everett, second senior pilot and flight commander, seemed to the 'bograts' (as junior sub-lieutenants and midshipmen were known) to take himself a trifle too seriously on duty, though off duty he was a creative and very artistic person. An amateur photographer of merit, his greatest talent was in organising the ship's theatricals and concert party, where he positively shone. None who served with him will easily forget the satirical sketches he could write and produce, lampooning many of the Navy's dearest traditions. Dark, agile, and resembling Chaplin in build, his impersonations of that great artist together with his sketches parodying the Cornish Floral Dance and Noel Coward's 'Stately Homes of England' had ships' companies in tears of laughter when he presented 'ARP' (*Ark Royal* Productions) every six months or so. Later he went on to command 810 Squadron in *Illustrious* in 1942, and eventually founded and directed the Deck Landing School at Easthaven in Scotland, which trained not only pilots, but also deck landing control officers or 'batsmen' for carriers.

Colin Ennever was Robert's observer, a ruddy-complexioned Master Mariner who had entered the Royal from the Merchant Navy, and was consequently well-versed in ships' routines. Of pleasant and gentle-mannered character, he lost no opportunity of encouraging and training his 'bograts' by example. Possibly the most unforgettable officer in 820 Squadron was Lieutenant Hugh de Graaf Hunter – Hughie to his friends, who were legion. A quiet and very self-contained person, he only raised his voice and became loquacious under extreme pressure. When Hughie 'blew his stack' he really meant it. His great chums were Sam Hankey and David 'Feather' Godfrey–Fausset, each with a somewhat adolescent sense of humour, indulging in such larks as stealing helmets from the Gibraltar Police, whose uniforms at that time were almost identical with those of the London 'bobby'. Curfew hour in Gibraltar in 1940 was 2100 hours, a practice this trio studiously avoided when ashore, continually thinking up schemes of the most devious nature to outwit the police and naval patrols. In fact, Sam had left the ship before I joined, but we met in Algeria in 1942, when he was senior pilot in 813 who were ashore in North Africa, but all the legends I had heard appeared to be founded on fact as our friendship developed. This fine trio were all killed, quite astonishingly, within a few weeks of each other, Sam in Tunisia, Hughie and Feather at Crail in Scotland, while instructing in the Torpedo Training Unit.

Hughie's observer was Sub-Lieutenant Tony 'Maxie' Mayes of the dark curls and dapper dress, what today we would call 'sharp'. He sported a reefer for flying, but refused to don the Mae West lifejacket, claiming that it ruined the hang of his clothes, nor would he wear the observer's parachute chest harness. The latter could be clipped to a 'monkey chain' or 'G-string' which secured observers and airgunners to the cockpit floor, a necessary procedure if violent changes of aircraft direction were likely. One day Hughie decided to teach Maxie a lesson and without warning carried out a 'Chinese Immelman', a sort of half-loop, which left Maxie hanging half-out of the cockpit, holding on to the compass mounting and screaming his head off. Thereafter 'Maxie' was always properly equipped for flying. His great love was water polo, which he played boisterously and well. Although he survived the war, 'Maxie' died at the early age of 50, ironically of pneumonia brought about by playing water polo too soon after recovering from influenza.

An excellent combination was Michael Lithgow and Geoffrey Topham, both extremely competent and conscientious. Michael, known as 'The Red Mullet' on account of his pink complexion and pale blue eyes, was one of the most accurate pilots it was possible to meet. It came as no surprise when in late 1942 he was taken out of operational flying to become an 'Acceptance Pilot', testing aircraft which the Royal Navy was contemplating purchasing from the United States. After the war he became Chief Test Pilot for Vickers Supermarine, and I met him many times at Battle of Britain displays, where he and Jeffery Quill demonstrated poetry of flight in a Spitfire and a Hurricane. After holding the World Airspeed Record for a short time, flying the Supermarine 'Attacker', he joined the British Aircraft Corporation in 1961, and was most tragically killed while testing the BAC-111 airliner prototype in 1963. Geoffrey Topham, known as 'Toom', was a pre–war RNVR observer, 'pale and interesting' as a Wren-friend once described him. His reliability and accurate navigation made them, with 'Geordie' Galloway, their bearded airgunner, a very competent crew.

Alan Swanton and Norman Charles Manley-Cooper were another good pairing. Manley-Cooper, usually known as 'Scruffy' because of his juvenile appearance and engagingly disreputable dress, whether in uniform or plain clothes, always looked a permanent 18-year-old. Alan was rather more serious, probably because he was one of our few married sub-lieutenants, but they seemed to enjoy each others' company ashore as well as at sea.

Murray Willcocks having gone temporarily sick, I crewed up with

Tony Dixon, so 'Duke' Norfolk went to Alan Owensmith, both of whom I have described earlier. Tony and I did not jell completely at first, probably because I was resistant to the switch, having become used to Murray and he to me. Tony had come to us in January 1941 with considerable carrier experience, having served in *Ark* in the Norwegian campaign, where his aircraft was on one occasion badly shot up while attacking a heavily-defended iron-ore plant. We both came from Lincolnshire, he from Stamford, I from Boston, and we discovered many mutual friends in the farming community. After this we got on very much better, and flew together for about four months until another shuffle occurred, and I went back to Murray. When we left *Ark Royal* in mid-1941, Tony stayed behind to join 825 Squadron, after which I lost touch with him until many years after the war, when I 'discovered' him in a neighbouring Devonshire village.

Our youngest pilot was Nigel Gardner, nicknamed 'Mouse' because of his rather fragile stature. 'Mouse' flew with Leonard Mann, a rather mature observer in years though not at this time in experience. Our 'babies', sadly lost in the attack on Genoa, were Midshipmen Attenborough and Foote, both 19.

These then, were the stalwarts of 820 Squadron, with most of whom I was to spend my first operational commission.

Several 'characters' from other squadrons are recalled with pleasure – Tony 'Bud' Beale of 810, who couldn't stand sleeves on his shirts, and hacked them off as soon as purchased. It is impossible to forget the look of sheer horror on the face of Gieves' Gibraltar tailoring manager, who, when measuring 'Bud's' chest for some new uniforms, encountered a somewhat damp armpit. Hector 'Dilly' Dangerfield, who with Kit Halliwell and 'Buster' Crabbe, would play their two or three Gilbert and Sullivan records from 'Mikado' until we knew the words by heart. Freddie Willet, known as 'Flossie' for some long-forgotten reason, another course-mate with a rabelaisian sense of humour, who once took off at night in full mess kit after returning from a shore party just as the ship was leaving Gibraltar. 'Flossie' was last heard of as Professor of Military History in Melbourne, Australia, after having fulfilled an equally unlikely post at Cambridge. Little Bill Urry, 'small but beautifully marked' as he was wont to say, continually bemoaning the fact that by accident of birth he was a snottie still whilst his older course-mates were sub-lieutenants and drawing 13/6d a day while he drew a measly nine bob. Worse, as a midshipman he was not allowed spirits, though we managed somehow to give him a gin occasionally to stop him going berserk. Together, we juniors shared a large cabin flat, known always as 'Brothel Alley' for reasons which to this day aren't clear to me.

Promotion in the Navy in those days was on a time basis, so that we had senior lieutenants who had not the required eight years in for promotion to lieutenant-commander often commanding squadrons. Such a one was Lieutenant Richard Smeeton, CO of 800 Skuas. Similarly, flight commanders, which in the RAF would usually be flight-lieutenants, were often senior sub-lieutenants. It was much later that a squadron of nine aircraft or more carried automatically a lieutenant-commander's rank. In the RAF, wartime promotion came quicker, not only because of their higher casualty rate, but also on the basis of responsibility rather than length of service. Some of their squadron-leaders and wing-commanders were very young indeed. The legend went that in one London hotel during the war a notice was displayed above the bar to the effect that group captains under the age of 21 years could only be admitted when accompanied by their parents. Apocryphal, of course, but it was possible to be a group captain below the age of 25.

Some time in 1941 or 1942, Their Lordships seem to have appreciated that the RAF offered rather better chances of promotion (and hence of pay) than did the naval air branch, as a result of which we might be losing in the race to recruit the 'best types'. Whereupon improvements were introduced, albeit slowly, at least so far as acting ranks were concerned for greater responsibility.

Chapter 5
Looking for Hipper and the Elusive Sisters

The bombardment of Genoa and the neighbouring industrial north of Italy completed, we spent a mere 24 hours in harbour before a report was received that the heavy cruiser *Hipper* had intercepted one of our Sierra Leone – Britain convoys in the Atlantic off the Azores, and like a fox among the chickens, had quickly sunk seven out of 19 ships (12 February) before withdrawing to Brest. Our task was to search for, and if found, to sink *Hipper*. In any case, we would take over the protection of a very important convoy bound for Gibraltar from Britain, and known to be within *Hipper*'s range. Once this convoy was out of danger, we were to intercept and escort another convoy bound from Britain to the Far East.

Weather conditions in the North Atlantic were atrocious, and the few reconnaissance aircraft flown off saw nothing. The flightdeck was pitching about 40ft, making take-offs and landings most hazardous both to aircrews and handling parties. But with speed and surprise being of the essence, our Captain was not anxious to have too many of his precious aircraft damaged, which would reduce his reconnaissance and striking-force potential. So for long periods flying was suspended altogether, especially as *Sheffield*'s radar could sweep for 50 miles all round, ten times the visibility of an aircraft. Another fair assumption was that in such vile conditions of visibility and sea, limited further by rain, sleet and snow showers, no U-boats were likely to surface, so anti-submarine patrols were only flown in emergency.

In these weather conditions the mechanics and deck-handling parties had a most difficult task. The carrier would be making best possible speed, probably 15 knots, which enabled day to day routine to be carried out without equipment sliding all over the place, and, most important, watchkeepers could get meals and rest without too much discomfort. On the flightdeck there might be a wind of 30 to 50 knots, giving relative windspeed over the deck of 45 to 65 knots, in which conditions bringing of aircraft from the hangars to the flightdeck, known as 'ranging', was extremely hazardous.

Accurate choreography was essential, since aircraft were stowed below with wings folded for economy of space. Once on the flightdeck, they had to be moved into the correct position for take-off, which allowed of no mistakes on the aircraft brakes and chocks. Once in correct position, aircraft were kept there until the aircrew had been briefed and ready to take off. At this point the carrier turned into wind, and in any sort of sea heeled over, and the handling party had to ensure that the aircraft did not slide on the wet deck. This manoeuvre complete, the wings were spread into the flying position and secured in place by a locking device. The engine was then started and run up so that the aircraft was ready for take-off.

In those days there was no specialised clothing for the mechanics and handling party, no waterproof overalls, skullcaps or gloves. Ratings wore their own clothing, a miscellany of boilersuits, oilskins, balaclavas or caps lashed tightly under the chin, and at all times their inflatable lifebelt, suffering the wrath of the storm as they steadied the aircraft and its chocks to prevent movement, as freak gusts of wind eddying round the island superstructure tried to get leverage under the mainplanes. In conditions like these, the rule rather than the exception, the aircrews' job was less dangerous once they were airborne. Yet only once do I recall a rating being blown clear of the safety nets and over the side. By the time the alarm was raised, in this case within seconds, there was no hope of rescue, even had we been able to get a boat away.

The air mechanic's moment of glory was when his aircraft was ranged and awaiting his pilot, as he sat in the pilot's seat. Often he would start the engine to warm it up. Swordfish were probably the last service aircraft not to have an automatic cartridge starter. Instead, a manual or 'Hucks' starting handle was inserted into the engine, and wound furiously by two mechanics until the flywheel had gained sufficient momentum to start the airscrew revolving. When, as often happened, the engine misfired, the groundcrews' cursing would have made an Irish navvy blush as this tiring performance recommenced. Manoeuvring of the aircraft called for a quick ear and hand as they were moved into the centre of the deck for take-off, with men hanging on to the handles on the outer edges of the lower mainplanes. Deck collisions at this stage can be serious in terms both of aircraft and human life, nor does the captain want to be on his straight flying-off course too long if crews have to move into the spare aircraft always ranged for emergencies – engine faults at the last minute, such as magneto drop or rough running.

Yes, the mechanics and flightdeck parties were a spartan bunch, with an intense loyalty to their 'own' aircraft and crew and second to their squadron. In those days, an aircraft was assigned to one aircrew, who had their own fitter, rigger and armourer, all caring for their charge much as an enthusiast looks after his sports car. In 1942, for reasons of efficiency, 'centralised maintenance' was introduced, a sort of garage

A prewar photograph of Fleet Air Arm (actually RAF) fitters at work on the Bristol Pegasus engine of a Swordfish aboard *Ark Royal*. *Popperfoto*.

system, removing pride of individual ownership, though obviously making economical use of maintenance personnel at a time when so much new technology was being introduced.

Just as the naval aviator faced much greater natural hazards than his RAF counterpart, so also did the mechanics and flightdeck crews. Not only were their living conditions much more primitive and noisy at sea, they came down from a range, often tired, wet through and miserable, yet knowing that they might be called out within minutes for an emergency landing or other unscheduled duty. Many a visitor to a carrier in harbour walked round the flightdeck with trepidation akin to that of the biblical Agag. Few could imagine the hazards to which the mechanics and flightdeck handlers were subject to at sea in rough weather. Wherever you are, Chiefie Arundel, Mortimer, Herring, Dowler, Croad, Lemon, Waldron, Wilson, yes, even Hanson, I salute you all!

In such vile conditions another reason for not dispatching reconnaissance aircraft was that in areas regularly patrolled by the four-engined German 'Kondors' radio silence was strictly observed except for an enemy sighting report. On 13 February 820 Squadron flew off five aircraft for a search, and in rapidly worsening conditions of visibility, two out of five could not find the ship on return, though they were less than five miles away and searchlights were pointed at them. Eventually they had to request a D/F bearing, which was doubtless immediately picked up by the ever-vigilant German D/F operators along the French

Atlantic coast, thus inviting attack on us by aircraft, submarine or both.

On the 14th we were 800 miles west of Brest, on the 15th, 1000 miles west of Land's End, the ship's company swearing they could smell fish and chips, despite a screaming gale from the southwest.

The biggest problem in these conditions was to keep morale at a high level. Recently I had been appointed RAF ranks' Divisional Officer, to look after the welfare of the 10 RAF technicians in the squadron. Corporals Croad and Lemon were no great problem, being long-service men with excellent records and skills. Leading Aircraftsman Hanson was THE problem. Whether it was an inverted sense of humour or his chance to make someone else's life miserable, he was full of complaints. His boots didn't fit, his laundry had been lost or his overalls ripped. Hanson always had some problem. Small wonder that he was known as 'Drip' to his RAF and naval shipmates. This was my first taste of responsibility for my fellowmen at sea and there were times when I wondered if this was the career which I had dreamed about since first wearing long trousers. It looked like being a long, hard winter.

Then I hit on a bright idea. Obviously when there was no immediate requirement in the hangars to repair aircraft, which there shouldn't be if we weren't flying, I would institute educational sessions, getting some of the specialist officers to talk to the troops about, for example, meteorology, photography or even accountancy. It would not only be instructive, it might even spark off some ideas for another career when their RAF service came to an end. Most unfortunately it all came to naught, for on our next visit to Gibraltar, draft chits had arrived for all 10 RAF ranks. Croad and Lemon 'shadowed' their reliefs, ensuring they came to no harm that would jeopardise a return to Lee-on-Solent, where five of them were bound. The other five? Hanson included, they went to Dekheila (Alexandria), where perhaps a spell with the Desert Air Force would be preferable to life on the ocean wave.

We carried many guests in *Ark Royal* – newsmen, cameramen and diplomats. One who remains in my memory is Lieutenant-Commander Steadman Teller USN. His navy was not yet in the war, but was most anxious to learn what they could from our experiences, and sent over this seasoned carrier pilot as liaison officer. The US Navy's aircraft were designed specifically for carrier work, unlike ours, which were mainly compromises, so there was little for him to learn on design and performance, what was useful was the day-to-day operating routine. He was particularly interested in the catapult, where we seemed to be ahead, and in decklanding techniques where we used signals the complete reverse of theirs. Our decklanding control officer or 'batsman' raising his paddles indicated that aircraft was too low and must go higher. In the US Navy the same signal meant the aircraft was too high and must come lower. Since our being allies was inevitable, such items must be co-ordinated, or at least understood.

As an officer of a friendly navy, he was entitled to the full ceremonial when coming aboard or leaving the ship, that is, the bos'un's pipe and his country's anthem. We could not really muster the Royal Marine Band every time he went ashore or returned, and obtained a gramophone record of the 'Star Spangled Banner', housing it in the ship's broadcasting office. Upon sighting our American guest leaving or returning, the duty commanding officer, officer of the day, officer of the watch, midshipman and full side party including bugler and messenger would assemble. At a signal from the duty CO transmitted down to the midshipman, the broadcasting officer would put on the record. Steadman was no egocentric, and one morning, when I was officer of the watch, he sidled along behind me as I stood near the gangway, and said 'I'm going ashore Lootenant. Cut the tooting'. Protocol in the Royal Navy cannot be broken like that. We compromised by giving him the first 16 bars – ie up to and including 'first gleaming'. Thank God the needle never stuck.

Newsmen and cameramen were another story, all of them ever anxious to get 'exclusives' for their newspapers or film companies. Laurence Wilkinson of the *Daily Express* was with us for several months, Roy Kellino and little bearded Prosser with their newsreel cameras for rather less. The cameramen were anxious to fly on every possible occasion and would, I believe, have 'gone operational' if they could. Bob Everett was their favourite pilot, and because of his own deep interest in photography, gave them excellent shots and angles. The dedicated Prosser I remember well on Malta convoy runs, crouching on the flightdeck and shooting a high-level bombing run, hatless, shirtless, wearing shorts and sandals only, avidly photographing, panning, missing nothing. Months later, after he had departed for England, we had a special showing one night in the hangar cinema of his exciting films which he had specially sent back for his hosts' amusement. I'm afraid that we whom he photographed were better aviators than actors.

The remainder of February and March 1941 were spent in the Eastern Atlantic, now becoming an especially dangerous area for our convoys, with the battlecruisers *Scharnhorst* and *Gneisenau* as well as the heavy cruiser *Hipper* at large, sinking ships if the convoys were weakly escorted, and always retiring at high speed before our heavies could arrive on the scene. On 17 February we met the battleship *Rodney* and the cruiser *Birmingham* with 33 ships to be escorted to Gibraltar, *Rodney* turning smartly about for Britain after exchanging signals. Around this huge convoy in three columns we carried out continuous anti-submarine patrols, with dawn and dusk deep searches ahead and astern. It was argued that since we looked ahead more than we did astern, U-boat commanders would reason quite soundly that, provided they made visual contact before dark from the rear of the convoy, they could pick off stragglers possibly without retaliation if there were no explosion to see or hear. Later, during the height of the Battle of the Atlantic, 'wolfpacks' of up to 30 U-boats would work ahead of the convoy, and attack up and down the lanes all night if not quickly suppressed by destroyers or corvettes.

Often there was little to see on a 3½ hour patrol. My logbook for 18 February records sighting the Norwegian tanker *Sildra* and a dead whale. The tanker was directed to the convoy and Finney, who was short of practice, fired a few pans at the dead whale. This was not entirely for fun. It just might have been some new device to confound us – a mine? We reported both sightings anyway on returning, first to *Birmingham*, which would check credentials, later to our own ops room. We took no chances, as there were known to be a number of U-boat supply ships in the North Atlantic. A report that a small aircraft had been sighted would indicate to a supply ship that a carrier was in the vicinity, and if this could be disposed of, a 33-ship convoy would provide several days' and nights' work for a U-boat pack.

For three consecutive days we worked in virtually zero visibility due to continuous thick fog. On the 22nd we flew off a deep search, while the fighters sharpened up their strafing and the convoys' guns crews. In less than 15 minutes, the fog had returned and all aircraft were recalled.

One of the two defecting Vichy French Glenn Martin Maryland bombers on North Front airfield, Gibraltar in March 1941. Sub-Lieutenant (A) G W Roberts RN surveys the aircraft with the Racecourse Stand behind him. *Author's collection*

In such conditions speed must be reduced to 7 knots, then to 3 knots. Eventually fog-buoys had to be streamed, so that ships could keep visual station. Later we met *Malaya*, which took over from us, enabling us to return to Gibraltar with *Renown*. With no destroyer screen, double lookouts were posted and extra patrols flown. At this time, with pressure on us to guard valuable convoys in the Atlantic, some of them being brought through the Mediterranean for Malta and Alexandria, the volume of work on every member of Force H was excessive, and from being the exception, 17 and 18 hour days became the norm; for aircrew comprising two 3-hour flights, interspersed with duty in the Air Operations Room, on the bridge or in the hangar. It must be admitted in retrospect that in *Ark* we always felt, and were made to feel, part of the ship, not as happened in subsequent carriers, simply aviators, whose job was to fly and nothing else. The days were long and tiring, but when we returned to harbour, we relaxed with the non-aviators as members of the same family. I say 'relaxed' because quite often we played hockey or football at the Naval Officers' Pavilion or swam at Catalan or Sandy Bay, so our 'relaxing' was often as tiring as working.

On the afternoon of 28 February we were sunbathing at Catalan Bay in the warm spring Mediterranean sun when air raid sirens sounded. A French Glenn Martin twin-engine bomber-reconnaissance aircraft was circling the Rock at a respectful distance. The artillery lobbed a few markers at him before he flew off. The following morning two of these aircraft came in on the prescribed bearing, wheels and flaps down, they landed and were taken to dispersal at North Front – my runway-widening scheme giving plenty of room for manoeuvre. The crews were from the French naval base at Tafaraoui near Oran, and were taken away for interrogation. At this time we were not allowed to go over the aircraft, but later learned that one crew had got 'lost' on a navigation exercise while the other crew had 'borrowed' their CO's aircraft to effect their escape. One of the aircraft played a very significant part in the *Bismarck* operation less than three months later, being used from Hatston in the Orkneys to reconnoitre Bergen in Norway, where the German battleship was supposed to be, but was found to be missing.

Next day on board, a number of long-range tanks were being fitted to certain aircraft, one of which was mine. This looked rather ominous, since rumour had it that we were going back into the North Atlantic to immobilise the German heavies once and for all. Attaching a tank was simple, a cylindrical self-sealing petrol container being fitted in the observer's cockpit. This extends the Swordfish's range considerably, from the normal 4 hours' to about 6 hours' flying though periods even longer than this have been recorded. But there are several side-effects. First, anyone who has driven a car for 6 hours continuously will know that concentration fades periodically, and at sea there are no roadside hostelries where one can pull up for a rest and refreshment. Second, the observer flies with no airgunner, occupying the rear cockpit, which is smaller than his own. In this very confined space he has to navigate using a Bigsworth (chart) board and instruments; observe – that is reconnoitre for surface and airborne objects – keep a listening watch on one or more radio wavelengths; be prepared to issue an enemy report, which may involve using his coding machine; operate the rear gun if necessary; remember to reel aerials in and out, use the homing beacon; and in between times chat with the pilot to keep him awake. Apart from that, the observer's time was his own to do as he liked. Six hours of that each day, perhaps seven days a week, with an alleged self-sealing 100 gallon petrol tank nudging one's backside, was pushing patriotism to its furthest-acceptable limits. But that's what looked like happening, and we were somewhat less than enthusiastic.

After dining *Renown's* officers on 2 March, we fitted the 'Marathon' tanks next day and sailed for exercises before proceeding to the North Atlantic. There was just too much to do on these long trips, and my failure to recognise a large increase in the headwind caused us to be 45 minutes late returning to the ship, which meant she had to turn into wind specially for us. I was unpopular for a while, though after a few more days of flying exercises and manoeuvres, we returned to harbour on the 4th, feeling more competent with the Marathon tanks, even though observers flying in aircraft so equipped were instantly recognisable by their resemblance to Quasimodo.

This is the point at which to explode another Hoary Naval Myth. I cannot number the times that the top speed of the Fairey Swordfish has been proclaimed as 135 miles per hour. As a young man I saw this on the back of W D & H O Wills (the only brand) cigarette cards and later in *Jane's Fighting Aircraft*. Numerous works on naval air warfare confirm this figure. Vice-Admiral B B Schofield in his *The Attack on Taranto* and Rear-Admiral Sir William Jameson in *Ark Royal 1939-1941* quote 125 knots and 154mph respectively. Even in the Dominion of Canada's Museum of Aviation at Vanier airfield, Ottawa, 135mph is writ large on their Swordfish, so beautifully kept it brought tears to my eyes in 1978. It would now seem an appropriate time to disclose that this figure must have been quoted to discourage the enemy, since never EVER has a Swordfish, straight and level even with minimum equipment on board, been known to exceed 100 knots flat out in still air. The Marathon tank reduced airspeed by at least 10 knots. Perhaps it was this exaggerated claim which saved us so many times, as the flak burst way ahead of us, the enemy either believing what he had seen on the back of Messrs Wills' cigarette cards, or else refusing to believe that an aircraft could be flying so slow as his predictor suggested. So perishes The Best Kept Secret of The War.

Next day brought a captains' conference during my watch, and the operational smell began to permeate quite distinctly. Diffused, but detectable. Panic stations came on 6 March as.*Malaya*, returning home with a convoy, had sighted *Scharnhorst* and *Gneisenau* off the Cape Verde Islands. The battlecruisers had beaten a hasty retreat, not because they could not have handled the ageing battleship, but because their job was to harass and sink merchant and small warships, to stay at sea as long as possible without sustaining damage, to live off their own supply ships, and finally to avoid engagement with larger ships of the Royal Navy. Accompanied by *Renown* and the cruiser *Arethusa*, we left harbour at 2045 with only two destroyers for a screen, making 25 knots in the general direction of the Canaries, intent on intercepting the unholy nuisances on their way back to Brest.

Reconnaissances on the 10th and 11th revealed nothing, though a very wide area was searched, and our instructions were now to stay with the convoy, hoping that it might be the goat to attract the tigers, who would then get a nasty surprise.

The convoy was the biggest we had yet escorted, 55 ships in all, and a best speed of 7 knots. We had heard during our training that the speed of any convoy is the best speed of the slowest ship, but never expected it to become so wearing. At 7 knots the convoy seemed scarcely to move, developing an alarming pitch which from time to time incorporated a sort of mid-pitch-shudder. Flying operations involved the carrier moving out of her central position in the five lanes of ships, and from time to time there were near-collisions with our flock. Of the squadrons, 818 had more hard luck than most, losing two aircraft in barrier prangs, while Lieutenant 'Tan' Tivy executed a quite magnificent steeplechase jump over the barrier after missing all arrestor wires. This sporty character had only a few weeks earlier achieved local fame by pursuing a fleeing Cant seaplane firing his .45 service revolver when his front gun jammed.

There were many compensations. The merchant ships, with whom very few of us wished to change places, huddled close to us for protection. Occasionally the Admiral would ask the convoy commodore for more speed, but every attempt brought dangers of engine break-down, or worse, excessive smoke that might give away our position. Every aircraft going on patrol or returning flew up and down the lanes, the merchantmen returning cheers and waves all the way. Whenever possible both fighters and bombers carried out dummy attacks, always making certain beforehand that their aircraft was known to be friendly.

This time the weather was fine, sunny and warm, and in off-duty hours we would find a sheltered spot for sunbathing and 'goofing', that is, watching take-offs and landings. The weather always has a tremendous effect on my spirits, a sunny day bringing out the best in me, a dull day the worst. Here we had the best of all worlds when off duty. As Chiefy Mortimer commented one morning 'If you was a civvie, sir, you'd be paying twenty quid a day for the luxury you're enjoying here'. At which precise moment John Callendar made a heavy landing, depositing on the deck an aluminium dust sea-marker which exploded, covering us all with silver dust. Twenty quid a day would not have included that.

On dull days, Bill Roberts and I operated a photographic 'firm', having bought equipment including a second-hand enlarger. In league with the ship's photographer, we pursued an interesting and rewarding hobby, blowing up our shipmates' negatives, mainly prangs and portraits. Unfortunately, the photographer, who did the initial developing, discovered that we were giving him the hard stuff to do, and dealing only with the profitable work. So he became a little difficult, and since we could not store flammable chemicals in our cabins, our get-rich-quick scheme soon came to an end. The photographer, who had probably engineered things his way, bought our enlarger.

These lazy days soon became just a memory. The German heavy group had captured or sunk 13 ships off Newfoundland on 15–16 March, 1500 miles away to the northwest. So tight had been the escort situation that the two convoys which were almost annihilated had no escorts and were easy meat. We were the other side of the Atlantic and tied to a convoy as other German raiders were known to be in port and ready for sea all along the French Atlantic coast. On the 19th the cruiser *Kenya* took over the homeward-bound convoy from us, leaving us free to make maximum speed to intercept the German ships. Information had also been received that several of the ships captured might be taken by their prize crews to French ports, and it was known that several supply ships were between us and Gibraltar. 'Flossie' Willett had sighted a suspect on his dusk patrol the previous day, and she was earmarked for interception and action on our return. Capture of such ships intact could provide useful information on U-boat equipment, tactics and morale.

Taking off for the dawn patrol on 20 March, our aircraft A4H developed a disquieting engine noise, calling for an emergency landing. Herring, our Leading Airfitter, quickly diagnosed 'doof ploogs', the changing of which would take time as the engine must cool first. So we took the spare, A4F, which unbelievably recorded alarming magneto drop shortly after take-off. Again we returned, wondering what had happened to the normally reliable Bristol Pegasus engines. 'Wings' was not amused as we took off for the third time, having delayed the ship for at least ten minutes as she turned 100 degrees to port for each false start. Fortunately our third choice, A4C, behaved in an exemplary manner.

In the early afternoon, we intercepted two of the German prizes *Bianca* and *San Casimero*. Ordered in international code not to lower boats, as we wanted the ships intact, they disregarded our signals, abandoning their scuttled ships. A few pans of tracer, aimed wide overhead, encouraged them back on board to unscuttle, but both ships eventually sank. *Renown* rescued the crews from the overloaded boats, giving them a tongue-lashing, since she was stopped at the mercy of U-boats which might have been meeting their supply ships. Many years later, in Canada, I met Walter, who had been a *Bianca* crew member. 'Your fliers very bad shots,' he said, not recognising our chivalry, and thankfully not knowing of my participation, as he was a very large man.

A final dusk recce was flown off ahead of the force, this time by the faster Fulmars. In the gathering darkness, Rupert Tillard, the CO and Mark Somerville – the Admiral's nephew – as observer, sighted the two enemy battlecruisers heading at high speed for Brest. Mark transmitted his Enemy Sighting Report in plain language, but due to a radio malfunction, it was not received in Force H. Realising this possibility, they returned at maximum speed of 270 knots over the 100 miles, landing on in darkness at 1700, passing their report earlier by Aldis lamp. Our aircrews being completely inexperienced in night torpedo attacks, it was deemed too dangerous to get a strike off at night. In any case, the probability was strong that the Fulmar had been spotted or their message intercepted, so the Germans would go flat out to open the range. The battleships *Revenge* and *Rodney*, escorting a homeward-bound convoy from Canada, were ordered to join us. Throughout the night we closed at full speed of around 30 knots, every loose piece of equipment rattling as the engineers squeezed every ounce of power from the engines. But such is the luck of war. After searching tens of thousands of square miles for the enemy ships, we found them too late to attack that night. Had they been seen only two hours earlier, up to 30 torpedo aircraft would have been available to make repeated attacks in what was left of daylight, in near-perfect conditions for our antiquated but efficient biplanes. There was some cloud cover, and a setting sun

The German supply ship *Bianca* scuttles at about 1300 on 20 March 1941. Photographed by the author from Swordfish A4C with *Ark Royal* behind. *Author's collection*

would have made an excellent stage for a decoy on the bright side, while the main force attacked from out of the gathering darkness.

Fulmars went off at dawn, but encountered thick fog up to 3000ft. Although we stood at readiness all day, and flew off searches as the weather improved, reports from Coastal Command in the late afternoon indicated that the two ships were only a few hours' steaming from Brest, and were already under cover of the *Luftwaffe* and U-boats. Tragically that day Peter Opdall, Charlie Hearn and 'Baron' Biggs, of 818 Squadron crashed into the sea with their depth-charges on after being catapulted for an anti-submarine patrol. The carrier was lifted out of the water by the explosion and the aircrew killed instantly. Many of us were resting between flights in our cabins and imagined we had been torpedoed. Three more splendid young men had gone.

Next day the main quest terminated, though we continued to search for enemy supply ships en route to Gibraltar for refuelling after our 16 days at sea, many of which were at high speed. If we were looking for a few days' leave, this was soon forgotten as we docked at 0830 on 24 March and sailed after refuelling at 2200. Bob Everett left us to become CO of a squadron reforming at home and took passage in the trooper which was taking the German prisoners. A few of his impersonations with prophecies of what lay ahead for them could have struck terror into their uneasy hearts!

Although after our protracted 'spring cruise' only three of our nine aircraft in 820 were fully serviceable, we exercised night take-offs, flare-dropping and night landings, another deficiency recently revealed. After which, we set out once again for the Bay of Biscay and began to encounter some very heavy weather. Mess furniture was skidding all over, aircraft straining at their lashings in the hangars and the sliding of cabin doors which crashed to and fro with monotonous regularity, since in most cases they could not be locked. We hadn't enough serviceable aircraft, so everyone turned to in the hangar, in Drake's phrase 'the gentlemen hauling with the mariners'. Unintentionally I revealed a talent for repairing instruments, and was appointed assistant to the instrument fitter.

After the excitement of the previous week, a somewhat depressed mood descended on us all. However, Bob Woolston and Mike Fell of 800 Squadron organised a cockroach derby. Regrettably the best source of these was the galley, where they lurked in daylight in the shadows, issuing forth only at night. By switching the lights off and waiting, Bob and Mike gathered a dozen of the larger 'seagoing' genus, which were then put into strict training by their owners until after dinner, when the Biscay Spring Handicap would be run. The first home was owned by Callingham of 800, but a protest was entered as he'd been observed doping it with gin. The surgeon commander demanded a saliva test on both cockroach and Callingham, declaring the race void. So a re-run was ordered for the next evening. All perhaps a little crazy, but it removed the depression entirely. At least for the moment.

April's beginning meant that the 'sprogs' who joined in October had now been operational for six months. It was interesting to see how we had developed in that time. Arriving full of the knowledge of our trade, it was plain to see now that what we lacked was experience. It was equally true that some of our instructors would have had heart failure were they to see how many of their sacred tenets were ignored. For example, it had been instilled that we must 'Find a wind' every half-hour when on reconnaissance, to avoid big navigational errors. That was fine at Lee-on-Solent where the objective was to complete a good navigation exercise which would be analysed, the marks going into our Progress Reports. How different, when to parody Kipling's immortal poem:

> If you can keep control of your dividers
> And Bigsworth Board and Gosport tubes and pad,
> Or listen to the pilot and the wireless
> Talking in unison and not go mad....

And how much easier to let it slide for another half-hour when the present chaos must have calmed down a little, when one could think about releasing a smoke-float or dust-marker and flying reciprocals for three minutes. 'Ownership' of an aircraft meant keeping it in first-rate fettle, everything stowed away properly, compasses swung regularly, the radio crystal-tuned daily in the hangar, guns fired, adjusted and dismantled for frequent cleaning. All this, and the dozens of other experiences which would turn 'sprogs' into aviators, though there was still a long way to go. Somewhere was a Rubicon into the Land of Inattention to Detail that must not be crossed if one was to survive. Occasionally very experienced pilots and observers let their concentration droop. Sometimes luck would be with them and the lesson would be learned. Sometimes luck would be absent, and conversation in the wardroom that night would be wondering how such an experienced chap could do whatever he had done in error. There was a very fine line between something going wrong and the same action turning the perpetrator into a hero. Flying folk called it 'joss' – which some people had in great abundance, and others not at all.

While continuing to show proper respect for the CO and the senior officers in the squadrons, we had learned to be slightly more informal and more at ease with them. Some 'bograts' had been given responsibilities as divisional, maps and charts, stores, training or intelligence officers. Mike Lithgow became adjutant, dealing with the mass of paperwork, assisted by a Leading Writer, an ex-local government character to whom paper was the end-product. Responsibilities which would have awed us six months ago were now accepted as routine. The maintenance personnel, our fitters, riggers and armourers, most of whom had been with the squadron much longer than ourselves now appeared to have looked us over and approved, possibly feeling in some way that they had helped us over the initial hurdles. They were an interesting bunch to talk to, many knowing much more than we about the mechanics of aircraft engines, guns, radio and compasses. One could, if interested, learn a great deal of value.

Possibly our greatest triumph was the selection of Nigel Gardner and myself for the squadron soccer team. While this disqualified us from the wardroom team, to play for 820 was a greater honour, because it was achieved on merit.

A Fulmar lands on *Ark Royal*, its hook down to engage the arrestor wire visible on the right of the arrestor system's hydraulics drum. Astern are the battlecruiser *Renown* and the old carrier *Furious*. In two May and June 1941 operations the two carriers successfully flew off 90 Hurricanes to Malta. *Author's collection*

Chapter 6
Flying for Force H
at sea and ashore

On 1 April Rupert Tillard and Mark Somerville were both awarded the Distinguished Service Cross for leadership, courage and devotion to duty as CO and Senior Observer of 808 Squadron, awards well-deserved by two officers of great skill and perseverance. Naturally, a 'gong party' followed that evening. During the day *Argus* had arrived from Britain with 12 Hurricanes for Malta, and it had been decided to fly them from *Ark*. Consequently the RAF pilots had come aboard us, and were included in the celebrations. It was a great night, as they 'sang for their supper', bringing songs and games we hadn't heard of before.

The reason for the transfer of the aircraft to *Ark Royal* was simple, we had a longer flightdeck than *Argus*, and were much faster in the water. Consequently, the Hurries could take more fuel if flying from *Ark*, and could be flown off at a greater distance from Malta. This would invite less curiosity and bombs from the *Luftwaffe* and the *Regia Aeronautica*. The latter we didn't mind too much, but the *Luftwaffe* were now becoming very accurate, and, more important, more firmly established in the Men's End, as the more frequently attacked Eastern Mediterranean was now known.

Leaving harbour at 0300 on 2 April, we aimed for a position 150 miles southwest of Cagliari, where they would fly off, escorted by a pair of Skuas from 800 Squadron. RAF Glenn Martins were to meet them over Pantellaria and escort them to Malta. Everything went very well. With the flightdeck full of Hurricanes there was no flying, though some Fulmars were kept ranged forward and to starboard of the barrier ready to be catapulted should enemy bombers attack. But just what would happen in that event doesn't bear thinking about. The *Ark's* lifts were all oblong shaped, and the Hurricanes' wings did not fold, as was the case with all naval aircraft at that time. Thus to land the Fulmars on again after combat would have meant bringing all the Hurricanes forward of the barrier, with a prayer party fallen in to invoke interdenominational Divine Protection against a Fulmar fouling the flightdeck, or even worse, ploughing through the barrier – which had been known to happen – and writing off some of the Hurricanes so badly needed in Malta.

Dilly Dangerfield and I had prepared some charts for the RAF pilots with a mass of detail of courses both magnetic and true, recognition signals and colours of the day, callsigns, silhouettes of any ships and aircraft they were likely to meet, in fact, the complete 'gen'. It was a job well done, both the Squadron Leader and our own signals officer, Charles Coke, offering us congratulations.

So, after a final briefing, we approached the fly-off point without incident. It was a tough proposition for these RAF pilots. Their aircraft had been run-up and found to be in good shape, but hadn't been flight-tested since leaving Britain. Now they had to fly in formation nearly 400 miles over unfriendly waters after taking off from a very mobile and heaving airfield. Small wonder that at moments we felt very slightly superior! But we nevertheless gave them a rousing heartfelt send-off.

Whether it is due to the engine torque or a nameless fear of the island superstructure, I do not know, but all RAF Hurricanes veered away to port whenever we flew them off. Our own aircraft seemed always to incline to the starboard bow. Since the Fulmar and the Hurricane had very similar Merlin engines, one must conclude that it was the island that caused the problem. On this occasion, at 0630 on 3 April, a Thursday according to my diary, one Hurricane flew right over the port fore gun director, dipping slightly, and smashed off its port long-range petrol tank, slung under the wing, together with its tail wheel. Not a whit deterred, the pilot carried on, and all 12 aircraft arrived safely in Malta. We were becoming quite expert at this now, and what was better, Malta was sending back to us the crews of the escorting Skuas, instead of as previously, pressganging them into 830 (Swordfish) Squadron.

Later in the forenoon two of the ubiquitous Cant 506s came to shadow, together with a Heinkel 111 – the first time we had seen this aircraft in the Mediterranean. Our Fulmar pilots Royal Marine Lieutenant Ronnie Hay and PO 'Buck' Taylor shot down one Cant, and during the afternoon a benign mist descended upon us, aiding our getaway to the west. Maybe the prayer party idea did work for us?

Late in the afternoon, as we were to the north of Algiers, visibility improved sufficiently to allow Murray Willcocks and me to carry out an anti-submarine patrol. Nothing was seen, and perhaps our euphorious mood caused Murray to lose concentration awhile. Whatever the case, a rather shaky landing caused us to proceed crabwise to port, almost going over the side with our depth-charges still on. With the memory of Peter Opdall, Charlie Hearn and 'Baron' Biggs still very fresh in our memory, we felt we had received a timely warning not to let concentration slip for a moment. Maybe it wasn't entirely that, since the experienced Alistair Kindersley who had 'borrowed' Bill Roberts' Fulmar, went into the barrier rather expensively later on.

Next day, 4 April, brought quite a shake-out, shortly after our arrival in harbour at 1045. The Ugly Sisters – *Furious* and *Argus* – were both there, with *Renown's* sister-ship *Repulse*. Colin Ennever, our senior observer and 'Duke' Norfolk were going home for re-appointment, Colin to be replaced by Tim Cardew. The departure of Colin and 'Duke' called for considerable farewell toasting, on their near-virgin wine bills lasting until their boat came alongside to take them to *Furious* and home. At this point 'Duke' suddenly remembered that he hadn't told his batman to pack his gear, and a pot-valiant gang of well-wishers hurried below to assist him. 'Duke's' method of packing would have made a Burgundy grape-tromper envious, consisting of throwing all his gear, suits, flying clothing, books, personal possessions, the lot, into all available cases and kitbags, then treading it into the receptacle, wisely removing his boots first.

At 1900 all the big ships, escorted by destroyers, left harbour, plus two merchant ships, which according to rumour, were full of female charmers, plus Colin and 'Duke', who had managed to get their homeward accommodation switched. James Stewart-Moore called a conference that evening to introduce Tim Cardew and to indicate re-arrangement of crews. Murray and I were to be together again, which suited us both, since we had become accustomed to each others' methods, and a certain confidence had grown between us, though this was a 'flying friendship' only. Our tastes on shore leave differed. I liked sports, while Murray and his bosom pal, Pat Campbell, sought nothing more energetic than elbow-lifting in a cool bar, known to them as 'Egyptian Calisthenics'.

The maintenance personnel from 800 Skua Squadron had left us the previous day for passage in *Furious*, being replaced by the troops from 807 Fulmar Squadron under Lieutenant-Commander J S Douglas. After completing what appeared to have become our routine dawn A/S patrol and returning, Murray and I went down to breakfast, to find the wardroom full of strange faces. All of 800 had gone, leaving one aircraft behind for what purpose we knew not. A number of old friends had departed, a number of course-mates had arrived in 807, plus one special friend, though he wasn't in the wardroom. Johnnie Underwood and Ken Grant were the course-mates, and Richard Leggott the special chum. Dick and I had been at school together at Boston, Lincolnshire, and had both been keen on the sea as a career. He had gone to HMS *Ganges* as a boy seaman, specialising first in diving, but finding the air to be more his metier, later qualified as a rating pilot. Though of good education and enviable skill as a pilot, he steadfastly refused to take a commission, and was now awaiting promotion to CPO. Of an extraordinarily tough physique (one of only 43 who survived *Glorious'* sinking off Norway in June 1940) he had an attitude I could never understand, which seemed to boil down to the fact that most of his friends were in the Lower Deck, and he didn't want to forsake them. He was certainly not without ambition, and I spent many hours trying to convert him, but without success. Fortunately for the Royal Navy, he did cross the floor later and eventually · commanded 1831 Corsair Squadron of the 13th Carrier Air Group in the British Pacific Fleet during 1944-45. He retired as a lieutenant-commander, having been chief flying instructor at several training establishments after the war, where he maintained his reputation both as a pilot and as an instructor.

Returning to Gibraltar to refuel, collect stores and to effect a minor engine repair we spent two whole hours there before an emergency signal was received, indicating that the German battlecruisers were again at sea. So at 0500 'Special Sea Dutymen' was piped, and we left, having completed none of the allotted tasks, accompanied by our stablemates, *Renown* and *Sheffield*, with the cruiser *Fiji* and a destroyer screen. Rumour had it that we were to be the southern strike force, while the battleship *Queen Elizabeth* and other Home Fleet heavies were to look after the north. It seemed that *Furious* and *Argus* might have to put scratch striking forces together, since they were only about 400 miles north of us, heading homewards. Whatever happened, it had all the signs of being an exciting and interesting trip, since on 'swap-day' we had received four new Swordfish fitted with a miraculous new airborne radar device called ASV (Air to Surface Vessel). It was said to have a quasi-optical range, ie at 1000ft it could detect surface vessels at 10 miles, at 2000ft, 20 miles; 3000ft – 30 miles and so on. It sounded like magic, and in April 1941 it certainly was. There would be one ASV aircraft per squadron, with one aircraft kept as a spare. All observers were looking forward keenly to our training period which would begin shortly. On 7 April visibility deteriorated very badly after our fruitless afternoon recce. Nothing remotely resembling a German warship was seen, though Charlier of 810 reported seeing a Focke-Wulf four-engined 'Kondor' at the far end of his patrol.

Next day, all available aircraft not required for a search were loaded with 18in torpedoes, so that we could dispatch a strike immediately on receipt of an Enemy Sighting Report, and crews stood by, kitted for flying and all ready to go. However visibility became steadily worse, and was down to about 400 yards by 1500. Stan Keane, senior pilot of 818, made a remarkable landing just before dusk, missing all arrestor wires, and coming to what he later described as 'a thankful halt' on the port catapult. A signal later from RAF photographic interpreters indicated that the enemy ships were still in Brest, and meteorological information was that the fog was likely to be with us for several days, so an old-fashioned blockade of the French Atlantic ports was set up, Home Fleet ships returning to Plymouth to refuel and re-victual when necessary, our force doing likewise to Gibraltar.

In this dank and dismal weather, flying was restricted to A/S patrols since the roll and pitch motion was likely to be heavy on undercarriages, and we did not want to put ourselves into a situation where the fog lifted, the enemy emerged, and we had no serviceable strike aircraft. RAF Bomber Command attacked Brest nightly in an effort to cause sufficient damage to the town and to the ships so that they would be forced to put to sea, straight into the arms of our heavies. As the fog lifted occasionally, we would fly off Fulmars for a search. This they could carry out more rapidly, but less efficiently than Stringbags, but in the case of a strike being launched, they were not vital for the attack on surface ships, but would be very necessary for our defence against enemy aircraft.

After 12 days of constant searching all over the southwestern approaches to Brest it was reported by the Admiralty that *Gneisenau* had been damaged in harbour and had entered drydock for repairs. It was unlikely that a single battlecruiser would emerge to attack convoys, and anyway could be dealt with by fewer ships. So the Home Fleet went home, and we returned to Gibraltar, hoping this time to collect the fuel stores and food not collected last time.

Bad news awaited our arrival on 17 April at Gibraltar. Captain Holland was to be relieved, and was to be promoted. Though extremely pleased about the latter, the former caused no joy whatsoever as we would lose an extremely kind, capable and sensitive 'owner' who knew the value of flying machines. This is not to imply that his sensitivity was limited to aircrew – every manjack in *Ark* knew that 'Hooky' would back him all the way. There is little doubt that the 12 months of his command had been doubly onerous, since he had seen more action in that year than most captains see in a war. He had operated off Norway, Dakar, Oran, Cape Spartivento, Genoa and in numerous 'club runs' taking valuable convoys to the Eastern Mediterranean. So, on the 18th we dined him in the wardroom, where many compliments were paid and many dry tears shed. Even the case-hardened 'Maxie' Mayes was quietly thoughtful. Now we had to train his relief, Captain L E H Maund. If he was half as good as 'Hooky' for starters, we would have promising material on our hands.

Prior to entering harbour on the 17th, aircraft 'Able', 'Baker', 'Harry' and 'King' of 820 had been flown ashore to North Front. The ship was likely to be undergoing minor repairs for several days, and the German Navy was attempting to infiltrate U-boats into the Western Mediterranean. If we had been conceited, we might have believed that Force H and especially *Ark Royal* had become a number one priority on the Nazi liquidation list. It was becoming apparent from the determination of their attacks on aircraft carriers that they were getting extremely worried about the constant flow of additional Hurricanes to Malta, together with tanks, guns and men to reinforce the Army in the desert. It seemed that there was to be another 'club run' to Malta the following week, and our detached flight was to stay ashore to carry out various duties. We were billetted at the Grand Hotel, which, though Grand in name only, was at least a change from eternal sea-going accommodation.

The native Gibraltarians, like the Maltese, were British subjects and very anxious to impress their loyalty upon us. The hotel manager was courteous, helpful and very efficient. Our personal laundry, near-vandalised on board, now became very well looked after. Our white shirts became white again and decently ironed, socks again felt like wool instead of cardboard. The menu, whilst by no means up to the standard of the Berkeley Buttery, showed more variety, and the chef responded to our occasional suggestions, on more than one occasion producing curries and Spanish specialities. In the evenings we could walk around Gibraltar, at least until curfew time of 9pm and drink with friends in the various bars – Bristol, Capitol, the Rock and the Yacht Club. Perhaps one of the great delights was to wake in the morning to find the sun streaming through the curtains, to make a leisurely toilet, then go down to breakfast and to read TODAY'S newspaper – even though it was the *Gibraltar Times* with most of its reports through Reuter's Agency. Then a walk down to North Front, just over a mile, and to work.

The RAF carried out the dawn patrols in one of their large variety of aircraft. There were various flying boats, Londons, Singapores, even RAF Swordfish on floats, and usually one or two ships' Walrus amphibians disembarked for compass-swinging or repairs and in need of flying time. Several of *Ark's* pilots were also disembarked for dummy decklanding practice, their flying having become rather expensive in the last couple of essays into the Bay of Biscay. There were so many naval personnel ashore at North Front that we opened our own operations room, though it was subordinate to RAF operational control.

On the night of 21 April Murray told me that we were to have Admiral Somerville as a passenger on our dusk patrol of the Straits. He would fly in my normal observer's cockpit and I would operate as Observer/TAG, navigating (if necessary) and signalling both by radio and Aldis lamp. This should be a piece of cake after having done it for extended periods with a marathon tank, but on reconsideration, that inflammable item would have been preferable to the eagle-eye of Vice-Admiral Sir James Fownes Somerville KCB, DSO, especially as he was known to be better than a raw hand with the morse key. Part of the exercise was to inspect the lights of the colony. At that time, and so far as I know, throughout the war, there was no black-out, so that the Rock could not be distinguished from neutral Spain by enemy bomber crews.

We took off at 2000 without incident, though both our CO and senior pilot seemed twitchy lest I should commit some new *lèse-majesté*.

The Admiral had flown with me on a previous occasion, shortly after I joined the ship. On that particular morning my normal TAG, Finney, was absent, and a rather grizzled character, clad in a green Sidcot suit clambered aboard. Sidcot suits were not normally worn, except in very cold weather, even though we had open cockpits in Stringbags. Last time I had donned mine was in the early days at Lee to have a photograph taken to impress the incumbent girlfriend. But there was a shortage of airgunners, and some of the old 'barrack-stanchions' who had been looking forward to a leisured life at Signal School, or the two observer schools, or at Worthy Down, training more TAGs, were being drafted to ships as a temporary measure. It was not unnatural for me to suppose that such an Ancient Mariner had now joined me. The exercise was a dummy torpedo attack on our own ships, so little would be expected from the rear seat unless we ran into some sort of emergency. We didn't, simply carrying out two climbs to 6000ft, followed by two ear-popping dives at 180 knots, dropping a smoke bomb to simulate a 'fish' and landing on. After landing my 'airgunner' got out first, and I called to him to take my gear – Bigsworth Board, binoculars, instruments etc, while I climbed out. This he did, I took them from him, thanked him, and then walked up to the operations room. I suppose I should have wondered why such a piece of Old Ming didn't know the routine. Reporting to Commander Bentinck, I was transfixed by a basilisk stare 'Why?' he asked, spacing his words to give added emphasis, 'Why, Woods, are you behaving in such a bloody familiar manner with the Admiral?' As Bernard Miles used to say, 'There ain't no answer to that', as I stood there, rather like the little man in the H M Bateman *Punch* cartoons, quite shattered by the meteoric promotion of my airgunner, and could only stammer in a pale green voice that I hadn't recognised him, which happened to be true. 'Be sure Woods', went on Commander Bentinck, 'That he will in future recognise you.'

So obviously we had to box clever this time. I lurked in the shadows until The Great Man appeared, and wore my goggles down over the eyes to conceal as much as possible of my face. But all to no avail. None of it did us any good. We managed to make two sweeps across the Straits to Ceuta, then up to Tarifa and across to Cape Spartel, keeping always well outside international limits. After this, it had become reasonably dark, and Sir James requested Murray to circle the Rock so that he could take a look at the lights. Gibraltar is well-known to pilots for its strange air currents and eddies, which can lift or drop an aircraft several hundreds of feet without warning. Indeed, there have been many accidents there, some of them fatal, which were attributable to these unpredictable currents. So it was with some trepidation that we approached the town, and flew on down to Europa Point, Sir James making notes as we dropped or lifted. Just as we turned the corner to fly up to Sandy Bay, after which we would request permission to land, every light in the aircraft went out. With nerves sticking out like piano wires, I asked Murray if he was OK and if the lack of light would interfere with his continued flying and landing. Always cool and collected he replied over the Gosports that everything was under control. The Admiral somewhat testily (had he recognised me I wondered?) commanded me to rectify the lighting malfunction, which is difficult enough to do on the ground if one is not an electrician, which I wasn't, and almost impossible in the air. So I went through the motions, searching with my torch for some disconnected fuse, most being either in the pilot's or airgunner's cockpit and in some ridiculously improbable place.

So, I went through the motions, unscrewing leads, checking what I could, but all to no avail, though fortunately the airscrew continued to go round and we landed without any problems. As we taxied to dispersal, all the lights came on again, and to be honest, with no help from me. I gave the thumbs-up signal to Sir James, who gave me one of those 'you can't fool me' looks which all senior officers and especially vice-admirals, reserve for idiot juniors. Next day, of course, the electrician could find absolutely nothing amiss.

Admirals, like elephants, never forget. Eighteen months later, in Eastern Fleet, I was once again to serve under the very kindly 'Uncle James'. One day, in *Formidable*, we were being inspected by him. As he came along the ranks of 820 Squadron, our eyes met. His eyes stayed just that split second longer. No word was said, no word was needed. If he was going up for a night view of Colombo, Ceylon, there was one chap he was definitely not flying with.

Which was a pity, because that incident led me to take an unofficial course in aircraft electrics, and I could have guaranteed no problems in our new Albacores, with which we had re-equipped in 1941.

Alan Swanton had now rented a car from Sergeant Garcia of the Gibraltar Police Force. Automobile petrol was almost unobtainable, except for official purposes, which is why the car was for hire. We discovered that 97 octane aviation fuel plus a judicious admixture of paraffin gave an acceptable blend which would neither burn out the valves nor push out the choking clouds of smoke that advertised the illegal use of paraffin. So each morning we left the Hotel for North Front, 'Scruffy' Manley-Cooper beating a devil's tattoo on his passenger door to warn unsuspecting pedestrians of our approach. Alan would drive, with passengers Tony Mayes, myself and John Hedges a Fulmar pilot who had recently come to join 807, but needed to brush up his decklandings. John was a Manxman, quiet, but with an extremely dry wit. We discovered a mutual interest in rowing, and decided to try to join the Gibraltar Rowing Club, which could frequently be seen taking a 'four' round the outer harbour. Unfortunately nothing ever came of this, since our visits were so unpredictable.

The day after my flight with the Admiral, I was duty officer at North Front in the naval section when our new Captain Maund arrived for an unofficial inspection. Fortunately as 820 Squadron had practically built the airfield, I knew where everything was; the number of fire-extinguishers and fire-points, and all the trivia with which COs try to trap their underlings. A thought flitted through my mind that perhaps Sir James had expressed his displeasure at the previous evening's performance, and this visit was to check on my IQ; though it was hardly likely that a carrier captain would make such a visit himself. My self-esteem must have been rather low at that time.

The Dutch submarine *Dolfijn* had come to work from the base, and next day we carried out search and strike exercises with her in Algeciras Bay, with one of their officers as a passenger. Murray took the opportunity to show off some fairly 'split-arsed' turns. I don't know whether they impressed the Dutchman, they certainly surprised me, since he was normally such a steady and accurate no-nonsense pilot. But I suppose even the most orthodox aviator has, now and again, to cut loose a little.

Gibraltar was now becoming quite a busy airfield. RAF aircraft of all types were arriving, mainly to fly on to Middle East. There were Bombays, Blenheims and Wellingtons arriving in half-dozen lots, which must have had the Nazi spies in Algeciras working overtime. Especially as on 25 April that grizzled veteran and hero of the Dunkirk evacuation, Lord Gort VC, arrived to take over as Governor of the Colony. Rumours were rife – an invasion of Spain, a siege of the Rock or an evacuation? The air was thick with buzzes, each more far-fetched than the last. The day previous to the new Governor's arrival, Force H left harbour to fly off 24 Hurricanes to Malta, Bill Urry navigating the leader of the three escorting Fulmars. Simultaneously, the cruiser *Dido*, the fast minelayer *Abdiel* and 5 destroyers were to go through the Narrows to reinforce the Mediterranean Fleet. The fly-off was delayed for 24 hours as Malta was under a heavy mistral. So we 'ogo-pogoed' until Malta signalled that all was clear and the Hurries could now be received. Despite this delay and our being spotted by a Heinkel 111, no attack developed, the aircraft were flown off, and we returned to Gibraltar. All aircraft arrived safely.

In harbour we had our own excitements. On 25 April an RAF Wellington, giving its position near Cape Trafalgar, made an SOS. Four aircraft from 820 made for the spot where the Wellington was reputed to have ditched, but found no sign of the crew. Later, while making a further low-level investigation, RAF Gibraltar signalled that all the crew had been safely picked up by a Spanish boat. Next day they were brought to Gibraltar.

A very strange party now arrived at the Grand – Belgian airmen who had decided to join the Allies, and had been passed to Gibraltar via the 'rat-lines' through France and Spain. All had been pilots of Fairey

69

Ark Royal straddled by 12 Italian bombs on the late afternoon of 8 May 1941 as seen from HMS *Renown*. *Author's collection*

'Battle' bombers in the Belgian Air Force, and not having flown for some time, were anxious to try their skills on the Fulmars at North Front, viewing these aircraft as 'modified Battles'. An embarrassing situation arose, since despite the patent authenticity of their identities, too many strange people were arriving on or leaving the Rock, and since the last batch of French aircrew to arrive had 'borrowed' their CO's aircraft at Tafaraoui, this was a situation that would not make good press at the inquest if anything went wrong. The supreme diplomacy of our acting CO, Hughie, saved the situation. Agreeing that they should fly the Fulmar, but since they hadn't flown for some time, they must first take an air medical from the North Front doctor. Most surprisingly, they all failed due to slight irregularities in blood pressure and vision, which a few weeks' rest would undoubtedly cure. By which time we hoped they would be in Britain, thinking not one whit worse of their new allies.

So much clandestine work went on at that time with the various underground movements and the most improbable people arrived out of nowhere, that we lived some of the time in a state of acute scepticism, wondering if anyone (including ourselves) was who he or she represented themselves to be. With people of our own calling and nationalities there were certain tests which could be applied quite discreetly and without giving offence. Our recent friends at the Grand Hotel quite obviously were from Belgium, unquestionably they were pilots, and a few discreetly-worded questions had been properly fielded. What we didn't know was whether this was part of some deep Vichy or Axis plot to steal one of our aircraft on which there were still quite a few pieces of secret equipment, for example IFF which, as the initials imply, identified friend from foe on ship or shore radar screens. There was the homing beacon, which brought us back to the carrier in bad weather, and doubtless a Fulmar's radio and armament would have been of interest to the enemy.

Our new friends' credentials were, to say the least, straight out of a 'Sapper' mystery. One of them, whose real name escapes me today, had a British passport, probably issued by the British Embassy in Madrid, representing him to be Sir Anthony Marmol, a name so improbable that it might have been true of someone. Another, whose real name was Jacques LeGrand had the identity of John Thomas Large, obviously the brainchild of some whimsical character in the Madrid Embassy. But I suppose the Gestapo would have had greater difficulty in believing the name of our Ambassador to Spain at that time – Sir Samuel Hoare.

One evening in the small back-bar at the Grand, our guests announced that they were leaving us shortly, so we decided to give them a farewell party. The obliging hotel manager prepared us a punch which he christened 'Stringbag Special'. Our official wine-taster, 'Maxie' Mayes, opined that just a touch more boost was required to attain quickly the requisite flying speed, and added another bottle of Spanish brandy. Another – probably 'Scruffy' – knowing nothing of 'Maxie's' action, added further bottled produce, and the party climbed to operational height very quickly. Our guests, who numbered five or six, then gave us a few of their squadron songs – remarkably similar to our own in terms of anatomical reference and lubricity. We had now rendered 'Cats on the Rooftops', followed by 'O'Reilly's daughter' and the first forty or so verses of the 'Ball of Kirriemuir'. 'Maxie', known on board as 'The Bathroom Baritone' was in his element, pounding on the piano, and covering his numerous bum notes with his fog-horn-like harmonies. The Belgian Air Force songs were now including actions, and all of a sudden the manager appeared at my elbow requesting a word in my ear. Fully prepared for a request to raise the tone of the lyrics, I was embarrassed to be led to a couple of extremely well-groomed ladies, by their accents obviously French, who wished to know more of the party's origins. I explained that we were saying farewell to some Belgian friends, apologising meantime for the questionable quality of some of the songs. The senior lady, of quite striking, almost masculine, elegance said 'Please ask if we might join you for a little singing of jolly songs. If it helps, my name may possibly be known to them. It is Françoise Rosay.'

Never ever, before or since, have I seen so many expressions pass so quickly over so many embarrassed faces. Here was one of their idols, l'Etoile, the one and only, the incomparable Françoise Rosay. And she had heard their lewdness. 'Quel embarras' moaned Sir Anthony. He need not have worried. She made us all feel perfectly at ease, talked to us all, sang beautifully and nostalgically for us, so that even 'Maxie', for the second time in a month, became misty-eyed. Finally she consented to join us for dinner. It is an incident, so implausible that even today, almost 40 years later, I wonder if it really happened. But my diary says it did, and I have checked that the late lamented lady was in Gibraltar at that time. Ergo it is true.

What Madame Rosay was doing in Gibraltar I never thought to ask, but have since then learned that she took an active part – a very active part – in the French Resistance Movement, making many broadcasts from Britain, and later, after the invasion in November 1942, from Algiers. Ever since that meeting I have never failed to see her films, usually when re-run on television.

Next morning's flying was a little tentative, though a couple of 180-knot dives proved that the cure is often worse than the illness. Later we heard that two Wellingtons had been lost out of the latest half-dozen coming out from one of the Devon or Cornish airfields. Rather surprising, since this only entailed flying south for a more or less predetermined time, then turning left. Maybe the RAF's phobias about flying over the sea were akin to ours when flying over the land. Maybe a couple of naval observers should be loaned the RAF to navigate their aircraft to Gibraltar.

Force H was back next day, 28 April, and it appeared that at least for a time, 4 Stringbags and 3 fighters would be retained ashore. Four from 810 and three Fulmars from 808 landed at North Front in the afternoon, and we flew on at 1800, just prior to the ship entering harbour. Dick Charlier had a nasty incident on the last trip. Due to a strong wind at take-off he had no option but to turn to starboard as he passed the bridge superstructure, but in doing so, his wingtip struck the bridge and he crashed into the sea. Dick and his observer, Jefferd, were rescued, but his airgunner, Evans, could not be found, despite a long search.

Someone up there must have been reading my mind, since next morning, when I went to North Front to supervise some compass-swinging, two RAF Sunderland flying boats arrived, followed soon afterwards by six Beaufighters. The Beaufighters were in two vics of three, each vic navigated by a Sub-Lieutenant (A) RNVR. To complete the picture, later that afternoon, a Sunderland arrived from Malta, this one navigated (he later claimed) by Bill Urry. Though not at all improbable, the navigation equipment in a Sunderland is akin to that of a small ship, with astrodomes, automatic pilot and every modern convenience, like galleys and toilets.

Bill brought the sad news that two old chums had been killed in Egypt – 'Muscle' ·Griffiths and 'Budge' Dixon, the former an Oxford University and Northamptonshire cricketer. 'Budge' and I had realised that pilot's wings were not really for us, and had both volunteered to become observers rather than poor pilots, possibly condemned to ferrying or drogue-towing for the rest of the war. He was a delightful friend, intelligent and thoughtful, an excellent pianist in both classical and ragtime mood, modest to the nth degree. I well remember in our initial training at St Vincent in the late summer of 1939, the physical training instructor requesting volunteers for a cricket team to play the

Three Fleet Air Arm Fulmar fighters prepare to lead 23 RAF Hurricanes from *Ark Royal* to Malta at 0630 on 26 April 1941. The Fulmar had a much longer cockpit cover (for pilot and observer) and wider wheelbase than the Hurricane. Sub-Lieutenant (A) Charles Friend RN of 810 Squadron walks forward to the island. *Author's collection*

officers. The usual slashers and comic bowlers volunteered, leaving the PTI one or two short. 'Anyone else play cricket?' 'Budge' said 'I have, Chief'. 'Well do yer want to play or don't yer?' asked the PTI. 'Love to.' said 'Budge'. At that time we had only been together a few days, and none knew of 'Budge's' prowess with bat and ball. He skittled the opposition out for a meagre total, which could have been less had he not decided to rest and let them get a few 'on the board' in order to make a game of it. At the interval, the PTI called him over 'You played afore, ain't yer?' Budge agreed. 'Where?' asked the PTI. 'Oxford University and Northamptonshire' said 'Budge'. 'Can yer bat an'all?' asked the PTI. 'Not too well' said 'Budge', feeling at this time like a criminal found guilty of fraud. He was put in at 4th wicket down, since miracles, even at *St Vincent*, didn't happen twice in one day. So after the first four wickets (including mine) had fallen cheaply, 'Budge' went in, and with a few classic shots including a couple of sixes, drew us just short of the wardroom total before throwing his wicket away so that someone else could have the glory of making the winning hit. 'Budge' was just that sort of person. I don't think they're made any more.

Our Straits A/S patrols continued while my new-found expertise in compass-swinging was utilised to the full, and we soon had every aircraft on top-line in this and all other respects. Knowing that we would shortly again be at sea, I made it my business to get the ratings' work finished each day by 1500 to 1530, so that they could enjoy sunbathing at one of the many beaches, Sandy, Catalan, or Rosia Bays or Europa Point. It was still a shade cool for swimming, but getting better. And so April came and went.

Our new senior observer fell sick on 4 May, necessitating his passage home, leaving 'Maxie' Mayes as temporary incumbent.This we were prepared to tolerate for a short while, and would support him in every way, but since 'Maxie' hadn't yet passed his W/T proficiency test, we were less than enthusiastic about his technical decisions since his navigation was also based on somewhat cavalier and insupportable principles, plus a great deal of luck. But we backed him up in front of the CO, as none of us knew when we ourselves might not be thrown into a situation which was too big for us. In fact, Geoffrey 'Toom' Topham would have made a better choice, being more efficient all round, but sadly, in the Royal Navy, it is usually seniority which wins the day, not always ability.

To everyone's surprise, we left Gibraltar on 5 May and steered westward into the Atlantic. Not surprisingly, the ship was once more rife with buzzes, mainly because no one really had a clue as to what we were doing. In the afternoon, Captain Maund continued 'Hooky's' practice of putting everyone in the picture as soon as possible, telling us that we were going to have a fight a desperately important convoy through to Alexandria in the next few days. The Desert Army was short of tanks and the newly-arrived German general, Rommel, was pressing towards Cairo. The situation there was at best described as 'grim', with Tobruk besieged, Greece overrun and Malta taking a hammering daily. Normally the convoy would have gone round the Cape route, but Winston Churchill had insisted that the risk of losses among the vital 240 tanks of Operation 'Tiger' was acceptable if the extra 42 days at sea was saved by avoiding the Cape route. The thought of a few more days in 'Bomb Alley' caused sharp intakes of breath all round, since we knew that huge *Luftwaffe* reinforcements had been flown into Sicily, Sardinia and Italy, all capable of making life extremely noisy and unpleasant for Malta and Alexandria convoys.

Taking off at 1535, Murray, Finney and I searched ahead of the Force, rendezvousing with the battleship *Queen Elizabeth*, which, with cruisers *Naiad* and *Phoebe*, was to help escort the convoy through to Alexandria. Re-entering the Straits at night, once more we passed through an astounded Spanish fishing fleet, setting our course for the Skerki Bank, our turnabout point when we flew off the Hurricanes on Malta runs. We took station to the north of the convoy, to intercept enemy bombers before they could attack the slower convoy, and to give ourselves better manoeuvring room. That afternoon, clocks were put two hours on, making a shorter working day, but a later sunset. Initially it had been planned to bomb Cagliari airfield using delayed-action fuses. In the past this had kept the Italians on the ground, but we felt it wouldn't deter the more vertebrate *Luftwaffe* and might, in fact, do more harm than good, as on the last run, Force H with its Hurricanes had escaped detection altogether. For better or for worse, no bombing of Cagliari this trip. And so passed 6 May.

Next day was my father's 49th birthday, and I made a note to drink his health that evening, if I were spared. Visibility was delightfully poor, but shadowers were detected on *Sheffield*'s new radar, and we breathed again as the 'bandit' turned out to be one of our own aircraft appearing from a direction whence it should not have been coming. All day long we carried on through the drizzle and low cloud, flying only A/S patrols at low level to avoid their being detected by enemy radar, and also kept them in touch visually with our ships, which in the rather eerie weather were inclined to shoot first and ask questions afterwards. At 1930 two large aircraft were reported coming from dead ahead, and fighters were scrambled to intercept. A few seconds later two very surprised and startled Sunderlands switched on their IFF sets and continued on unmolested to Gibraltar. In view of the very poor visibility it was again considered whether 820 should not take part in a 15-aircraft raid on Cagliari, but for the same reasons as yesterday, the idea was shelved. So we carried on unmolested through the night, and I drank to my father's continued good health, coupled with that of his elder unmarried son. Darkness fell at 2200.

It seemed now that A4H was The Peoples' Choice for 'Operation Sparrowfart' as the dawn A/S patrol was known, and at 0700 on 8 May, Murray, Finney and I were on our usual routine. Most ships went to action stations at this time, since it was the hour at which submarines were unusually active in the belief that all shipping tended to be a bit sloppy then. Half-an-hour later, it was usual to release to defence stations, but this day, it was action stations all day, going to meals in watches. The murky weather of the past few days disappeared with the sunrise but fortunately visibility was still rather limited. It was going to be a very long and probably exciting day.

A shadower was picked up by the radar at 0855, but chased immediately by Fulmars, disappeared into cloud. Since it was obviously going to be a day for the fighters, most TBR pilots and observers were allotted secondary duties, some as officers i/c the 2pdr eight-barrelled pompom mountings, some as 'shadows' to senior officers who might be wounded and immobilised. My action station was in the operations room understudying Commander Bentinck. At 1355 four sub-flights of torpedo-carrying SM 79s appeared, concentrating on the carrier. They were discouraged by intense AA fire from the destroyer screen and from the bigger ships, which forced them to drop their 'fish' outside the screen, so that *Ark, Renown* and *Sheffield* were able to turn and comb the

Hurricane reinforcement for Malta being prepared for take off by a RAF sergeant pilot aboard *Ark Royal* on 26 April 1941. *Author's collection*

tracks. The SM 79, unlike the Swordfish, could not turn away after dropping because of its lower manoeuvrability compared with a biplane, but endeavoured to fly low and fast between the columns of the convoy. While this of itself was dangerous for the SM 79s there was usually some indecision from the AA gunners, who found themselves not only with a prime enemy target, but a fair possibility of firing through to a hitherto friendly ship in the next column. On this occasion, the SM 79s were out of luck, losing three out of eight, two to ships' gunfire and one to Jimmy Gardner of 808. Rupert Tillard, CO of 808, and Mark Somerville, the senior observer, failed to return to the ship. They were last seen engaging several Fiat CR 42 biplane fighters of extreme manoeuvrability, similar in type to the famed Gloster Gladiator. The deaths of these two courageous and experienced officers made us realise that the Mediterranean sea war was no longer the jocular affair it had sometimes been when fighting the Italians alone. Their moral fibre now strengthened by the arrival of *Fliegerkorps X*, we could expect the battle to be much tougher henceforth. Our fighters suffered a great deal that morning. Starting with only 12 out of 18 serviceable for combat, the two lost left us with 10 only. However, the other crew shot down, 'Buster' Hallett and TAG Smith, were rescued by the destroyer *Foresight*.

Next, at 1515, came high-level and dive-bombers, one of which was shot down before our fighters drove them away. Petty Officer 'Leslie' Howard, one of my former instructors, took a cannon-shell in the leg, but insisted on staying up to fight until recalled for refuelling and rearming. A short pause followed this attack, then three small formations of SM 79s came to highlevel bomb between 1630 and 1730. Two of the formations were forced to jettison their bombs outside the destroyer screen after determined attacks by Fulmars, the third, escorted by CR 42s dropping a stick of 12 bombs which straddled *Ark Royal*, drenching the flightdeck with spray, but doing no physical damage. Then came the lull before the storm.

During this intense period of action, what interested me most was the unexpected transformation that came over Commander Bentinck, normally a very reserved and correct senior officer. When all guns were firing and cracking our eardrums and the bombers and torpedo-carriers were being pursued hotly by our fighters up and down the shipping columns, he would run between port and starboard portholes of the Air Information Office (AIO) cheering like a schoolboy watching the First XV, once throwing his gold-braided cap in the air as a SM 79 came to a fiery end almost alongside.

Snatching a hasty meal after my AI0 duty was complete, I hastened to my second action station on M4 pompom. The 'Director Officer' was a recent addition, since it had been found that the regular guns' crews were so involved watching their target aircraft, especially torpedo-planes coming in fast and low out of the darkness, that they could fail to see a less obvious but more dangerous one elsewhere. The control of the mounting remained quite properly in the capable hands of the Leading Seaman 'Captain of the Gun', though the extra pair of trained eyes seemed to help. So far I had taken part only in dummy-runs, with none of the 8 barrels firing. I hoped that my nerve would hold up in this exposed position under actual combat conditions. Though there were still three hours to go before sunset, at 1900, we began to feel a quiet confidence, while realising that darkness could lend cover to some nasty surprises from submarines, mines, E-boats, destroyers or even night torpedo-bomber attacks. Just as we noted with pleasure some huge black clouds moving in from the north, a large formation was reported by radar to be approaching from the direction of Sicily, fine on the port bow. About 30 Ju 87 Stuka dive-bombers, escorted by Me 110 twin-engined fighters, were in three sections. It looked like the enemy's last desperate throw, and we could not help remembering that it was the kind of attack which had in a matter of minutes transformed *Illustrious* from a proud fighting ship into a smoking shambles.

Three more Fulmars had been damaged too badly for combat, and every fighter on board bore its honourable scars by bullet and cannon-shell. As the remaining seven prepared to fly off in three sections of two and one rover, we knew that the dice were heavily loaded against them, and consequently against us. No one dared think of what would happen were the carrier to be sunk or damaged, when further air defence would be impossible, the fighters ditching wherever they could, the convoy left vulnerable to continuous night attacks from air and surface.

As the escorted bombers approached out of the darkling sky, the grey-blue heavens were spotted with black AA bursts. With a courage born of desperation, yet with cool heads, our fighters tore into the bomber formations, and though heavily outnumbered, made head-on, beam, quarter and tail attacks as opportunity presented itself. Miraculous to relate, not a single bomb was dropped on the convoy or its escorts, every bomber jettisoning its load and heading flat out for Sicily. It was unbelievable that such strong German formations could have been chased out of the sky by seven tired Fulmars flown by tired pilots and observers, most of whom had made four sorties each during the day. Puzzled analysts next day submitted that the only explanation was that the Fulmars were mistaken for Hurricanes which had achieved an enviable reputation in the defence of Malta. Whatever it was, the facts are that during the day at least 8 enemy fighters and bombers were shot down by AA fire and fighters for the loss of 2 fighters and 1 crew. Even allowing for the fact that the crew shot down was probably the finest partnership in the Royal Navy, the arithmetic was good.

But the day was still not over, and as dusk became darkness four more SM 79s, each with twin torpedoes, attacked from ahead, making straight for the carrier. Ronnie Hay and Giles Guthrie at readiness, flew off, but couldn't intercept before the tinfish were launched. My M4 pompom was going full blast, scoring hits on the tail of the last aircraft as it turned away aft. Though I still think it was 'ours', later reported on fire and in the sea, I am not really sure, but nevertheless advanced the gun's crews' claim for a probable. Our ships combed the tracks and sustained no damage.

Thankful for the gathering darkness at 2100, we posted double lookouts all round and with rousing cheers for their safe arrival, left the convoy to turn back for base. Of the 12 Fulmars with which we had started the day, only 3 were now still fully operational should we encounter trouble next day, though by cannibalising, 6 could be made serviceable. Although the pilots and their crews had been exceptionally courageous, it should not be forgotten that without the sterling work of the maintenance crews, their efforts would have been less praiseworthy, slaving away as they did all day in a hot and noisy hangar deck, knowing little of the battle going on outside. Captain Maund had caused loudspeakers to be rigged near all action stations so that ship's company was kept informed. It was hot, noisy, sweaty and dirty, but we had again won the day. Meals in the circumstances were excellent, and prepared and served by a galley staff, who, having action stations too, were just as vital in our success. All through the day our 16 high-angle/low-angle 4.5in guns in twin mountings had been firing as the ship manoeuvred in all directions, yet all members of the ship's company on deck and in the air worked together with the skill and cheerfulness one came to expect from this very efficient ship.

It was a day never to be forgotten, though the convoy did not get through unscathed. *Empire Song* was sunk by a mine off Malta, another one damaging *New Zealand Star*, which managed to reach Alexandria. The 8th Destroyer Flotilla had escorted the convoy right through the Narrows, but returning to Gibraltar next day was bombed and *Fortune* damaged. For the remainder of the return passage we kept guard on her since Italian submarines were known to be in the vicinity. She reached Gibraltar safely.

Rome Radio put on their customary comedy show that night, claiming to have sunk one aircraft carrier, a battleship and a cruiser, while 30 Hurricanes and 12 Bristols (whatever they may have been!) had been shot down for the loss of only 5 of their gallant – and lying – aviators. This happened all the time, and one really had to wonder why we didn't run out of carriers and battleships, so many had they sunk.

Despite an 18-hour day on 9 May, Murray, Finney and I made our customary dawn and reconnaissance patrol next morning, followed by another at dusk. Three French merchant ships were sighted sailing from Marseilles to Algiers, just off the eastern tip of Minorca. Impressed by the surprise effect of the low-level Italian torpedo attack, Commander Flying had us carry out a replica next day with runner torpedoes. I don't know if flying at nought feet out of the darkness scared the carrier, but by God, it scared us. At 85 knots we were sitting ducks.

Our humorous RPO Mortimer on Rounds that evening commented 'Don't know what's the matter with me, sir. Up every morning at dawn, work through until midnight only, yet I feel tired out. D'you think I'm getting too old for the job?'. I was so tired myself that his point didn't sink in immediately, and I woke up hours after turning in, laughing my head off.

Back in harbour on 12 May, the next few days were spent in getting our fighters back to full strength. In spite of the fact that one of our major tasks was to keep Malta and the Western Desert Air Force supplied with replacement fighters, we didn't seem to carry enough spares for our own fighter defence, which was odd, because if we could not fulfil our own role, we could not carry out our assigned tasks. Our Air Engineer Officer, 'Finkle' Fensome was fortunately well endowed with better-than-average senses of humour, proportion and persuasion. Added to which he seemed to be pretty good at his job despite (or perhaps because of) the single wavy stripe on his sleeve. Flitting between the ship, North Front airfield, Dockyard engineers' workshops, RAF Coastal Command depot and any ship in harbour carrying aircraft, he managed to keep the maximum number of aircraft serviceable. At this time, when an engine was repaired or overhauled, this was done in situ, after which the aircraft was brought up on deck, run up, and if satisfactory, test-flown. Now unveiled on the flightdeck was his new masterpiece, known as 'Fensome's Fearnought'. Simply this was a test-rig, on which an aircraft engine could be affixed by a small number of bolts, brought up to the flight deck and run up. If not satisfactory, it was worked upon until it was so, avoiding the time-wasted by replacing an engine on an airframe, finding it was not quite right, and eventually having to dismantle again. Provided we carried sufficient spare engines, we could test them before replacing in the airframes and achieve greater serviceability.

On the 13th we heard of Rudolf Hess's arrival in Scotland. This seemed just too far-fetched to be true, especially as we had recently read *Flying Visit* by Peter Fleming, describing a fictitious descent by parachute on London by Adolf Hitler. But all was later confirmed by the BBC Overseas News. An even ruder shock came later that day when I was informed by the pay office that I was due to pay income tax. Shattering news! The war was now becoming personal. After risking my neck several times a day for a miserable £20 gross monthly in pay and

The rear cockpits of a Swordfish Mark II. Observer's cockpit: Starting at the wing edge and going round clockwise one can see the port compass mounting, the airspeed indicator and altimeter dial and the observer's morse key. His parachute is stowed beneath the high coaming (supposed to cut down some of the slipstream). Finally there is the starboard compass mounting. There are identical compass mountings on either side of the air gunner's cockpit for use when a long-range fuel tank was fitted in the observer's. Air Gunner's cockpit: Aft is the Vickers 0.303in gas-operated machine gun on its ring mounting. To the right of the port compass mounting is a Vickers ammunition drum and below it the wheel for winding in and out the trailing W/T aerial next to the fire step. There was one each side for the gunner to stand on when firing. They were hollow and used to stow W/T spares. *Ian Huntley Collection*

RAF armourers fit smoke-floats to the bomb rack of Swordfish L7672 aboard *Ark Royal* before the war. *Popperfoto*

allowances, a grateful government was now asking for £25 back annually. As Mr Lord – the aptly named Warrant Paymaster pointed out – 'There is a war on you know'.

Next day, our big squadron soccer match versus communications. Again Nigel Gardner and I were selected – a great honour. We both played very well, despite being a trifle out of condition, and won 3-1. This moved us into the final against either the Royal Marines or Engineroom XI. It appeared that 820 was the only soccer team with officers playing, and I am not sure of the significance. Later Nigel and I went on to join John Hedges, Alan Swanton and 'Scruffy' at the Yacht Club. Also there was Giles Guthrie of 808, relaxing quietly with Jimmy Gardner after the excitement of the last convoy, when they flew four sorties each on the last day. They were very cut up at the loss of Rupert Tillard and Mark Somerville. The Admiral, they said, took the loss of his nephew very well, but commented that it might have been better had he (the Admiral) been killed after his full and rewarding life, while Mark's promising career had just begun. Giles suggested that we should start hunting for 'rabbits' – sailor's slang for gifts for home – especially silk

81

stockings, now almost unobtainable in Britain. He would say no more, other than that he had heard a well-found 'buzz'. The Admiral perhaps? After all, even Admirals gossip occasionally.

Next day a squadron reshuffle was announced. Paul Compton was being relieved and was going home, leaving Hughie as senior pilot to fly with James. 'Scruffy' showed great aptitude with the new ASV radar, and would operate it on all strikes. Murray now became a flight commander, with Tony Mayes as his observer, and I moved over to Alan Swanton, with whom I had already flown several times. Murray was due for his second stripe within a few weeks.

Chapter 7
Hunting and Sinking the Bismarck

On 16 May leave was allowed until 1630 only, as Force H went to sea for more practices. The first was a night navigation exercise, but just as we were getting into our flying gear, a heavy fog rolled in from the Atlantic, and the exercise was cancelled, since even with everyone regaining the ship correctly, there were strong possibilities of accidents during landing-on. If any aircraft got themselves lost, the resultant chaos either homing them or searching for ditched aircraft would nullify any advantages gained. This was just as well, since I had that day sustained a rather shattering attack of 'Gibraltar Dog', unpleasant enough on the deck, but much more unnerving in an open cockpit at night.

The next morning found the fog burning away quite early, giving way to clear blue skies. *Renown* decided to have a throw-off shoot with her main 15in armament, and I was selected to do the spotting for her. My persecution complex surfaced immediately. I was beginning to get a 'thing' about the Admiral, and suspected that this was yet another trial of my ability, and mentioned it to Alan. 'Come off it' he said, 'I saw the Admiral climbing into the ASV aircraft with 'Scruffy'. They're off doing some ranging, and he'll join us in an ALT later on.' It appears that there were several dignitaries from the Rock, including senior Army and Air Force officers who had been pressed by the new Governor, Lord Gort VC, to take a look at what their sister service was doing.

The throw-off shoot went very well, thanks to a short chat with our own gunnery officer just before take-off to ensure that I would be using the right procedures. We climbed to 3000ft to ensure that we were well clear of the zenith of any erratic projectiles, and were immediately in touch by radio with *Renown's* gunnery control officer. Perhaps the day was too perfect, there being neither roll nor pitch and only light winds, but after two ladders, the target was straddled, and continued to be straddled. Each of the three turrets took its turn, and the exercise was complete. Then we joined the rest of the squadron which had now formed up to climb for a dummy torpedo attack. Because of the almost cloudless skies, we climbed to 10,000ft, at which height one's breathing becomes slightly laboured, as we lacked refinements such as oxygen masks, at least in Stringbags. A fairly 'split' dive preceded an attack on the flagship, which was doubtless exercising her guns' crews. It was a perfect sector attack, and whichever way *Renown* turned, she encountered a sub-flight of three. I'm sure the 'Visiting Elks' were impressed.

On return, both Wolf Bentinck and Charles Coke, the signals officer, extended their congratulations on our flying and spotting procedures. It was a most encouraging start to a new partnership, destined unfortunately to be of brief duration.

Lieutenant-Commander Charles Coke was our signals officer at that time, and a very good instructor to the inexperienced. His office was a small 'cuddy' off the main operations office, where he would sit very quietly most of the time, browsing through signals manuals, making corrections. One would never know he was there, save for the giveaway pungent smell of his perennial 'Erinmore' tobacco. Charles never seemed to enthuse over anything, but was always punctiliously polite, even when handing out a rocket for some misdeed, so polite, in fact, that his reprimands hurt more than those handed out by more irascible seniors.

Laurence Wilkinson of the *Daily Express* had been with us in his role as official war correspondent for the past six months at least, and was now recalled to the Bomb Alley of Fleet Street for further orders. That evening we drank long and hard courtesy of Beaverbrook Newspapers as we wished Laurence a fond farewell – he never dreaming that he was shortly to miss the 'scoop' of his career.

Furious and the cruiser *London* arrived at dusk, the old carrier mooring with her stern to ours, which was unusual. However, we saw the reason shortly afterwards as a wooden bridge was put across the gap to join the two flightdecks. She had brought out 48 Hurricanes for Libya, and we were to take 22, 'Scruffy' was in his element, as he had been urging a simple modification like this for some time. Instead of flying off a dozen at a time, two carriers could now bring 48 or so, as *Furious* had stowed them below decks for the passage out by the simple expedient of detaching the wings, which working parties spent all night re-attaching to get ready for the fly-off.

At 0030 on 18 May, having put Wilkinson ashore, giggling and hiccuping, we went to sea, making our usual feint into the Atlantic. *Furious* stayed in harbour revictualling and refuelling, joining us with *London* next day at 1600 when we all proceeded up towards the Men's End (this small conceit we continued to grant them in Alexandria). The following day was uneventful, apart from a Spanish commercial aircraft flying over us at 1345. As his approach was from a not unfriendly direction, fighters were not scrambled as he was recognised at about 25 miles' range.

Captain Maund was getting slightly worried these days, since so much of our work was predictable. When we left Gibraltar, this fact was pretty certainly made known immediately to Berlin and Rome. If we had no convoy with us and fighters on the flightdeck, it was a pretty safe bet that these were for Malta or Libya, needing no Sherlock Holmes to determine our approximate ETA at the flying-off point, give or take a few hours or miles. Something pretty nasty could be cooked up for future trips. Were the boot on the other foot, we would certainly have done so long ago – mines, submarines, MTBs, night or day torpedo attack. We were beginning to stick our necks out and we knew it, but there was no quicker way of delivering these priceless aircraft to where they were so urgently needed. The alternative was to fly them across Africa starting on the Gold Coast at Takoradi.

Swordfish A4C of 820 Squadron going in to attack *Bismarck* about 1920 on 26 May 1941. The author sits between Sub-Lieutenant (A) F A Swanton RN (pilot) and Leading Airman J R Seager (telegraphist/air gunner), both of whom were wounded in the attack. The 18in Mark XII torpedo has an arming pistol in its nose and the Swordfish has smoke-floats under the lower wing. *Author's collection*

Dawn on 21 May sent us to action stations preparatory to flying off the Hurricanes, 8 of which were to formate on each of 6 Fulmars, Mike Tritton leading. But hardly had his brood attached themselves than he had to return with a choked oil line landed on, repaired the fault and took off again, urged by 'Wings', who wanted to get off his straight and level course quickly. Another Fulmar, piloted by PO Sabey, could not retract its undercarriage, and so would never make Malta unless it were fixed – a 400-mile flight and tight under normal circumstances. Sabey returned, circled, signalled, and a relief Fulmar took off, but the Hurries refused to leave Sabey, invisibly attached, like piglets to Mum. Finally Sabey and his observer, Bernard Furlong, flew away, hoping to turn their charges over en route. Malta later reported the safe arrival of 47 Hurricanes and 5 Fulmars. The lost Hurricane had for no obvious reason dived into the sea off Cape Bon, Tunisia, while Sabey and Furlong's Fulmar also ditched. They had shown outstanding devotion to duty, knowing it to be an 80/20 chance of turning out a one-way ticket. Fortunately both Sabey and Furlong were rescued, Sabey being awarded the Distinguished Service Medal. As for the Hurricane, we had lost them before mysteriously, so perhaps removal of the wings was a cause, perhaps not. All in all, a very satisfactory operation.

The remainder of the day was unusually quiet, the only excitement being our afternoon A/S patrol sighting a Blenheim pilot in his dinghy, and organising his pickup by a destroyer. One shadowing Cant appeared from the direction of St Elmas, Cagliari, was intercepted by a Fulmar, but escaped into a cloud. If anything, it was too quiet, but few of us expected the storm which was to burst around our ears before the next week was out.

David Moxey of 818 Squadron was in charge of the observers' office, where all charts and equipment were stored. David was going home, and I was appointed to take over. It involved also keeping the ops room charts up to date, which I proceeded to do on the afternoon of 22 May. It was there that the signals were coming in apace from the Eastern Mediterranean, now truly the Men's End, for the Battle of Crete was in its third day, both the cruisers *Fiji* and *Gloucester* reporting being hit.

At 1645, Alan and I took off for an A/S patrol, returning after 15 minutes by way of emergency landing when a main oil line had broken, leaving me in the rear cockpit about two inches deep in oil. As we dripped our oily feetmarks up the deck, even 'Wings' had to smile. Leaving A4G, our brand new Blackburn-made Swordfish, we climbed into A4L, the spare, and to show that the mechanical breakdown had in no way disturbed us, did a voluntary all-round patrol. The destroyer HMS *Foresight* joined us from Malta at 1745 and at 2300 we were entering harbour. May is a beautiful time in Gibraltar as it is not yet that 'siesta' type heat, and there are cool, rather than warm winds blowing. On the flightdeck that night it was cold enough for an overcoat, but good to see some lights ashore again.

Even ashore 23 May was ominously quiet, eerie would be a fitting word. Most of us felt that something was about to happen, we knew not what. To get our minds going in a different direction, Bill Roberts, Dilly Dangerfield and Bill Urry and I went to Sandy Bay in the afternoon to sunbathe, having completed our shipboard duties in record time. We figured that harbour time was now going to be at a premium, so we should get ashore at every opportunity. At sea the 18-hour day would be the norm.

Naturally it was my duty watch when the order came to lash everything down securely and proceed with all dispatch to sea at 0230 on 24 May. Heavy weather was expected. Twice I woke the wrong Duty Petty Officer. News slowly came in and by the time I was in the observers' office, getting out the requisite charts, a grim picture was beginning to form. By breakfast the dread news had been broadcast that the once-mighty battlecruiser HMS *Hood* was no more, sunk apparently with no survivors (subsequently 3 were picked up out of a ship's company of 1419). A great feeling of depression came over us, since *Hood* was considered unsinkable, the Navy's pride, but above all this we had so often received calls for help from convoys being attacked by surface raiders, always seeming to arrive too late. It seemed that this might be just one more of those wild-goose chases, where we would spend a couple of weeks rolling about in the North Atlantic searching night and day for something which had gone to earth the moment we crossed the boom at Gibraltar.

So many stories have been written of the *Bismarck* action by more erudite folk than I, that I will merely try to describe the sector in which 820 Squadron were involved. There was a strange and personal prologue to this action. Before I knew that I would join *Ark Royal*, my last leave was spent in Boston, Lincolnshire, my home. A neighbour and friend there was Robert Gooding, Chief of the local Customs & Excise Waterguard, whose job was to inspect all ships entering that small East Coast port. One evening he called me over for a drink and showed me a photograph which had been given him by a young Scandinavian seaman in a ship which had recently escaped to Britain. Some weeks earlier, the ship was in a Baltic port, and all scuttles were ordered closed and blacked out as a secret warship was coming past. Being young and intending to escape as soon as possible, this aroused his curiosity, and when he saw this enormous ship draw past, he took a snapshot. With no idea what the ship was, he gave the snap to Robert Gooding, who gave it to me. It had to be *Bismarck, Tirpitz* or a scaled-down version such as the heavy cruiser *Prinz Eugen*, since we knew where all other heavies were, and had not yet seen any of those mentioned.

In turn, when I joined *Ark Royal*, I passed on the picture to Commander Bentinck, who compared it with known silhouettes of major German warships, and by elimination we deduced it to be either *Tirpitz* or *Bismarck*. We must have been the only ship to know what the enemy looked like, since both ships had been completed after the outbreak of war and therefore had not appeared in *Jane's* or in the press as would have been normal.

All through the 24th and 25th we slugged northwards with *Renown* and *Sheffield*, heading for the dreaded Bay without a destroyer escort, which was pushing our luck a little. However, this was urgent business, which if grasped now, would make our life so much easier in future when we didn't have another raider to worry about. But we rolled and yawed corkscrew fashion, knowing that any U-boat captain with sense was lying on the sea-bed waiting for the storm to pass. New situation reports kept coming through as the cruiser shadowers, *Norfolk* and *Suffolk*, slid wraith-like in and out of the mists of the Denmark Straits. It seemed all so far away, yet with the two forces closing each other at combined speeds of say 45 to 50 knots there seemed a remote chance of action. The Germans knew now that they had been spotted by superior numbers and were being shadowed. In the 20-minute action with *Hood* and the new battleship *Prince of Wales*, *Bismarck* had suffered very slight damage, but *Prince of Wales* had been hit several times. Since the latter was not fully operational, but still working up (she had civilian workmen on board), Captain Leach wisely decided to disengage and assist *Norfolk* and *Suffolk* to shadow. Meantime *Rodney*, which was on passage to Norfolk, Virginia, for a refit, was ordered to about turn and join the battle. What we did not know at that time, and had no way of knowing, was that *Bismarck's* damage was most serious in her fuel tanks, and because of this, did not realise that her only hope was to make for Brest for repairs. Right up to the moment of the final search it was assumed that she was bent on accompanying *Prinz Eugen* on a worldwide convoy-raiding mission.

Late in the evening of 24 May - ironically 'Empire Day' - Lieutenant-Commander Eugene Esmonde led 9 Swordfish of 825 Squadron from *Victorious* on a torpedo-attack. The situation could not have been worse. The squadron was still working up, and many pilots had made their first decklanding only a few days previously. Weather conditions SW of Iceland were foul, with cloud-base at about 1000ft and thereafter 10/10ths up to 8000ft. The sea was running high, almost gale conditions, and understandably, the strike took almost 1½ hours to cover the 100 miles to the target. In those northern latitudes darkness does not fall until after midnight at that time of the year, and Esmonde attacked into the setting sun, thus silhouetting the target. With a squadron not completely worked up, it is hardly surprising that twice their ASV radar homed them on to a friendly ship, first the British *Norfolk*, later the US Coast Guard cutter *Madoc*. The Americans must have been startled to find themselves in the midst of a battle.

The attack was made at midnight, Percy Gick, the senior pilot going round again as he was dissatisfied with his initial approach, and reporting a column of smoke from *Bismarck* after he left the scene. This was confirmed by the shadowing Fulmars. Gick's observer was my old friend 'Duke' Norfolk, who had taken a very large camera in the rear seat to photograph any hits. With this, the size of a 3-gallon bucket tied round his neck, he was trying to get a shot of *Bismarck* while Percy was making violent evasive action after his drop. The story – probably quite true – is that 'Duke' shouted to Percy 'Keep the bloody thing straight. How do you expect me to take pictures if you're throwing her all over the sky!' Percy Gick's reply is not recorded. The Swordfish all made it back to the carrier, many of the pilots making their maiden night decklandings. Two Fulmars were unfortunately lost (though one crew was picked up some days later by a Canadian ship, SS *Beaverhill*, luckily some miles off her proper course. The observer was my old course-mate John Hoare of Montreal, Canada).

All of this information was coming through on signals, and as *Bismarck* was now reported to be making 20 knots, it was assumed that she had not been damaged by the hit claimed by 825 Squadron. In any case, her shadowers, *Norfolk* and *Suffolk*, were engaged by gunfire every time they got too close, until dramatically at about 0300 on 25 May, contact with the enemy was lost. Apparently this fact was not known to the German Admiral Lutjens, who was becoming very worried about the unremitting terriers snapping at this heels, whose persistence he attributed to the superiority of British radar. So, believing himself to be still shadowed, Lutjens then made an unbelievable mistake – at 0854 that morning, he began a series of long signals to *Kriegsmarine* Group West. It was unbelievable, but a gift from heaven as our shore direction-finding stations made a clean cut giving us a positive position again. Skilled radio operators can identify ships' morse emissions exactly, and the character of the key operator indicated almost without doubt that it was the enemy battleship. However, between them the Home Fleet flagship and the Admiralty made a mistake in the positions deduced from the cut, and it was almost seven hours later before the latter issued a correction, indicating that *Bismarck* was probably making for Brest or St Nazaire, the only two French Atlantic ports able to berth the 50,900-ton battleship, then the largest at sea in the world.

This was where the professionals came in, and as it became known through Force H that we were the only ships who could stop the *Bismarck*, excitement became high and the adrenalin began to flow. If present courses and speeds were maintained by both forces, it was likely that contact could be made in the late forenoon of next day, 26 May.

All night of the 25th/26th *Renown, Sheffield* and *Ark Royal* ploughed and plunged north through the rising sea into the teeth of a north-westerly galeforce wind. Speed had to be reduced progressively through the night from 25 to 17 knots to avoid heavy damage to our ships' engines, since the propellers were churning out of the water almost as much as they were submerged, and damaged propeller shafts were the last things needed now we were deep into the Bay of Biscay, and shortly to be within range of shore-based aircraft, U-boats and even small fast coastal craft. The *Bismarck*, steering southeast, had a following sea, which would cause less damage to her propeller shafts.

That night there was very little sleep for anyone, either because of apprehension of what the morrow would bring or the realisation that so much depended on us. Those who had no such worries, and there were a few, could not sleep because of the noise as everything not secured rattled away. Aircraft in the hangars were double-lashed and guards posted to deal with any breakaways. It was forbidden to go on the flightdeck as the wind was now touching 50 knots, and even though this was 60ft above the water-line, waves were washing over it. *Renown* and *Sheffield* were taking seas over their superstructure most of the time, and were probably used to it, but we had never before operated in such frightful conditions. Slowly we began to realise that even if we did get to the area on time, flying might be impossible.

At 0500 on 26 May I made my way from the crew room to the ops room. It was indeed the sort of black morning when the conscience has to be searched for reassurance that this is indeed one's choice of profession. Just the few yards between the companionway and the watertight door in the island took my breath away, and almost my body too. The waves were frightening to look at, dark green and capped with monstrous white foam. IF we got our aircraft off the deck; IF they found the target and dropped torpedoes – there were still the twin prospects of being shot down by enemy gunfire known to be accurately radar-controlled, or making a bad decklanding and going over the side, either meaning almost certain death in these mountainous seas. Even a normal approach was going to be dicey in the extreme as the flightdeck was now rising and falling about 60ft, and this, in a length of 800ft presented an interesting mathematical problem. At what point did you stop climbing and start rolling down the flightdeck? We would soon find out in a practical way.

The principles of aerial torpedo warfare are simple – Find, Fix and Strike. So first we must send off a search to locate the missing enemy ships – and it should be remembered at this time that we were looking for two ships, being unaware that *Prinz Eugen* had parted company and was making off independently. Lieutenant-Commander Pat Stringer, the flightdeck officer had, a monumental task on his hands as he tried to organise the range of 10 aircraft from 810 and 818 with wings folded on a deck as slippery as an ice-rink. Even double the normal number of hands could hardly hold the heavy biplanes in position as they tried alternately to crab sideways over the side or to commence an unmanned take-off down the wildly rising and falling deck. Eventually the ship turned into wind and Commander Traill used all his judgement and experience to get them off as opportunity presented itself. The ungainly

Stringbags still crabbing slightly dueto the eddies round the island, found themselves first climbing up a very steep incline, then as the bow fell below the horizon, rolling down into the raging sea. But somehow, they all managed to become airborne safely, though some reported feeling their wheels hit the sea as they cleared the carrier's bow. Understudying Commander Bentinck in the operations room I asked 'Anything I can do, sir?' He gave me his thoughtful half-smile and replied 'We wait, Woods. We pray. And we hope'.

And a long wait it was. But success attended our efforts, though the initial first sighting report came from an unexpected quarter. At about 1030, two hours after our search had taken off, an RAF Catalina flying boat piloted by Pilot Officer D A Briggs flying from Northern Ireland spotted our quarry through a hole in the clouds. But the quarry fired at him, causing him to seek refuge in the clouds. However, that was enough, the hunt was on, and about 30 minutes later Swordfish A2H of 810, piloted by Jock Hartley, with Peter Elias and TAG Huxley, also radioed their first sighting report, but were not sure if it was *Bismarck* or *Prinz Eugen* below them. Since the ships were of almost identical outline, but differing in size, this was a pardonable mistake in the foul weather conditions. Shortly afterwards John Callendar's aircraft, with Peter Schonfeldt and TAG Baker, also made the sighting, confirming that it was in fact, the *Bismarck*. Both aircraft were instructed to remain in contact until relief shadowers with long-range tanks could take over and therefore remain much longer in the air. The enemy was reported to be on a south-easterly course, making 20 knots with a following sea. Lieutenants T W B Shaw and V Graves, senior observers of 810 and 818 Squadrons respectively, were then both sent off as experts in ship recognition. Both independently identified positively and remained as relief shadowers.

The German battleship *Bismarck* about noon on 26 May 1941 photographed by Lieutenant Vernon Graves RN, senior observer of 818 Squadron, in a shadowing Swordfish. *Captain T W B Shaw DSC, RN*

Now came the time for calculations. Our ships were beginning to get low on fuel, and we would shortly begin to come within range of the *Luftwaffe* and U-boats, though neither was likely to be a great worry while the present weather continued. Other heavy ships, including the battleship *King George V* and *Rodney* were on the way, but still 135 miles away, and likely also to be anxious about fuel supplies. We had to assume that *Bismarck* was still in top fighting condition, and that *Prinz Eugen* was somewhere in the vicinity. Therefore we had a simple situation – *Ark Royal* must get off striking forces to sink or slow down the enemy until our capital ships could arrive and engage her with comparable gunpower.

Orders went out immediately for a strike of 15 Swordfish from 810 and 820 Squadrons armed with torpedos. It was also suggested, but quickly dismissed, that a squadron of Fulmars might make dummy dive-bombing attacks as a diversion; but as the heavier Fulmar needed a long take-off and a long flat approach for landing on, with the present sea conditions, it would be tried only if all else failed.

Meantime, Force H had crossed *Bismarck's* track ahead, this manoeuvre giving us more sea-room to operate aircraft, since every time we needed to fly-off or -on we would have to turn into the north-west wind, in other words, to port. If we lay on a parallel course, but to the south, we would be turning into the enemy each time aircraft were operated. With no knowledge of *Prinz Eugen's* whereabouts, *Bismarck* could lead us into a trap. *Renown* was a battlecruiser, lightly armoured, and with memories only two days old of what had happened to another battlecruiser, *Hood*, the Admiralty had instructed Admiral Somerville not to engage the *Bismarck*. *Sheffield*, with her radar expertise, was similarly instructed. The vital thing now was not to lose enemy contact, and shadowers with marathon tanks relieved each other throughout the afternoon. Their job was no sinecure, *Bismarck's* accurate radar ranging enabled her to fire on any aircraft which came within range, in cloud or not.

Our torpedo-bomber resources were stretched to the limit, and the striking force could not be ranged until all the search aircraft had returned. Landing on was extremely hazardous, with the 60ft rise and fall of the flightdeck and a 40-knot wind over the deck. Here was another problem. Because of the wind, the carrier had to slow down to about 8 knots, which increased the pitch and roll, but if the speed were increased to lessen this, the wind over the deck could easily equal the Swordfish's stalling speed of 55 knots, and the aircraft might be blown back over the round-down. Thus several aircraft had to be waved 'round again' two or three times until the flight deck officer, Pat Stringer, was satisfied he could get them down on the deck. Though several almost 'did the splits', they all got down safely, and were struck quickly down in the lifts to the hangars to be loaded with their deadly torpedoes.

As soon as this part of the operation was complete, *Ark* had to turn to starboard and steam at full speed of 30 knots to regain station on the enemy.

Just before 1500, the 15 Swordfish, led by James Stewart-Moore took off. Only sub-flight leaders carried observers, since the distance from the enemy was only about 60 miles, and weight could be an important factor. The pilots without observers would rely on their telegraphist-airgunners to get them home by radio or homing beacon. Though I was disappointed not to be in this attack, it was very probable that there would be a succession of attacks throughout the rest of the day and possibly the night too, provided the wind and sea abated. Shortly after take-off Nigel Gardner had to return with engine trouble, and landed with his torpedo still secure. This was a magnificent effort, though his undercarriage made a near-perfect impersonation of a circus elephant sitting down.

Now came the near-tragedy. The Admiral, anxious to ensure that our quarry did not again elude us in the increasing mists, detached *Sheffield* to maintain radar contact. A signal was made to this effect by *Renown*, but arrived in *Ark Royal* after the strike had taken off, and was not yet decoded in the carrier. As Stewart-Moore approached the last-known position of the enemy, he sighted a warship below which he naturally assumed to be *Bismarck*, having no information that any other ship was in the vicinity, save perhaps *Prinz Eugen*. Putting his strike into echelon, he ordered a sub-flight attack, which appears to have been extremely well executed, but unfortunately on the wrong ship – *Sheffield*!

Something was gained from this ghastly mistake. All the torpedoes had been fitted with magnetic heads which would explode on striking a metal object but many exploded on hitting the water. On this day the seas were so rough that they had a consistency of concrete, causing the pistol in the nose to detonate the explosive. The first sub-flight realised their mistake as soon as they got within dropping range, did not drop, and fired off red Very lights to warn the following aircraft. However, when one is all hyped-up for a death-or-glory attack of this nature, the obvious is not always so, and the red Verys were mistaken by some pilots for enemy flak. Captain Charles Larcom of *Sheffield* realised immediately what had happened, increased speed and combed the tracks as best he could. He had at one time served in the carrier *Furious*, which must have sparked off his intuition.

Back came the crestfallen crews. All that danger endured – the take-off up a pitching and rolling deck, instrument flying through clouds with base at 1500ft, the anticipation of the attack, and eventually another hazardous encounter with the flightdeck to land on. And all to no purpose. In the operations room Stewart-Moore and Hughie Hunter stood talking to Commander Bentinck. It was the first time I'd seen Hughie let himself go. Cynically he said, 'It was a perfect attack, sir.

Right height, right range, right cloud cover, right speed AND THE WRONG FUCKING SHIP!'

Three aircraft had been pranged on landing, and another strike was being got ready to take off as soon as the crews had rested a little, been fed, and the aircraft reloaded. I was glad to be among those detailed for the second strike, flying with Alan Swanton, in A4C. The strike once more would be 15 aircraft, which was in fact all the serviceable ones we could muster. But this time we would use the reliable 'contact' pistol to detonate the torpedo, this actuating only on contact with metal, which should prevent heavy seas jeopardising our efforts a second time. Our leader this time was to be Lieutenant-Commander 'Tim' Coode, CO of 818, who would lead the first wave, James Stewart-Moore leading the second. Orders were that we should first make visual contact with *Sheffield*, now believed to be shadowing from between 10 and 12 miles astern, and on *Bismarck*'s starboard quarter. After a hairy take-off at 1910, we formed up in sub-flights of three, and headed straight for *Sheffield*, which directed us to the enemy, bearing 110 degrees, distance 12 miles.

The plan was to climb to around 5000 ft above *Sheffield*, and to make a co-ordinated attack by sub-flight. Thus, five sections of three aircraft each would attack simultaneously from different bearings, dividing the enemy fire, so giving us better prospects of hitting and getting away scot-free. At least, that was the theory.

The practice was somewhat different. Cloud base was down to about 1000 ft, and solid right up to 6000 ft. Going through this dark-grey murk was quite frightening with a ton of torpedo slung underneath, climbing in sub-flights. After a few minutes we realised that in these conditions formation flying was dangerous, but it would be even more dangerous to try to break out of it. So onward, ever upward we climbed 'hanging on the prop'. Just what happened inside those clouds will never be known but it seemed on comparing notes later that each aircraft came out independently of the others, each pilot taking a look round, deciding he'd lost his fellows and diving back through the dark grey cotton wool. Miraculous to relate, as we came out of the perfect cloud cover at about 1000 ft, we were almost back in sub-flight formation! I remember Alan saying to me over the Gosports 'OK, shall we go in?' and my reply, in a voice half-an-octave higher than normal, saying bravely 'Fine, let's get it over with'. Then we flattened out, ready for the run-in.

The minute or so which followed will be forever engraved on my memory. There she was, a thousand yards away, big, black, cowled funnel, menacing, with every close-range weapon stabbing flame as we steadied on our approach, 100 knots, 100ft, 1000 yards just as the textbook says. 'Flash' Seager, the TAG, was sensibly crouching down in the cockpit, sitting on a lead-covered codebook. Later he told me I was shouting my head off as we ran in, probably true, but what it was I have no idea. All I do know is that as we dropped our 'tinfish' A4 'Charlie' almost leapt into the air, and as we turned away aft tightly, we were suspended motionless for a split second that felt like an eternity as every gun seemed to concentrate upon us. The flak ripped through the fabric-covered fuselage·like peas on a drum. 'Flash' yelled, and then Alan said 'Christ! Just look at this lot' as *Bismarck* put her 15in guns on a flat trajectory, firing ahead of us, either intending to blast us off the face of the earth, or as happened in fact, to make a Breechers' Brook of water-splashes 100ft high through which we must fly, and which might bring us spinning down into the raging sea. 'Flash's' normally sallow complexion looked grey, but at that time it didn't worry me, because I had no idea what colour I was, probably even more grey than he.

As we sped aft, opening the range, and out of immediate danger, I asked him if he was all right, and he said yes, but did not look at all happy, and went on to say he had been hit in the buttocks, so I turned and spoke to Alan, telling him this and giving him a course back to the ship. I saw that Alan's flying overalls were torn in the right shoulder and asked if he was all right. He said yes, but there was blood seeping down his back. 'How long before we're there' he asked, 'About 25 minutes.' 'OK, I can hold on.' That was about the sum of our conversation. I had escaped injury but the burst which must have wounded them both had gone clean through my Mae West life jacket near the left shoulder, and the kapok was welling out. At first I thought it was my tripes, but realised they weren't up there.

Meanwhile, we had formated on 'Scruffy' Manley-Cooper with his beloved ASV radar set, and on the other side was Jock Moffat, as usual laughing his head off. And so we came back to the carrier. During the trip the other two aircraft had informed that I was going to request an emergency landing priority, and they went away to allow me to fire off red Very lights and signal with the Aldis lamp. Quickly *Ark* acknowledged the fact that pilot and airgunner were wounded and cleared the deck for what might be a very ropey landing. But all was well, Alan held her off until the last moment and she sank lightly on to the deck. Straight up and through the lowered barrier we went and stretchers came alongside for the wounded. Alan was able to walk to the sick bay, but poor Seager, in great pain, had to be carried.

Slowly the strike returned. The news was encouraging, but in the conditions, not very definite. Bud Beale lost his sub-flight in the clouds, re-located *Sheffield* and got a fresh bearing and distance, then carried out a solo attack, probably scoring a hit amidships. 'Feather' Godfrey-Fausset and Pat Patterson both attacked from the starboard beam, were both hit by shrapnel, but claimed one possible hit. Alan Owensmith was fired on while still in cloud which he stated later was 'a little startling'. He had also made a solo attack, and ran into the same type of 'hedge' on his run in as we had on our run out. Alan noticed an unusually large rudder correction to port just after his drop, which later had great significance.

Time seemed completely irrelevant that night. We had flown about 100 miles in total to and from the attack, about 1¼ hours' continuous flying, but from take-off to landing was three hours, so we must have spent almost an hour climbing up through the clouds and coming down again. Having seen Alan and Seager down to the sick bay, I reported back to operations room and told my story, adding little to the scoreboard as in those conditions of sea and enemy fire, no one could be sure whether he had scored a hit, though Bud Beale and Patterson seemed those most likely to have succeeded.

Our shadowers were still in the air, and it appeared that *Bismarck* was still in full fighting trim as she occasionally loosed off an accurate radar-controlled burst at them, or at *Sheffield* if the latter became too inquisitive. Not a single aircraft had been lost in combat though three had strained undercarriages due to doing the splits on that pitching flightdeck. There was nothing also to do except load our remaining serviceable aircraft for another strike at dawn. It had been another very long day, and at 2330 was beginning to get dark. A comforting report came up from the met office to say that the 'front' had now passed through and next morning would probably bring better weather. Very comforting. The weather just had to get better since it could hardly be worse than today.

The last two shadowers had come home to roost after five hours in the air, which in the North Atlantic in an open cockpit can turn a man into a zombie. So it was with some skepticism that we listened to 'Long John' Longmuir's statement that he had seen *Bismarck* turn two complete circles after the last attack, and she was now steaming, not exactly under control, in the general direction of Newfoundland. But true it certainly was, and reports came in, suggesting that one of our 'fish' must have done damage to the rudder or steering gear, jamming the rudder hard to starboard and immovable. At last we'd done the job right. The rest was up to the heavies and perhaps the destroyers, now moving in as darkness fell.

The 4th Destroyer Flotilla, under Captain Philip Vian in *Cossack*, comprised *Maori*, *Zulu*, *Sikh* and the Polish *Piorun*, the latter's captain having several times to be restrained from ramming the enemy battleship. Instead, torpedo attacks were made in the night, and of 16 fired, two hits were claimed. All night long the destroyers fired their guns and starshells, making sure the enemy were kept awake and tired out.

As usual, the met office had made a mistake. The weather was worse than the previous day, and though a shadower was flown off at dawn – 0430 – aircraft for the strike could not be ranged on deck. In the hangars double lashings were necessary. The 12 aircraft strike was finally ranged at 0930 and flown off immediately, aircraft crews being warned to stay clear until signalled to do otherwise, as *Rodney* and *King George V* were about to open fire, and might include some Swordfish in their targets if they were below the safe trajectory height of 3000 ft. An hour later *Bismarck* was out of control, but still firing accurately – so much so that *Ark* was continuously being ordered to keep out of the way by Admiral Somerville – until at last, a blazing wreck that would not sink was given the coup de grâce by the cruiser *Dorsetshire's* torpedoes.

One had to feel some sadness at the loss of so beautiful and courageous a ship, even if her purpose was to get amongst our conveys and sink them. This sympathy very soon disappeared as we were attacked by 'Kondors' and Heinkel IIIs just as we were recovering the striking force and unable to get off an extremely eager flight of Fulmars, the pilots of which were getting fretful at being left out of the operation. At 1040 on 27 May *Bismarck* finally sank, leaving around 300 survivors in the water. *Dorsetshire* and *Maori* had rescued about 110 when the *Luftwaffe*, seeing *Ark* on a straight flying-on course, decided to intervene. *Renown* and *Sheffield* put up an AA barrage, which probably caused the bombers to drop their load some 500 yards astern, or did they – as the Fulmar boys asserted later – anticipate attacks from the dreaded 807 and 808 *Jagdstaffeln*? Meanwhile another destroyer reported a U-boat contact and rescue work was abandoned. Every ship in the action now needed refuelling, so at 25 knots, with everything lashed down, Force H made for Gibraltar, the Home Fleet for the nearest British Isles port.

Alan and 'Flash' seemed to be comfortable in the sick bay, both heavily sedated. Having seen their wounds the previous evening, their cheerfulness was surprising, though perhaps they had considered the alternative to being wounded. Alan's shoulder had the flesh laid back in layers to the bone, whilst considerable ribaldry and lewd comment had been generated by Seager's unfortunate experience. I had to report to them both that A4 'Charlie' was no more James, Fensome and Pat Stringer had helped me count the bullet- and shell-holes. We got to 200 of all sizes, when Air Engineer Fensome said he had decided long ago that 'Charlie' was a complete write-off, and in fact, it was a credit to Fairey Aviation and to Alan Swanton that we got back at all. Theoretically we should have fallen to pieces shortly after the attack. So, after only 40 hours' flying on her Form 700, she was put below, to be disembarked to North Front and cannibalised for spares. So now I had no crew, and what was worse, no aircraft.

Euphoria following the victory lasted for several days. Swordfish had to fly up and down taking film for the newsreels back home. The BBC lauded us to the skies, and congratulations came from Winston Churchill himself. Later, most unfortunately, the Walrus amphibian from *Sheffield* flying for more filming, crashed into *Renown's* quarterdeck killing all four on board.

Our entry into Gibraltar on 29 May will always live in my memory. Black Watch pipes played us into harbour, and every resident and serviceman had the day off. Every mole, every wharf, every window was full of flags and people, and as we moved gracefully to our usual berth, boats laden with sightseers, buzzed, sailed or rowed around us. A small ray of sunshine in a rather depressing part of the war. That evening came what we'd hoped for, a signal from *Sheffield* – 'Request the pleasure of your company for drinks tomorrow noon. All is forgiven and forgotten'. What a charming gesture!

On the 30th, all the best-looking chaps from those who had taken part in the torpedo attacks, which obviously included 'Scruffy', Jock Moffat and myself, had to hold a mock post-mortem on the action for the benefit of Gaumont-British News. With neither instruction nor rehearsal, we hammed it up, 'Scruffy' in his element, miming with his hands in true Fighter Command style. My mother didn't think so. Several weeks later, the newsreel was shown at our local Odeon in Boston, Lincs, and the dear lady was almost ejected for her ecstatic cries as she recognised her firstborn son. But the manager, God bless him, gave her a free show next day when he heard the true facts behind the uproar. Such is fame.

Later on 30 May all Swordfish crews were summoned on board *Renown* to be presented to Lord Gort VC, and to have more film taken for a news-hungry British public. The Admiral, as was his wont, sought a quiet corner where he could converse with his sub-lieutenants and midshipment of the Air Branch, as he put it 'To find out what REALLY went on'. He was even cordial to me, and later that evening came aboard *Ark* with *Renown's* officers for further drinks, dinner and conversation. He came over to speak to Alan Swanton, who had been given leave to join the party, but not to drink alcohol. I was standing next to Alan. 'How, Woods', said 'Uncle James', 'would you describe the action?'. Taken momentarily by surprise, in the circumstances I produced one of the few original quotable quotes of my lifetime. 'To paraphase Oscar Wilde's views on hunting, Sir', I said, 'I would describe it as the pursuit of the unspeakable by the unsinkable'. From that moment on, he seemed to take a better view of me, and even today, I think it was a pretty good effort.

We got that delightful intestinal feeling, almost bubbling over with bonhomie, that at last we were fully paid-up members of the First Eleven, and today had the same standing in Force H as the veterans. Well, maybe not quite, but we'd won our spurs, something which eight short months ago had seemed unattainable. It was good. We all stood ten feet tall, from the Boy Seaman Bugler to Captain Maund. Dinner that night was 'Chef's Surprise', his own tribute to his ship – 'Swordfish Supreme', which it really was, and delicious too. As Jock Moffat remarked during dinner – the Chef did not have too much choice, it had to be that or *Bismarck* Kipper!

The wardroom cartoonist in *Renown* had made an excellent drawing which the Admiral was showing round. It depicted a boxing ring in which was a German heavyweight, on his last legs, whilst the old 'pro', *Renown*– was clearly on top and about to administer the knockout. The promoter, a thinly-disquised Admiral Jack Tovey, C-in-C Home Fleet, was saying to *Renown's* seconds, *Ark Royal* and *Sheffield*, 'Let me bring my new boy in for the last round, I gotta build up a reputation for him'. The new boy was, of course, the battleship *King George V*, flagship of the Home Fleet, until this action unblooded.

They told me next morning that it was a very good party – I can't remember much, other than that Alan was going up to the Military Hospital next day, and was worried about 'Scruffy' driving him there. He felt he'd be safer walking.

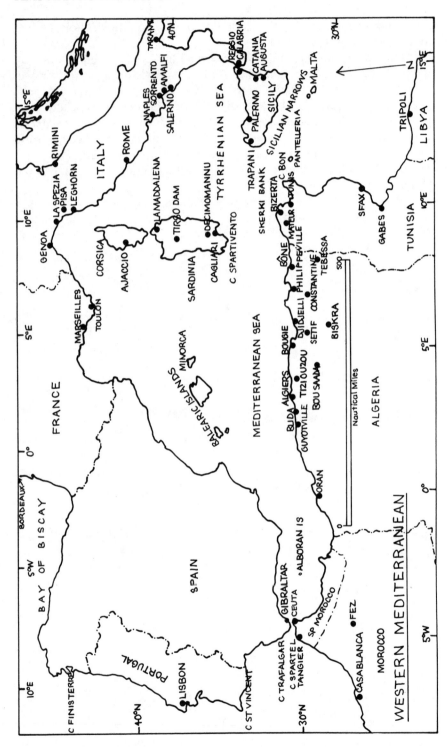

Chapter 8
820 Squadron transfers

Later that evening came a reminder that if the war goes on, the work goes on. *Furious* had arrived with more Hurricanes for the Eastern Mediterranean, and just before sunset *Argus* was signalled with a similar cargo. This looked like another Malta club-run, though some news brought later by Leighton Rowland from *Furious* made us pause awhile. It appeared there had been a slight scuffle between ourselves and Vicky forces off the coast of Tunisia, near Gabes. The Vichy forces had gone away with a flea in their ear, and there could be some reprisals taken, either against us en route to the Narrows, or an attack on Gibraltar airfield or harbour in our absence. Though obviously such stupidity could only result in a further 'Puce a l'oreille', the political overtones were not at all nice. Supposing they gave a temporary Tunisian base to the *Luftwaffe* for this trip alone, or suppose alternatively that in trying to drop a bomb on Gibraltar, they overshot, dropped one on Spanish territory for which we got the blame. The situation was a trifle fraught. Fortunately the Admiralty instructed the expedition to be delayed until *Victorious* arrived, also probably bearing more fighters for Malta and the Desert.

And here came confirmation of Giles Guthrie's advice to us of a week earlier, to start stocking up on gifts for home. It was a strength 10 rumour that *Victorious* was to bring out a relief squadron to *Ark Royal* when she became involved in the *Bismarck* operation, and made the first torpedo attack with untrained crews. She also had 24 Hurricanes for a final run to Malta before crews were exchanged. Some defects were revealed in *Victorious* during the operation and she put back to Britain for repairs. But, said the rumour, she could be here in a few days with our reliefs.

The minor casualties from the recent action caused yet another reshuffle of crews, even though on our return to Britain it was more than likely that we would lose some of our senior aviators to strengthen newly-forming squadrons anyway, since the great expansion of the Fleet Air Arm was now under way. Lieutenant 'Pig' Lucas joined us as senior pilot, flying with James Stewart-Moore, our CO and I became observer to Hughie Hunter, second pilot and sub-flight leader. Lucas' nickname has always intrigued me, for in a short acquaintance, he seemed extremely courteous, if somewhat lacking in sociability, though by no means unsociable.

In this ambiguous atmosphere, we took on 24 Hurricanes from *Furious* by the wooden bridge method, which much to 'Scruffy's' delight, had become standard operating procedure. We crossed the boom on 5 June with *Furious, Renown* and *Sheffield*, with the object of flying 44 Hurricanes to Malta. A new plan had been devised for the transfer, the predictable pattern of which had begun to worry the Admiral and his staff, who feared a surprise attack while the fighters were being flown off, the carriers were on a straight course, and the Fulmar squadrons could not be used to deter enemy bombers of either dive-, high level- or torpedo variety. In short, if the *Luftwaffe* decided to launch a saturation attack, it could be very tricky, if not fatal. The obvious thing would be for one carrier to stand by with her naval fighters as the other flew off her Hurricanes, then reverse the roles, but nobody seemed to have thought of such a simple solution. All Hurricanes flew off almost simultaneously with the two carriers unprotected. The Hurricanes couldn't protect us without the possibility of sacrificing some of their precious fuel, in which case, they might not arrive in Malta. If a surface or U-boat attack were made on the carriers, they would not be able to get their Swordfish deterrents off to make depth-charge attacks. It was all rather worrying. However, there had been some improvement in the plan.

The day before we left Gibraltar, nine RAF twin-engine Blenheim bombers had landed at North Front. A minor panic had been caused, leading to action stations all over the colony, as they had overshot the lefthand turn into the Straits, and finally approached the Rock from the general direction of Spanish Morocco. With the rumoured threat of some retaliation from Vichy forces, trigger-fingers were a trifle twitchy, especially in the Rock's AA defence, since they didn't often get a chance to shoot in anger. And especially at friendly aircraft.

The Blenheims would leave Gibraltar the day after ourselves, and take over the escort duty to Malta, the Hurricanes being fitted with wing overload petrol tanks. This was a good move, assuming the Blenheim crews had no aversion to flights over the sea, since it meant we would not deplete our meagre fighter complement when they were most needed. On this trial trip all went well, the bombers rendezvoused on time, and all the Hurricanes got off without mishap. They all got off all right, but one developed engine trouble shortly after take-off, returned to *Furious* and landed on, to loud cheers from the 'goofers' who always packed the gallery for Hurricane trips. Since this courageous gent had neither decklanding experience nor an arrestor hook, it was quite a remarkable performance. It strengthened the rumour that Hurries would soon be modified to fleet fighter standards, but now presented a problem – what do we do with a lone Hurrie and pilot? This was solved on return by flying him off to North Front, where he became RAF Fighter Command, Defence of Gibraltar.

We were shadowed all day from the south, probably a Vichy aircraft, but nothing more happened, and flying off fighters from a more distant point from Bomb Alley seemed to be a dividend-payer. The balance of naval power in the Mediterranean had shifted since the retreat from Crete, where we had lost 3 cruisers and 6 destroyers, plus 2 battleships, one carrier, 6 cruisers and 7 destroyers damaged. German fighter and bomber bases in Sardinia, Sicily and Italy had heretofore been directing their effort against the gallant defenders of Malta, and the convoys bringing in their vital supplies, but now the Cretan bases meant that the whole of North Africa from Algiers to Suez was well within their range. Continuous reinforcement of Malta was our only hope of interrupting Rommel's supply lines until our Desert Army and Air Force could build up sufficient strength to counter-attack. It was a situation which emphasised strongly the necessity for Force H to retain command of the Western Mediterranean and the approaches to Gibraltar and Malta.

On our way back to Gibraltar on 6 June, Johnnie Johnstone, CO of 810 with his senior observer, Terence Shaw, flew over Oran to check whether the battleship *Dunkerque* was still in harbour. Rumour had it that she was making ready to proceed to Toulon where, despite Vichy French assertions to the contrary, there was every likelihood that she might become part of either the German or Italian Navy, and yet another nuisance to be coped with in the Mediterranean. All was well, said Terence, *Dunkerque* was in her usual berth.

As we entered harbour next day, two remarkable sights greeted us. First was a Catalina flying boat executing a sensational cartwheel whilst landing in a relatively calm sea. Very soon afterwards we saw the Cunliffe-Owen experimental aircraft, aptly named 'The Flying Wing' take off for her return flight to Britain. An almost futuristic design, akin to those depicted in the science-fiction magazines of the period, she was all wing and engines, with no visible body.

After a stay of only 12 hours to refuel and re-victual, we sailed the same evening in company with *Renown*, *Furious* and *Sheffield* to rendezvous with *Victorious*, which was bringing yet another cargo of Hurricanes. The rumours were now on the boil that we were going home. Apart from the feeling almost like the day one left school for good, there was a new cameraderie abroad. James and Hughie would occasionally join the 'bograts' and buy us a drink at the bar. The old barriers seemed almost completely down. We were now fully 'blooded' and were apprentices no more. But still paramont was the warm feeling that comes when one knows that just around the corner are leave, home, and all that means – above all a short respite from this all-consuming war.

Late next afternoon, 8 June, *Furious* and *Sheffield* parted company to go home. All 820 aircraft returning from an unrewarding armed search for a U-boat reported in the Straits by a Catalina, gave *Sheffield*, our 'chummy ship' for so long an imperial beat-up. She was a most efficient escort as well as a forgiving friend.

At 0700 next day *Victorious* was sighted, and came to join us, her flightdeck full of Hurricanes. Her design seemed rather more modern and warlike than *Ark Royal*, less ladylike and lower in the water. Most important from the ship's company's viewpoint was that armoured flightdeck.

Though none had yet been seen, there were reports that U-boats were patrolling the entrance to the Straits, waiting for targets of opportunity or the opportunity to break in. The aircraft Straits patrols, performed either by ourselves or by the RAF amphibians and flying-boats by day, and by naval motor-launches at night, probably persuaded the U-boat commanders that this was not a healthy area for them to be. On 10 June, Nigel Gardner and Leonard Mann sighted a U-boat on the surface only ten miles distant from *Ark Royal*. On sighting the Stringbag made best possible speed towards it, but the U-boat dived. Nigel continued and completed his attack, his zeal unfortunately outrunning his performance, since the semi-armour-piercing bombs did not detonate. Surface craft later joined in, but without positive result. It can, however, be assumed that a badly-scared U-boat crew kept their heads down whilst the force passed through the Straits.

Transfer of stores and personnel started on 11 June. Several old chums were in *Victorious*, Colin Ennever, as apple-cheeked as ever, Bobbie Lawson of quiet mien and a dry wit, the perfect foil for his extrovert compatriot, Jock Moffat, and also the 'Duke'. The wooden bridge between flightdecks was operated and Hurricanes transferred. Meanwhile paymasters and other stores personnel conferred and arranged what items would be left and what would be taken home, bearing in mind that a spare engine was of infinitely more use to the war effort in Gibraltar than it was at Lee.

Everyone got ashore as much as possible, not only to collect presents, but also to intensify our suntans, which (or so the media said) all women admire. Food in *Victorious* was a little more homelike than in *Ark Royal*, where rice was offered in lieu of potatoes after three days at sea, and thereafter until the next convoy arrived. Moffat was in his gastronomic element 'going round the buoy' – having seconds – whenever opportunity occurred. There was only one thing Jock preferred to eating. Internally, *Victorious*, commissioned two years later than *Ark Royal*, was a more business-like ship, with many modifications incorporated in the light of wartime experience in naval aviation. With more armour in the flightdeck than *Ark*, her hangar space was smaller, but without doubt, it was the armour which had saved *Illustrious* from total destruction and enabled her to fight another day. The overall impression one gained initially after serving in *Ark Royal* was of the lower headroom, and the smaller scale of everything. But a fighting ship she certainly was, and others of her class, *Illustrious* and *Formidable* were identical, while *Indomitable* and *Implacable*, which came later, were given more hangar space.

The reunion with friends followed the set pattern, a pleasant pre-prandial session at the bar, wine with dinner and a few brandies afterwards. Then the anticipated wrestling started, with 'Digger' Morgan, the Australian Air Engineer, challenging all comers. 'Digger' was a bit over the hill for that sort of statement and was swiftly 'struck down'. The main bout of the evening was between the incumbent champion of *Victorious*, Percy Gick, and the dark horse from *Ark Royal* – Jock Moffat. The grunting and groaning as these two totally unfit and semi-inebriated sportsmen tangled in their hitherto spotless whites on the wardroom floor was heartrending. Eventually Jock was declared the winner, though in Percy's favour it must be admitted that he was giving Jock about five years, a stone in weight, was about three brandies ahead, and was without his monocle. All good clean fun.

Colin Ennever, with whom I always enjoyed a good rapport, buttonholed me next day and asked me to join him for lunch. It was quite surprising to hear him ask if I would consider joining 825, who were relieving us, as observer to the second senior pilot. It was a big decision to take, and he asked me to meet the CO, Lieutenant-Commander Eugene Esmonde, a slight, dapper officer with quite piercing eyes and an obvious anxiety to get his squadron worked up to a high peak of efficiency. Though it was flattering to feel one could become part of that, and more experience comes with more responsibility, I felt I needed some leave. True, the eight months in *Ark* had taught me a great deal, most of which I could feel in my daily duties, and maybe another eight months with Colin might help complete my apprenticeship. Promising to think it over, I discussed the matter with newly-arrived friends and those in 810 and 818 whom we would be leaving behind. The consensus of their opinion was simple – get some leave, you might not get another chance – so regretfully I thanked Colin for his kind offer, but made my decision to go home. James Turner had just joined 820 and, anxious to gain more experience, happily took my place.

I often wonder what might have happened had I stayed with 825, which later became known as an unlucky squadron, since they appeared to have a somewhat higher casualty rate than average, and were disbanded and reformed several times during the war. Eventually, when *Ark Royal* was sunk, some five months later, Esmonde brought 825 home, later winning a posthumous Victoria Cross carrying out his incredibly gallant sortie against the German heavy squadron, comprising *Scharnhorst*, *Gneisenau* and *Prinz Eugen*, which broke out of Brest in February 1942, sailing up the English Channel back to Kiel. It is not impossible that I could have been in the reformed 825, but such odds are incalculable in wartime, so speculation on these lines is not fruitful.

Five days after the Allies invaded Vichy Syria, we were ready to leave on the Malta club-run, and in anticipation of the possibility of retaliation against Gibraltar by the French forces in North Africa, 808 Squadron was left ashore at North Front for fighter defence of the Rock. At sea, *Ark* was to fly off her 24 Hurricanes first, and two Gibraltar Hudsons would rendezvous with us to take over and lead them to Malta. Fifteen minutes after this, *Victorious* would fly off her 23 Hurricanes, to be led by a further two Gibraltar Hudsons. All worked according to plan except that much later in the day we learned that one Hurricane had dropped into the sea en route, while another had last been seen trailing black smoke as it headed for North Africa, there to be taken prisoner by the Germans, or worse – to be interned by the allegedly neutral Vichy French. A further two Hurricanes crashed on landing in Malta. Later in the day we realised we had sailed on Friday 13 June.

To confuse the Spanish spies, we returned to Gibraltar with our remaining Fulmars ranged on deck, since it had been alleged, probably with some truth, that the Germans could not distinguish them from Hurricanes. Whether it confused them or not I don't know, but confusion did exist in *Victorious* next day, where I was doubly involved as both duty squadron officer and officer of the day. The switchover of squadrons, with *Victorious* at the detached mole, called for administrative genius to cope with boats transferring officers' and ratings' kit, lighters of stores, plus normal boat traffic, libertymen, captains, commanders and others going to and coming from conferences, as well as the myriad things of everyday routine. Far better had I known my way around *Victorious*, and who the various officers were. None of this was improved by my temporary mental aberration that we were still in *Ark Royal*, so that some of my signals dispatched that day would have made interesting reading.

When not watchkeeping it was almost as if the 'hols' had begun. A sprightly air ran through the ship, an impatience to get to sea, and thence home. Above all, James was smiling most of the time. *Neptune*, a cruiser, had attacked and sunk the U-boat supply ship *Gonzenheim* in the Atlantic on 4 June, taking 11 officers and 56 ratings prisoner. These all came aboard in the afternoon for passage to England, a mean and dispirited-looking lot, though one stroppy officer observed to the Royal Marine sentry that the bogus *Ark* did not fool him – he KNEW she had

HMS *Victorious* in June 1941 probably bound for Gibraltar with two of her cargo of Hurricanes on deck. The flightdeck windbreak of perforated steel (operated from 'Wings' bridge on the island) is up to shield personnel at work while the ship's radio masts are lowered on either after beam. *Author's collection.*

107

sunk a year previously in the Norwegian fjords, so that this parade was yet another example of British duplicity, who were now even trying to deceive their own people. 'Quite so, sir,' replied the Royal Marine sentry who was shepherding the captives to their quarters. 'Let's just keep it a secret between ourselves, shall we, and I'll promise not to tell Adolf that we sunk his bloody *Bismarck* last week.'

So, at 2000 on 15 June, we left Gibraltar for the United Kingdom. It may be hard to believe, but we were a little misty-eyed as we saw the Rock receding in the late twilight, the lights of downtown Gibraltar shining away – a sight we should not see again for many long months, now that we were heading for blacked-out Britain. Most of all, we felt emotionally moved as we stood on the quarterdeck, taking our last look at *Ark Royal* with the Rock as a backcloth, serene, almost majestic, even as she lay in harbour on Ragged Staff wharf, her signalmen busily sending out messages to her consorts. It would not, in fact, be our last sight of her, since she was escorting us part of the way home, and we still had to transfer 825 Squadron, but we should never again see her in what had become her natural habitat.

At lunchtime next day 825 flew off *Victorious* and landed on *Ark Royal* and three aircraft only of 820 Squadron joined *Victorious*, all others being left behind at North Front as spares and to act as part of the Rock Defence Force. We could only hope that nothing more serious than submarines was to be encountered on the way home, since the carrier *Glorious* had been sunk in similar circumstances while returning from Norway in June 1940. These thoughts were going through my mind as I lay sunbathing near the starboard after turret, and nearly jumped out of my shin as the twin 4.5in guns fired at a surface target towed by *Sikh*. Obviously we were taking no chances, though with *Renown* and *Ark* still in company, we were unlikely to be taken by surprise for the next couple of days, after which we should be fairly comfortable under cover of Coastal Command from Britain.

Hughie decided that we should get to know each others' flying habits better, and we flew a couple of A/S patrols together in the balmy afternoon air. Obviously feeling his oats a little, he did a beat-up of *Ark Royal* on return, flying very low alongside to wave to his old chum 'Feather' who was having his late afternoon constitutional on the quarterdeck. Unfortunately he didn't judge, or didn't care about, the strange eddies curling about in the lee of the ship, and for one dreadful moment it seemed he had misjudged, as our wheels hit a wave. Maybe it was for 'Feather's' benefit, it was a bit unlike the normally safe and reliable Hughie.

The 13th Destroyer Flotilla spoke to us next morning. Returning to Gibraltar, they had sunk U-138 and taken 40 survivors prisoner. Unfortunately we could not take them on board as it would have meant stopping in an area known to be traversed by U-boats, and an unguarded minute is all that is needed for a ship to be sunk when stationary. The po-faced Marine sentry made sure that his charges knew of the sinking, adding that there wasn't very much food in Britain for prisoners, hence their being taken to Gibraltar. 'I expect, gentlemen,' he confided, 'that after you've had a few months' interrogation in England, you'll be sent back there by sea.' Buster Keaton wasn't in it for straight-faced comedy.

A final mail-call had been made in Force H, and sacks could be seen going by jackstay from all ships to *Ark Royal*. It was fitting that Hughie, probably the most popular pilot should be the last mail-man. *Victorious* had collected all the ship's company's Gibraltar money, and I was entrusted with handing this over to *Ark Royal's* Paymaster Commander. With such onerous duties to discharge, Hughie was ultra-careful, making a sensational first-wire landing to the plaudits of the flightdeck party. Leaving the Swordfish on deck, we reported to the Captain, Hughie's 'pusser' salute belied by the wide grin on his face, as well as his reputation for being one of the less disciplined of regular officers. Captain Maund, together with Commanders Taylor, Bentinck and Traill cracked a bottle of champagne, then another, but even Hughie thought that more would be imprudent.

And so we took off for the last time from *Ark Royal*, cheering and being cheered as we soared over the bows, and made a mild beat-up down the flightdeck, mild because the troops' mail was in our care, and I had the paymaster's money. Then a similar last hurrah to *Renown*, especially for the Admiral, and away to land on *Victorious*.

Ark and *Renown* left us next morning, 19 June at 1000, with many fond farewells signalled. She was my first ship, and true to the sailor's legend, the happiest I ever served in. It is almost impossible to say why. Perhaps she had more experienced officers and men than subsequent carriers, owing to the enormous expansion of the Fleet Air Arm, and the consequent dilution of career men. Other carriers I served in didn't have *Ark's* panache, her spark which made her so different. Subsequent ships seemed to regard aviators as interlopers who must be suffered, but were borne for gin and flying only. It is certainly true that many aviators took this same view, and did little to form good relationships. Again, as the Fleet Air Arm expanded and more reservists commanded flights and eventually squadrons, the anti-regular lobby strengthened, and reservists did not bother to take part in ships' activities as much as they should have done, or in ships' duties. In *Ark Royal* it was a privilege to be recommended as suitable material to be trained for a watchkeeping certificate. In most other ships one was regarded as a passenger.

An Italian proverb says that fish goes bad from the head, and this may be more to the point. *Ark* was fortunate in having two excellent captains in 1940 and 1941 – A J Power and C S Holland. Only serving under the latter, I was told that 'Hookie' took on what A J left behind; a

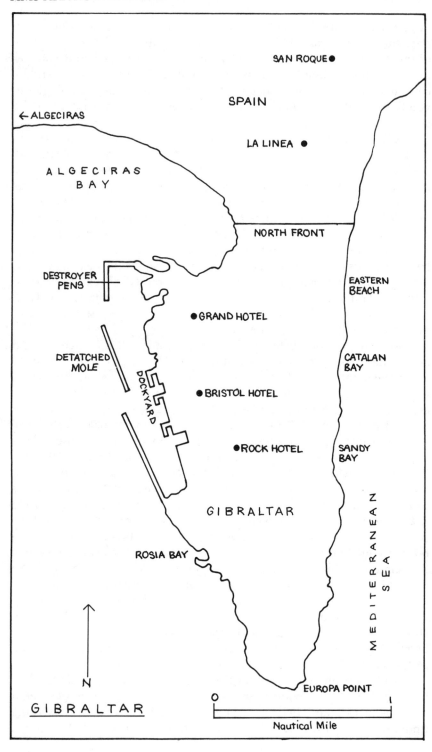

SAN ROQUE ●

SPAIN

← ALGECIRAS

LA LINEA ●

A L G E C I R A S
B A Y

NORTH FRONT

DESTROYER
PENS

EASTERN
BEACH

● GRAND HOTEL

DETATCHED
MOLE

CATALAN
BAY

DOCKYARD

● BRISTOL HOTEL

● ROCK HOTEL

SANDY
BAY

G I B R A L T A R

M E D I T E R R A N E A N   S E A

ROSIA BAY

EUROPA POINT

↑
N

O   I
Nautical Mile

G I B R A L T A R

ship full of fighting spirit. Certainly under 'Hookie', every manjack on board was made to feel that he and his job mattered a great deal – everyone from the lowliest Ordinary Seaman to the Departmental Commanders. I served later under Earl Mountbatten in India and Ceylon. Though he certainly had an incredible memory, and was very popular with the troops, Lord Louis worked for that, not so much because he wanted their esteem, but he realised that by having their esteem, he could have their co-operation also, and get things done. Captain Holland wasn't like that. He really didn't care whether you liked him or not, but he would prefer that you did. What was to him much more important was that YOU knew that he cared about YOU, which I believe is a better route to getting things done.

A couple of years later I was in London on leave. It was probably November 1943, when I had just come back from North Africa, and had vistied Queen Anne's Mansions to hear about my next appointment. In the Mall I encountered 'Hookie', now a Rear-Admiral, and I a Lieutenant (A) RNVR. Tearing him off the sort of salute that a lieutenant reserves for admirals, he acknowledged it, then stopped, paused, extended his hand and said, 'Woods, isn't it? How are you and what are you doing now?' So he kept a couple of Captains RN waiting while he chatted for a few minutes with one of his Old Arks. The sort of incident which puts four inches on your chest and two feet on your height. With him it wasn't to gather popularity, he really wanted to know. Now Lord Louis wouldn't have used the interrogatives: he would have known it was Woods, because his photographic memory would have told him so.

The rest of our trip home was – happily – uneventful, as escorted by *Cossack*, *Sikh*, *Hesperus* and a Norwegian destroyer – *Stord* I think ('Hookie' would have known!) – we arrived in Greenock on 21 June. On the way I flew a dusk patrol with Lucas, taking off at 2300 in those northern latitudes, and landing at sunset (0045!) rather heavily, says my logbook, and with depth-charges on. Next morning our three remaining aircraft flew to Abbotsinch airfield and *Victorious* dropped anchor in the Clyde at 0730 on 21 June 1941, the day before Hitler attacked Russia.

James' last act had been to appoint me officer i/c rear echelon, which meant that I had to get the squadron stores and ratings to Lee-on-Solent, where we were to re-equip with Fairey Albacore aircraft, a sort of streamlined 'Stringbag' if report spoke true. But first we had, cat-like, to mark out our terrain there, get rid of our redundant stores and send the troops off on leave. Like me, they would all get extra time for the extra work they had done, plus a day, and all of that I could leave to our splendid RPO, Mortimer.

It was a long and dreary journey from Glasgow to Fareham, Hampshire via Crewe, most of the time being spent talking about the prospects now that Hitler had for reasons best known to himself, decided to attack Uncle Joe Stalin – or so he was known at the time. We all seemed to be thinking too much about leave, and the conversations weren't too serious.

We were going on leave. At least the troops did, and I was intending to. That evening, I reported to the Commander of the shore establishment HMS *Daedalus* – Lee-on-Solent, who asked me where I'd come from. I told him that my last ship was *Ark Royal*. 'Pity,' he said, 'You just missed an exciting action against the *Bismarck*.' 'No, sir, that was our last big action before I left her.'

That did it. Next morning I had to report to the office of Rear-Admiral Bell-Davies VC, DSO, Rear-Admiral Naval Air Stations, to give my graphic firsthand description of the action. It must have been a good delivery, because I got a bit worked up when describing the approach and turn-away of poor old A4 'Charlie'. Ralph Richardson was among those present, then on the staff as a Lieutenant-Commander, and he congratulated me. I always thought this was on my histrionics, but no film offers ever came my way.

Pity, telling the truth cost me a day's leave. This was the first time I recognised Murphy's Law No 1 'No unselfish deed ever goes unpunished'.

Chapter 9
Interlude at Lee

The leave looked forward to for so long was slightly disappointing in that I had not realised that almost all of my contemporaries would be away in the various services. Bomber Command had now moved into Lincolnshire en masse and airfields existed or were fast being constructed all over the country. One of my few friends on leave, John Marris, was in the RAF civil engineering branch, engaged in this work, and prophesied, accurately as events turned out, that in a couple of years the entire country would be one mass of Bomber Command airfields, This was natural, Lincolnshire being flat and not more than 400 miles at any point from Hamburg as the bomber flies. In the process of moving in, the RAF had spoken for most of the available unattached local talent, the Army regiments billeted locally coming second by a nose. Having been away from my native heath for almost two years, with no one carrying the torch for me, it seemed that romance would have to wait until I settled down somewhere for an appreciable stay. If ever.

My father, a local headmaster, had unfortunately, but with pardonable pride, leaked some of my adventures to Lionel Robinson, editor of the local weekly newspaper, with the embarrassing result that a keen young reporter called for an interview. Not knowing what was permissible conversation, I asked him to bring along his syndicated reports of *Ark Royal*'s operations, on which I would comment as a local boy.

I was not at all prepared for the headlines a few days later in the *Lincolnshire Standard*, and my lunchtime and evening rendezvous with friends tested my capacity for alcohol very keenly. There are, it seems, some situations in which you cannot win, since in an effort to avoid well-meaning but dangerous liquid donations in the local hostelries, I shed my uniform and appeared in sports jacket and slacks. One morning, while waiting for a bus to take me to town, a middle-aged lady approached to ask why a well-built young chap like me wasn't in uniform. 'Madame,' I answered, preparing for a teasing session, 'because I don't choose to'. Whereupon she told me that I should be ashamed of myself for letting others do my fighting for me, and pinned a white feather on my lapel, which I wore proudly into the bar of the White Hart. Standing at the bar was a uniformed Chief Petty Officer torpedo-coxswain from one of the minesweepers in the local docks. To the delight and hilarity of my friends (in plain clothes because of their reserved occupations) he proceeded to try to inveigle me into joining the Royal Navy. Again, attempting to tease him, I replied that the Navy wasn't my field at all, since I was prone to seasickness even on a damp lawn, which he countered darkly, suggesting that it would be better for me to volunteer now rather than wait to be conscripted into some unit I wouldn't like, such as the Pioneer Corps. With this I had to agree, promising the Chief that I would think it over.

There was a duty visit to my old school, which brought on a strange feeling, similar to that described by Erich Remarque in *All Quiet on the Western Front*. The Headmaster, who had gained a Military Cross and lost a leg in 1914-18, and my old maths master became over-jingoistic as old soldiers are wont to do. A much better feeling came from chatting with the Cadet Force after school, when a short lecture on navigation and signals was expected and given.

During this visit I had promised to attend the school sports, and a few days later found myself lurked into the Old Boys' Race. Normally, this would have been quite enjoyable, as I was a keen sprinter at school, but one of my contemporaries, now masquerading as an Army subaltern, had brought along a case of beer in his car to fortify us. By the time the Old Boys' Race was called, we were all very nicely thank you, producing the slowest 100 yards' time since Aesop's tortoise.

Another old friend, George Wilkinson, formerly a chief officer in the Merchant Navy, and now a lieutenant RNR, commanded HMS *Ouzel*, a minesweeper based in Boston and patrolling the Wash. He invited me for a trip, which I was happy to accept, since not only did it give time to exchange reminiscences, we also shot a trawl and caught some splendid fish. I didn't know it then, but it was the last time I should see George, as less than a year later he and most of his ships' company were killed by a swept mine exploding prematurely when they were trying to put a safe distance between mine and ship preparatory to a conventional detonation.

It was good to see my parents and family, and to be with them again, but a little of Britain in wartime went a long way with me. The teenagers of yesteryear had grown up and had seen things they didn't want to talk about. Mother cooked all my old favourites, but offset this by having a long visiting list for me, mostly taking tea and making polite conversation. All this kindness, this respite from war should have made me glad, but having no permanent attachments, it seemed to be lacking in something. At first it seemed possible that the town was too small, but making comparisons after leave was over, it appeared that even in the big cities, apart from London, there were problems in finding sufficient congenial things to do. It wasn't that we were keen to get back to the war, but in retrospect it may have been that our new and more disciplined way of life had taken over, and our new shipmates had replaced the sort of friendships we used to have. Our lifestyles seemed to have been reshaped. Certainly many years later, when peace broke out, it was equally difficult to become re-accustomed to civilian life.

And so the two weeks passed, until finally, almost with relief, I made my farewells on 8 July, something which embarrasses me even today. Passing through Waterloo Station, in wartime chock full of naval personnel, I met Alan Swanton, seemingly recovered from his wound and hoping to be passed fit for flying duties. Arriving at Lee-on-Solent, the wardroom was a-buzz with rumour, the principal one being that 820 was to be split into two flights, one specialising in dive-bombing, the other in torpedo and reconnaissance work, each comprising nine aircraft, another flight of fancy so barmy that it might even be true.

The Lee-on-Solent of summer 1941 was vastly different from the No 1 observer school of just over a year ago. Expansion had filled the barrack blocks and new hutted camps were springing up all over the place. The old and rather grand officers' quarters were also overflowing and local hotels were being commandeered. I was fortunate in being billetted in Haylands Court, where life was much easier and detached from the signals, messages and routine that always attend the HQ of anything. Lots of aircraft were arriving, but none for us, the majority going to squadrons already operational and in need of replacements. And 820 was also going through a reshuffle.

Lieutenant-Commander Stewart-Moore was leaving us to take command of 827 Squadron in *Victorious* and Walter Elliot, another observer, was taking over command of 820. We knew nothing of him except that he had played for the Navy and England at rugby in the mid-1930s in the stand-off half position, which boded well for our sporting aspirations. One of the good things about living at an HQ was that there were always people passing through, giving a chance of meeting friends, so that lunchtimes and evenings were from time to time enlivened by such fortuitous gatherings. John Hoare, a Canadian course-mate (though his schooling and university in England seemed to have deleted any accent he may ever have had) turned up one day, and we brought each other up-to-date on present disposition of our numerous mutual friends. Telling me of his experiences adrift in a dingy for several days after his Fulmar force-landed off Iceland during the *Bismarck* operation from *Victorious*, which were terrifying, he then shattered me with the news that Pat Goodger and David Beattie, two mutual good friends and course-mates had been lost in similar circumstances at that time. Bob Morris of 818, 'Duke's' wrestling opponent, was also reported killed, but the worst news of all was the death of Lieutenant-Commander James Tillard. A cousin to Rupert Tillard, the recently-deceased CO of 808, James was our course-officer at *St Vincent* and also a fighter pilot. We had seen him many times doing aerobatics at Lee and Arbroath, his favourite being a nought-feet beat-up of the station in a Sea Gladiator.

It was a depressing time, but the Fleet Air Arm was involved in a great deal of action in those days, far removed in many cases, from the types of combat envisaged in peacetime. It was only after the sinking of the German cruiser *Königsberg* off Bergen in Norway (10 April 1940) for the loss of one Skua out of the 16 employed that the full role of the bomb and torpedo began to be realised. *Königsberg* was the first major warship to be sunk by aerial attack in wartime, and after the Taranto action in which three battleships and two cruisers were sunk for the loss of two Swordfish, no fleet could ever again feel safe in harbour, as we knew from our experience in Gibraltar. The sinking of *Bismarck* at sea was a classic example of what the far-seeing senior officers (and there were a few of these, but far too few) had always prophesied – that the capital ship of the future was not the battleship, but the aircraft carrier. It we were to win this war by seapower, we must always be ahead in techniques, and our current enemies, Germany and Italy, had no carriers. Germany had already launched her first, *Graf Zeppelin*, though she never went to sea.

Ivan Fisher, our new senior observer, arrived. Straight from training in Trinidad, he was a Master Mariner, a lieutenant RNR, and could pilot service aircraft. Probably just about on the age-limit for operational flying (then 38 years) he seemed a very reasonable type. An RN lieutenant observer, Donald ('Bud') Abbott, was appointed flight commander. Also straight from training, he was about 23 years old and very enthusiastic. So it seemed that we 'experienced sprogs' would have to wait a little longer for our own promotions to flight command. Ivan appreciated this problem quite cannily, and asked me to be his assistant, a wise move since he had never before been in a first-line squadron.

'Scruffy' Manley-Cooper and Alan Swanton were re-appointed to 821, then operating in the Western Desert, and keen to be going, since they would probably by flying together. A good combination, the serious Alan and the perpetually ebullient 'Scruffy'.

Another of the more amusing things at this time was meeting our old instructors in the control tower and radio office. Most of them were very experienced petty officers and Leading TAGs, good at their craft, and knew their gunnery and radio operating inside out. 'Shorty' Roberts, a Welshman from Pontypool had been one of my favourites and happily he was now to join 820 as petty officer and senior TAG. Good news, as he would certainly smarten up the raw young TAGs now being drafted to us. 'Shorty' survived a hair-raising experience before the war, when his pilot's scarf caught in the winch mechanism of a drogue-towing aircraft and began to throttle him. 'Shorty's' ingenuity and enterprise in slashing the offending scarf with his jack-knife saved them both as well as the aircraft.

Possibly because our full complement of aircraft hadn't yet arrived, four 820 observers were sent on an army co-cordination course with No 16 RAF Squadron at Weston Zoyland, Somerset. At that time it seemed a pointless, if pleasant, exercise to fill in some spare time, but the knowledge gained came in very handy some time later. No 16 Squadron was mobile, living in tents and marquees, and hoping shortly to take its Westland Lysander single-engined high-wing monoplanes to the Western Desert. Used during the war for numerous duties, and especially, because of its low stalling speed and short take-off run, for dropping and picking up agents at night in occupied countries from September 1941, it was an ideal aircraft for army co-op work. The crew normally consisted of a pilot and a wireless operator/airgunner (or Wop/AG). The pilots were an odd breed, rather like their naval opposite numbers in that their first loyalty was not to aircraft, but to their parent service, the Army. Many were seconded to the Air Force, but obviously all of them retained great pride in their original regiments to the extent that they dressed in army uniform for dinner, though wearing RAF battledress by day. Their CO was Wing-Commander Peter Stansfield; second-in-command Peter Dudgeon (an old Egypt hand, known as 'Dudgeon Pasha'); Adjutant Charlie Zorab; while the younger pilots were Robin White, 'Chunky' Chegwin, Micky Coombs and Fred Malcolm. Two genuine 'Pongoes' John Bury and Jimmie Earthrowl were in charge of photographic reconnaissance and intelligence analysis.

Fred Malcolm had an interesting story. Arriving home on leave in Scotland on 10 May, some six weeks earlier, he was called out at night by the local constabulary to identify a German pilot who had bailed out of a Messerschmitt 110 in a very lonely part of the country. The captive had told the police he was Rudolf Hess, and requested an interview with the Duke of Hamilton. The story sounded so daffy and the bucolic local sergeant of police was not prepared to accept the story, and hence responsibility, without some independent identification, and Fred Malcolm, the only known officer and gentleman in the vicinity, was dragged protesting from his bed to make the necessary identification. As Fred commented in the bar of the 'Dolphin', Wincanton, 'I'd never met Rudolf Hess. Who the hell in Britain had? But to me he looked like a lot of newspaper pictures of Hess!'. And as the world knew a few hours later, Hess it certainly was. I sincerely hope that Fred is still dining out on his unique story.

The following week seemed like a month, we crammed in so much work. Lectures on strategy, tactical reconnainssance, spotting for artillery, all new territory to we four 'Tarrybreeks' as we were known –

Ivan Fisher, Leonard Mann, Frank Norman and me. Each morning a new tactic was exercised, and another each afternoon. Somerset was beautiful that summer, and the squadron full of bonhomie. Working hard and playing hard, we flew from dawn until 1800, then a quick supper and off to the local hostelries. We visited Old Sarum, Larkhill, Frome, Wincanton, Chedzoy and many more delightful towns with delightful names and even more delightful pubs. The locals just could not understand what the hell sailors were doing on Salisbury Plain and in Somerset, neither particularly well-known for maritime affinity. One night we came back to find everything and everyone gone. 'Dudgeon Pasha', who was duty officer, had decided in the CO's absence that if 16 were truly a mobile squadron, it was time to test this, ordering everyone to pack the gear as quickly as they could and move to Wincanton racecourse from Weston Zoyland, leaving only the aircraft behind. Peter Stansfield was somewhat less than enthusiastic about 'Dudgeon Pasha's' usurpation, but as the latter remarked, 'If the Krauts had attacked, would I have had to await your return before counter-attacking?'. The Wingco agreed, getting his own back by collapsing Peter Dudgeon's bell tent in the small hours.

At Colerne one morning we saw a force of Halifax and Wellington bombers going to attack Brest in daylight – an unenviable task, as *Scharnhorst* and *Gneisenau* sheltering there would be heavily defended by flak batteries and aircraft. If those ships could be eliminated, the war would go along much faster. Whirlwinds and Beaufighters went over later on a fighter sweep of France.

Many were the novelties, like riding in new Churchill tanks over Salisbury Plain. As riding in tanks is dirty, we borrowed army denim fatigues to wear over our naval reefer jackets. Halfway across the plain, Ivan Fisher's tank threw a track, and he had to thumb a lift to the nearest army camp while his former hosts repaired their tank. The sentry, who had been carefully briefed to look out for parachuting nuns and other suspicious characters, was confronted by this startling apparition in a naval uniform under denims, with the most peculiar stripes on the sleeve, surmounted by wings, which everyone knew were worn on the left breast. Add to this the fact that the visitor had a crew cut, wore a monocle, and claimed his christian name was Ivan. What would any self-respecting sentry do? Right! And it took us a couple of hours to bail him out of the slammer. Dudgeon was all for keeping him there overnight, but we had to live with Ivan. Next day 'Dudgeon Pasha' got his come-uppance when a friendly AA battery fired on him maliciously as we were dropping dummy parachutists over Bristol. The Wingco decided it was time to move on.

Though the 'Lizzie' was an excellent aircraft for army liaison in 1940, its low maximum speed was likely to be a hindrance in the ever-increasing pace of modern war. They were soon displaced by single-seat US Curtiss Tomahawk fighters, some arriving when we were there. These pilots were specialists, and given the improvements attained in the range of the radio-telephone communication from air to ground, there would be little need for a Wop/AG, since the Tomahawk had enough speed to wiggle out of nasty situations.

And as all good things eventually come to an end, this joyous interlude was no exception. So, at 1030 on Sunday 27 July we flew back in one of four Lysanders to Lee-on-Solent, arriving just as the bar opened, to give our hosts of the preceding two weeks a stimulating session there, followed by the renowned Lee peacetime-style lunch. At 1500 our guests took off for Somerset, but (they alleged) ran into some thick haze and all four Lysanders returned. Dinner and a noisy evening at the Inn by the Sea followed, our new friends leaving early next morning.

It was about two years later that I ran again into John Bury, by then a major, in Algiers, where he was in some 'private firm' of parachutists in the cloak and dagger section of Combined Operations. His duties were to parachute or otherwise effect entry into captured enemy cities and headquarters, preferably before the defenders surrendered, to seize important dossiers, documents, secret codes and any other items likely to benefit Allied forces. Much later I met him again, in India, and sometime around 1944 heard that this very courageous gentleman had been killed in action during one of these dangerous missions in Burma.

The 820 Squadron stay at Lee-on-Solent lasted three months, slowly but surely collecting replacement aircraft and crews, for several more of our senior people had left to form the nuclei of new squadrons. The new pilots, observers and airgunners, as well as the new aircraft were straight from the production line, all needing tuning up to operational standards. Hughie Hunter and Nigel Gardner went off on courses, and the new pilots – David James, Clifford Wearden, Teddy Reed, Jock Marr, Jimmy Bridge and 'Red' Knight plus the new observers – 'Sprog' Norman, Jimmy Perrot, 'Fanny' Adams, and one with whom I could already see confusion, named Wood – all spent long hours becoming acclimatised to Albacores and to squadron workings. Mike Fuller and 'Gubby' Allen had joined just prior to our quitting *Ark Royal*, so had made a few operational flights and decklandings.

The Fairey Albacore, though from the same stable as the redoubtable Swordfish, and reputed to be a sophisticated version, was not to everyone's liking. The Taurus engine was more powerful than the old Pegasus, but early production engines were prone to rather catastrophic oil leaks. But, for the first time, naval torpedo-bombers had enclosed cockpits with sliding hoods. An all-metal aircraft, unlike the fabric-bodied Swordfish, she was much heavier, and therefore less manoeuvrable, but from an observer and airgunner viewpoint, undeniably more comfortable and better equipped. We must obviously take our time to

Albacore 5Q of 820 Squadron flying from Lee-on-Solent in August 1941. The pilot is Sub-Lieutenant (A) S W ('Davy') James RNVR with the author behind the perspex to the rear. The TAG, probably Leading Airman Keel, is checking the rear gun. *Leonard Mann*

Four 820 Squadron observers on detachment to 16 Squadron RAF at Weston Zoyland, Somerset, 21 July 1941. Left to right: Sub-Lieutenant (A) Leonard Mann, the author, Midshipman (A) F J Norman, and Lieutenant Ivan Fisher RNR. Flying Officer Fred Malcolm RAF pilots the Lysander behind. *Author's collection*

120

'fly them in', and correct our techniques accordingly. From an armament angle, the Vickers GO gun mounted in the rear cockpit gave greater confidence against attacking fighters, but obviously, we must still depend upon turning in ever-decreasing circles against fast enemy monoplanes.

Our earlier doubts about Lee-on-Solent began to disappear as soon as we got into the social swim. Many senior active and retired naval officers lived in this pleasant area of Hampshire, and most of them seemed to have nubile daughters or other young female relatives, most of whom served under some strange engagement in the WRNS. They were known as 'Local Wrens' and were not, at that time anyway, subject to the Naval Discipline Act in many respects. Most of them seemed to work in transport, sick bay, signals and administration. Most of them were attractive, or had we been at sea too long? At any rate, after we had found the various social meeting-places, romances began to thrive.

The favourite spot of the younger element was the tennis club, where a peacetime 'anyone for tennis' atmosphere prevailed, with afternoon teas and a dance on Saturday nights. It seems some tennis was played, and unfortunately there was no bar so far as I remember, but there were abundant local hostelries, where we 'got flying speed' before the dance started and it was a pleasant way to spend one's Saturday or Sunday after the barrenness of Gibraltar. Two of the tunes remembered from that time, which still make me go all nostalgic when I hear them, were 'Deep in the Heart of Texas' and 'Yes My Darling Daughter', though I preferred Adelaide Hall's 'The Things I Love' on the flip side, unfortunately not a dancing tune. Alverstoke, a few miles nearer to Gosport seemed to be the most desirable residential district, the inhabitants thereof being known as 'The Alverstokracy'.

Lee-on-Solent was now the main drafting air station, as well as being one of the forming-up stations for new squadrons. Thus a lot of old faces from training days were still there, and other familiar faces arrived almost daily. It was, as 'Klondyke' alias John Hoare remarked in the Canadian idiom, 'Just like Old Home week'. Leslie Holmes, recovering from his leg-wound, and 'Darkie' Carlyle, both former instructors, were passing through. I had seen 'Darkie' earlier in Gibraltar when he was in *Berwick*, shortly after an Italian 8in shell had gone through their catapult aircraft's hangar off Cape Spartivento, turning 'Darkie's' swarthy complexion, it was said, six shades whiter. There was the tall dePass, from one of our destroyer escorts, now a sub-lieutenant, Bill Roberts and Randolph Pearson with eye problems and dark glasses; Dick Charlier and 'Pig' Lucas, the latter 820's senior pilot for a short spell, and now commanding 811 Squadron which was forming up in American Chesapeake dive-bombers, lease-loaned. This seemed to be the basis of the rumour that 820 was to split into two sections, since we flew on a great number of exercises with 811, and marked their dive-bombing practices on the Stokes' Bay range nearby. A two-seater monoplane with pronounced dihedral, the Chesapeake looked to be an extremely purposeful aircraft, but for some strange reason was never adopted by the Royal Navy.

I developed a certain ambivalence about Lee. Living there was good, flying by day and often by night, but being able to spend every free evening gassing with old mates or new arrivals, or dating some of the local talent, mainly the Wrens. The local ladies viewed all operational officers as their special charges, and we were spoiled rotten. It was a fact, the reverse of my home-town syndrome, as was perhaps only to be expected. Here the girls had grown up to regard the air station as the local industry, when suddenly it had become near-operational with a constant but not too rapid flow of bronzed and seasoned warriors returning awhile from the wars. What else could they do but console us? It was, nevertheless, soon obvious that the daughters of the senior naval or retired naval residents consoled the RN regular aviators with greater enthusiasm than was accorded to the impermanent RNVR.

Against this lotus-eating time, I didn't feel that we were moving fast enough in our re-equipping, and ought to be getting back to the war before we became too soft with too much 'poodle-faking'. I confided these thoughts to my father who said very simply, 'Gather ye rosebuds, my lad – you never know when you'll get another chance to do so'. I suppose he was right.

And within a few days the point was driven home. On 7 August 'Gubby' Allen and I, with Leading Airman Shields, were due to take part in an Albacore ALT over Stokes Bay. There had been some complaints about the Taurus engines 'fading', a fault subsequently discovered to be due to a carburettor weakness. Just as we were gathered in the crew room for briefing, Ivan Fisher, the senior observer, came over and asked if I'd mind stepping down, as Fairey Aviation's technical officer, Mr Goddard, had come over specially from the factory to get some firsthand experience of the fault. Having done all the ALTs I ever wanted to do, since the observer is practically a passenger in all torpedo attacks except the real thing, I gladly agreed. Half-an-hour later, the aircraft took off, and I was helping in the squadron office. Suddenly the telephone rang, and a slightly incoherent voice said, 'This is the control tower. One of your aircraft has just gone straight in. Could you confirm that the crew were Allen, Woods and Shields?'. I remember saying, 'Oh, my God! No, it's Woods speaking' and the voice the other end said 'Thank Christ, this is Bill Roberts. Must go'. And we severally dashed to do what we had to do in emergencies. We sped to the seaplane slipway, to see a crash boat circling a piece of the undercarriage which was all that could be seen of the crash. There were no survivors. Although 'Gubby' wasn't my regular pilot, I was flying with him as a sort of tutor, he was a delightful youngster, just 20 years old.

Shields, the same age, had been with me for a couple of months, and had some operational experience. Both were North country men with a good sense of humour.

We shall never know what went wrong. The aircraft was recovered next day, the bodies removed, and a gloom descended over the squadron. Leonard Mann seemed to know 'Gubby' best, and volunteered to pack his kit for sending home. The only person who seemed not exactly unhappy about the whole affair was Bill Roberts, who confessed that he really was upset to think I'd had it. Shields' messmates, in naval tradition, auctioned his kit for the usual ridiculously high prices, the proceeds going to his parents.

Next day more bad news, this time that Clive Jewell and Ian Gay had been killed in *Ark Royal*. Apparently one of their bombs had hung up, though every indication was that it had been released. A bumpy landing in a period of rough sea had caused the bomb to fall on to the flightdeck, where it had exploded, killing them instantly. Incidents like these two on successive days made one realise how tenuous was the thread between life and the alternative. Moreover, it also indicated that however careful a pilot or observer might be, there was always the unexpected lying in wait to trap the unlucky.

Even in these sad circumstances, a wry twist of humour arose. Wally Elliot, our CO, was a little dubious of the ability of the squadron maintenance personnel, who were, after all, fitters, riggers and armourers, to put on the necessary ceremony at the forthcoming funeral. Seamen from a ship's company would do this perfectly, but our deceased shipmates had to be escorted on their last journey by a guard of honour from their own squadron, led by an officer and the Regulating Petty Officer. The latter was easy – this had to be Mortimer, but which officer? It so happened that one of my party pieces was a take-off of a Whale Island Gunnery School instructor rehearsing the funeral party, and I'm sure that this was why I got the job, and was flattered to have been selected, everything going off promptly and with decorum.

Some few days after this episode, spares had to be transported in a hurry to the new fighter station at Yeovilton, Somerset, and there I saw the first squadron of Sea Hurricanes forming up. So the rumours were correct, at last some decent fighters for the carriers. The necessity was underlined that evening back at Lee when Bob Woolston arrived with dire news of the disastrous 30 July attacks against Petsamo and Kirkenes in Finland, a sop to the Russians, who were now our gallant allies; and it was rumoured, an order from Churchill himself to show that the Royal Navy was a vital striking force. The reverse seemed to have been proved, and in all, something like two-thirds of the aircrews of 827 and 828 had been either killed or taken prisoner, among them several contemporaries; Alec Bulford becoming a prisoner of war. No fewer than 16 out of 51 aircraft launched had been lost from *Victorious* and

Furious, and the operations appeared to have been a complete shambles. According to Bob, the biplanes had been jumped in broad daylight by Me 109s, their own fighter escort of Fulmars having failed to make the rendezvous. What a difference a few Sea Hurricanes would have made. At least they would have knocked down some enemy fighters, but more important, would have given the TBRs' morale an enormous boost. There were a couple of light moments – Nigel Ball, pilot of one of *Victorious'* Albacores shot down a Ju 87 Stuka dive-bomber, which was also masquerading as a fighter, and had strayed into the sights of Nigel's single Browning .303in front machine-gun. Ever afterwards, Nigel was to be known as 'One-gun Ball'. Gordon Gorrie, an observer, was last seen paddling his dingy roughly in the direction of Russia, where he was, in fact, rescued and returned to us at Scapa many months later, clad in Russian winter clothing and looking rather like a commissar, by which pet name he was thereafter known.

More old Arks passed through, each adding a little to our knowledge of what was going on in the various carriers and shore stations, Paul Lennard, 'Cockie' Cockburn as vague and as charming as ever. 'Cockie' had been (or so he said) first commissioned into a Highland regiment, though it was hard to imagine all 5ft 5in of him in a kilt. Nevertheless, when suitably fuelled, he would give a passable demonstration of some of the more complicated Highland dances, our favourite being the Sword dance. Bill Roberts arrived back from leave with an enormous motorbike, which he proceeded to ride far too fast down country lanes at night, with me clutching his waist from the pillion seat. I was beginning to have a feeling that my close chum hadn't quite grown up, but felt extremely sorry for him when he was pinched by the local constabulary one morning for speeding in Lee, and the same afternoon was logged at the airfield for low-flying in a Fulmar. Follow that!

I had meanwhile moved back into the wardroom from the Haylands Court, and spent most of my flying time with David James, known to his intimates as 'Stoker' since he had volunteered in that category before transferring to the Air Arm for training. We had a complementary sense of humour, both being 'Popeye' fans, and conversed in a strange dialect on the intercom. Slowly we trained practically the whole squadron to use Wimpy's 'Greetings' as a morning salutation, and even today, I find I'm still doing it. David was almost unflappable, to the extent that sometimes I felt he was asleep up there in front. We began to enjoy each others' skills in the air, though our tastes on the ground were somewhat different. Our selected airgunner was 'Fuzz' Keel, a serious, competent young man, who, once he had become used to the fact that he was flying with a couple of strange characters who nevertheless took their jobs very seriously, became very much an integral part of the crew of Albacore 4Q – for 'Queer' as David would announce to air control. A new observer arrived about this time, Jack Stokes, an unusual combination of RNR sub-lieutenant's stripes, a Canadian accent and about 6ft 6in tall. An ex-Merchant Navy cadet, he was a great help to any who struggled with seamanship, and his dry, patient wit was a tonic. Happily, I met him recently in Vancouver, and recognised him immediately, he not having changed a bit in 37 years, though he had to take three or four looks before he could be certain it was me. I hate people who don't change in 37 years!

As the rainy August moved into a sunny September, rumours of our leaving began to circulate. We had sharpened up our flying, after sundry blasts from Wally and the station brass, done our night-flying and night-dummy decklandings at Worthy Down where the wardroom seemed to be full of Old Vic actors masquerading as naval pilots – Laurence Olivier, Ralph Richardson and others. The awards for the sinking of the *Bismarck* were now announced, and DSCs were awarded to Hughie, Colin Ennever, 'Duke' Norfolk, Bud Beale and Peter Elias, which, by common consent were well-earned and representative, though I would liked to have seen Alan Swanton's courage and determination recognised. In fact, my worries were groundless, as he later collected a DSC and bar, and then a DSO in the Korean War. So, that night in the wardroom there was a 'gong' party for Hughie. Any excuse for a party, but this was for a most popular and self-effacing shipmate, and something special.

Aircrew of 820 Squadron hold a post flight inquest aboard *Formidable* in the Indian Ocean. An Albacore with folded wings is behind them. From left to right: Sub-Lieutenants P H ('Prune') Chambers, 'Gutty' Snelgrove; 'Francois' Du Cane; J M ('Hank') Henry; Smuts Smith (in cap); Frank ('Skeezix') Norman (in cap); the author (in cap back to camera); P A ('Pussy') Grant (foreground); Geoffrey Topham (in cap); 'Davy' James; and Lieutenant J N ('Bushy') Shrubsole RN. *Leonard Mann*

An 820 Squadron Albacore lands on *Formidable* off Ceylon in the summer of 1942 with another behind. The batsman is *Formidable*'s senior DLCO, Lieutenant-Commander (A) 'Sandy' Cubitt RN. The holes in his 'bats' are to minimise wind resistance as they were otherwise sometimes blown out of the batsman's hands which could cause unnecessary delays in landing. *Leonard Mann*

Chapter 10
The Road to the Isles

On 26 September, part one of our work-up was deemed complete, or as complete as it was likely to be, and orders came for our move up to RNAS Crail in the Kingdom of Fife. By this time I seemed to have achieved a reputation as an anchor man, possibly due to my playing for the squadron as goalkeeper at soccer and hockey, full back at rugby and wicket-keeper at cricket. Or maybe I'd got the routine off pat, having done it several times, so, the aircraft having left in the morning, my rear echelon troops cleared everything up, trucks took us the short ride to Fareham railway station, and we began our long journey north to Scotland. For some strange reason, either one pilot sick, or a spare aircraft had to be taken, Ivan Fisher, the pilot/observer was given an Albacore to fly north, and he was the last to leave.

Leonard Mann met us at RAF Leuchars, the end of our rail journey, with the news that the weather had closed in on the squadron, and they were told to proceed independently instead of in formation. A real Muldoon's Picnic had ensued as the cloud base and visibility dropped alarmingly, pilots putting down wherever they could see an airfield. Taking the west coast route, most of the kites had put down either at RAF Sealand near Chester or in south Lancashire. Poor Ivan had managed to crash land at Speke airport, Liverpool, and had bent his Albacore rather badly.

And so we arrived in Crail with all the squadron stores and no aircraft, though they came in over the next few days. Rather cautiously. A number of old Arks were at Crail as instructors in the Torpedo Training School, which was looked upon by their Lordships as tantamount to a rest from operations. In fact, it was anything but a rest, many senior and valuable pilots being killed instructing at Crail, due usually to over-zealousness or sheer hamfistedness on the part of their pupils. Most of them had come straight from training schools and had no experience of torpedo work. Among those decorating the bar that evening were 'Tan' Tivy, Carl Appleton, Stan Keene and Paul Whitfield; all senior lieutenants, and all at least operational flight commanders, if

127

not senior pilots. That night I slept very well.

Crail was much colder than Lee, and the hours we worked were long. Almost as soon as we arrived, rumours began to circulate that we would soon embark in a carrier, though it was obvious to anyone with operational experience that we were far from ready for front-line work. Nevertheless, I prepared myself physically for such an eventuality, for after all, had not Esmonde's 825 attacked *Bismarck* during a working-up trip in *Victorious*? So I went to the dentist to have any cavities sorted out – rather important in these northern climates, and fortunate, as things turned out that I did so. I also had all vaccinations that might be needed anywhere in the world, not wishing to be feeling under the weather should a 'pier-head jump' occur.

We worked long hours polishing up the finer points of reconnaissance, navigation exercises and formation flying. Wally had appointed me officer in charge of sports and signals, a strange combination, but the former I never regarded as a duty. Armed with some authority now in matters of radio and radar, courses were organised with RNAS Arbroath for a week's training of all observers on the inner workings, repair and maintenance of ASV sets, something hitherto neglected, probably due to the lack of knowledge and shortage of instructors. So sub-flights went to HMS *Condor* (Arbroath) to be put through numerous air exercises by Sam Inderwick who often affected a bowler hat when flying his ASV-equipped Walrus amphibian. On the ground were several of our old TAG instructors from Portsmouth Signal School and Lee-on-Solent, notably 'Cuts' Edwards, Watson and Whales, now all petty officers. Also there was Mosedale, my favourite radio instructor from Lee, a very amusing yet strange character. In 1939 he had completed his 12-year engagement, successfully avoiding promotion of any sort, and as a three-badge TAG, was ready to leave the Navy, go on to the Royal Fleet Reserve, and set up a radio repair and sales business in Gosport with another shipmate who was also hoping to be an ex-TAG. Unfortunately, war broke out, so 'Mose' and partner were kept in for the duration. In those early days of the war, he still – like many others – thought that it would all be over by Christmas, and again very successfully avoided promotion. However, their Lordships decided in 1940 that all flying personnel should have at least the rating of Leading Airman, so 'Mose' accepted defeat gracefully and shipped his hook. His wife, more ambitious than he, finally persuaded him to take the long view, and much later in the war (1945 I think) who should I meet one day but Warrant Officer Mosedale. It would have been regrettable if his great technical ability had been wasted in the lower rating, when he had so much knowledge to impart.

Arbroath had a new captain, none other than R M T Taylor, who had been Commander in *Ark Royal*, and among his officers were none other than Bob Everett and 'Feather' Fausett. Whether 'Feather' had wangled the appointment, or whether it was just good luck we shall never know, but Hughie Hunter decided to marry his fiancée on 4 October at Broughty Ferry, and 'Feather' was Best Man. A great occasion, and a number of old Arks at the church and at the reception, Hughie making the longest speech anyone had ever heard from him – about one minute flat. Maybe it was the gin, or the ceremony or the gathering of old chums, but altogether it was a very emotional occasion, and one felt that we were members of a very exclusive club, as indeed we were.

Back at Crail, there were signs in the air that something was happening, we knew not what. Our torpedo exercises were stepped up, we dropped a number of 'runners' ie torpedoes identical to the real thing except that they contained no explosive, and surfaced after completing their track, to be picked up by drifters or the target vessel and re-used. Dive-bombing also became a priority, and on as many exercises as possible we had observers working the radio sets, since in this particular expertise, they had become sloppy, leaving the technical side to their TAGs. This was all very well, but supposing the TAG was absent, wounded, or we had a recurrence of long-range petrol tanks? Rear-Admiral Dennis Boyd, now Flag Officer Air, came over one day to give us a pep-talk and stayed to witness night flying exercises. Happily, the weather was kind, and he appeared to be suitably impressed. Next day 'Streamline' Robertson, Crail's Commander Flying, came up in David James' Albacore, with me working the radio very successfully. David was at his very best on the dive-bombing range, getting four practice bombs in the 50-yard ring out of six shots. 'Streamline' was most impressed, at least until the newly-fitted 'Wurlitzer' radio set swung out of its housing and almost crushed my right knee-cap. With all this attention from the Top Brass, we should have known that there was something unpleasant coming up.

About this time, a new member joined who was to be one of my greatest friends for the time we were together in 820 Squadron. Patrick Hawkesley Chambers, a short-service sub-lieutenant pilot entered the wardroom somewhat tentatively one evening, to be greeted by Nigel Gardner and Mike Lithgow as a long-lost brother. Pat was a Manxman and had been wounded in Malta, where he flew 830 Squadron Swordfish, mostly at night. Malta was a hot spot, and even the Navy only allowed its aircrews to stay there for six months before being relieved. There were two situations in Malta for aircrews – you were either flying or being bombed. Add to these, the facts that food was severely rationed, aircraft spares were unavailable and there was little or no entertainment, it all added up to a rough time. Pat was a very soft-spoken character, hiding an astutue wit under a bland, almost rustic, face. Just at this time, the RAF had produced a monthly training magazine called 'Tee Emm' - persumably short for 'Training Manual'.

One of the star characters therein was a Pilot Officer Prune, who was always doing the wrong thing, so that each month he demonstrated how NOT to do something properly. Also awarded each month was the Order of the Irremovable Digit, the winner being selected from the mass of accident reports received by the Air Ministry. The legendary award was an index finger rampant, surrounded, I believe, by a laurel wreath; the 'award' title being, of course, derived from the age-old exhortation from instructors to pupils to 'pull your finger out'.

The resemblance between Patrick Hawkesley Chambers and Pilot Officer Prune was quite fantastic. Physically only, I am more than delighted to say, since later we flew together quite a lot, and I found him very much above average. Pat's rather happy nature accepted the new role, and he became 'Prune' to all his friends, even adopting a raised index finger as his salutation.

Saturday 30 October saw the beginning of the end to this relative interlude. Mike Lithgow, who had acquired a rather clapped out car, invited three of us to accompany him into the nearby city of St Andrews for shopping and a few beers. As might be expected from one who later held the world's airspeed record, Mike had a breakdown in the rain on our way home, and had to be towed ignominiously back to Crail. We were a trifle late arriving, to be met by Mike Fuller, officer of the watch, who informed us that we were leaving next day for RNAS Hatston in the Orkneys, the air base for Scapa Flow, and reputed to be the last place God made.

By now I had the rear echelon drill buttoned up neatly, and having got the aircraft off at 1030, we were ready to move off at 1600. As so often happens in the Air Arm, we had to go south to travel north, and went first to Edinburgh, then on to Perth. Provided the rear echelon didn't wander into the fleshpots at our various stops, we could leave a small guard over the stores, and the rest could go and get drunk as they liked. Several did, realising that their opportunities of doing so in future were likely to be limited, but Mortimer knew his 'skates' and kept a watchful eye on them. We arrived at Thurso at 0100 on 2 November in the snow, had a hearty Scottish breakfast, then embarked in the MV *Morialta* for the passage across the Pentland Firth, arriving at Hatston by 1700 that evening. Having got rid of the stores to the station's security and seen that the ratings were properly settled in, I went over to the wardroom, handed my own travelling gear over to my steward (our heavy items having gone on ahead by truck), and strolled into the bar. Who should be there but Alan Swanton and 'Scruffy' Cooper, with whom we'd had a farewell party a few weeks earlier before they departed, allegedly for the Desert. 'Scruffy' had an instant explanation – this was a desert, wasn't it – not a tree on the .... island, all the dogs with prostate trouble.' Alan claimed that 'Scruffy' had given him a reciprocal course to steer. They were shortly off, anyway, taking Johnny

Buscall, another course-mate, with them, persumably this time, to the Desert.

We ourselves didn't waste too much time at Hatston, a really bleak airfield, and nearer to Norway than to Newcastle. But the food was good, eggs were plentiful, and the local inhabitants (every one of whom seemed to be named Shearer, or was related to the Shearer family) made us feel very welcome with their beautifully-modulated voices and their soft accent. Kirkwall was the nearest town, more Scandinavian than British in appearance, and for a population of 3000 they certainly had an excellent social life, with a dance at least once a week at the town hall, and some extremely elastic licensing hours. The town was about 1½ miles' walk away from Hatston across the isthmus, and the largest in the Orkneys.

Only three days after our arrival, six of our Albacores joined *Victorious* in Scapa Flow and we left for Iceland on 3 November. Hughie was acting CO with Ivan Fisher as senior observer. Other crews included Lithgow and Topham, Chambers and Mann, Teddy Reed and myself. So far I had flown only occasionally with Reed. Though his flying was most impressive, and his decklandings almost impeccable, he tended, as pilot, to override my instructions sometimes, which was not only bad discipline, but also rather dangerous for one so recently out of flying school. On a reconnaissance one day, having been given a course for the final leg home, Teddy thought he saw the carrier on the starboard bow, and disregarding the course given him, edged to starboard, despite my repeated instruction when I noted that my compass was not giving the correct course. After about half-an-hour, he realised that what he thought was the carrier was, in fact an island, so that we landed on almost an hour late. Unfortunately Teddy would not accept the blame, and I could see that we were going to have a few personal problems unless he changed his ways.

And so we came to Iceland, not the cold country we had been expecting, though at this time of the year it was more often than not in the grip of a gale. Britain had taken over this island on that fateful 10 May in 1940, much against the will of the inhabitants, though our intention was to forestall the Germans from using it as a base to attack Allied shipping in both the Atlantic and the Arctic Oceans. The Icelanders made no secret of their dislike and studiously avoided any sort of contact. A pity, since their almost white-haired girls were most attractive, but had been threatened with head-shaving if they were seen with any of the 'invaders'. Thus our sallies into the capital, Reykjavik were few, and usually via a landing craft that made a tour of all ships for libertymen and officers going ashore. One thing puzzled me here. The small convoy we had brought in with supplies for the Allied garrison there, unloaded quantities of silk stockings and confectionery, mainly chocolate. The troops going ashore bought huge quantities of these same goods which we shortly took back to Hatston, which didn't seem to make sense. But did anything make sense in those days?

In Hvalfjord, a large natural harbour, where we anchored, were several US Navy heavy ships – the battleships *Idaho*, *New Mexico* and the heavy cruiser *Tuscaloosa*. Although not yet in the war, American warships had been escorting convoys to Iceland since July. The Royal Navy took over for the final leg to Scotland. It was rumoured that Douglas Fairbanks Junior and Robert Montgomery were aboard this flotilla, but I never saw them, though we did exchange visits with these ships. The reason? The US Navy was 'dry' but had different, and unusual superior food to ours. What simpler then, than to invite the Yanks over for aperitifs, go back with them for dinner, often delicious Virginia ham or some succulent fish. Sometimes this was followed by a movie, and then all returned to *Victorious* for a nightcap. Just one problem – there is nowhere in the world that a gale can spring up without warning as it can off Iceland. The officer of the watch had to be very careful to get our guests back to their own ships at the first signs of a change for the worse in the weather, since we were also at short notice for sailing should any German raiders decide to venture out.

One day, Admiral Sir John Tovey, C-in-C Home Fleet, came aboard and gave us an appreciation of the naval situation. This was the first time that anyone had given us the reason for our being there – to attack *Bismarck's* sister the *Tirpitz* and the 'pocket battleship' *Admiral Scheer*, which were known to be in Norwegian waters, should they come out to attack our Russian convoys. It was obvious, as we loftily said to 817 and 832 Squadrons, who 'belonged' to *Victorious*, that a few real professionals were needed to stiffen up these 'sprogs' who hadn't yet had a whiff of grapeshot. In fact, it was a bit unfair, since even a few weeks of Iceland had become a trifle depressing, and these squadrons had been operating between Scapa and Iceland for some time.

Number 832 had been searching unsuccessfully for the German heavies *Tirpitz*, *Scheer* and *Prinz Eugen* and had lost their CO in the process, Peter Plugge, who had been a course officer during my training at Ford and Lee. *Victorious* was not a happy ship, at least insofar as the aircrews were concerned; 832 and 817 occupied separate sides of the ante-room – fair enough – but they rarely seemed to mix, and certainly didn't with the visiting 820, though there were a few mutual friends among them willing to talk. Jim Broadburn was from my observer's course, and also two engineer officers, Chambers and Cramb, whom I'd known in other ships. The big problem seemed to be that there wasn't the camaraderie in *Victorious* that we had enjoyed so much in *Ark Royal*. Maybe it was the area; after all, Mediterranean sunshine lifts the spirit more than the cold and damp of the Arctic, but then, *Ark* had her share of the Arctic during the Norwegian campaign. So, the 12-man detachment from 820 tended to keep to itself, and communicate with the other squadrons only when it was necessary. Hughie, that most gregarious of people, and an excellent listener, had no more success than we had, despite his reputation for skill, courage and alcoholic capacity.

As anticipated, flying in these latitudes, even with enclosed cockpits, sorted out one's dental cavities, and once again I had to visit the 'toothwright', who embarked on a long campaign to get rid of an elusive ache. A further problem was that compasses became most unreliable so far north, due to the North Pole's magnetic field. On some reconnaissance flights, they would vary by as much as 45 degrees, so that the onset of foggy weather would make crews flying very apprehensive about making a good sighting on the final leg. To minimise such problems, we carried out a series of exercises on the ship's homing beacon, which gave us great confidence.

On 13 November we were back in harbour and *Rodney* had anchored a few hours before. My old chum, John Hoare (always known to his intimates as 'Klondyke') was on board with his Walrus aircraft. A signal came over for me to dine with him, which I accepted with alacrity. The atmosphere in a capital ship is so much different from most carriers as to make one imagine it is a different navy. As John commented, *Rodney* 'had style'. True, there appeared to be none of the pettiness met in some of the carriers. At dinner that evening I met a long-lost chum, Lieutenant (E) May, and some new friends, Jimmy Ness, a watchkeeper and Captain Bill Teak, Royal Marines, who seemed to be members of a floating poker school with John. The Marine band played during dinner, and as the ship had recently been to USA for a refit, many popular tunes were included in the programme. One of these was a tune, originally Scandinavian, I believe, called the 'Hut-Sut Song', very popular throughout the war. John leaned over and said, 'We've got a first line to a parody, but can't go any further. Can you help?'. Knowing my reputation as an amateur rhymster, John and Jimmy crooned softly –

> There's a ballsup on the quarterdeck and the Wavy Navy done it
> There's a ballsup on the quarterdeck and they don't know who to blame...

A splendid dinner ended, and as the Royal Marine Band played the 'Hut-Sut Song' during dinner, the tune and the challenge to find a lyric were in my head all next day, most of which was spent line-fishing from the quarterdeck of *Victorious*, a favourite pastime when in Hvalfjord. Suddenly the first verse took shape, and I dashed off to my cabin to get it on paper. Next day, fishing again, and by chance in a very choppy swell, one of the officers' boats came off second best against one of the gangways, which gave me the second verse. After that it was easy. Two days later, having got everyone worried by locking myself in my cabin most of the day, it was finished, and John and Jimmy were invited over.

We played it over in the deserted ante-room, made a few corrections, and knew that we had the lyric as right as it would be. So after dinner that night, when the customary sing-song was under way, it being Guest Night, 'ush was called, and the new song delivered for approval by 'Klondyke' and me:

There's a ballsup on the quarterdeck and the Wavy Navy done it,
There's a ballsup on the quarterdeck and they don't know who to blame.
    The Owner's walk is disturbed by the talk
    Of the fishermen round the rail
    Exchanging dirt, discussing skirt
    From Hatston, Twatt and Crail.
There's a ballsup on the quarterdeck and the Wavy Navy done it,
There's a ballsup on the quarterdeck and they don't know who to blame.

There's a ballsup on the gangway and the Wavy Navy done it,
There's a ballsup on the gangway and they don't know who to blame.
    The DSB Mid's gone to tea,
    The cox'n can't be found.
    The cutter's prow has smashed the brow
    And the Bos'un's Mate's been drowned.
There's a ballsup on the gangway and the Wavy Navy done it,
There's a ballsup on the gangway and they don't know who to blame.

There's a ballsup in the wheelhouse and the Wavy Navy done it,
There's a ballsup in the wheelhouse and they don't know who to blame.
    The KG 5's ten miles astern,
    She should be twelve ahead,
    Since every turn by the makee-learn
    Was Blue instead of Red.
There's a ballsup in the wheelhouse and the Wavy Navy done it,
There's a ballsup in the wheelhouse and they don't know who to blame.

There's a ballsup on the Flightdeck and the Wavy Navy done it,
There's a ballsup on the Flightdeck and they don't know who to blame.
    Reds galore from an Albacore
    Helldiving for the drink.
    Di-da Di-da comes from afar
    As a Fulmar starts to sink.
There's a ballsup on the Flightdeck and the Wavy Navy done it,

There's a ballsup on the Flightdeck and they don't know who to blame.

The song was an instant success, encored and encored until 'Klondyke' and I could sing no more, despite generous lubrication donated by an appreciative audience. The Commander brought the Captain into the wardroom, for us to give one final 'Royal Command' performance. It was quite a night, and many nights after that our new song became a request number.

There were two strange side-effects. First, it applied to all departments of a ship, most of which employed some RNVR officers, so that departments would compose their own verses, often extremely technical, sometimes downright lewd, and bring them along to me for approval. As if I cared, so long as people were happy! Some years later there must have been fifteen to twenty verses, most of which were new to me. Second, by lampooning ourselves, we took away from the sometimes critical regulars the very stick they beat us with – our amateurishness, our inexperience. We showed that we understood not only our failings, but also their feelings, and implied that we wished to take remedial action. Whatever, it was, almost immediately a happier atmosphere was created in the *Victorious'* wardroom with less noticeable friction.

The song became a Fleet Air Arm classic, and is, I am proud to say, included in the official song book, probably the cleanest among a collection that would make even a Billingsgate porter blush with embarrassment. This one wouldn't, but it gets right down to the way reserve officers regarded themselves, not only in the Air Arm, but throughout the Royal Navy.

About thirty years later I emigrated to New Zealand, which Dominion produced a high percentage of our aircrew – for some reason nearly all pilots – and was invited to one of their reunions in Auckland. As usual, there was a singalong of all the old nostalgic numbers, especially including the 'A-25 song' a wonderful classic, with almost as many verses as the 'Ball of Kirriemuir'. With great pride I noted that 'Ballsup' was included on the printed programme. One of the few people who knew of my connection was Peter 'Dusty' Miller, with whom I served in *Formidable* just after the song originated. Banging a gavel, 'Dusty' said, 'Friends, please give a welcome to the author of this song, who is with us this evening, and will sing it for us.'.

I do wish Peter hadn't done that – I couldn't remember the words!

News came through on 14 November that *Ark Royal* had been torpedoed and sunk by a U-boat (*U-81*) not far from Gibraltar, and a great sadness came over us, relieved to some extent by the news that only one man had been lost, but it was a great blow, especially as the Navy was at this point low, very low, in carrier strength, with only *Victorious* actually operational of the new carriers. *Hermes* in Ceylon,

Furious somewhere in the Home Fleet, *Formidable* and *Illustrious* under repair and not due back for a few months. This would have been a moment for the *Kriegsmarine* to have brought out their warships from Norway and the French Atlantic ports. But they didn't.

One morning in Hvalfjord, I walked after breakfast on to the flightdeck to see a tanker alongside oiling us. My God, I thought, the Japanese are here already! But it was not the Japanese, it was a crew of Eskimos, clad in fur jackets and hoods. These boys must know what they're doing, I thought, and promptly drew an Irvingsuit from stores. This fur-lined leather suit made life much more comfortable, though I never quite felt at ease wearing the trousers, which made me walk bowlegged. There were many other aids to keeping warm; long underwear with chemical heating pads and another type which plugged in to the aircraft's electrical circuits. Many inventions were on trial at this time. One day Mike Fuller dropped his Albacore into the sea, with Leonard Mann and Leading Airman Hilton as observer and airgunner respectively. A destroyer had been keeping watch astern as was usual during landings and take-offs, and had them out of the water in about five minutes, but it was touch and go whether they would avoid getting frostbite, gangrene or other rather dreadful after-effects. Fortunately they all recovered. The sea was cold, and in those latitudes, about 15 minutes maximum, even in a calm patch, was the most one could expect to survive at that time of the year.

On 18 November Hughie was relieved as senior pilot, to go for a six-months' 'rest' instructing at Crail. He was naturally pleased to go, since he could take his new bride with him, but sad to leave the squadron in which he'd become almost a fixture. He would also join his close chum, 'Feather' Godfrey-Fausset, but sadly, both of these two fine friends would be dead less than a year later, as also would the third of the trio, Sam Hankey, killed in North Africa.

Towards the end of November, it appeared that despite the many searches and reconnaissances we had carried out – sometimes feeling a little like the cheese in the mousetrap – the *Tirpitz* and *Scheer* did not seem to want to come out. The carrier headed back for Scapa, where 820 would hand over all its new aircraft to 817 and 832 and await our own new ones prior to going to sea again. M for Mother, our aircraft, did not take off with the others, due to oil pressure troubles, now besetting many Albacores, and becoming a bit of a bad joke. Eventually after no fewer than three further attempts; twice returning for the same reason after take-off and landing on, we finally landed at Hatston. After our second landing on *Victorious*, the Captain was beginning to get a little waxy through having to turn into wind so often to present a juicy target for any U-boat lurking off Scapa Flow, and I think Teddy would have departed anyway, with or without his aircraft.

A strange happening the night before we left. Having had a few valedictory drinks, Lithgow and Topham were having a mild argument, the sort that goes on between close friends, when Mike pretended to hit Geoff with a stool. Ducking the wrong way, Geoff collected a fearful blow on the head which gave him slight concussion and a somewhat rambling speech. However, he stayed on board next morning, to disembark later by boat.

On 7 December the news came that the Japanese had treacherously bombed Pearl Harbor, making the Americans our new gallant allies. Immediately their catapult aircraft, mainly Vought single-float biplanes, began to practice with us, several of their officers being billetted ashore. Some language difficulties arose, mainly of a technical nature. For instance, we had a number of Swordfish on floats in the hangars known to us as 'Stringbags on boots' whereas the US Navy called them 'Twin pontoon, three-place scout-observation-torpedo ships'. But we understood each other, which was the main thing, and they certainly enjoyed the luxury of a bar.

Only a few days after the news and shock of Pearl Harbor, came a further blow as the battleship *Prince of Wales* and the battlecruiser *Repulse* were sunk by Japanese Navy bombers off Singapore, and it was obvious that our combined depleted forces would be stretched to the maximum to hold the present situation, let alone begin to counterattack. A new sense of urgency was obvious everywhere, as daily more sombre news came in of Japanese advances, though there was some consolation in the reports that the Germans were becoming bogged down in Russia as the winter set in. Whenever possible we flew on every sort of exercise and when flying wasn't possible owing to the weather, which was often, training lectures were arranged. This was another ardous duty I had assumed, arduous because to hold the attention of aviators anxious to be moving on could only be done if the subjects of the lectures were interesting. During the remainder of our time at HMS *Sparrowhawk* (RNAS Hatston), we had ship and aircraft recognition competitions; armament, radio and engine repair and maintenance; rifle and pistol firing on the range; survival, semaphore; and even had talks from officers who had been to China and Japan. Anything to keep the minds moving and interested.

When the weather wasn't good enough for flying, but not raining or snowing, we played soccer, rugby, hockey, went cross-country running or clay-pigeon shooting. It wasn't always easy but we managed to keep everyone fit. Our squadron rugby team started off as a bit of a joke, since several soccer players were pressganged to make up a team, one I remember having to be persuaded that it wasn't done to head the ball in a line-out. Our CO, Wally Elliot, had been England's fly-half in the mid-1930s, and with his encouragement, we managed to improve considerably the tackling and scrummaging of the novices, which previously had resembled inexpertly attempted rape, eventually producing a reasonable fifteen. Once we challenged the Scottish regiment who guarded our airfield. They turned out a man short, so I played for the squadron in the first half, and for the 'Pongoes' in the second. The Scots won 5-0 and I scored the try for them, which made it an extremely expensive night for me in the bar.

Leave was granted in three watches, and looked as if this would be the last before embarking around the end of January 1942, and the probability was that we would join *Formidable*, recently returned from repair yards in the USA. Sailors are notoriously superstitious, and it seems that when this ship was launched at Belfast on 17 August 1939, several Harland & Wolf employees were killed due to an accidental dislodging of parts of the launching cradle. Our senior prophet and harbinger of doom muttered darkly that the ship 'had been launched in blood' which boded ill for all who sailed in her. In fact, *Formidable* survived the war intact, as also did the harbinger of doom.

Shortly after leave was completed, all squadrons were briefed that they would be going into Kirkwall for a talk from Admiral Commanding Orkneys and Shetlands, short title (as Paddy McGrath would have said) ACOS. A day or two before this top-level pep-talk, Jack Stokes, our tame RNR Canadian, was duty officer and supervising work in the hangars. Chief Air Artificer Arundel, the senior technician, reported to Jack that some work had been completed. 'OK Chief', he replied. At that moment, the captain, a somewhat irascible character and a stickler for discipline, happened to be passing, and called Jack over, giving him a monumental dressing-down and emphasising that there was no place in the Royal Navy for such expressions as 'OK Chief'. The correct phrase should have been 'Very good, Chief Air Artificer'. Jack took his rebuke, saluted and was dismissed.

Two days later, all officers were embarking in a bus to go to the lecture by ACOS, and in correct naval tradition, all were seated, awaiting the captain's arrival. When he climbed aboard and was seated, the bus driver, a Londoner, looked into his driving mirror, and half-turning his head said, 'OK behind?'. From the rear of the bus came a voice with accent redolent of the Rockies demanding 'Whaddya mean OK behind? You mean 'Aye aye astern!'. The captain turned half around and solemnly raised his cap.

On 31 December the annual assessments were inscribed on our logbooks by the Commanding Officer. I felt that his 'Above Average' for me had been well-earned. Leave was more enjoyable than usual, probably because I made myself enjoy it, and being over Christmas and New Year, many of my old school associates were home too. Unfortunately at this time, all my romances were coming successively to an end, and much of this was my fault, since a feeling had been growing inside me that this would be my last leave. There was no major reason for this, since my professional ability had unquestionably improved and my duties were not causing me any worries. It was an accumulation of little things. The Albacore's engine had given a few frights. The casualty list included several very competent senior aviators and a few of my contemporaries, even though it was said that, if one survived the first three months, one was usually safe for a couple of years. It just depended on how this yardstick applied to my pilot, I suppose.

Overall, it seemed pretty certain that we should shortly be going somewhere out east, and the almost unbelievable success of the Imperial Japanese Navy and especially its modern air arm was probably at the bottom of it all. They seemed to go where they liked and sink anything they sighted. One might rationalise this by saying that they had been preparing for the conquest of South East Asia for twenty years, and had struck treacherously at Pearl Harbor; but nonetheless, they had sunk two British capital ships, (one brand new, the other rather ancient) on the open sea in something like two hours. It had taken *Ark Royal* almost two days to slow down *Bismarck* for the heavies to sink. Moreover, stories were coming out about the 'Zero' shipborne fighter, which had the performance of a Spitfire at certain altitudes, and their aircrews seemed to be not just unafraid of dying, but positively to crave a warrior's death.

The CO seemed to have been having similar thoughts on his leave, since on our return, he invited Spitfires and Hurricanes from nearby RAF Skeabrae to make dummy attacks on us during our torpedo and bombing runs. The Spitfires were flown mainly by Norwegian pilots, who made the most split-arsed head-on, quarter, off-the-top of a roll and other varieties of attack before, during and after our runs. This was extremely good practice for both them and us, out of which we devised some new evasive methods.

A wild rumour began to circulate that six of our aircraft were to be flown to the Shetlands, and stationed permanently at Sumburgh to carry out torpedo attacks on German convoys taking raw materials (iron ore and the like) for armaments from North Norway to the Fatherland. Now Sumburgh is a strange airfield, with its one runway (if it could be called that) making take-off imperative in one direction, regardless of the wind direction, boasting a high cliff on one side and a cliff edge dropping to the sea on the other. Never having been there, we requested information from pilots who had. They usually shuddered and changed the subject. Sumburgh had been used by Skuas from Hatston earlier in the war after it was discovered the hard way by several pilots and observers that the Skua lacked the fuel to get to Narvik, or any other target, and back, especially if there were a change in the strength of the customary head wind on return. Aircraft had been known to make 'dead stick' landings, and several had dropped into the sea during their final approach at Hatston. So, they had flown from Hatston to Sumburgh as an intermediate measure, refuelled there and gone on to their target, which seemed to do the trick. That is, if one disregarded the dangers of landing possibly out of wind with a somewhat sensitive load of bombs or torpedo slung underneath. Happily this rumour must have been a planner's brainstorm, as it never eventuated, though squadrons from Hatston did go there from time to time during the war. Today Sumburgh is an important helicopter base for the North Sea oil rigs, a role that makes a great deal more sense.

Towards the end of December 1941, 818 Squadron arrived, having survived the *Ark Royal* sinking by being flown off to Gibraltar just before the fatal torpedo struck. Jock Moffat presided at the wardroom piano that night, and we enjoyed the best sing-song we'd had since parting company the previous July. Terence Shaw, former 810 senior observer, was now CO and as with ourselves, there were many new faces, though most of the new pilots seemed to be of the same vintage as many of our new boys. Jock was a great friend to have in Scotland, since he either had relatives everywhere we seemed to go, or if not, his brass-bound cheek obtained entrance to places that would have been out of bounds to ordinary Sassenachs.

Our move was now officially promulgated. Both 818 and 820 Squadrons would move across the Scottish Highlands to Machrihanish as soon as all replacement aircraft had arrived from Lee-on-Solent. The 817 and 832 'swaps' were beginning to get towards the end of their engine life, and it would be preferable to have new aircraft if we were going out east, where spare engines were few and far between. Cliff Wearden and Teddy Reed managed to force-land and prang respectively on their way north thanks to a blizzard encountered over the Grampians. This also delayed our departure for a few days. The January weather in this part of Scotland is quite unpredictable. A clear but cold day, ideal for flying in the morning, could be turned into a leaden sky by noon, and a snowstorm by nightfall. Daylight is short too, it rarely being light before 1000 and dark by 1530. Of course, in the summer, the situation was reversed, the Orkneys being light enough to play football until 2200 and light again about 0330. But it was rarely what a Sassenach would call warm.

Eventually all aircraft were mustered, and just to vary the routine, I left this time with the advance echelon on 28 January 1942, though still with the squadron stores. The route to RNAS Machrihanish – or Machri-bloody-hanish as we knew it – was obviously planned by the author of 'The Road to the Isles', since it led from Kirkwall to Invergordon, where we accepted an additional ten tons of squadron stores and mail, and thence to Glasgow. Here we had trouble finding accommodation for the ratings, eventually installing them in the minesweeper barracks. At that time, Glasgow was not exactly the World Centre of Nightlife, and after a brief survey of unpromising possibilities, I dined where I was staying, at St Enoch's Hotel, which one of the few resident naval officers said might as well be St Eunuch's for all the talent passing through.

Next morning, another boat for the crossing to Campbeltown, and thence by road to Machrihanish, all round the winding roads of Argyllshire. The air station had certainly expanded since 820 were last there, with runways and every evidence of a real airfield, instead of the grass of 1940. Regrettably, the living accommodation had not been completed quite so rapidly, being known locally as 'Nissen City'. This, of itself would not have been too bad, but there was a dearth of baths, showers, toilets and even hot water, but an over-abundance of rain and mud. *Formidable's* fighter squadron, 888, in their Grumman Wildcats, had arrived first, and naturally had staked claim to all the best billets. Their CO was Captain F D G Bird of the Royal Marines, a splendid pilot and a good CO. He needed to be, having a mixture of experience and inexperience to knock into shape.

The senior pilot was Guy Brockensha, a South African, with flight commanders Stewart ('Tiny') Devonald, 6ft 6in tall, and Dennis Jerram, all three RN 'A' officers. Dennis had been loaned to the RAF for the Battle of Britain, scoring 4 victories against the *Luftwaffe*. Conversely, 'Tiny' had been shot down by the RAF over Britain, obviously not recognising the naval Skua as a friendly aircraft. This had made a sorry mess of one of 'Tiny's; legs, giving him a permanent limp. Jerram was short and a trifle portly, rarely going anywhere without 'Tiny', reminding me always of Don Quixote and Sancho Panza. Much later, when I commanded my own squadron, these two both commanded squadrons of Hellcats forming our fighter escort. I met 'Tiny' again in October 1982 at Yeovilton in a wheelchair, after having finally had the leg amputated. Regrettably, this remarkable character died in November 1983, Dennis Jerram having died some years earlier.

'Tiny' played the guitar, if not expertly, at least with sufficient enthusiasm to get a sing-song going wherever he was. I can still recall Don Quixote and Sancho leaving the airfield or the ship for a party somewhere. 'Tiny' striding limpingly along, guitar slung over his shoulder, Dennis hurrying along. 'Spreading a little 'appiness', as Dennis was wont to say, in his Mayfair-cockney.

Hughie's relief as senior pilot didn't stay very long, and shortly we were joined by Nick Shrubsole for this position. Known as 'Bushy' to his intimates, he had previously been in 832 in *Victorious*, and was therefore no stranger to us. 'Bushy' was Merchant Navy before becoming an RN pilot and subsequently got on very well with the senior observer, Ivan Fisher, who came from that illustrious background. Much more gregarious than Hughie, and possessed of a very infectious laugh, he quickly became one of us.

Sadly about this time I learned that my former pilot in *Ark Royal*, Murray Willcocks, had been killed somewhere off the east coast of

Spain, though I never heard the details. A splendid friend, whose death made me very sad.

There was now a great hustle to get our decklandings completed, both TBR and fighters. Prior to this, I was given a further responsibility, but still no promotion – now in charge of compasses, which could be a bit of a nuisance in Albacores, since there was much more metal in the construction. In three days we had swung all 12 aircraft, no mean achievement as we spent half the time sheltering from heavy downpours. Ivan gave me some consolation by appointing me Deputy-deputy-deputy senior observer, ie next in line to himself, Abbott and Topham. I cannot at this distance say what was the real reason for the anxiety to get aboard *Formidable*, which we knew was now in the Clyde. With some, like Devonald and Jerram, it was the duty-free gin; with others an anxiety to get on with the war, but with everybody, a burning desire to get away from the glue-like mud and rain of Argyllshire.

Chapter 11
Back to War in
Formidable

On 4 February we flew to rendezvous with *Formidable* off Lamlash in the Isle of Arran, and landed on successfully, though Pym's 818 Albacore went over the side, just as Percy Guy of 808 had done in his Fulmar the day I landed on *Ark Royal*. The ship seemed an improvement on *Victorious* though nominally the same design, and one problem quickly reared its head which, it is certain the designer and builder had not forseen. The advance of technology meant that quite a lot of newly-invented electronics and radar had been incorporated. This meant quite a few additional officers and also, for the voyage, we were carrying the Admiral and staff, so that sub-lieutenants and midshipmen had to share cabins. This, in retrospect, was no great hardship, but we did have a great deal of equipment, blue, white and khaki uniforms for instance, plus some of our flying apparatus which had a habit of 'disappearing' if left lying around or stored where we couldn't keep an eye on it. I drew 'Pussy' Grant, with whom I had shared rather more spacious quarters at RNAS Lee. We took turn and turn about sleeping on a camp-bed, the other having the regular and relatively sumptuous bunk.

Aircraft carriers of the *Illustrious* class had only one hangar, unlike *Ark Royal* which had two complete decks for aircraft stowage. The reason for this was that the newer class had much more armour on the flightdeck, and a more complicated system of watertight doors below decks. All of this increased the weight of the ship, making her settle much lower in the water. Junior officers' cabins were almost all below the waterline, and since all watertight doors would be shut immediately if we were hit by a torpedo or bomb, to prevent flooding below decks, we were informed that when the ship was in waters in which these damages might arise, juniors would have to sleep in makeshift cots above the waterline. The same restrictions applied to ratings, as a result of which the decks which were above the waterline were strewn with sleeping bodies at night, similar, but not so thick on the ground as the sights we had seen at night in the London Underground stations.

My squadron was assigned the forward end of the hangar deck for aircraft stowage when at sea. Our ratings had spread themselves out, almost like domestic pets marking out their territory. Leading Air Mechanic Pontefract was the resident squadron humourist, and on the forward bulkhead, he had drawn the 820 Squadron crest, which displays a rather annoyed-looking flying fish leaping out of the water. Below this were chalked the battle-honours since the beginning of the war, which went something like 'Norway', 'Oran', 'Dakar', 'Malta Convoys', 'Genoa', 'Spartivento', 'Bismarck'.

Some wag, probably from another squadron jealous of our reputation, and mindful of the near-tragedy of 26 May the previous year, had daubed in very large letters underneath our imposing list: 'AND WHO PUT THE SHITS UP THE SHEFFIELD!!'

Fair comment.

Our new Captain was A W La Touche Bissett, a short, rubicund and paternal-looking gentleman with a passion for cats, of which he had at times five or six in his cabin. The Commander was 'Ted' LeMesurier, of aquiline features and a great sense of humour, who nevertheless was a stickler for discipline, as I was later to find out. Commander Flying was C G Ermen, a former CO of 820, though that didn't cut much ice, as he treated everyone the same – like automatons. Short, balding and somewhat irascible, he was not especially popular, though his intention was, as he once explained, not to win popularity contests, but to win a war. The Air Staff Officer was Commander P Yorke, who dealt mainly with COs and senior observers, juniors being dealt with by Lieutenant Richard Kearney, who had been my instructor at Lee, subsequent to achieving passing fame in December 1939 as observer at the Battle of the River Plate, when from a Seafox seaplane he spotted the fall of shot for the cruisers *Exeter*, *Ajax* and *Achilles*. Most unfortunately, it appears that he was on the wrong frequency for most of the time. Another though more junior officer was Mr Langley, the Warrant Officer Bos'un, who had been another of our instructors at *St Vincent*. A rather dapper chap, he subsequently became a lieutenant-commander and captain of Nelson's *Victory* in Portsmouth Dockyard. All in all, there was a better atmosphere to this ship than we had found in *Victorious* – a first impression, but these are often very accurate.

For the next few days, we exercised with the old carrier *Eagle* and the cruiser *Charybdis* off Arran, returning each night to shelter in Lamlash, since we were not doing any night exercises yet. All day we practiced torpedo attacks, dive-bombing on towed targets, and my special duty was to help calibrate the ships' guns. This entailed making straight and level runs over the ships at accurate heights and courses while maintaining radio contact with them. A little tiring, but well worthwhile. Cliff Wearden piloted on these runs, and we received a 'bouquet' from all ships.

Paddy McGrath and Barney Rowland were in *Eagle*, and invited me over to dinner one evening. Paddy was dying to tell me of an incident in London where he had recently been on leave. While passenger in a taxi, two obviously inebriated Americans stepped right into its path, signalling the driver to halt. 'Blimey, not tonight', said the driver, commenting that though excellent payers and tippers, their demands to be taken 'where the action is', wasted a lot of time, and frequently to near-fisticuffs, with the added hazard that they often were sick in the back. 'Leave it to me', said the fearless McGrath, and as they stepped into the cab on the near-side, Paddy opened the off-side door, saying 'This way, gentlemen', so that they stepped right through the cab into the street. As the driver drove off, leaving his two American would-be passengers standing in the street, wondering what had happened, Paddy handed him half-a-crown. 'What's this for, guv'nor?' enquired the puzzled cab-driver. Paddy said, 'He tipped me'. This and others, plus Barney's rapid-fire Liverpool anecdotes had our corner of the wardroom in an uproar most of a very pleasant evening. One of Barney's expressions apropos carrying out a good piece of navigation stays with me to this day – 'It's like peeing yourself in your best blues', he commented, 'gives you a lovely warm feeling, but no one notices'. Very apt.

Formidable's solitary communications/target tug Swordfish with arrestor hook down attempts to land, 6 February 1942 (off Ailsa Craig in the Clyde). The Stringbag carries two 250lb depth charges. *Author's collection*

145

Our decklanding training, though apparently successful was not without a few incidents, some of them serious. Matt Wotherspoon hit the round-down on 5 February and dropped into the sea in his Albacore right in the ship's wake, but he suffered no injury, Dyson and Hank Henry pranged theirs on the flightdeck, and Jack Bennett, a young New Zealand Wildcat pilot, was killed when he went into the sea. A few days later during a spell when the fighters were being catapulted, one of them went through the crash barrier, while landing and into the for'ard 4.5in gun turret. But in the circumstances the percentage of successful landings was acceptable. One pilot was given further solo landing practice in the communications 'Stringbag' which we carried. This aircraft was deliberately lightened of all gear for the purpose, and the pilot made almost a dozen swoops at the deck, either overshooting or bouncing off into the air, unable to get his arrestor hook to connect. I have one photograph in my album of the flightdeck crew running for cover almost on all fours as another hair-raising pass is made. Finally 'Wings' said, 'If the idiot doesn't make it this time. I'll have him shot down'. Fortunately this time, he made it successfully. I will never understand how this pilot was accepted for first-line work, since subsequently in India, he was transferred to the pool, and continued to get himself into the most extraordinary and dramatic crashes, forced-landings and the like, ferrying aircraft around the sub-continent. I was sure he must have written himself off somewhere, when to my surprise, attending a meeting of ex-FAA officers in a London pub, probably in 1956 or so, I was astonished to hear his unmistakeable voice behind me. Not only had he survived the war, he had been given a permanent commission, and had also won a decoration. There's a moral somewhere!

On 13 February we heard the dreadful news of the annihilation of 825 Squadron in the stupidly-planned but incredibly gallant attempt to stop the *Scharnhorst, Gneisenau* and *Prinz Eugen* forcing the Channel. As the pieces of the news were assembled, one had to wonder, with so many more suitable RAF aircraft available on the South Coast, why Esmonde's heroic flight had been called upon to make such a useless sacrifice. Two weeks later he was rightly awarded a posthumous VC and all the survivors – five of the eighteen taking part were given the highest decorations possible. But what a shambles! We felt proud to have been part of a service which could produce such men, and at the same time ashamed that their deaths had been so futile. There were other squadrons, such as ourselves, which were in a better stage of training who could have taken on this task, if it had to be done by biplanes. One could only wonder. And hope that it wasn't repeated.

On the 14th the Flag Officer Eastern Fleet came aboard with his staff, including a US Navy observer. Of course, it HAD to be Sir James Somerville, whom I felt was waging a personal vendetta upon the luckless Woods. However, a few days later, when we were on our way to the war, he gave a small party to the squadrons one by one, and I warmed as he shook my hand and said – with no trace of animosity – 'We have met before, Woods, haven't we?'. 'Yes, sir. Delighted to see you again, sir', was the best I could stammer, as 'Prune' whispered 'Creep' in my ear.

Rodney and *Malaya* anchored nearby the day before we left, John Hoare and Jimmy Ness coming over for pre-prandials and lunch. The convoy began to assemble around us; *Eagle, Malaya,* Hermi-One (as the cruiser *Hermione* was known), *Newcastle* and a small troopship collection including some we had escorted previously, but whose names, apart from *Pasteur,* I cannot recollect. So large was the convoy that it had attracted the attention of the *Luftwaffe,* and for several days in home waters, all escorts, including ourselves, stood to all day, expecting an attack from German bombers. The Wildcats of 888 stood by on deck, very anxious to get first blood for the Eastern Fleet before we left Blighty. It was quite possible that we might be attacked by both bombers and U-boats as we slowly passed through the western fringes of the Bay of Biscay, and anti-submarine patrols were flown all day, with fighters and TBRs being shuffled about the deck for take-off and landings.

As we came abreast of the Straits of Gibraltar on the 21st, *Eagle* and *Malaya* turned to port with the part of the convoy due for Malta. We were never to see *Eagle* again, as she was torpedoed and sunk by U-73 on another Malta convoy in August. Another tragedy occurred the same day – as Rogers and Garland of 818 failed to return from an Albacore reconnaissance flight. There was some hope that they might have reached land in Spain or Portugal, but alas, they were never heard of

Sub-Lieutenant (A) Matt Wotherspoon RNVR drops his Albacore into *Formidable*'s wake on 5 February 1942 off Lamlash (Isle of Arran, Clyde, Scotland). Another Albacore makes its landing approach. *Captain T W B Shaw DSC, RN (Retd)*

again. There was some resentment that a search had not been flown off to look for them, but it was clearly not on to risk the lives of thousands of soldiers and sailors for a crew of three, since the carrier would have to have been detached and turned into wind twice. With a 10-knot convoy, this would have exposed *Formidable* to considerable danger from U-boats – it being know that several were in the area of the Straits, waiting to pounce on convoys and especially stragglers. It is probable that the word went up to the Admiral, in view of what happened off Capetown some two weeks later in similar circumstances.

The slow speed of the convoy was a nuisance, though its commodore – none other than our former Rear-Admiral Naval Air Stations, Bell Davies VC, DSO, RNR – knew our problems better than anyone, and tried his best to make life easier for us. At 10 knots we rolled, but kept together. At 12 knots we rolled less, but the troopers began to wander, and at any higher speed, the convoy would not only begin to break up, it would also make too much smoke, for many of the merchant ships were old, and some were still coal-burners. So while the 'sprogs' were ill and 'parked custards,' as Jimmy Clark so nicely put it, at least the troops were being steamed to the battle areas as quickly as possible.

The slow speed was probably responsible for some of the prangs we suffered; Hayes of 818 made a very colourful one on 21 February, followed by two more from the same squadron next day. Just to balance things, Teddy Reed, who had shown himself to be an excellent decklander, pranged one of 820's Albacores returning from A/S patrol on the 23rd.

We had reports of a German tanker being sighted in the area south-east of the Azores into which we were now passing, and on 25 February Nigel Gardner and I flew off with six 250lb semi-armour-piercing bombs to look for her, bring her to a rendezvous with a destroyer if possible, and if she did the usual German trick of scuttling, our orders were to sink her with the bombs. The destroyers were not going to waste their time picking up survivors from a scuttled ship, especially since the scuttling might well be a ruse for U-boats to attack a weakened convoy. In the event, though our ASV worked beautifully and the visibility was excellent, we saw nothing and returned for Nigel to make his landing with due care and attention. Next day, this time flying with Davy James, we made dummy torpedo and fighter attacks on the convoy to sharpen up their gunnery. Unfortunately one fighter got too ambitious and force-landed in the sea, the pilot being picked up by a destroyer. Later we joined Dicky Bird, whose birthday it was, in celebratory drinks and a sing-song.

Now we were west of the Azores, a well-known U-boat rendezvous area with their supply ships and tankers, so we flew special dusk and dawn searches, as well as A/S patrols all day. On the 28th Nigel and I were selected to do an extended search abeam and ahead, husbanding the fuel of a long-range petrol tank as well as possible, to check the Albacore's endurance. It appears that this had never been done before, and there were some doubts about the answer being a simple mathematical problem, since the centre of gravity was shifted quite considerably when this extra tank was fitted, altering the flying angle of the aircraft. In the event we stayed aloft 4½ hours, but discovered quite a large error in our final fix – some 30 miles – so obviously either our compasses needed swinging, or the extra load had somehow made an unsuspected difference. As we would be anchored off Freetown in a couple of days, this could be investigated at the compass base ashore.

After flying from 0939 until 1430 on the 28th, I returned to find I was duty officer until 2230. In the heat which was slowly increasing as we sailed south, it was a very long and exhausting day, but, as we moved on into dangerous waters, 18 hours a day became the norm. As RPO Mortimer said encouragingly to his troops 'Think yourselves bleeding lucky you ain't living in a desert foxhole'.

Ashore next day to Freetown to swing 5F's compass, I had my first experience of the deceptive heat of Africa. Accompanied by Nigel Gardner, PO TAG 'Shorty' Roberts, and two maintenance men, Herring and Phillips, we worked from about 0900 until noon, swinging the compasses and checking radio frequencies with HMS *Spurwing*, the local FAA Station. By noon we were through swinging, both with and without the long-range tank, which did appear to make a difference to the deviation card. In short-sleeved khaki shirts and shorts, we had not noticed the strength of the sun, and endured nasty blisters next day. No leave was allowed in Freetown, ships refuelling and revictualling only, though next day, swinging round the buoy, we traded with the local bumboat men. Our padre was a rather prim type, and strolling round the quarterdeck, he was hailed by the bumboat men, who seemed to know all the naval ranks and ratings – usually promoting the object of their hail by at least one rank. 'Hello, Massa Jesus!' they hailed the padre, who ignored them and continued his stroll, their shouts being unnoticed. After their third hail had elicited no recognition, the bumboat men called out 'OK Massa Jesus, no black womens for you tonight!'

Leaving Freetown on 3 March for Capetown, we resumed our patrolling, now adding a second aircraft, so that ahead, astern and both sides were completely covered. Our confidence in the ASV was increasing, but eyes were still considered more reliable. On one occasion, I remember getting an enormous 'blip' on the screen where nothing should have been, some 10 miles ahead, but at 5 miles it had disappeared from both visual sighting and ASV. Maybe there WAS a submarine there, and it had dived on hearing our engine. We shall never know exactly how many U-boats were forced to dive, and thus miss a shot at a convoy because an air patrol had been detected. Of course occasionally that 'blip' was a whale surfacing, and one day we sighted a lifeboat, with two bodies on board. It was reported to *Formidable* by Aldis lamp (radio silence being in force except for enemy sighting) and a destroyer varied her course to investigate, finding two badly decomposed corpses.

The Admiral decided next day that he would like to come up for an ALT 'to clear his sinuses' as he put it. My fears were groundless, since though he did select his favourite observer – myself – for the trip, everything worked perfectly, and David made a superb first-wire three-pointer which impressed no end. Hardly had we struck the aircraft down to the hangar than a radio report came in from St Helena that three unidentified aircraft had flown over the island 200 miles SSW of us and we altered course to investigate. Because of the possibility of this being a decoy, we did not leave the convoy, but stayed with it at 10 knots, to arrive off St Helena at dawn. Midshipmen While was my pilot next day, and though we searched 60 miles ahead from bow to bow of the convoy, saw nothing. The destroyers went in to refuel and investigate the report, which would have indicated, if anything, a Japanese presence. This seemed unbelievable because of the distance involved, but not impossible. Moreover, we knew very little about the ships of the Japanese navy, and they might have had a small carrier in the southern seas, or perhaps a seaplane carrier, like the old *Pegasus*. Certainly no friendly ship with three aircraft was nearby, and to this day I have heard no rational explanation of the report, other than 'gin spots'.

With calmer seas south of the equator, our convoy could speed up another knot, but more important, the ship's deck hockey league could be resumed. For the uninitiated, deck hockey is played on the flightdeck, or in smaller ships in any clear space. I have seen it played in cruisers and have heard that it is played even in destroyers, where one would not imagine enough room to be available. In a carrier, departments of the ship played against other, eg Torpedomen v Stokers; obviously squadron rivalry was keen, both officers and ratings producing their own teams. The 'blood matches' were either between squadrons, or between squadron officers and the same squadron ratings. Equipment was simple, a walking stick bent in the shape of a hockey stick, and a rope puck, properly spliced into a circle and steeped in aircraft dope to harden it. Pucks had to be in abundant stock, since many disappeared over the side. Rules were almost non-existent, though I believe biting and gouging were frowned upon, and ten minutes each way – which may seem a short half to the uninitiated – was usually enough for all but the staunchest players. Weird and wonderful too were some of the teams' clothing including anything from goalkeepers in boiler-suits and cricket pads to centre-forwards in swim-trunks. Teams were usually 7 a side, which meant that in a ship's company of 2000 as we had, assuming only 50 per cent participation, there would be up to 100 teams, so that knock-out was the only type of competition possible. On one occasion the Captain summoned me when Rear-Admiral Dennis Boyd was taking passage with us, asking if we could fit him into a game as he was anxious for some exercise, but cautioning me neither to disclose his identity, nor to allow the game to become too rough since the Admiral was no longer a young man. So we fitted him into the squadron team playing the Royal Marine Band. After a close and somewhat robust game, the band team's captain approached me, a player who whirled his hockey stick with the same enthusiasm as the band's drum-major whirled his mace. 'Who, sir,' he enquired in an aggrieved tone, 'was the older orficer playing on your side?' 'Rear-Admiral Boyd. Why do you ask?'. 'Because, sir', replied the Marine "e's a dirty bastard – beggin' 'is pardon. Kneed two of my blokes straight in the goolies'. It was just as well that the Rear-Admiral Aircraft Carriers wasn't a younger man, he might have kneed the whole of the team.

On the night of 7 March we were nearing the Cape of Good Hope, where it was rumoured that German and Japanese submarines were operating, though at this stage of the war it was unlikely, but not impossible. Unlikely because with the language and communications barrier, there was always the possibility that they might attack each other by mistake. However, it was certain that U-boats were active in the area, mainly off the Agulhas Bank, since this was a focal point for huge numbers of merchant and warships to pass through, and some merchant ships had been lost in this area. As the running of convoys through the Mediterranean had become so much more expensive in terms of ships lost, due to the *Luftwaffe* taking over, everything except vital supplies were sent by the Cape route – taking 40 days longer to get to the Middle East, but being very much safer. So, to sharpen up the convoy's lookouts and gunnery, we would carry out a dusk search first, and on return make dummy attacks. Several of us had made one 3-hour flight that day, searching for a reported armed raider. Nothing of this type had been seen, but Jack Stokes had sighted a straggler from some previous convoy which had identified herself correctly. As we began to move into our operational area, we could feel ourselves getting more tense.

The first excitement was of an unexpected kind. At 2045 on the 7th 15 Albacores took off in the dark to make a step-aside search 100 miles ahead of the convoy. After this, assuming no enemy reports, we would return to the ship, identify ourselves independently, form up in the dark, and make our dummy attack. The first part went well, nothing was sighted and each aircraft identified correctly on return, our IFF sets ensuring that we were not shot at. All aircraft had checked in, and now went away to form up on the southern side in sub-flights, navigation lights on. Formed up, we now broke off into five separate attacking sub-flights, ours having been assigned the carrier whose lookouts would note where the flame-floats fell and assess the attack. Sub-flights reformed as planned, and we flew around the convoy awaiting a 'C' on the ship's searchlight, which would signal us to close, go into line astern and land on. The night was dark, the sea relatively calm, and everything seemed to be under control. David put 5Q down easily, and we reported to the operations room as usual for an inquest on the practice. But only 14 aircraft had returned, and as the last one to land made her identity letter, we realised that Mike Lithgow and Geoff Topham were missing. Mike was probably one of the finest pilots ever produced by the Navy, as witness the fact that he became the world's airspeed record holder and later a chief test pilot. Anyone who had flown with him could testify to his almost casual accuracy. Topham was one of our best navigators and the bewhiskered 'Cab' Galloway, who had flown a lot with me, was very experienced. Half an hour went by, and no sign of them. The Admiral wasted no time, and knowing that they had reported in prior to the ALT, ordered the majority of the warships to reverse course and explore the area at that point, leaving the convoy with only a light escort.

At 0030 next morning, nearly three hours after they had last been identified, the most southerly destroyer heard a whistle being blown to port. In other words, had the destroyer not been so far to the south, with keen lookouts, the sound would have been missed. Mike, Geoff and 'Cab' were clinging to the only part of their Alabcore left afloat, a main landing wheel and part of the undercarriage. They had been flying low after their ALT, and apparently had hit a wave-top which had upended them. This rather shaken trio admitted afterwards that they were beginning to despair as the icy water began to bite into their legs, and they believed that sharks were nosing around the vicinity. It need hardly be said that the action of Admiral Somerville gave a tremendous boost to our confidence, feeling that here was one who would be loyal to his men, as he would expect them to be loyal to him. Our three lucky shipmates were reported in good health by the rescuing destroyer.

Before entering harbour, we were given a pep-talk by the Captain on the perils likely to await us – not the usual ones predicted by the principal medical officer, but more of a political nature. Not all South Africans were in favour of the war, moreover, some of the Afrikaner extremists were actively pro-Nazi, a few even joining the German forces. Capetown was not likely to give us any great problems in that direction but we had to avoid being lured into native quarters, where one would certainly be robbed, beaten and probably killed. So no lone wolves. Always go about at least in pairs. Don't get into political arguments. Be careful of Cape brandy, even it is 3/6d a bottle. Above all, don't go near District Six. Most of this, was of course, for the younger ratings who had never been out of England before, and who might just be stupid enough to be lured into the seamy native bordellos, there to be mugged or killed. Warnings were issued to all ships, both Navy and Merchant Navy, that behaviour ashore had to be of the best. Apparently a convoy of Australian troops had come through only a short time before, and the local and service police had fought what was tantamount to a pitched battle with the 'diggers'. The reasons were obscure, though I've met few Australians who needed a reason for a free fight.

The senior pilot of 888, Guy Brockensha, an RN lieutenant, handsome and of great charm, who had won a DSC in Norway flying Skuas, was our guide to South Africa, since he hailed from Durban, where his father was a magistrate. So, after the chat from Captain Bisset, we got the 'real oil' from Guy. Certainly avoid politics; the *Ossewa Brandwag*, the extreme group could be quite nasty, but best of all, Capetown ladies ran a hospitality service, and he gave us the numbers to call as soon as we got ashore. There were dances, weekends up-country, in fact everything the young sailor or officer could need, and apparently a-plenty.

Table Mountain at 0630 is a most impressive sight, especially when the orographic 'tablecloth' cloud surmounts it. The air was clean, brisk and clear. We hadn't spent any of our pay since leaving England five weeks earlier, so 'Prune' and I went ashore with Ivan, our senior observer, largely, as 'Prune' commented, to protect him from covetous females. Our first stop was for some cool beer, at a hotel I seem to recall was named the 'Carlton'. I recollect it, since at about 1600, some four hours after we had left the ship, we had walked about half a mile, drunk about half-a-dozen lagers, and had seen nothing of the city. Moreover, we had to call the hospitality service, otherwise the ladies of Capetown would feel cheated. Which we did, and then took a cab back to the ship to change into our longs, 'Prune' saying that dancing in shorts made him randy. After five weeks at sea, very few would need such an aphrodisiac.

Ivan decided that a second jolly ashore was a bit too much for him, so off we went to meet Muriel and Edna, our blind dates for the evening at the 'Bohemian' night club, where among the few things I do recollect clearly from that evening was that the doorman/cloakroom attendant had a steel hook instead of a right hand, and this tended to keep gatecrashers quiet. Muriel, my date, lived on Kloof Road, Sea Point, and this being only Tuesday, we were invited up for the weekend for a swimming/fishing/sailing party, though in our hearts we knew that the possibility of our being in harbour for longer than it takes to victual, refuel and turn round was about 10 to 1 against. But 'laugh it up while you can' was the squadron's unofficial motto, and that we did. The Bohemian was not licensed to sell alcoholic liquor – their laws were very strange indeed. 'So', I asked the girls, 'what do I do to get a bottle to take in?'. Giving me the look reserved for congenital idiots, Muriel said, 'You go and ask a policeman'. And that's exactly what I did. Outside the night club was a very large Afrikaner policeman, about twice my size, so I asked respectfully where I could get a bottle. Again I submitted to 'The Look' as he directed me to a store nearby, adding 'Tell them Sergeant DeVries sent you', in his delightful 'Yarpie' brogue. DeVries wasn't, of course his name, but I hope he got his commission on the bottles of Canadian Club I purchased for about 6/6d. This was about twice the price of Van de Hum, a liqueur we had been warned not to mix with Cape brandy in the local and (for a novice) near-lethal custom. An excellent party, the club full of *Formidable*, Brock, 'Tiny' and Jerram forming the relief cabaret. Later I was rebuked by 'Prune' for falling asleep, but the lost hours of sleep over the past few weeks were slowly catching up with me.

The following day we decided to see a little more of the environs, and our new-found lady-friends arranged transport to Muizenberg, where we swam, surfed and drank more delicious cool beer. Later we saw the University, the Rhodes Memorial and the Zoo, followed by a short kip, and then changed for another evening at the Bohemian.

Naturally, as happened with all the romances of my youth, just when things were going well, we were recalled, and sailed next day. Though everyone seemed more than a little upset, too long in the lotus-land would have sapped our moral fibre, and sadly we remembered that we had come out to fight a war.

As we left Table Bay, the Captain came on the tannoy and gave us the information we'd been waiting for. Our task was to join Eastern Fleet in Colombo (Ceylon), where we should find *Indomitable* and *Illustrious, Renown* and other heavies. After a short working-up period, we would then have the task of stopping any further Japanese advance towards India, working in close co-operation with the Army and Air Force. As yet no Supreme Commander had been appointed, but this was expected shortly. Frankly, beyond the level of captain of our ship, we were not at that moment interested in the Top Brass, though obviously Supremo would have to be a first-rater. I note some thoughts to myself as the master plan unfolded – not much hope of coming back in one piece from this trip. In retrospect it is one thing to have confidence in one's immortality, at least for the threescore years and ten, but if one is resigned to the fact that it may be a short life and a gay one, then it is essential to get more enjoyment for the time that is left.

As we steamed in a north-easterly direction, passing south of Mauritius, the air became hotter, and for the troops, working in the hangar was nigh unbearable. As a mute protest, many of our maintenance ratings shaved off their hair, looking like a bunch of Martians. Unfortunately the dawn ranges for searches and A/S patrols were chilly, and they had to dig out the woolly hats they had worn on the Iceland trip.

So, on 23 March we came to Colombo, after another unceremonious crossing of the Line. There was an increased sense of urgency here, to the extent that all 818 and 820 aircraft flew ashore to Ratmalana airfield, where we swung compasses, tuned radios, IFFs and other electronic equipment. Our fighter squadron, 888, had flown ashore also, and largely, to improve the morale of the local citizens, we did a combined low-level formation flight over the city. One of the Wildcat fighters, landing on an airfield on which a metal mesh, known as 'Summerfield Track', had been laid to give a firm surface on top of grass, forgot that he didn't need an arrestor hook ashore, dropped it, and formed himself into a sort of metallic Swiss roll. Expensive, but the point was taken by his fellow pilots.

Having settled in temporarily at the wardrooms, we decided to explore the city, and finally came to a swimming club, which would have been ideal this sultry afternoon. However, the local sahibs did not seem to be too welcoming, quite a change from our reception in South Africa. So we decided not to push the point, but to negotiate for honorary membership here or elsewhere, making a mental note that we hoped the gentlemen would one day need our help, when we should politely suggest that they tried swimming instead.

Next day, during my stint as officer of the watch for the last dog watch followed by the first, two shots rang out on the flightdeck. We had armed guards up there when in eastern harbours, and all sorts of wild rumours flashed around, so I sent the midshipman up to investigate. Two sentries had mistaken each other for saboteurs, had challenged each other and fired without waiting for a reply, wounding each other. Oh God, another day's leave ashore lost writing out reports, or so it seemed. But it wasn't quite as simple as that. Our doctor, Surgeon-Lieutenant 'Bugsy' Drummond, hadn't been satisfied with the evidence, and so called in the First Lieutenant, who brought in the 'Gestapo' as the Regulating staff were known. Then tragedy as one of the sentries died, probably of shock, since neither wound was critical. The survivor, now in considerably deeper shock by this turn of events, probably imagining that the same fate might overtake him, confessed that they had made a 'Blighty Pact' to wound each other and obtain a discharge, or at least a home posting. But such was not to be, and the survivor certainly had time to contemplate his errors in one of the less fashionable Indian Service gaols during the 8 years awarded him by the subsequent court-martial.

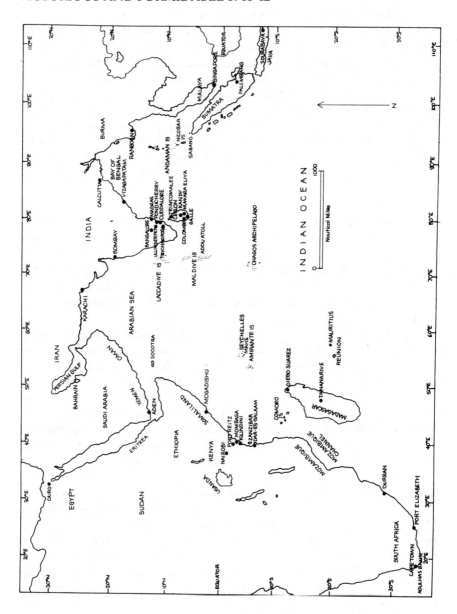

Chapter 12
Eastern Fleet 1942

For the next few days we had the opportunity to visit friends in the many ships now assembled: the carriers *Hermes, Indomitable* and *Illustrious;* battleships *Resolution* and *Warspite* (the latter Admiral Somerville's flagship); cruisers *Enterprise, Dragon, Caledon* and *Cornwall;* plus a destroyer flotilla including *Lightning* and *Laforey*. Since *Eagle, Argus* and *Furious* were the only carriers not in the party, the aviators had many reunions, but one face nearly all were pleased to see was that of Chief Yeoman Spencer, now of *Laforey*, who, as our instructor in *St Vincent*, to use his own words at our passing-out party 'taught you all I know, and still you stupid bastards knows nothing'. As irrepressible and talkative as ever.

Extraordinary rumours were circulating: (a) the Japanese were going to invade the Andaman Islands in the Bay of Bengal and/or (b) we were giving up the defence of India and Ceylon, withdrawing to Perth, Australia, to fight the war from there. Delightful though the latter sounded, the former was the more likely, since Singapore had surrendered in February and the Japanese were advancing steadily up Burma after taking Rangoon. But the social and speculative chats were rudely interrupted after morning church service on Sunday 29 March, when we went to action stations, and the following day went to sea before dawn, silently and without panic.

It seemed that the Fleet Air Arm's model attack at Taranto, where the Italian Fleet was rendered inoperable for the rest of the war, had been copied successfully by the Japanese at Pearl Harbor, and this type of attack had now become their pattern. If they could succeed in knocking out the greater part of Eastern Fleet at one blow, nothing could prevent their onward march through Burma into India, eventually to join up with the Germans and Italians in the Middle East. If this succeeded, then most of Asia and Europe would be Axis-dominated and the end of the war could be in sight, though not the end that we had in mind. In short, Admiral Somerville, like Admiral Sir John Jellicoe at Jutland in 1916, could literally lose the war in an afternoon. With this sobering thought, our Fleet, large in number but long in the tooth overall, went a-hunting, to be joined later in the day by three more 'R' class vintage battleships; *Revenge, Ramillies* and *Royal Sovereign.*

Captain Bissett, a very humane soul, apologised in advance for the trial we were to endure, but he had no intention of being caught with his pants down. So we flew our normal patrols, and those who were not doing so were flown off or squirted from the catapult to make dummy torpedo, bombing and fighter attacks on the Fleet. Our drogue-towing Swordfish worked overtime giving the ships practice with both high-angle/low-angle and close-range AA weapons. As one of the gunnery officers remarked – if we were not careful, we would use up all our fuel and ammunition before meeting the Japanese and have to resort to hand-to-hand combat.

The four Rs were built or before or during World War I, and because of their heavy side-armour had to sacrifice fuel space, so that they could only exist at sea for about four days. We had a secret anchorage in the Maldive Islands, southwest of the southern tip of India, known as Addu Atoll. So small that it rarely appeared on maps in those days, it was a hollow coral island into which our tankers came from the Persian Gulf. Approaching the atoll, it looked to be straight out of Somerset Maugham, except that no one seemed to live there, and later we found out why – one of the atolls in the group was a leper colony! A lone RAF civil engineer officer was surveying the place for an airstrip, which was built much later, and is today known as Gan, until 1976 a most important international junction for the Western Powers. But in 1942 we rarely spent more than half a day there, just time enough to refuel, obtain fresh water, shower, shave and feed the lone 'Crabfat' engineer, then get back to war.

On Good Friday 3 April, while en route for our patrol line, we heard that the Japanese Navy had bombed the Calcutta area, sinking much merchant shipping in the Bay of Bengal. *Hermes*, which had earlier been ordered to Trincomalee on the east coast of Ceylon, was sent to investigate and intercept, while the cruisers *Cornwall* and *Dorsetshire* were detached from their present patrol southwest of Galle, and sent to the southeast tip of the island. They were to report any enemy shipping sighted and to fight delaying tactics until our larger striking force could arrive with heavy guns, torpedoes and bombs.

In the clear skies and hot sun, we worked up to our maximum speed of 30 knots, and as everything on board rattled, *Indomitable* sent off a six-aircraft search ahead. With the rest of the Fleet at top speed, this only gave a swept area ahead of 100 miles, but that was infinitely better than nothing. Radio silence was in force unless the enemy was sighted. Meantime other carriers prepared their strikes and armed their fighters, since it was most probable that several Japanese carriers were in the area equipped with Zeros, certain to outperform any of our shipborne fighters at that time.

Despite advance warning of the probability of such an offensive and an enemy report from a Catalina of 413 Squadron flying from Koggala Lagoon, we were caught with our pants down on Easter Sunday, 5 April. It was assumed that the attack would come to Colombo from seaward, perhaps a surprising assumption when the Japanese always did the unexpected. Instead, flying overland from the direction of Galle, they first bombed and strafed Ratmalana airfield to crush fighter and bomber opposition. A second wave from the 91 bombers and torpedo aircraft attacked what little shipping had been left in Colombo harbour. During this time, six Swordfish armed with torpedoes arrived from China Bay to help out. They mistook enemy fighters for an expected escort, and encumbered by their torpedoes, were shot down like sitting ducks. Among the pilots killed was Sub-Lieutenant Anthony ('Bud') Beale DSC, credited with dropping the torpedo which a year earlier had jammed the *Bismarck's* rudder.

Confusion ruled in the air and among the detached ships. The C-in-C had expected the enemy to approach much closer than 200 miles before launching aircraft and defending fighters were not scrambled early enough. The shore-based Fulmars were hopelessly outclassed by the Zeros, leaving the brunt of attacking to the RAF Hurricanes who could only gain advantage if they had superior height which takes time to regain after the first pass. For some reason, said afterwards to be due to watch changeover, radar plots of the enemy were not signalled quickly enough, many of the somewhat primitive radar installations also believing that the approaching aircraft were from Eastern Fleet. In short, a most disastrous shambles.

Every signal that day was bad news. The enemy strikes returning from Colombo had landed, re-armed and sunk *Cornwall* and *Dorsetshire* with dive-bombing, in 22 minutes. Fortunately 70 per cent of the crews survived and were rescued by *Enterprise,* as well as the destroyers *Paladin* and *Panther.* Meantime, back in *Indomitable,* their search had returned, one Albacore making an emergency landing. Jefferd, the observer, had sighted six enemy ships, but closing to identify them, had his radio shot out of action by enemy fighters before he could make an enemy report. Taking the only option available, his pilot flew back flat out at 95 knots to report.

It was now 1600 and Admiral Somerville, after receiving this report, decided to close the enemy forces until dusk, in other words until about 1800, when he would fly off two night strikes to give our slow aircraft less fighter opposition. As there seemed to be two enemy forces 60 miles apart, each strike would have a different target, one southeast of Galle, the other southeast of Trincomalee. So we continued at full speed, aircrews being prepared for a dusk briefing. The galley had laid an excellent mixed grill supper, though meditating our maiden night torpedo attack, few had much appetite. The 'Kelso Bull' (Jock Moffat) had either no nerves or an insatiable tapeworm, possibly both as he 'went round the buoy', eating everything his more sensitive shipmates couldn't stomach.

If we had success, we would strike again before dawn, when the Japanese would be very busy arming and preparing their aircraft for strikes on Ceylon, as it seemed probable that their intention was to soften up the island preparatory to an invasion and subsequent takeover of the whole Indian sub-continent.

The 4 Rs, now low on oil after the high-speed steaming, would soon need to refuel. Just as we were about to assemble for briefing, the strikes were postponed, as the Admiral had been ordered not to risk his carriers unless confident of total victory, which in those uncertain conditions, he could not be. At that time we did not know how many ships and types we were up against, and if we lost the battle, the aircraft and ground organisation in Ceylon would take such a beating that an invasion would be a pushover. So with mixed feelings of relief and frustration, we turned back for Addu Atoll. Having, in the words of Lady Macbeth 'screwed our courage to the sticking place', we would have had some success, even in the face of heavy fighter opposition, but at what cost will never be known. The Admiral and all senior officers were equally frustrated, but knew nevertheless that had we not been completely and totally successful, Ceylon could have been overrun in a matter of days.

Three days later, on 9 April, the Japanese dive-bombed Trinco-malee, sinking *Hermes* and the destroyer *Vampire* as well as several merchantmen, and inflicting further serious casualties on the fighter squadrons at China Bay. Their objective seemed to be to lure our fleet into the Bay of Bengal, where they could call up shore-based bombers to assist. Eventually Blenheim bombers of 11 Squadron counter-attacked the Japanese Fleet, losing 5 out of 9, including Sub-Lieutenant Tony Peace, a course-mate, flying on ship recognition duties. His father, gunnery officer in the armed merchant cruiser *Rawalpindi*, had also been killed at sea. Our failure to engage was disappointing, but with hindsight the tactic of keeping our Eastern Fleet in being, as a constant threat to enemy incursions, saved India and Ceylon and gave a breathing space until, with material superiority, we were able, in 1944, to chase them out of South East Asia.

One of our main propeller shafts had been damaged in the high-speed chase, entailing repairs in the comparative safety of Bombay, much preferred to Colombo, where the old destroyer *Tenedos* had been blown out of the drydock in Walkers' Yard. There was also a pressing need to obtain great efficiency out of the TBR squadrons, causing the temporary disbandment of 818, their aircraft and crews joining 820, but such is squadron tradition that it was some time before complete loyalty was transferred. It obviously made more sense to have one TBR and one fighter squadron per carrier, thus cutting down aircraft spares, less bodies and paperwork. The wonder was that it hadn't been done before.

Our Wildcat fighter squadron, 888, had a number of New Zealanders in its ranks, Gerald 'Doc' Burke and Peter 'Dusty' Miller were two I recollect well, the former a stocky and somewhat truculent character, the latter mild-mannered and drily witty. They were heavily outnumbered by 'Pommies' who adopted a Kiwi accent and phraseology, while the Kiwis reversed the mickey-taking by adopting upper-class English accents. Thus a newcomer would become very confused, which was exactly what 888 Squadron intended.

Arriving back in Colombo on St George's Day, 23 April, the weather became very overcast as the monsoon season approached, our met friends at Ratmalana prophesying like a bunch of undertakers that it would be with us for four months at least. Next day we left harbour to take on 10 Fulmars of 803 Squadron, some of which had been operating in the Western Desert, the remainder being survivors from Trincomalee. Fighter operations in Ceylon were now taken over by the Hurricane squadrons at China Bay and Ratmalana, happily reinforced by aircraft which we had seen at Juhu, Bombay, a couple of weeks earlier, and of a later mark. It was encouraging to see better fighters at last arriving in this theatre so long starved of up-to-date equipment. We had seen aircraft in Ceylon that had been flown out of Singapore so obsolete that even our Albacores looked modern by comparison. There were Brewster Buffalo fighters, ancient TBRs such as Vickers Wildebeests, Westland Wapitis and even a Fairey Seal flying boat of which we had 'heard talk' from nostalgic aviators now too old to fly operationally. And these aircraft had been in the front line defence of Singapore, the Eastern bastion of what we used to call 'The British Empire'. Small wonder that the Japanese had made such short work of capturing that fortress.

On 1 May *Formidable* dropped anchor in the beautiful harbour of Mahé in the Seychelles for no obvious reason, but the shuttle service of captains' barges made it obvious that something was afoot, The lower orders meantime went ashore, our heads full of the latest 'buzzes' – Capetown – Durban – Australia – UK – to sample the primitive delights of the island, reputed to be the original Garden of Eden, as well it might have been, with luxurious flowers and silver beaches. The beautifully clear water which half a mile out from the shore only came up to the armpits gave a fantastic view of the coral, out of which darted swiftly fish of all colours and types. The language in the Seychelles was a strange patois, a mix of English and French due to the occupancy by both nations over the centuries. 'Prune', who claimed to be fluent in French, had the local children in fits of laughter as he tried to discover the whereabouts of his aunt's pen. Such beautiful, natural kids, who brought us coconuts and wanted little for their efforts at climbing the tall trees, other than to talk with us and perhaps have a souvenir. None of the clamour for chewing gum, cigarettes or invitations to visit their sisters which we encountered in other more frequently-visited, but less attractive places. Alas, our stay was only to oil and confer, and after having planted a rough idea of how to play rugby with partly-trimmed coconuts for a ball, we returned to the ship at dusk, and sailed during the night, never again to return.

Back on board, Captain Bisset told us that it was suspected that the Vichy French in Madagascar were lending support to anti-Allied forces, probably to the extent of allowing fueling and repair facilities to Japanese submarines that were supposed to be entering by the Mozambique Channel, between the African mainland and this large island. Madagascar was therefore, to be invested and the assault would be made by Royal Marine Commandos in landing craft. *Illustrious* would give air cover to the landings with *Indomitable,* and the battleship *Ramillies* would carry out bombardments if necessary. We were to be longstop in *Formidable,* maintaining continous searches by Albacores, with Wildcats and Fulmars taking turns to give fighter protection to our small force, our escorts consisting mainly of ancient cruisers, among which were *Dragon, Dauntless* and *Enterprise.*

The invasion was over in about three days, though the Vichy resistance was much stiffer than expected. In four days, from 4–7 May inclusive, I flew on four search patrols with long-range petrol tank, a total of 18 hours, about the average for a whole month at that time. The crouching position in the airgunner's seat, and the equipment which had to be crowded in (Bigsworth chartboard, coding machine, navigational and radio equipment, binoculars, on top of the normal radio and pans of ammunition) gave me the beginners of a dowager's hump, but fortunately the Vichy forces surrendered at Diego Suarez on 7 May and the majority of the Fleet sailed for Mombasa in Kenya. We dropped anchor in the wide Kilindini river on the morning of 10 May. Kenya has always been my favourite part of Africa since that day. The sight of green grass, red roofs to the European houses and a reasonable climate was delightful. Admittedly, there was little here in the way of social life, but later when we were invited out by the planters for the weekend, or could make a trip to Nairobi, we found the atmosphere, the friendliness and the opportunities for sports hard to beat.

Mombasa itself in those days was quite primitive, a few stores, the Manor Hotel and the Mombasa Club were all the night-life it had to offer. Some of our aircraft had flown ashore to the local grassfield airport, Port Reitz, a few miles outside the city, and reports of the RAF mess were very good. Fortunately loads of delayed mail caught up with us there, so much of our time was spent writing airgraphs home. Because of the abundance of grass, we played a lot of soccer, rugby and hockey, against teams from other ships, the RAF Port Reitz, and a detachment of the South African Army who had chased the Italians out

162

of Ethiopia the previous year, and were resting prior to moving back north again. So soft was the grass, or so tough were these 'Yarpies' that many of them played rugby in bare feet, kicking with tremendous precision. Work on board began early, and most afternoons were make and mend for the non-duty watch, so that they could go ashore or get rid of the backlog of games in the ship's deck-hockey knockout competition. Many, of course, preferred just to get their heads down and recharge their batteries for the weeks ahead when we should be back to 16 hour days again. But for the enthusiastic, there was boat-pulling in whalers and cutters, sailing, boxing, and a new craze – commando training with the Royal Marines. To remember those days brings back just one major thought – we must have been fit!

One incident sticks in my memory. I had arranged for one of the powerboats to take a party up to the Port Reitz area each afternoon. There, despite the fact that the river was full of crocodiles, swimming was fairly safe because of a wire net which had been erected by RAF Port Reitz for their own troops' safety. The boat was supposed to call back half-an-hour before dusk, normally about 1730 all year round. When night falls near the equator, it falls with great suddenness – none of the long twilight one is used to in Northern Europe, so we didn't particularly want to hang around with a river full of crocodiles, as well the other hazards ashore such as snakes and lions. One evening, and it was the only one on which it occurred, the boat forgot to call for us; there being only two officers ashore that day and no ratings, which is probably why it happened. Anyway, by 1745 it seemed we had better do something just in case, so Jock Moffat and I started to collect large pieces of driftwood, which we lashed together with vegetable creepers to make a raft. By dusk it was obvious that the boat had forgotten us, and using an oar-shaped piece for steering, we went out from the beach on the ebb-tide. *Formidable* was about two to three miles downstream, and when we got within hailing distance, began to shout for all we were worth, since we were both seeing and imagining things all round us in the water from crocodiles to sharks. Eventually a boat came out and took us to the ship. Not only did the duty officer get a rocket, so did we, which seemed somewhat unfair, as we were sinned against rather than sinning. Further, as we put it to the First Lieutenant – we had no choice, for if we had tried to strike inland to the Causeway, a mile and a half distant, we would probably have encountered snakes, lions and perhaps crocodiles too, since they were known to come ashore for their dinner after dark.

A few days later a seaman painting the hull of the seaplane carrier *Pegasus*, which lay opposite us in the anchorage, fell from his painting cradle, and was seized by the crocodiles almost as he hit the water. We never went back to swim at Port Reitz.

For a special treat one night, we had a film in the hangar entitled

'Ships with Wings', a hearty patriotic British film of the type made early during the war to show those at home what heroics were being performed by 'The Brave Lads Out There'. Michael Wilding and John Clements were two of the actors, most of whom went though every emotion from A to B. The story doesn't really matter, but from memory a pilot was wrongfully dismissed the Navy. Later, after war has broken out, he lands on the carrier, somewhere in the Eastern Mediterranean, to warn that the dastardly Italians are up to some no good ahead of the Fleet. Everything was overdramatised, and failed to even approach reality, everyone salutes everyone else, heroic understatements are made, and for some strange reason chubby-cheeked midshipmen are tossed in blankets.

Every cliché since 'The Middle Watch' was dragged out and milked. The only parts of the film worth watching were the magnificent footages shot by Roy Kellino when he was with us in *Ark Royal*. In the final elaborately romanticised sequence, our three Intrepid Aviators take off into the sunset – surely going the wrong way – ready to give their all in a sub-flight comprising a Swordfish, a Skua and a Fulmar, keeping the most awful formation. It must have been the very worst in a series of dreadful wartime films, and everyone loved it! The villians were hissed, the heroes cheered, with lots of admonitions to 'look behind you' and so on. The whole audience was falling about the place, and for days afterwards the whole ship was re-enacting the clichés. It would have been a wonderful film to keep for showing as a restorative on those hard days when nothing went right and the heat and humidity made everyone a trifle niggly. In fact, our Captain and Commanders allowed a great deal of latitude to minor offenders. Not too much, but the absence of petty crimes made life just that bit more bearable.

Illustrious and *Indomitable* returned from Madagascar on 22 May, sending over calling parties to tell all about their gallantry. There appeared little evidence of any intention to allow the Japanese to use Madagascar as a base, but plenty of anti-Allied sentiment was expressed by the Vichy French. Apart from some unique fauna and flora, such as sloths and lemurs not found elsewhere in Africa, Madagascar appeared to have little to commend itself, being largely a barren swamp. Robert Everett had been shot down while leading his squadron to bomb, but had been released after about an hour, and 'Prangler' Pike, an amusing and witty character, flying a Swordfish from *Indomitable* had forced-landed on a desert island away from the mainland, where they had drawn enormous SOS-es in the sand, being rescued after a few days. There were lots of souvenirs to show us, but we got the impression that no medals were likely to be awarded. A submarine, two merchantmen, a sloop and two aircraft had been destroyed, so that on balance, things were about even. In fairness, we had to know if facilities had been made available to the Japanese, and a small holding force was left behind as caretakers.

Fortunately my various duties as sports, signals and training officer kept me fully employed when there was no flying for Albacore 5B. In sports we had four teams from the squadron in the quarter-finals of the deck-hockey; at soccer we were beating more teams than beat us, numbering the fast minelayer *Manxman, Enterprise* and *Dauntless* among our victims, but succumbing to *Dragon.* At rugby we won more than we lost, and several of our players in each sport were in the ships' teams. There was only one major problem – as squadron sports officer, I was expected to fill in for every vacant position when players went sick or could not play for any reason. To compensate, I introduced handball to *Formidable,* and apart from the hazard of losing the ball overboard at sea, it was taken up most enthusiastically. Indeed, on one occasion, we mustered three officers' teams from the ship, even getting some of the barflies enthusiastic. 'Prune', who could loosely be put into the last category, objected strongly to my enthusiasm for sports, claiming that I was a Notifiable Disease.

The Madagascar business over, we felt rather safe in Mombasa, and some more problems with the main propeller shaft had been rectified. However, one morning, a yellow warning – enemy aircraft approaching – was broadcast, sending everyone scurrying for their anti-flash gear and battle bowlers. Closed up at action stations, the gun trainers and layers were busily waiting for the order 'Commence, commence, commence' when almost at treetop level from the other side of the river came a Walrus amphibian, to execute a perfect landing, completely oblivious to the panic its failure to identify itself had caused. There were several Walruses in the Pool at Port Reitz, known to the local native boys employed there as 'motor-car belong Jesus'. A rather apt description if you think about it.

Another strange thing happened at Port Reitz. One day, when up there for some flying practice, we saw a lady pilot officer in the officers' mess. this, of course was no rarity, but we had never before seen one with a pilot's brevet. It appears that on the outbreak of war, appeals were made in East Africa for private pilots to join the RAF in Kenya, and this charmer volunteered. It also happens that her name was Evelyn, and the recruiting people accepted the application, imagining that the name was similar to and as in Waugh. Surprise, surprise when she arrived, booted, spurred and wearing wings over the left breast – probably the first time the regulations for uniform were 100 per cent correctly carried out. Anyway, Evelyn was there, and God bless her, there she stayed. I understand a very good pilot too, though her work couldn't include combat. At least not in the air.

It was about this time that we carried a company of East African Rifles across the Indian Ocean, en route, we were told, to Burma. The huge and very smart troops came abroad, saluting everything that moved and were billetted in every spare space all over the ship, mainly around the pompoms. Every morning at dawn they fell in for PT on the flightdeck, breakfasted and took up very smart but quite unnecessary sentry positions all over the ship. Their British officers explained that they actually loved doing this, and competitions took place amongst the various platoons for the smartest askari. Their fellows blancoed the candidate's equipment, blacked their boots, including the soles, and also their knees. Then the candidate was carried to inspection for the elimination process, and the winner was finally selected. The prize? Extra turns of sentry duty! Our troops shook their heads in astonished disbelief. It so happened that on this particular crossing we carried out night exercises with *Illustrious, Warspite* and the cruiser *Gambia*, including flare-dropping and night dummy torpedo attacks, which impressed our passengers greatly. Not that they ever had any doubts about who was going to win this war – King George's Men.

Exercises, exercises, exercises. Every day and most nights for the rest of May and throughout June that summer we flew until we were honed to razor sharpness. There were some casualties. Jimmy Clark of 888 all but wrote himself off pranging his Wildcat; Cy Ballard, his squadron-mate made a splendid kangaroo-jump over both barriers, landing on the first starboard pompom, to the astonishment of the guns' crew who were sunbathing. One of 803's Fulmars went over the side, and though Nicholson, the pilot, was rescued, his airgunner was drowned. Observer 'Fanny' Adams of 820 was delayed at briefing one morning, and his Albacore was catapulted without him, much to the embarrassment of the flightdeck officer and the pilot of the aircraft. A rather dicey exercise one day involved squirting off an Albacore across wind, just in case we were faced with this problem some time and 'Prune' either volunteered or was pressganged into this one. His Albacore took off with a sideways motion, rather like a Giant Mexican Landcrab, skimmed the wavetops, but finally made it, much to everyone's relief. Mr While, our tame midshipman, who flew mainly on less hazardous trips because of his youth, was one day towing a drogue for *Gambia* to fire at and thoughtfully streaming it a few hundred feet astern, with 'Bud' Abbott, our second senior observer, operating the winch. For some strange reason, *Gambia* ignored the drogue and put some bursts unnervingly close to the Swordfish itself, so close that the aircraft crashed into the sea, but fortunately without harm to the crew.

On this voyage, as on several others, we crossed the Line a dozen times in the same night as the Force zigzagged as part of the exercise. 'Gutty' Snelgrove, one of our younger observers, on another occasion got into my aircraft instead of his own, and took off. He was 'spare' that morning, and somehow had been given to understand that I was sick. What was not surprising perhaps was not that these incidents happened, but that they didn't happen more frequently. With three carriers operating, from time to time flying off simultaneously, the

Four of the six Seafire IB fighters aboard warm up for take off from *Formidable* in the Indian Ocean, June 1942. *Author's collection*

margin for error was wide, especially as most of the time radio silence was in force.

Laundry facilities on board were not of the best, since fresh water had to be conserved, and many were the cases of that dreadful complaint prickly heat. Since the baths and showers were salt water when at sea, washing generally made the rash worse and the only remedy in the oppressive conditions of heat and humidity was to 'burn it off' by sunbathing, though it was a long and tedious business. Sleeping with prickly heat was nigh impossible, and it would sometimes disappear, only to come back a few days later. Red-haired people, because of their pigmentation, suffered more than most, and Shrapnell-Smith, one of our engineers, endured the problem for most of the commission, the heat and oily conditions in the enginerooms doing little to help matters.

'Shrappers', in fact, got me into rather fearful trouble one evening. He was in the wardroom, wearing his short-sleeved white shirt outside his shorts, since he claimed it gave most draught to his affliction, The Commander suggested that he was improperly dressed, and should tuck the shirt-tail back in. A little horseplay then ensued after the Commander had moved on, with 'Shrappers' and I pulling out each others' shirt-tails. We were both requested to report to the Commander next morning at 0900 to explain our behaviour, 'Shrappers' getting away with it because of his obvious rash, but I got a talking to – about the behaviour expected of gentlemen, and a promise of some extra duty at some future and unspecified date. Having been thoroughly dressed down by Commander Ted leMesurier, I forgot all about the incident and the promised punishment. Ted didn't.

167

On 22 June it was voted to put on a ship's concert party to relieve the tedium, and this was yet another duty which fell to me. We chose to rehearse one of Bob Everett's sketches entitled 'Commissioning Night', a burlesque of all the things that can go wrong when a ship commissions with a raw ship's company. The sketch had been done many times, but had wonderful opportunities for the insertion of unmistakable lampoons of senior officers and of situations which require emphasis. In *Formidable* there was much opportunity for both, so much so that the person originally selected for the principal part of the Commander became slightly nervous of what the reaction to our caricatures would be, and declined to continue. As usual, it fell to my lot to substitute, and ham it up we did, even inviting Bob Everett over from *Illustrious* to give us the author's own criticism at final rehearsal. He thought we were well within the bounds of permitted stage licence.

We had just come into Kilindini Harbour for three nights. Barring panics, ideal timing for the presentation, so the show commenced, with offerings from each part of the ship. All the traditional pieces were there: the Stokers' can-can; Moffat with his guitar; banjo and mouth-organ cowboy group; Mr Bayliss and Mr Browning; the Warrant Gunners with their fantastic cutlass drill; the Sparkers' choir; a stand-up comedian from the Royal Marines, with feeds placed strategically in the audience; all the traditional hoopla, which everyone loved and applauded to the echo. Then came our sketch as the finale, rehearsed to a hair, milking the laughs and going over better than at any rehearsal, poking charlie at everyone from the Commander downwards,. and including not only the Lieutenant of Marines, but also the master-at-arms and the canteen manager. The troops and the officers loved it, giving us a great ovation.

Next morning *Formidable* was asked to supply an officer for the harbour anti-submarine night patrol in a small powerboat going to and fro across the boom where the river joins the sea. The Commander chose that night and the next for my extra duties, but not until the show was finished. There was not the least malice in this, of that I'm sure, it was just that Ted thought logically, and would have given me the duty whether there was a show or not. As a result it was just too bad, and I missed the wardroom party after the last night, when all the cast, officers, ratings and Marines, were entertained to food and drinks in the wardroom. Instead, I spent the night dropping 10lb depth charges to discourage saboteurs and as a side-effect to provide a great deal of fish for next day's meals. And it rained, all night, in fact, both nights.

The following evening, when I went into the bar for a pre-prandial, the chief steward whispered conspiratorially in my ear 'Commander's compliments, sir. There was two rather large gins left over after last night's party'. Thank you Ted, it was a nice thought.

On 6 June the CO sent for me to report to his office. My heart sank – what have I done wrong this time? We were young then, most of us under 23 years old, and liable to do silly things either because of the stress and strain under which we lived, or sometimes out of boredom when a week or so would go by without any sign of action and only routine flying to keep us busy. Not that routine flying was without its perils as witness the numerous prangs which always seemed to attend us. Some of us had other problems too, especially the ratings, many of whom came from such cities and Coventry, Plymouth, London and a great number from Liverpool. The bombings of these cities, when reported on the BBC Overseas programmes caused great huddles around the numerous radio sets, but it was customary for telegrams to be sent to next of kin of any casualties serving in HM Ships, and we were luckier than many. If an urgent case arose, a married man bereft of his wife or children, would be sent home as soon as possible, and I remember few cases this deserving. Nigel Gardner had the misfortune to hear of his brother's death at Tobruk on 2 July. So, musing on these and other thoughts (was it my own behaviour or bad news from home?), I reported to the Boss.

It wasn't bad news at all – he had recommended me for accelerated promotion to Lieutenant, largely because of my 'cheerful acceptance of extra responsibility'.. Unfortunately I wasn't allowed to mention it as it might not be confirmed by higher authority. Anyway, it felt good to have one's self-confidence lifted.

And so we continued our 'milk run' across the Indian Ocean, from Mombasa or Colombo. There were few sightings of ships outside the few convoys we escorted, and not a great deal of information about Japanese operations until after they had happened. Whereas there was little doubt that earlier in the war, the enemy had been underestimated, their recent successful run seemed now to make us overestimate their strategy. Rumours of Japanese potential submarine bases were as numerous as ever, and occasionally we widened our area of operations to cover the Amirante Islands, west of the Seychelles, and 10 degrees south of the equator, or the Maldives and Laccadives 10 degrees north. It was essential that they shouldn't find our secret refuelling base at Addu, and in fact, they never did, even though their submarines sank ships far north of this haven. Now that the civilian population at both ends of our patrol had come to recognise us, life became more contented. The locals, especially at the swimming club in Colombo agreed to our honary membership, and even invited us to dinner both at home and in the city. The same applied, and had for some time at the Kenya end. Almost invariably when we arrived off Mombasa or Colombo, and were going to fly aircraft ashore in case patrols were required, by agreement with the local services commander, we would give the AA guns some practice by doing a formation flight over the city first, and then strafing the place. In fact, the first time this was done, shortly after the Easter Sunday raid on Colombo, hundreds of Sinhalese workers dropped everything and headed for Nuwara Eliya up in the hills. One bank manager complained to us that he had to remain closed for a week owing to the absence of his clerks. But after a while, they got used to it. Mombasa anti-aircraft defences used to fire rockets and Very lights at us, which heightened the realism.

On 25 June we left Colombo for a sweep around the Chagos Archipelago, again 10 degrees south of the equator, a submarine having either been sighted or having made a radio signal which had been plotted by direction-finding (D/F). But despite wide searches, nothing was seen. During our return trip to Mombasa we streamed a fog-buoy to give dive-bombing practice to *Illustrious* aircraft, when a most frightening accident occurred. One of their Swordfish, piloted, I believe by McCaulay, had its wings fold in the dive, the crew of three being killed instantly. The aircraft went straight in at something like 200mph terminal velocity. There was nothing anyone could do. A destroyer circled for some time without result. Next day they lost a Wildcat, though this time the pilot survived and was rescued.

A Martlet (Wildcat) II fighter, piloted by Major F D G Bird, Royal Marines, CO of 888 Squadron, lands on *Formidable* in August 1942 with one half lowered wheel, the other had broken. Both pilot and aircraft were soon flying normally again. Above the port wing can be seen the turrets of *Formidable*'s port after 4.5in/45 calibre QF Mark III high angle/low angle guns. *Author's collection*

Chapter 13
Farewell to 820
Squadron

Of all patrols, the dawn search had its own peculiar beauty for me, and this flight had now become almost the prerogative of 5B. Usually we were shaken at 0400, then dressed and up to a sepulchral wardroom for coffee, toast and to have our thermos filled. Then up to the operations room, while David went into the hangar deck to check that the aircraft was serviceable. If not, we took the spare. At this hour everyone is more cheerful, probably the common bond of fellow sufferers. Our maintenance crew, Phillips, Post and the duty electrician would be grouped round the aircraft, now on deck, as I came down with all the navigation, signals and other 'gen'. Then into the aircraft to see that all necessary equipment was present and working; check with TAG 'Fuzz' Keel that the radio and guns were OK, then on the intercom to David 'Greetings – ready when you are', to which came his standard reply, a formula used by a lewd instructor at flying school – 'Right – orf we fucking go!'

We didn't always fly off, sometimes we were 'squirted', ie catapulted, depending on wind strength and whether the Captain wanted to turn into wind, which itself depended upon whether the area was safe or questionable, for a carrier flying off aircraft is very vulnerable for several minutes, on her straight course. I didn't like 'squirting' too much, with its bigger element of chance, and remembering Opdall's aircraft breaking in two with depth charges on, killing all three crew in *Ark Royal*. But today it's a fly off, so then 'Wings' gives a green light from the flying bridge, the flightdeck officer (known as 'Little F') dips his flag, chocks are pulled away by the ground crew. 'Davy' revs up, we move, and the tail is up before we reach the bridge, his eyes focussed on the bow, mine through the starboard window to catch any late information from the ops room – usually a new wind offered by 'Seaweed' the meteorological officer, or an alteration to the Force's MLA (Mean Line of Advance) which correction will have come in from the flagship. Then suddenly, we feel the wheels become unstuck, and we're airborne, soaring over the bow. Both 'Fuzz' and I note the time to start our records, he for his radio log, and me for navigational plot as we're away to commence our search and patrol.

It's still dark, but we're heading east, and we climb through the mist low down, and over the ships ahead of us, giving them all a wave as we go past. 'Davy' likes this bit, and often stays down low, flying at bridge level. I suppose those poor devils have got a more monotonous job than we have, and need a bit of cheer now and again. We are sometimes tempted to flash them a message, but with all eyes on us at this time of the morning, we don't. That is how mistakes happen, and one day we'll maybe need some help, and they'll think it's only those fancy fly-boys fooling again. So, immediately we pass the screen of destroyers, we get up to our patrol height.

First we do a quick sweep with our eyes, 'Davy' taking the ahead sector, 'Fuzz' and I alternately taking quarter-hours to port and starboard. After this first visual sweep we try the radar, though most naval observers prefer to rely upon their eyesight, and use the ASV set for about 5 minutes every half-hour. The point is that if you get a blip from a submarine, it will dive immediately, unless it wants to try a shoot-out. This is most unlikely since we have depth charges on, and our sighting report will have alerted the carrier, so that another aircraft or pair of them will be with us in about 10 minutes, and anyway, our destroyer leader will probably detach at least one surface hunter, all of which will be bad news for a submarine, unless he is acting as a decoy. So far as we are concerned, while it would be great to sink a submarine, (and 18 were sunk by Fleet Air Arm carrier aircraft alone in World War II plus another 16 shared with surface ships or the RAF) it probably serves almost as good a purpose if we keep him submerged so that he cannot get too near to the ships.

Of course, every ocean and every theatre of war differs. In the Atlantic the U-boats worked in 'wolf-packs' and frequently offered a decoy from ahead as the pack came in from the rear. Alternatively, the decoy would be offered from the rear of the convoy, with the pack waiting ahead to go through the lines of the convoy at periscope depth just as attention was concentrated on the search for the decoy astern. But this was the Indian Ocean where such tactics had not yet started.

The sky gradually changes from blue-black to pearly-grey and the sun begins to lift over the horizon, clearing the remaining mists away. It is cold, despite our heavy turtle-neck sweaters, flying boots and gauntlets worn in addition to uniform reefer jacket and trousers. In about an hour, it will be getting warmer. I take a back-bearing on the carrier, check it against my chartboard plot. The rod aerial goes down and we also check our track against the ship's beacon, which at 2000 ft will be audible and accurate at 20 miles, but since our orders this morning are to go on a box-search 40 miles ahead, then drop back ot the normal anti-submarine range of about 10 miles ahead, we shall not use it, as in this theatre, visibility is usually about 40 to 50 miles at 2000 ft.

But this can change very quickly. One day I was off on a search with Hank Henry, and we could see the ship about 50 miles away, but since we were heading into a strong wind, and *Formidable* was going away at about 20 knots, our airspeed of 90 knots had us gaining at a relative speed of about 30 knots. In short, it would be nearly two hours before we were on the deck, though we could see her clearly. I think Hank at that time was doing some mental arithmetic, trying to discover whether we had enough fuel to get there, and as a subsidiary thought, had he remembered his shark repellant? Then, all of a sudden, the ship disappeared, one minute there, the next gone, obviously having vanished into a heavy bank of mist or fog. That meant that we were not too far from some type of hurricane or an inversion, or maybe just a heavy front. We had no radar that day, but the beacon was in good shape, and we came in on the beam, as they say. The landing was Hank's usual three-pointer, but as he got unhooked, and taxied over the lowered barriers, the engine stopped dead. Hank's usually ruddy complexion went deathly pale. We had run out of petrol, and he HAD forgotten his shark repellant. We had been airborne almost 5 hours!

So, as the morning warms up, we take it in turns to have a coffee, our vigil never relaxing. Occasionally we see something which might be worth investigating, get the binoculars on it, to find it's just another large piece of driftwood, and try to guess where it came from. In nearly 1000 hours of observing, I never saw an enemy submarine, and only rarely saw anything that was not expected to be seen. What one doesn't know is how many U-boats saw or heard us first, and dived to get out of the way.

We have now been up for 3½ hours, and in another quarter of an hour should be thinking about one large sweep forward to about 40 miles and another box search. If there is anything out there, it will dive, and when we return to the ship it may surface, so that our relief will have a go at it, assuming it's still surfaced. So, this done, we come back to our final position, 5 miles ahead and wait for the ship to flash 'C', indicating that we should close her, as she is about to turn into wind, and if we box clever, we can be in the groove for landing as our relief is having his chocks whipped away for take-off. And that's the way we do it today, as Mike Fuller rolls up the deck, and nears the island, we are over the round-down, not too close or we get his slipstream, which at stalling speed plus about 5 knots can be fatal. Hook engages, handling party grab the wingtips as we taxi up the deck, in response to signals and we go over the lowered barriers on to the for'ard lift. The wings are folded, but I manage to get out in time and run up to the ops room, reporting to Commander 'O'. He asks a few questions on visibility, wind strength and I am dismissed, joining Davy in the wardroom where we get a well-earned breakfast.

Later on we shall all meet again and discuss anything worth

discussing about the performance of engine, radar and radio, and to clean or repair anything needing it. We were a good crew, trusting each other, yet making allowances for the minor mistakes even a good crew makes. It was one of the proudest moments of my life one day in Mombasa when I overheard Davy say to one of the South African pilots 'Gerry is without doubt the finest navigator in the country'. I blushed and simpered, and said 'Thanks, Davy, that's good to hear', whereupon he replied 'I hadn't finished, had I?' then continued to our 'Yarpie' friend, 'As I said, Gerry's marvellous in the country, but no bloody good at sea'. It is so nice to feel such trust.

Our only point of mock difference was that of seniority. This gave me command of the aircraft under RN tradition. It rarely mattered, since the duties of attacking or reconnaissance clearly made one or the other, the leader. Davy felt nevertheless that as in the RAF, the pilot should be the captain. One day at Port Reitz, we decided to settle this once and for all by a beer-drinking competition, the one sinking most bottles to be senior for all times, with no further arguments. This competition, unfortunately, was after quite a heavy pre-prandial session, and we both passed out, lying in the sun by the swimming pool up at the officers' mess. Some two hours later, we awoke almost simultaneously, burnt an unattractive purple by the afternoon sun. To alleviate his burns, Davy dived into the swimming pool and sank, happily being retrieved by Mike Lithgow with a boathook.

Now things became more exciting. On our return passage to Colombo, an armed raider was reported on 23 July, believed to be German. Here again, we knew the drill, and were loaded with six 250lb semi-armour-piercing bombs. The force altered course to the southeast in the direction of the Seychelles, and an unarmed six-aircraft search flew off diverging to twice visibility distance between aircraft, and on turning made a 'step aside', maintaining their distance apart to cover the widest possible area without leaving any holes. Despite this cunning mathematical arrangement, the 'armed raider' turned out to be nothing more dangerous than *Shikola*, a stray allied merchant vessel off the Amirantes, and heading for Colombo. She was too slow for us to escort her, and after a brief exchange of signals matters, the master seemed quite unperturbed, so we left her wallowing along at 10 knots to Colombo, which I believe she eventually reached without further incident. Alas, 5B did not get airborne at all that day.

After we arrived back in Colombo, the buzz-mongers had it that we were to make an offensive sweep into the Bay of Bengal, where several Japanese raiders were reported to be playing havoc and picking off unescorted merchant vessels at will. For once the prophets of doom were not far off the mark.

Going ashore that afternoon to the Colombo Swimming Club, quite a party of old shipmates were there – 'Dilly' Dangerfield from *Warspite*,

Bill Roberts, 'Ossie' Hutchinson, 'Buster' May and Outwin from *Indomitable*. Later we were joined by the two Richmonds from 803, Mike and Jock. A strange pair, who flew together in Fulmars, and though not related, were both red-bearded Scots, Mike the pilot was a quiet, self-contained character, in direct opposition to the extrovert observer, Jock. Ruminative and rumbustious Richmond, as they were sometimes identified, I believe the main reason they flew together was to confuse people in authority, though they certainly made an efficient crew. However, that day, to preserve our recently awarded honorary membership, we made Jock swear to behave himself, and later all repaired to *Indomitable* for a sundowner or three. Back to *Formidable* for dinner, we found a calling party from the small Royal Netherlands Navy squadron, which comprised the two light cruisers, *Heemskerck* and *Tromp*, all of which had escaped from bases in Sumatra ahead of the Japanese advance. To pay for their supper, the Dutchmen later entertained us with some delightful folk-singing and folk dancing, Lieutenant Fairwether RNN excelling in the latter.

So, towards the end of July, we put to sea, all Albacores flying ashore to Ratmalana for compass swinging. Unfortunately when we returned, *Formidable* had her radio masts stuck in the 'Up' position, so that we had to land on *Illustrious*, whose captain broadcast later, telling us that we were to make an offensive sweep into the Bay of Bengal to winkle out two Japanese 8in gun cruisers, reported there by the submarine *Truant*. By next morning repairs had been effected to the radio masts, so we returned 'home' and proceeded into enemy-dominated territory.

Early next morning a Catalina flew overhead – at least that was the verdict of the air lookouts, who later modified their positive identification, by which time it was too late to do anything about it, the 'Cat' having been at 10,000 ft. Both carriers had sent off Fulmars on the first search, since with their faster speed they could cover a larger area, but alas, the weather closed in on us, and two Fulmars failed to return. One from *Illustrious* was seen to ditch, and the crew – Gardner and Shaw – were rescued by *Heemskerck*. Our missing crew was Des Ellwood, a delightful and talented Kiwi, with his observer, Chris Christellis, from South Africa. Though 820 searched for the rest of the day to the limit of endurance, and again next morning no trace was ever found of them. Two splendid shipmates, Des was a fine cartoonist who caught not only the face of his subject, but the mannerisms too. I am proud that I still have one of his best efforts, lampooning 820 squadron, in my den. Some revenge was taken that afternoon when Johnnie Scott and Cy Ballard of 888 shot down a four-engined Navy 97 Japanese reconnaissance aircraft.

But the profit margin was shortened later in the afternoon, as we turned for Trincomalee to refuel, Peter Miller of 888 ditching his Wildcat, and an *Illustrious* Fulmar mistaking a Catalina heading for Trincomalee for a bandit, making one attack and wounding two of the crew before the mistake was realised. So, with no great profit to show, we made one more uneventful sweep north to the Andamans, then turned for Colombo, arriving there late in the evening of 5 August.

Next day, as we loaded three months' provisions and stores, the air was full of buzz and counter-buzz. Durban or Capetown, then home for some unspecified purpose, or the alternative and much more popular – to have 820 based ashore at Wingfield aerodrome, Capetown, thence to carry out anti-submarine patrols and searches to protect the ever growing numbers of tankers and troopers heading for the Middle East. Our minds boggled and our mouths watered at thoughts of no blackout plus wine, women and song with the infrequent interruption of a little flying. Never have I seen a ship's total company work as hard. At 1700 the work was complete and by 1900 we were heading for the open sea, on a tantalising course, slightly south of due west, heightening the buzz for Durban.

But of course, it wasn't, as we proceeded with *Manxman*, the cruiser *Birmingham* and destroyers in company. Some long patrols and searches were flown since our larger escorts were both short of fuel and had to go into the Seychelles to top up. Thereafter we carried out exercises, during which Tommy While in his Swordfish nearly rolled over the bow being ranged for the catapult, and 'Doc' Burke for some reason best known to himself opened up with his six 0.50in Browning machine guns when landing his Wildcat.

Next day occurred a mysterious tragedy to which no satisfactory answer has yet been given. Guy Brockensha, senior pilot of 888, disappeared from the ship during the night. Before anchoring in Mombasa, the ship was searched from truck to keel, but no trace was ever found. An enormously popular lieutenant RN already decorated with the DSC, he was an excellent pilot, a good sportsman, and so far as any of his close friends knew, including Dicky Bird, his Royal Marine CO, 'Brock' hadn't a care in the world. He was happily married to a beautiful Scots wife in Wick, though he hailed from Durban, where there was a strong possibility we should shortly be. In over 40 years since his mysterious disappearance, no satisfactory explanation has ever been offered. The whole ship was depressed over the loss of this popular and brave shipmate.

News next day of *Eagle* having been torpedoed and sunk in the Mediterranean, but with a small loss of life, brought yet another buzz into the possible destinations for us – Alexandria or Gibraltar, to replace her. Simultaneously came the news that several of our training course had been decorated, including 'Lucky' Sutton, who had been doing sterling work in his Swordfish at night with the Desert Army, one of the very strange roles the naval aviators adopted during the war. 'Flossie' Willett had been mentioned in dispatches and Johnny Buscall DSC listed as missing. Not one of our happier weeks, all in all.

But we were never depressed for too long, life could be so short. We had a debating society in which most subjects were far from serious. One evening came a discussion on 'Inventions which would end the war'. Though most of this was devoted to such items as training seals to detect submarines, or coating the flight deck with treacle which would be a cheaper and more effective way of stopping aircraft more quickly when landing on, several ideas which raised hoots of laughter were not too far from subsequent inventions that did curtail the war. For instance, Geoff Topham submitted that if a cable could be laid from England to Australia, then it should be easy to lay a submerged pipeline from Burton-on-Trent to naval ports, especially to Gibraltar, ensuring good and cheaper beer for the troops. Nigel Gardner thought that all we had to do was to duplicate the enemy's 'All Clear' siren, and incorporate this in the tail of our bombs, so that the enemy would run out of their shelters and trenches just in time to cop the lot. 'Prune', ever practical, suggested that as many of our pilots tended to swing to port on landing, could not the flightdeck be built diagonally with this in mind. Stupid thoughts at the time? But eventually came Pluto; atomic bombs dropped by parachute; and, of course, the angled flightdeck. Maybe we were wiser than we know, or genius really is akin to madness.

Gambia anchored next day with news that they had picked up three Dutchmen in a lifeboat 3000 miles out at sea, they having escaped from Batavia.

Our Army Co-operation experience now came in handy, as we engaged in exercises with the local garrison and Royal Marine Commandos. Leonard Mann, flying in the back seat of a Skua on these exercises was wrapped round a palm tree on take off, finishing up shaken but not badly hurt in sickbay. Ivan Fisher, our senior observer, went piloting for a change, and once more bent an Albacore at Port Reitz. Never a dull, as we used to say.

Then the important news. Captain A W la Touche Bissett was to leave us, and be replaced by Captain Talbot, known by his baptismals of Arthur George. So we dined Captain Bissett, a most popular and humane Captain, of whom frankly we never saw much. A most enjoyable evening, with many witty, and happily, short speeches and reminiscences. More changes followed, heightening the rumours of a change of base; Dai Davies, Gunnery Commander left us, and 803 Squadron moved ashore to Port Reitz. With all this excitement, my main priority was to rescue my laundry from Port Reitz before sailing, which now seemed imminent.

There were also some urgent spares to be collected from Nairobi and from the new airfield which was being built at McKinnon Road (or was it Mackinnon Road?). The point of the latter airfield always escaped me, since it was less than 100 miles inland from Mombasa, and if a naval airfield was required, it would have been easier either to extend Port Reitz, which was there already, or to have built the new field nearer to the port of Mombasa/Kilindini, where more abundant and intelligent native labour was available. I suppose there must have been a reason. Peter Large flew us there, and en route he suddenly said 'Hey, Gerry, just look at those pink elephants down there!'. Another of Peter's leg-pulls, I suspected, but no, he came down to about 100 ft, and there we saw by a waterhole, half a dozen of the variety. What had happened was that they had been bathing in the red clay, and with the waterhole less full of water than usual, much of the clay had dried on. For the record we took a few shots with the camera, alas only black and white film.

An Albacore being set up for catapulting from *Formidable* for Eastern Fleet's dawn patrol in May 1942. The figures in silhouette are Lieutenant (A) 'Pop' Cannon RN, decklanding control officer with green flag, 820 Squadron's senior technical rating, Chief Air Artificer Wyley (bending over) and the engineer lieutenant, i/c the catapult. Behind them is the Fleet flagship, the veteran battleship *Warspite*. *Leonard Mann*

A small detachment we had left at Mackinnon Road was anxious to get away and back to the ship, which was unusual. Freedom is freedom wherever it is. However, Chief Air Artificer Arundel explained that it wasn't the mosquitoes that worried them at night so much as the lions keeping them awake. Although the living area of the camp had been surrounded with barbed wire, they didn't feel safe. The Army officer in charge had told them that the chance of a lion penetrating the camp was a million to one, Chiefy had respectfully replied that just that once could be too much for him.

The Army Engineers had been drilling for water, relying on a map which showed an old watercourse called Maji ya Chumvi in Swahili. Countless drills had produced traces of water, but it was always brackish and salty. More recent borings were producing bigger quantities, but still not good for drinking. One of the more intelligent Kikuyu workmen, speaking as little English as the engineer spoke Swahili, had tried repeatedly to tell the latter that he would always get that type of water there, but the engineer didn't want lessons from his black inferiors. It appears that one evening, the engineer was discussing his frustrations with a local coffee-planter, mentioning the fact that 'local old wives' tales' suggested that his explorations were doomed to failure. 'Not old wives' tales, young feller,' commented the planter 'Your native informant is quite right. You will never get anything else from that watercourse. The name of the river, Maji ya Chumvi means, very simply 'The river of salt'. To borrow an exit line from *Punch* – 'collapse of stout party'.

Finally on 24 August, having rescued our spares, our troops, and most important of all, my laundry, we left Mombasa, heading south, and were given a valedictory low-level beat-up by Fulmars of 803 Squadron as, in true Hollywood fashion, we sailed into the setting sun. So we proceeded to Durban, where Brockensha's parents came abroad, and spoke to all his close friends in 888 and 820. A very sad interlude, with little we could say, except to offer condolences. At least they left the ship knowing that they were parents of a very fine and brave son.

Torn between shopping for presents for home – which now seemed a distinct probability – and having a last fling in near-normal conditions, we managed to do both. The gig was finally up when we saw our Commander – Ted – shopping for intimate garments, and plunged heavily. Knowing nothing about sizes, I asked the shop assistant what was the average size of ladies silk stockings to purchase, and found Davy buying two pairs of each size, the wider to spread his net. Later, when ashore with 'Prune', a large American car drew up alongside, with two charmers offering us a lift, which developed into a couple of days with the family, two nubile daughters and a retired father, who gave us a delightful scenic tour of the area, including the Valley of a Thousand Hills, Athlone Gardens and finally home for drinks. Father discreetly disappeared, leaving us to spend the evening at the 'Stardust'. Once more we found the licensing laws a trifle confusing, since the bars closed at 1900 and we again had to purchase a 'brown bag' from the nearest off-licence. Orange-juice only was provided by the 'night club', but thanks to some weird and wonderful admixtures, and an enthusiastic band, we spent a splendid evening, driving home in the full moonlight at 0430, which, as 'Prune' remarked, was better than taking off on A/S patrol.

The ship's company looked a trifle seedy at Sunday Divisions next morning, but leave was piped from 1130 to 1600 only, and woe betide anyone adrift. So sadly, we met our ladies for lunch and light conversation only, but were driven back to the ship in style. Such was the hospitality of the Springboks that few did not arrive back by car. We left in the early evening, to the traditional send-off, with thousands waving from the front, and the Lady in White singing 'Land of Hope and Glory' from the promontory, as she had for thousands of servicemen visiting this beautiful city.

The new Captain made his maiden speech next morning – Freetown first stop, but without escorts, so every finger had to be well and truly out, maximum speed and no time for unnecessary manoeuvres. In fact, the next day there was no flying, as the rolling round the Cape was excessive at 25 knots, and as we turned the corner, the wind was straight up our kilts, necessitating 180 degree turns. Risky perhaps, but this time we got away with it, posting double lookouts round the clock.

As we headed north for Freetown, searches were flown to maximum depth – about 150 miles ahead, and aircraft were all armed with depth charges in case we met a U-boat, many of which had been reported in the Freetown area, this too being a focal point for convoy assembly. One day I flew both dusk and dawn search, logging 6 hours 45 minutes. The only advantage to this type of flying was that it enabled us to complete the deck-hockey knock-out league. Both 820 aircrew and ratings' teams were in the two semi-finals. Though the officers' team were dismissed, the ratings went on to win the cup. Next day, some ironic niggling at me because there was nothing to do in the way of sports. I suggested water-polo.

Airborne in the early morning mist next day, we found one of our escorts, the destroyer *Wyvern*, and directed her to *Formidable*. *Vansittart* was most elusive, and not found until the afternoon search, and so into Freetown next dawn. The old place hadn't changed, dank, humid, sweaty, any number of unpleasant adjectives would do, though far from being the White Man's Grave of legend. Again more shopping, though the choice here was rather limited, consisting mainly of native carvings, parrots and monkeys. A strange happening came later when a Nazi spy was brought over for passage to England, having been caught in an American merchantman. The makings of a melodrama were added next morning when we loaded one million pounds' worth of gold ingots. Guarded by numerous askaris, it was brought to the ship by lighter, and loaded on board under a strong Royal Marine guard, the point of which I couldn't really see, since the ingots were so heavy that a man could only lift one at a time with difficulty, and certainly wouldn't be doing any 100 yard sprinting. Staying only 20 hours, we were off again at 1500 with our V and W class escorts for one day only. The Captain now informed us that we were going home, which seemed a little superfluous after loading gold AND a spy, but as well to have confirmation.

Formidable in the Indian Ocean, August 1942 with a Martlet (Wildcat) II fighter of 888 Squadron preparing for take off. Also visible are the port forward catapult and six starboard side outriggers for the ship's 6 Seafire fighters which had non-folding wings. *Author's collection*

The remainder of the voyage was fairly uneventful, though we sighted a raft with bodies looking very dead, and without escorts could not take the chance of stopping. One misty morning we found ourselves in the middle of the Portuguese fishing fleet from the Azores, who were more surprised than we. Signals indicated that a merchantman had been torpedoed by a U-boat some 50 miles away, so searches were flown, though we saw neither the torpedoed ship, survivors or the U-boat. It is not impossible that the message was faked, and it was known that we were in the area. Captain Talbot was taking no chances, and for the next two days until our final escort arrived, everyone slept fully dressed, boat drills were rehearsed frequently, air patrols and lookouts were doubled.

Two sailing schooners were sighted one morning, also an abandoned raft. A total of 30 U-boats were known to be in the Azores/Bay of Biscay/Land's End area, so that it was with great relief that our one Polish and two RN destroyers met us on 15 September. Now that we were in Home Waters, lookouts were relaxed a little, but an inquisitive RAF Whitley bomber with no identification showing almost had an eager section of Wildcats jump him some 800 miles west of Brest. Buzzes were now rife that squadrons would fly off to Lee-on-Solent, which raised many hopes for those with sweethearts and wives there, only to be dashed completely by a signal which instructed us to disembark to Machri-bloody-Hanish.

Almost as comic relief, a signal that day announced pay rises for the services. Sub-lieutenants would gain 2/– per day. Compared with today's rates, our pay then seems ridiculously inadequate, yet it was almost adequate. A midshipman, for example received 5/– per day plus 4/– flying pay; sub-lieutenants 9/– plus 6/–; lieutenants 13/6d plus 6/–, but as they could normally expect in peacetime to remain in that rank for eight years, received increments every three years. Marriage allowance was not paid to officers under the age of 26 years, but this latest signal rescinded that provision, largely because so many reservists were married before joining. A lieutenant in those days with marriage allowance would find it hard to live on his pay, and a lieutenant-commander, even with flying pay, some seniority pay and marriage plus childrens' allowances would find it hard if he had children to educate.

After spending days packing and repacking our gear for leave, separating those items which would go with the stores, we were all ready to fly off to Machrihanish. Happily one of the junior sub-lieutenants won the rear echelon duty, since after two years with 820 it was probable that a new appointment would be coming my way. At the last minute, owing to fog higher up the Clyde, it was decided to catapult the aircraft from Greenock since with 30-odd aircraft to leave, extensive manoeuvres in even light fog among merchant shipping would not endear us to our fellow mariners. Frankly we didn't mind how we left for leave, so long as we left.

Even in wartime, Customs and Excise officers examined our baggage, and many were the ruses to disembark our 'rabbits' – as gifts were known – without paying duty. One energetic entrepreneur had two dummy depth charges made, which no Exciseman in his right mind would go near. The great beauty of the 'Stringbag' was its fabric construction. Mainplanes could be cut open, 'rabbits' deposited inside, fabric doped over and sealed, none the wiser. The Excisemen were, in fact, pretty tolerant. The previous year, returning to the Clyde after the *Bismarck* sinking, as soon as the Customs men knew we were the happy warriors, it was 'open gangway', not that we had more than an extra bottle of gin and a carton or two of cigarettes, both severely rationed at home. But this year we wore no laurels after our fruitless frolics, but we were wiser and had reasonable excess dutiables plus intimate garments for our ladies. We were growing up, but we knew nothing of the form of Customsmen at Machrihanish. So all of us put into our aircraft approximately duty-free amounts of 'rabbits', while one aircraft was loaded to the gunnels with contraband. This one would fly off last, and would land last, preferably on a distant perimeter from the control building. There the passengers would get out, secrete the loot in one of the buildings with a watcher, the other climbing back in and carefully spilling a large tin of vegetable soup in the rear cockpit. When presenting the aircraft for examination, the Customs men usually took one look and felt ill themselves.

In the event, Hank Henry and 'Gutty' Snelgrove, custodians of the 'rabbits', went over the bows and into the Clyde, I gather that bottles of gin, silk stockings, cartons of W D & H O Wills (the only brand) and unmentionables were sighted as far away as Arran. But soggy and hard to light.

·Machrihanish was still hyphenated, though meeting old chums there relieved our feelings a little. The bathrooms were still not open, and we washed as best we could in hand-basins in cold water, shaving in hot water in the ante-room. Next day, all our duties discharged, 'Prune', Peter Large and I flew Albacore 5K to Abbotsinch, where I was lucky enough to get a lift in a D H Dominie to RAF Woodley, near Reading, and spent a very pleasant evening jawing in the mess there. Then on to King's Cross station in London next morning, and north to Lincolnshire. Changing at Peterborough with some hours to wait for the milk train, I visited my distant cousin Kate, married to a splendid man, who because of some minor ailment could not serve King and Country, but served some splendid drinks to those who did. Several of my friends lived in this part of the world, where we had an unofficial drinking school known as 'The Soaks of Peterborough'. And so to Boston.

My baby sister was home on leave, newly in the ATS, and though it is not good for sailors to have a pongo as a blood relative, you just can't win 'em all, and I had to admit that she looked very smart. The short leave – five days only – soon went, and seemed to consist of meeting old duckies who were friends of my mother by day and shooting lines in the local by night. Again, not too many contemporaries on leave at this time, and I wasn't too sorry – family apart – to leave for Lee-on-Solent.

Though I hadn't any real business at Lee, there was a very special girlfriend there and a chance to fly up to Machrihanish rather than do the Road to the Isles bit which was both boring and tiring. At Lee I found Jack Glaser, who lived there, now 820, Ossie Hutchinson, Johnnie Scott and Pat Campbell, the latter giving me a little more detail on how our mutual friend Murray Wilcocks was killed. Very sad. But there were a few of our Wren friends there, and we got a dance going to cheer ourselves up. My very special girlfriend seemed to have gone off me a bit. Lovely, very young and naive, it finally got through to me that we really didn't have too much in common. Her family background was top-drawer, father eventually becoming an admiral, which really wasn't my scene, especially as the Fleet Air Arm officers in those days were looked upon as slightly sub-standard types who were too dim to qualify in torpedo, gunnery, signals, submarines or any of the specialist branches. So, with a lot of regret, we finally said our goodbyes. We never met again, and eventually she married a pongo. I gathered later from mutual friends that she disappoved of my thirst, though my squadron mates regarded it as rather moderate.

No flights being available to Machrihanish, I eventually spent a couple of days in London, where I met an old flame, now a sergeant in the WAAF. She had more liberal views on alcohol, thank goodness, and did much to restore my wounded pride. Then on to Edinburgh and eventually to Machrihanish, where the squadron was re-assembling. Draft chits came floating in for the maintenance ratings, and practically wiped out my excellent sports teams. Former course-mates Johnnie Underwood and Jock Cunningham arrived, and many old shipmates were there too – Alan Owensmith and Pat Patterson from *Ark Royal*. But the weather was poor, winds of gale force and rain, which made flying impossible.

On 5 October we were signalled to move to an airfield in the Orkneys, very aptly named Twatt. At first we thought it was named after the man who built it, but it appeared that it was the real name of this swamp, which was, if anything, less desirable than Machrihanish. Gluey mud up to the ankles, no transport and a gale blowing most of the time. So it was with mixed feelings that when new appointments arrived for some of the older hands, my name led all the rest. Mike Lithgow was to go to the Service Training Unit, a good posting for such a skilled pilot, and I was to join the United States 12th Air Force in London for unspecified duties, which chilled me to the bone, since apart from the bare announcement there was no other enlightening information.

Chapter 14
Into the Wild Blue Yonder

So, I returned south the way I came less than a week earlier, via Abbotsinch, Edinburgh and a couple of days sneaked at home in Boston. At the Admiralty, I reported to Captain Keighley-Peach, who directed me to Lieutenant-Commander A J T Roe, of whom I had heard, carrying out some World War I secret operations in the Middle East. When one got to know him better, an extremely likeable officer. Others arrived; Freddie Harsant who had been trained with me, Alan Smith and Max Radford, a Kiwi. We were all observers, and as the job unfolded and was explained, it sounded as if we had been selected specially for it.

There was shortly to be a big operation codenamed 'Torch' in the Mediterranean theatre, and our gallant allies, the Americans, would be the major suppliers of air power. Unfortunately most of their crews had little or no experience of the sea and things which move on it. Having been fired at many times by our own ships, we could feel for them, especially as many of their aircraft would be unfamiliar to the average destroyer gunnery officer. Our job was to teach ship recognition and fly with their squadrons, at least until our educational efforts had begun to show fruit. John Roe took us along to meet our new colleagues at SHAEF in Norfolk House in St James's Square. Amid numerous 'Glad to know you's' we got a feeling that there was going to be a slight language problem, especially when one of the Americans asked me what ships I flew, but slowly we began to understand. Next day we were briefed – North Africa was the target – and some details of the various landing places were given us. We four could see ourselves flying in from Gibraltar, where the aircraft were assembling, landing at Casablanca, Oran or Algiers, then moving onwards towards Tunis, where we would hold the Axis forces at bay until Montgomery's 8th Army could catch up with them from the other end. In the event, of course, it was nothing like this at all!

After spending some four weeks in and around London, lecturing to US bomber squadrons, Boston, Mitchell, Marauder and Fortress crews, most of whom slept through it all, we had done as much as we could. The Americans loved London, as well they might, though on my new pay of 17/– a day, plus lodging allowance of about £3 weekly, we found it very hard going. Often we were invited to dinner at the Savoy, the Bagatelle or the Embassy, and it was difficult to refuse the people with whom we worked, even though they were most generous. Two of them I shall always remember – Eddie Bradford, then a first lieutenant and his great friend Captain Harry Mahon. Like me, they were Bostonians, but from the younger one. Our friendship was maintained long after the war, until both of them died, a few years ago. Eddie was from one of the *Mayflower* pilgrim families, though others mentioned the fact, not he; Harry was originally a graduate of the Royal Military College of Canada, but was on the administration staff at Harvard, whence Eddie had graduated years earlier, and with his twin brother Charles, won laurels in just about every sport there was. Eddie was modest, Harry a trifle regimental, and old fashioned, but both had great hearts and great camaraderie, not only for each other, but for all who knew them.

On 1 November my second stripe for promotion to lieutenant came through, and Gieves obliged in a couple of days. Our HQ had now been moved to Cumberland Place, and as the Intelligence (A-2) Section, of which we were now part had most of its officers staying at the Cumberland Hotel, it was all very cosy. Unfortunately the 12th Air Force was far less efficient than the Royal Navy, but we knew all that would change soon. And of course, it didn't. Much time was spent gathering useful information sheets, going to the Admiralty for photographs to copy, compiling talks, then translating them into American. We liaised with the RAF and the Army since both had useful intelligence for us. Because no one had given us very much instruction, we four naval aviators would spend a great deal of each day making our own plans, then going out to get the background material.

Eventually, with nothing further to do except wait, we took a few days' leave, and had hardly arrived home, before we were recalled. Things were moving. We went first to Liverpool, where we embarked in the trooper *Otranto* and lay out in midstream in the Mersey mist, learning just what it was like to be sailing in a convoy rather than our usual function of protecting them. We just prayed for good escorts, which finally arrived in the shape of 9 destroyers. Hearing that 820 had re-embarked in *Formidable*, I hoped they might provide our air escort. No such luck, they were already out there, and had covered the Algiers landings with panache and distinction two weeks ago, on 8 November. *Furious* had been at Oran, losing some aircraft to spirited French resistance, while out in the Atlantic at Casablanca, left to American forces, the invasion had been a breeze.

Eventually our convoy grouped up and sailed for Gibraltar, during which time we four learned the other end of the job. If ever we thought carriers were boring, we did not know we were born. Passage in a convoy is a painfully slow way of life, as we waddled along at 10 knots, hoping for action, yet getting none, other than fire and boat drills, daily 'formations' as the Americans call parades, and lectures on North Africa. To relieve our boredom, we gave talks on the Royal Navy, with emphasis on flying, taught them deck-hockey and organised concert parties. After ten days we finally arrived in Gibraltar on 4 December 1942, tying up at the detached mole, to find lying opposite us –*Formidable*! Having obtained leave from *Otranto*'s captain to visit, I repaired there smartly, ostensibly to obtain up-to-date technical information.

My old shipmates were glad to see me, some averring that as my departure had only been two months ago, they'd not realised that I'd gone. A few seniors had gone to form new squadrons, a few new 'bograts' had arrived to go through the well-known striving for acceptance. But noticeably the recent landings, hotly opposed in the British sector, had provided a 'blooding' of sorts, and already a few legends were being woven. My old friends 'Prune' Chambers and Jack Stokes had some hairy moments on 'C' beach, Algiers, being repeatedly fired upon by allegedly friendly guns. Alas, back in Britain, two old friends, Hughie Hunter and Jimmy Broadbent had both been killed in mid-air collisions instructing pupils. Whom the Gods love... . On a brighter note we heard that 'Lucky' Sutton had been awarded a bar to his DSC only two months later, doing sterling work with 826 Squadron for the 8th Army.

Furious' aircrews had taken a hammering at Oran, and next day, Colin Ennever and Ken Terry came over to *Otranto* with sad tales of the confusion there.

As night fell, a general alarm went out as Italian frogmen were captured penetrating the harbour boom defence nets. Naval divers inspected all hulls for limpet mines though none were discovered. Italian frogmen caused great inconvenience and delays to shipping in harbour and in the roads. Initially, it was believed that these raids were launched by a large parent submarine outside in Algeciras Bay. Dramatic laudatory and illustrated articles in the Italian magazines certainly fostered this illusion, misleading our intelligence people. The facts were so different and so obvious, but it took a very long time before the truth dawned and matters were rectified. When Italy entered the war in June 1940, an oil tanker had been scuttled in Algeciras Bay, less than a couple of miles from the harbour. Apart from resenting the occasional flow of oil from it, little notice was taken of the ship which to all intents and purposes was a wreck. However, the Italians, with extraordinary imagination, had converted it into a midget submarine and frogmen base, from which these very brave men ventured into

Gibraltar and operated virtually under our noses.

The airfield at Gibraltar had changed incredibly since our earlier days there. Now it had a very long runway, jutting into the Bay, capable of taking the largest aircraft, including B17 Flying Fortresses. Without it, Operation 'Torch' in North Africa would have been nearly impossible, at the very best difficult. Fortunately Major Chalk, Royal Engineers, was still there, and had been a guiding light in the construction, knowing the Rock like the back of his hand.

On 9 December, the North African part of our convoy left Gibraltar, soon arriving in Mers-el-Kebir, Oran. There, we disembarked, some-what inefficiently and God alone knows what a shambles it would have been if we had been opposed. The excess baggage carried by American units was incredible. There were boxes labelled 'typewriters', 'office equipment' and one, believe it or not, 'medals'.

I learned a new expression here, 'SNAFU', which means 'Situation normal, all fouled up' and it certainly applied to the next few days. Having no instructions, I held on to my identity as leader of four naval officers on loan to the US 12th Air Force. After all we HAD to belong to someone, and this at least got us fed and quartered. First we travelled to the French airfield at Tafaraoui by truck, which took most of the day, only to find that we should have been at the naval airfield of La Senia, where we finally arrived at dusk. We spent the night sleeping on the tiled barrack floor, wrapped in our one GI blanket. For the next few days it was all 'Snafu'. Nobody knew us or where we should go to find someone who did want us. Luckily I spotted an American lieutenant-colonel wearing a British DFC, and asked his advice. This turned out to be the redoubtable Larry Callahan who had flown with the Royal Flying Corps in World War I, and a greater anglophile one couldn't meet. He arranged for us to fly to Algiers, where he assured us we would be wanted, and as a parting present gave us each a roll of toilet paper, which he predicted was more precious than rubies. How right he was, the French equivalent was like wrapping paper.

I was overheard speaking French, and later that day was temporari-ly engaged as an interpreter with the French landlords of the airfield. Americans, I learned later, massacre foreign languages as well as English. As a result of this duty, we were invited later to a dance in the officers' mess, but unfortunately I became involved in a brawl with an American fighter pilot who had designs on the French nurse I was escorting. There is no memory of what happened, except that much later I woke up in the American hospital with a rather badly bruised face and a terrible black eye. I spent the night there, and on discharge next day went round the airfield looking for my assailant without success. A rather pleasant American named Barney Roche from New York said I was wasting my time, his compatriot had hit me from behind, and was being dealt with by his own colleagues.

Next day came our flight to Algiers, where the situation appeared more orderly, and we moved into the naval mess at the Hotal de la Régence, which housed the aircrew of a Walrus flight operating anti-submarine and air-sea rescue missions. We took a leisurely look at the city, which was quite beautiful, and aptly named from the Arabic 'El Jezhar' meaning 'The White'. None of the camel caravans we expected to see, just a modern city, almost in the category of any other Mediterranean port, though large numbers of Arabs in their traditional dress were in every quarter. Large numbers too of British sailors, mostly accompanied by the local talent. For once 'Jack' was getting in first.

Then up to the Allied Force Headquarters (AFHQ) at the Hotel St George, where we met our boss – Lieutenant-Commander John Roe – who was most upset that no one seemed to want to own us, and decided that Freddy Harsant and Alan Smith should return to Britain leaving Max Radford and I to cope with whatever work there was to be done. Max went on loan to the RAF, and spent many profitable months with No 38 Beaufighter squadron at Regehia who did need his knowledge of ship recognition, and put it to great use. As for myself, John suggested that I report frequently to AFHQ, and remain as RN liaison officer to the American Air Forces. Frankly, there were so many spare bodies in AFHQ on the hilltop that one could walk around there all day with a piece of paper in hand, and not have to justify one's existence. That is not to say that there was nobody working seriously – very many were – but there was an awful lot of surplus manpower that could have been better employed.

Most of my time for many months was spent working between the RN Intelligence Section and the A-2 of the 12th Air Force. I had offices in both HQs and could eat in both messes, living at the Régence, near the white mosque, around the corner from the Casbah. Though still imbued with drive and a desire to get on with the war, I never volunteered for anything, and am sure that I did useful work, but when meeting fellow naviators passing through, somehow felt slightly ashamed of what fate had handed me. However, most agreed that a 'lurk' like this came only once in a lifetime, so relax and enjoy it. So I did. The Army Transport section of the Royal Engineers had charge of motor transport, and a car was desirable, but not essential for my work, which entailed getting out to Maison Blanche airfield, Fort de l'Eau, Maison Carrée HQ and to various groups. Captain Cook found my request quite outrageous, but the sight of a couple of bottles of Johnny Walker produced a car almost magically – a 3½-litre Hotchkiss coupé – which gave me and my friends great opportunities to get out and see the countryside.

Eddie and Harry had now come to Algiers, and had rented an apartment, which was used as a dormitory for all friends passing through. My great friend was a young RN lieutenant of the engineering branch, 'Swede' Hansen, carroty of hair, and with a great desire to fly.

He offered in return, petrol and maintenance for my car, so naturally we became firm friends. Eddie and Harry liked him too, and many were the trips we made around the countryside, seeing Arab villages, Roman remains and so on. It so happened that we four were a reasonably quiet lot, not hankering after more than the occasional night out, but enjoying more a good dinner, at which the Algierian restaurants excelled, a few drinks and some discussion. L'Alsacienne was our favourite, and since Harry had now been promoted to major, Eddie to captain, the two lieutenants sheltered under their seniority. After all, was not Le Commandant a hero of La Grande Guerre? As also was Pierre, the *Maître d'Hôtel*.

As the British 1st Army and the Germans got themselves bogged down for the winter from the Atlas Mountains to the edge of the Sahara, so everything slowed down back to rear-echelon in Algiers. I made a few offensive trips with 12th Air Force reconnaissance aircraft, mainly to identify ships outside coastal waters, but nothing of any great excitement. The North African winter is a real winter of discontent, raining for weeks on end with no sign of a let-up, just as their summer is one of little cloud and a great deal of hot sunshine. Whereas our original welcome from the French had not been too warm, in fact definitely hostile, they now, like true Frenchmen accepted the reality, and many of their servicemen came to join us. As a result, my knowledge of French became most useful, especially when working with Americans, and I once had the temerity to give a lecture in French to a group of *aspirants*, or midshipmen, at the local naval college in Algiers – with a French lieutenant standing by as prompter, of course.

Chapter 15
Our Gallant Allies
in Algiers

On Christmas Eve 1942 all leave was suddenly cancelled, everyone being confined to barracks, ship and mess. The original rumour was that Marshal Pétain had been assassinated, but soon we learned the truth, that Admiral Darlan, governor of French Africa, had fallen to the assassin's bullet. Anyone's death is a tragedy, and murder more so, but the Admiral's decease solved an awful lot of problems, since he had always been somewhat suspect to the Allies. Unfortunately, this incident, plus an attempt by some extremists to plant a car-bomb near AFHQ caused the American Service Police, or 'Snowdrops' as they were called on account of their white helmets and webbing, to become even more uncompromising than usual. All cars had to park half a mile away from the Hotel St George, and all had to submit to challenges and searches. Unlike our military police the 'Snowdrops' fired first and challenged afterwards in many cases, and one night shot John Roe's driver, narrowly missing John. The death of his driver made John extremely cool with Americans after this, since he realised that no amount of protests would cut ice with the MP officers or the American top brass, which itself seemed somewhat reluctant to interfere where MPs were concerned. The advice even from Eddie and Harry was to 'back off – they'll get you for something else'. A great pity, yet later when I saw what the MPs did to their own, the advice was sound.

Since it now seemed that it would be ages before I once again sat in a naval aircraft's fragile cockpit, I decided that AFHQ should have the best possible information section on shipping and aircraft recognition. So over the next six months we worked to find every possible picture, photograph, sketch or likeness of every ship and aircraft in the Mediterranean theatre, obviously majoring on Allied and enemy, though neutrals were included if they might be met. We scrounged an epidiascope (optical projector), and made others. We borrowed time from a mobile printing works to produced 4-colour maps for briefing aircrews, and got them to print recogition posters. I was lucky enough to have an excellent assistant in Staff Sergeant A Z ('Bert') Lewis from

Daytona Beach, Florida. Later along came that treasure, Winston Potter, who could not only draw cartoons, he had a zany sense of humour, completely in tune with my own. This was invaluable, since we had long decided that aircrew get bored looking at pictures, so we gave amusing cartoons and rhymes at the top of our posters.

This was not original, but stemmed back to our training days at Whale Island, when some lewd gunner's mate was lecturing on the cordite charge for a starshell. 'Nah then,' he said, as all good GIs preface their words of wisdom, 'if I tell you this is an elongated, castellated cylindrical object, you won't remember it, will yer? But if I tell yer it looks like a donkey's walloper, you dirty-minded buggers will remember, won't yer?' And I did, and do. Even today I can draw a cordite starshell charge from memory. So we introduced humour into our offerings – not so crude as that, but pungent. Once, I recollect, after a lot of Junkers 52 tri-motor transports had been shot down in April 1943, trying to evacuate troops from Tunisia, we had to do a rush job, as a lot more Ju 52s would obviously be used in similar attempts. We had to give it a crisp piece of limerick-like doggerel to get attention paid to the photographs and sketch. Winston thought a minute, started to write and said 'How's that?' I forget the first line or two, but the final line said 'It's absolute lunacy to fly them in Tunisie'. It was most gratifying to find the the humour did work. Our gallant American Allies were obviously learning.

Some weeks after this, a combat training school was started at La Senia, and the ship and aircraft recognition school bcame my charge. However, all our compilation was done in Algiers as well as our printing and distribution to every American squadron in North Africa, copies being sent also to other theatres. In six months we also had instructions to send to British squadrons in North Africa. Later Frank Howie requested copies for the FAA in Malta, and Naval Officer-in-Command, Algiers for British ships. We were a success! After we had been recognised, we were approached one day by the Army to compile a series on tanks, but this, I felt was straining the naval aviator's versatility a little too far, and we said we would comply, but only if they couldn't get somebody a little more familiar with this arm of the service. We never heard again so I assume they did.

In mid-1943 I was over at Service Command, trying to get some pictures of gliders for a rush job prior to the Sicilian landings. The major in charge, said 'Like to help you, friend, but I guess you'd better go see Lootenant Woods of the British Royal Navy over at Shell Building. He's the expert!' I almost cried with laughter – and so did the major. But it was good to be recognised after all the hard work we'd put in.

It was difficult finding one's way around the US Army Air Force. To begin with, there was the language problem. Most Americans think they speak English, but there were New Englanders who couldn't understand their colleagues from the Deep South. Additionally there was a huge number of National Guard officers, equivalent to our Territorial Army or RNVR. But there was no distinction on the uniform from regulars, except that the reservists seemed to have higher ranks and more medal ribbons; notwithstanding that few had ever heard a shot fired in anger. Also, as I came to discover later, there were many 'pros' in the Army Air Force, disguised as officers. Many of the intelligence officers were in fact doing research for after the war. I knew several who worked for Shell or Standard Oil, and believe that they were listening and noting the possibilities of exploring and drilling in Algeria as soon as the last shot was fired. There were many politicians too, in the rear echelons, officers who were busy making contacts with the same objective as the oil men in other commercial areas. This is not to say that the British forces did not, but at least we were a little more energetic at getting the war over first.

Another strange department of the US Army was the Counter Intelligence Corps or CIC as it was more commonly known. I knew many of the officers, and a pleasant bunch they were. Unfortunately, somewhere, somebody injected from time to time a scenario which came straight from the pen of Al Capp, author of the 'Little Abner' comic strip. For example, during the summer of 1943, a series of mysterious explosions took place in Algiers, mainly in the harbour area. One day a cargo of land-mines was being unloaded from a ship when a thunderous detonation occurred, shattering windows right up to the St George Hotel, several miles away. A short time later, maybe ten days, an ammunition train caught fire in the goods yard by the harbour, just as a passenger train full of prisoners of war was passing it. Hardly had this mess been cleared up when another merchant ship, this time loaded with chemicals, caught fire in the docks, and rapidly the flames engulfed the ship. The British destroyer *Arrow* took a tow line, and moved the blazing ship into the outer harbour, where an explosion occurred, and some blazing debris caused great damage to the destroyer. In all three happenings and there was great loss of life.

Noting the coincidence, CIC moved in, and instructed half a dozen of their sergeants to disguise themselves in plain clothes, to mingle with the civilian population and get some leads. 'Plain clothes' was the understatement of the year. The NCOs to a man sported wide-brimmed low-crowned fedora hats. Their suits were unmistakably of the zoot variety, with peg-top trousers, and many of the wearers sported large cigars. As they tried to mingle with the Algerians, the locals scuttled sideways like crabs – there was never any possibility of contact.

Later, one of my CIC friends heard that a lieutenant in the paymaster branch, who happened to be quite a legal personality in civilian life in England, was having an affair with a Polish countess, who, presumably because she was Polish, was 'under surveillance' by the CIC. I was asked to effect an introduction to my friend the paymaster for my American friend in CIC. A tricky situation, but one with which I coped, albeit with some sense of being a double Judas. The meeting with 'the subject' (as CIC referred to my paymaster friend) took place in the bar of the Alletti Hotel on Boulevard Carnot, a favourite cocktail rendezvous. The American arrived in 'plain' clothes, and indicated a quiet corner where we should sit, then after drinks had been ordered, he asked the paymaster lieutenant – I swear, out of the corner of his mouth – if he was having an affair with the lady in question. Not even bothering to taste his drink, the Englishman said in a loud voice, 'Fuck off and mind your own fucking business'. End of conversation. Happily, both realised that I was an innocent go-between and bore no grudge.

The top US airman in North Africa was Major General James H Doolittle – 'Jimmy' to his men, a great character and a fearless pilot, who had led the 16 twin-engine B25 Mitchells from the US Navy's carrier *Hornet* to bomb Tokyo in April 1942. Loved by all with whom he came into contact, he didn't seem quite comfortable in this appointment, and was eventually replaced by General Carl ('Tooey') Spaatz, less popular and less well-known. Jimmy came back to London to command the 15th and 8th Air Forces, and later went on to Okinawa with the 8th. After the war, he received an honorary KCB from King George VI. The two senior executive aviators of the 12th Air Force, Colonels Hoyt Vandenberg and Philip Cochrane, were also at our HQ in the Shell Building. Both were excellent administrators and pilots, Vandenberg going eventually to the top rank in the US Air Force; 'Phil' Cochrane became a legend early in his own lifetime, and was depicted in the American coloured comic strip of the time 'Terry and the Pirates' as the heroic pilot 'Flip Corkin'. Despite this, he went on to the Burma theatre to head the air side of Wingate's Chindits, contributing greatly to the eventual defeat of the Japanese.

Life was busy, if nothing else. One week would be spent in Algiers, the next in Oran, with talks to squadrons all over North Africa. In the ten months I spent with 12th USAF, I visited Nouvion; Relezon; Casablanca; Ber-Reschid; Ras-el-Mar (Fez); Blida; Bône; Setif; Tizi Ouzou; Biskra; Bou Saada; Constantine; Djidjelli; Bizerta and Philippeville. That's from memory, there were many others whose names I forget and don't appear on maps any more. Fortunately a good contact had been made with the 51st Troop Carrier Wing with whom I had shared the convoy trip out, and who owed me favours, since they, alas, were 'dry' while I could obtain the hard stuff on board. The same applied to life ashore. They could buy liquor of inferior quality at the most exorbitant prices, and probably cut in strength, while friendly neighbour Woods became the 'hooch peddler' to the 12th Air Force among other things. Fortunately I had friends in the ships who could find me a couple of cases a month in return for American cigarettes, cigars and dollars. Everyone was happy, and I don't think I made a cent on the deals – it was oil to keep the wheels going. So far as the 51st was concerned, they would transport me or my friends anywhere, anytime.

The 51st's CO was an unbelievable character named Major Luke Williamson. One of the first sergeant-pilots in the US Army Air Corps, he was one of a trio of precision flyers known as 'The Flying Trapeze', and with the then Captain Claire Chennault and Sergeant Billy McDonald, dazzled millions across the States between the years 1933 and 1936 with incredibly daring aerobatics. He came from a place called Ninety-Six in South Carolina, was as Southern as hominy grits and loved fighting. He was then about 45, which seemed incredibly old to my 24 years, and affected riding breeches, leather high boots, and of all things, a swagger-cane. He professed to hate Limeys, but made a concession in my case because he claimed I was half Yankee anyway, being a Bostonian, and it was some time before I deduced that he thought the English Boston was named after the one in Massachusetts. His men adored him, he knew them all by name, and claimed he could outfight and outdrink and out-many-other-things all of them. The men, of course, allowed him to have this conceit. Luke claimed to speak French with a fair degree of proficiency. One evening this was put to the test. We went out from Maison Blanche to a small restaurant at Sidi Ferruch, where Luke entered and said 'Bongswah madame, mongsew-er, je ver le menyew'. Like a good hostelier the patron allowed him this, and played along with Luke's execrable French. Luke than ordered the speciality of the restaurant, which was no great shakes, but neat and clean. 'Je ver' he declaimed 'votter omelette doo mayzon mais avec dooz oofs'. The patronne looked surprised 'Douze oeufs?' 'Oui' said Luke, 'dooz'. So obvious was it that Le Commandant was the boss-ganger that she didn't argue, and Luke got his omelette with 12 eggs. He ate it, commenting only that 'these goddam Frogs don't understand their own language – 'dooz' means 'two' in Frog-talk'.

What hair he had left was red, to match his short-fused temper, which flared without warning. One evening a rather plummy English half-colonel requested transport from Maison Blanche to his HQ up near, but not too near, the front. Luke said 'Sorry, Colonel' and stated loud and clear in my hearing that he had no planes available. I knew he had, but it was none of my business. The colonel remonstrated, but to no avail, and after ten minutes' argument he departed with a last admonition from Luke to 'get some orders from Montgomery', and then he'd see what he could do. The colonel was not amused, and I was trying to pretend I was also having trouble with Luke. About half an hour later a bedraggled lance-corporal of the Black Watch came shambling into the control tower asking if he could have a lift back to his unit. It appeared he had got stoned the night before, missed transport, and was in deadly fear of being picked up by the the MPs for being AWOL if not a deserter. 'OK son,' said Luke,'Red!' – calling to 'Red' Harrison – 'take him in the pisser'. The 'pisser' was a light aircraft kept for local flying, a Reliant if my memory serves me well. I thought it timely to remind Luke that he had just turned down a lieutenant-colonel and given a lift to a lance-corporal, which didn't seem quite reasonable. 'Woody', he said, fixing me with a face the colour of a Turner sunset, 'We want fighting men up at the front, not goddam paper-shufflers!' They don't make 'em like Luke any more. I used to love listening to him telling tales of his days with Claire Chennault in China, working for Chiang-Kai-shek or in the American Volunteer Group in Burma. To live his life and to attain 45 years of it, you just had to be tough.

His 2 i/c was Captain 'Scupper' Geyer, a younger edition of Luke, and by many they would be taken for brothers. Months later I nearly shared the same grave with 'Scupper'. All his men were characters: 'Rowdy' Dow, the quartermaster and a warrant officer regular; Logan, small, and known to Luke as 'La petite Logan'; 'Red' Harrison was another; Max Schmitten; Ossy Warner; even Orland Wages the catering officer was cast in the same mould. One day I had to get to Oran in a hurry, and Luke called to 'Red' Harrison to take me in a Dakota, DC3; I protested that the 'pisser' would do, a C47 would use too much gas. Luke said 'Red' was better on the C47, the 'pisser' wasn't really available. So off we went, and Lieutenant Watkins, an RNVR engineer, came with us for the trip, a mess-mate who hadn't flown much before. We took off, and shortly began to climb over the foothills of the Atlas Mountains, when 'Red' asked if I'd like to sit up in the co-pilot's seat. There he was, smoking his usual and forbidden stogie. Just to converse, I asked 'Where did you qualify as a pilot, 'Red', civilian airlines or military?' Removing the cigar, 'Red' replied, 'I didn't, I got washed out at flying school.' Fighting back a rising panic, and hoping that Watkins wouldn't hear and start jumping out, I managed to ask 'Then how come you're flying this monster?' 'Well, y'see Luke wants me to get some more practice in, and he will then recommend me for another try at getting my wings'. In fairness, it must be said that Red's flying was impeccable, his landings excellent, but had there been any alternative, I would have used it to return to Algiers. This flight would not have sounded good at the inquest. I never told Watkins until about a year later, when we met in Madras. He nearly wet himself then, after all that time. But 'Red' did get his wings.

Another unforgetable character was Lev Corning, who claimed to hail from Texas, though most Texans claimed he came from Arizona. Lev squatted cowboy fashion to chat and had the most incredible collection of gamey aphorisms, so memorable that I can recall most of them today: my favourite – 'Busy as a one-armed paper-hanger with crabs'; 'Hot as a fresh-fucked sheep in a pepper patch OR Hot as a whore's dream'; 'Cold as a witch's tit OR Cold as a well-digger's arse in Alaska'. If broke, Lev was 'Clean as an angel's drawers OR Clean as a choirboy's thoughts'. 'Randy as a butcher's dog' was another of his expressions.

All of them seemed to have a double superlative, though sometimes they came from American folklore. For instance, one day at briefing, Lev, the briefing officer, gave a straight course to the target without diversions, which was unusual. One navigator asked 'A straight course, Captain?' and Lev replied, 'Straight as an Indian running to shit', which was beyond me, so I asked Lev for a translation. It appears that Indians always run in straight lines, but in this predicament, in a very straight one.

Naturally, all our American friends were not characters of this stripe. Hamilton Darby, the third Musketeer to Harry and Eddie was an architect from Long Island, and as quiet and pleasant as any architect you'd meet anywhere. Ray Holden, with the looks of Clint Eastwood, was about my age, and from Rutland, Vermont. Remaining in the Air Force after the war, I last heard of him as a colonel in the Pentagon. Ray and Pat Hoolahan were known as 'Little Abners in reverse' since most of their free time was spent chasing girls, French, American or British. Egbert Blackman had worked in Hollywood, and never denied being a producer, which he wasn't. It was too useful for rounding up the girls. Egbert's party-piece was to play the piano, which he did beautifully, but one piece only – 'Liebestraum'. Asked for an encore, he would play it again and again. It was hard to believe, but apparently in the Depression, he took a job as a piano salesman, and figured it would help is he could play a piece of music as a demonstration. So Egbert learned to play 'Liebestraum' by numbering the keys. People to whom this story has been told find it hard to believe, but I knew and partied with Eggie for almost a year, and never at many parties did I ever hear him play any other piece of music!

The Adjutant of A-2 was Bill Rice, a tall New Yorker not addicted to modesty. In the early days at Algiers his high-handed methods accompanied by a certain amount of 'bull' meant transfers for those who wouldn't play ball. One such was a Lieutenant Eddie Hillman, not the brightest of intelligence officers, but a millionaire who had married 'June' the former Lady Inverclyde. For some unspecified reason Bill took a great dislike to Hillman, and had him transferred back to the States for 'reclassification', whatever that might mean. Hillman, who was then approaching middle-age was heartbroken, as in all probability the only unselfish act in his own life, was in forsaking his chainstore business for this less comfortable life overseas. He pleaded with Bill, and doubtless offered all sorts of inducements for the transfer to be cancelled but Bill was adamant, and off went Eddie Hillman. Some months later, when at Casablanca, I met him again, on the staff of a general. It would have given me great pleasure to have told Bill, but by this time some of his own malfeasances had come to light and he himself had been sent to Pantellaria, a posting approximately equivalent to being Head Screw at Dartmoor.

Another celebrity frequently encountered at Maison Blanche was Elliot Roosevelt, who flew Mosquitoes in the Photo Reconnaissance Unit. In early 1943, when the US presidential campaign was beginning to warm up for the 1944 election, there was great anxiety, it seemed, to have Elliot complete his 25 missions so that he would qualify automatically for his Distinguished Flying Cross, apparently to aid father's campaign. This is no criticism of Elliot, a lieutenant-colonel and a courageous pilot, but it shed a little light on the cold-blooded attitudes of the American political machine.

What did give me considerable pleasure was the way my FAA and USAAF friends mixed together socially and enjoyably. *Formidable* came into Algiers from time to time, and 820 were disembarked then to Blida, an airfield in the Atlas foothills. When the ship went to Oran, they flew ashore to La Senia, Thus I was meeting Pat Chambers, Peter Large, 'Dusty' Miller, 'Doc' Burke, 'Tiny' Devonald, 'Thos' While, Ivan, 'Bushy' and 'Wallie', the CO, fairly often. In the cities, they had their own amusement. On the airfields the RN had access to hard liquor but the Americans' food was much better. Thus each needed the other, or so I thought, and arranged for the aviators to get to know each other, which they did, enjoying each others' company and 'goodies', as well as organising ship and squadron visits and flying with each other.

Walking along the main street of Algiers, Rue Michelet, one lunchtime with Patrick Chambers, we were approached by one of the hordes of professional beggars who were having a boom in their business due to the flow of Allied troops through the city. This worthy was one of the most revoltingly dirty Arabs imaginable, and would probably have given even Macbeth a nasty turn. Wearing a decidedly off-white djellabyah with an embroidered chéchia (soft round cap) on his head, he asked our charity. We each gave him a franc, whereupon he requested a cigarette, which was also given, and would probably be sold for much more than the two francs, so carefully was it stored in the headgear. His ugliness had to be seen to be believed, the least attractive part being his eyes which were the reverse of crossed, in other words, rather skate-like, and looking out of the far corners. Marty Feldman would have been jealous.

We walked on a few yards, when suddenly 'Prune' said 'Wait a minute, I must see that again'. In vain I protested that he would get taken for further largesse, so I waited and a few moments later was rejoined by my companion. 'What the hell did you want with him?' I asked, 'Couldn't get over those eyes, old boy,' replied 'Prune', 'What a wonderful observer he would have made, with 180 degree vision either side. He would only have to turn round once, instead of four times like you normal blokes, to see all round the horizon!'.

It was hardly surprising that the Arabs rebelled against the French after the war, finally winning their independence in 1962. Living near the docks, one saw in the mornings the most primitive sights. Many Arabs slept in shop doorways the year round, and it can be very cold in winter. The 'chain-gang' of manacled malefactors was marched down to the docks each morning, to work at unloading the ships, getting all the worst jobs to do. In fact, they didn't mind this too much, since many Allied soldiers and sailors would be unloading and checking cargo as well, and would see that the guards didn't inflict too much punishment on them, and ensure that they had enough food to eat while working on the ships. What we didn't see was what extra chastisement they received when back in the slammer. But the French colonial officials weren't rough only with the Arabs, they treated their European malefactors with equal cruelty. One of the mechanics working for 'Swede' Hansen, Henri, had tried to escape from Algiers a couple of years earlier to join de Gaulle, had been captured and given torture with lighted cigarette ends and electricity through his genitals. As Henri said, when revealing his scars – maybe the Nazis would have been kinder.

Colonel 'Red' Smith was chatting with me one day at the Combat Training School, and with his 2 i/c, Major Clint Frank, when 'Thos' White flew ashore in the drogue-towing Swordfish. 'Red' just could not believe that this was the aircraft which had wrought so much havoc among Axis warships. Like someone seeing the Crown Jewels for the first time, 'round his eyes with wonder grew', as he examined every part of the aircraft. 'Thos' had just shipped his first stripe, but still looked his 20 years –just. 'Red' wanted to fly the 'Stringbag', but 'Thos' could not allow this, but did take him and Clint for a flip. It was hours before 'Red' could stop shaking his head with disbelief. Some time later, at AFHQ, when 826 Albacores, under Bobby Bradshaw were due to attack Bizerta Lake which harboured some minor Axis warships, 'Red' tried to apply the veto and send his B25s instead. In the event, 826 sank several thousand tons of shipping there without loss, a mission which the heavier and less manoeuvrable Mitchells could not have done so well.

Clint Frank was a beautifully-built man, chest like a barrel, equipped with a surprising turn of speed on the baseball diamond, but wore very thick-lensed spectacles. One day, coming out of the showers, he was groping for his towel, when I advanced a somewhat left-handed compliment to the effect that it was a pity his eyes were defective, as he would have made a great football player. A roar of laughter went up from the other occupants of the shower-room, and I learned later that Clint was one of the superstars of American football, playing for Yale, and being selected for the 'All America' team – a mythical side which never plays anybody, but is selected by the press as the team which would, if it played, be the best available. Fortunately my blushes were saved by Clint's assuming this to be English humour.

One day at La Senia, I had returned from Tafaraoui at dusk, when an air raid siren sounded. A convoy just arrived had attracted enemy attention. Flying control was not too well organised with British Spitfires, American P38 Lightnings and P39 Bell Aircobras having their own flying control procedures and signals. Suddenly there was an enormous noise and explosion. Hurrying down to the operations tent, it seemed that a Spitfire and an Aircobra had taken off from opposite ends of the runway, colliding and exploding. It was horrible, and the fire-truck was having great problems in putting out the flames. 'My God,' I said to the controller, 'they must have been killed instantly'. 'No', he replied, 'thats them over there'. And sure enough it was, both alive, and apparently suffering for nothing worse than the fright of their lives. By some quirk of chance, both pilots had their hoods open, and had both been ejected by the force of the impact. Truth indeed is sometimes stranger than fiction.

Allied air strength was being built up fast in the rear areas, and I was asked one day to go to Ras-el-Mar, near Fez, to talk to a newly-arrived group. Having heard that this airfield was in Riff country, where it was not safe to wander outside the camp perimeter at night, I asked it I could have a 'Goolie Chit'. 'A what?' enquired the Air Executive. I explained that the Riffs were still a wild lot, and given to somewhat primitive and painful customs with infidel prisoners. A quick check with the airfield at Fez confirmed that my suspicion was correct, but not very likely. As it happened, I had with me a scarf – and still have – which was the 'Goolie Chit' issued in Eastern Fleet, promising gold galore for the return of the wearer unharmed and physically intact. In a matter of hours, and probably in fun, 'Goolie Chits' were being printed for American aviators who might encounter unfriendly desert warriors and so qualify for the gelding stakes.

Late in April 1943, the Combat Training School moved back from La Senia to Casablanca, the war in North Africa being almost won. The 8th Army was in hot pursuit of the *Afrika Korps* from the east, and now that the winter rains were over, the 1st Army was advancing to form the Tunisian anvil for Monty's hammer. The atmosphere in training became more relaxed, and I spent a week in Casablanca setting up my part of the school, and training the instructors, since the routine had become fully established, and an occasional visit was all that would be required of me, to check and advise. We arrived in a C47 one mid-afternoon, just as dark clouds were sweeping in from the east. The airfield was in a modest uproar, and eventually I gathered that the 'clouds' were in fact hordes of locusts approaching. Never having seen these biblical insects before I got into the 'Goofers' at the control tower. It was quite unforgettable to see these large creatures, some as big as sparrows, defoliate everything in a matter of seconds. Trees lost their leaves as one watched, grass was devoured faster than a mower could operate. Most intriguing was the sight of Arabs rushing out and beating all round with sticks to kill the unwelcome visitors, which seemed a little late in the day. 'Not at all' said one of my neighbours, 'locusts are delectable when cooked'. Good luck to the locust-eaters of Casablanca. It's definitely an acquired taste.

Returning to Algiers, I was sent for by Captain A G Talbot of *Formidable*, who asked if I would be interested in a permanent job with AFHQ, looking after all naval aircraft based in North Africa, whether ship-or land-based, and wherever in the Mediterranean they might operate. Having served under Arthur George for a few weeks, I felt I could answer respectfully without giving offence. Obviously the war would continue for some time in this theatre, and the present job, though executively responsible to John Roe, left me free to pursue many varied interests with the American, French and British Forces' training requirements. It was very interesting work, the lifestyle good, and boredom seldom arose. Above all, I wanted to get back to shipborne squadron life, and a hiccup such as this could upset it all. So, with considerable respect, I declined the offer, but felt from that day forward I was being watched carefully in the context of 'Baby's very quiet, see what he's doing and stop him immediately'.

The medium bomber wings of the 12th Air Force, consisting of B25 Mitchell and B26 Marauders, called for our services quite frequently, since they were becoming more involved with low-level attacks on shipping in the Tunisian, Sicilian and Italian harbours, and some of the heavy groups of B17 Fortresses were going for harbours such as Naples, Cagliari and Taranto, where the remnants of the Italian Fleet were to be found as well as supply vessels. So damaging were the attacks by daylight raiders that most Axis shipping was pushed through by night, across the narrow part of the Mediterranean between Sicily and Tunis, well-known to us two years previously when we were pushing convoys through to Malta. To balance this, the air strength in Malta had been stepped up, and aided whenever possible from other bases in North Africa and the Western Desert, almost non-stop attacks were made, though on a much lesser scale than the bombing by the RAF and US 8th Air Force in Western Europe.

One day I was visiting a wing of medium bombers near Tebessa, on the borders of Algeria and Tunisia. Toilet and ablution facilities were rather primitive as a rule, but this airfield had an enterprising young officer who had decided to improve matters. He had managed to scrounge a large section of concrete pipe about 2ft in diameter normally used for sewage or water-carrying in cities. About 18ft in length, the pipe had suitably-sized holes cut into it at intervals along the top, with an inflow at one end and an exit at the other. Toilet seats had then been attached, thus making a '12-holer' and affording, by hessian screens, at least a little privacy for such an intimate daily ritual. Conveniently nearby was a spring, and a water-wheel had been constructed in the Egyptian fashion, driven by a perambulating donkey, alleged to have been pensioned off from one of the seamier bordellos of Alexandria.

It was a comfortable latrine – too comfortable in fact, so that incumbents were seen to enter equipped with magazines and *Stars and Stripes*, the US Army daily newspaper. Following the advice of Lem Putt in *The Specialist* (an early paperback on his task), the hygiene officer (for such was now his title) roughed up the seats a little to discourage too long a period of meditation. The users replied by taking in sandpaper and smoothing down the seats. It looked like being a drawn-out struggle until one morning the hygiene officer hit upon a novel idea. Hearing that the compartments had been occupied for an unreasonable length of time, he took a piece of wood about 12in long, 3in wide and ½in thick weighted it so that one side would always be on top and to the top side he affixed some cotton waste which he soaked liberally in high octane fuel. This was lowered into the water inlet end and a match applied to the cotton waste. A succession of ear-splitting screams rent the air as the miniature fireship sailed down the line. 'Operation Burnham on Crouch' ensured that there was no more time-wasting in the toilets.

The Walrus squadron had moved from Algiers so the Régence mess was now mainly salt-horse and 'pussers', with a few specialists in shipping movement and control – no one to talk to on matters other than shop. I took an apartment, rations being issued by the Régence and supplemented by local purchase. 'Woody's Place' became the centre for visiting aviators. On the eastern corner of Boulevard Carnot, it overlooked the harbour, a splendid view except during air raids when we were liable to get overthrows from our own or enemy aircraft as well as the local ack-ack, noted for its enthusiasm rather than its accuracy. At such time, ships would loose off not only guns but also smokepots to obscure the docks, the smell of which lingered for days. Fortunately the frequency of air raids had diminished considerably.

Sitting on the verandah one lunchtime, we saw a B26 Marauder come in low over the harbour, presumably heading for Blida, though the approach would normally have been from further west, near to Guyotville. Suddenly it went into a stalled spin at 2000ft, from which, with the high wing-loading of this type of aircraft, a recovery was quite impossible. An enormous splash followed by an explosion, then petrol ignited on the water. There was no survivor from the South African crew.

A frequent visitor to the apartment was Bobby Bradshaw, commanding 826 Albacore Squadron, then moving up and down the coast between Blida and Bône depending upon targets of opportunity. With Brian Cooper and Gaston Revett, he came frequently to AFHQ. Tall and handsome, he joined 826 in 1939 as a midshipman, and was now sole survivor of the original pilots. Social life in Algiers was good, and improving as the war receded. Bobby was fancied by a rather strapping lady of my acquaintance, known to her friends as 'La Marquesa'. One evening she was endeavouring unsuccessfully to lure Bobby away for a quiet tête-a-tête, with untypical resistance on his part. Out of the corner of my mouth I asked him what the problem was, and it appeared that Bobby had learned something we had not told him – 'La Marquesa' was an amateur lady wrestler, and though curious, Bobby was not anxious for an amorous experience culminating in a Boston Crab. I seem to remember that Ray offered to step into the ring as substitute.

Another drawback to the apartment, apart from air raids, was being near to the Foreign Legion barracks, where reveille sounded at 0500, and until 0600 there was musical PT. I say 'musical', but the French military bugle was never my favourite instrument. Naked to the waist, summer and winter, the Legionnaires exercised at the double, rain, wind or shine. At 0800 they had a colour parade – the equivalent of our divisions, and all of this took place seven days of every week. Rather like the national music of any country, it was very interesting at first, but palled quickly. So far as we were concerned, the only remedy was to close the shutters or wear earplugs.

'Swede' called me one morning from his base engineer's office in some excitement, asking me to call with car soonest. Some days previously he had discovered in his rope and chain store a 5-gallon demi-john all encased in wicker, and supposed it to be part of his stores. However, he had become suspicious when nothing appeared on vouchers, opened it, to find it contained rum. This he had decanted into smaller gallonage jars, and replaced the original with coloured water. He waited several days but nothing happened, and now decided that the owner (probably a rating who had stolen the rum from RN stores) had finally got windy and decided to leave it. I am glad to say that we had several very enjoyable parties on this windfall.

We had many girlfriends at this time. Juliette, whom I inherited from one of the intelligence officers at AFHQ, was a splendid girl, but anxious to leave Algeria, and after some months she broke a date to say that she was now engaged to an American major. When she met him and how I'll never know, because she was with me most nights of the week. Her friends Simone and Suzy were also good fun, and strongly attached to the Royal Navy, Suzy preferring 'Swede', and Simone HMS *Formidable*. After Juliette forsook me, I met Lucille, a Corsican, black-haired and tall, beautiful, but with a fierce temper. She also walked like a cow with foot-rot, but that could be cured in time. Unfortunately she didn't like me for some incredible reason, and played me off alternatively with 'Swede' or Ray Holden, whom I warned to be cautious since I'd heard that Corsican girls wore knives in their stockings to protect their honour. 'Not to worry', said Ray, 'in Vermont when I'm around they carry a set of carvers'.

Some time later, our landlady at the apartment revealed some hitherto unsuspected talent. Married to a husband some 25 years older than her 35 to 40 years, she had obviously more love than he could handle. Several of my trusted friends were given keys to my apartment, but I'd forgotten that she had one too, and was almost raped one afternoon. I say 'raped' but as my old friend 'Flossie' Willett was wont to remark, 'the word suggests a certain amount of unwillingness, and is therefore inappropriate'. It seemed she was anxious to share her love too, since 'Swede' and others were similarly surprised.

As the summer came along, we spent many off-duty hours at Guyotville, about 20 miles west of Algiers, near the spot where General Mark Clark landed from HM submarine *Seraph* prior to the invasion to confer with Robert Murphy, the US Algiers ambassador. We would swim and sunbathe there, taking a meal at the Normandie Restaurant, beneath which Clark and party had taken refuge while the police searched for them. Unfortunately this became a very popular rendez-vous for officers. For no obvious reason aviators had a problem ashore with submariners – perhaps too many of them had been attacked by friendly aircraft. One night we had provocation, ending in a bout of fisticuffs, and though quite amicably settled, I was to remember it a few weeks later.

'Swede' Hansen's opposite number was Lieutenant (E) Geddes, who was building a 'Flying Bedstead', a high-powered sports machine based on a truck chassis, with about three times the horsepower of any known car. Its only snag was that in cornering at high speed, the rear wheels tended to leave the ground in a startling manner. Geddes, no whit deterred, built an extra seat over the differential, rather in the manner of a Lancaster rear-gunner, but facing forward. Having rapidly exhausted his 'volunteers', Geddes now had to resort to detailing men under punishment for this exhilarating experience. Now he joined our beach outings, and there was always an unsuspecting mug conned into keeping the rear end on the deck. One day Suzy's mother was shopping in Rue Michelet, the main street of Algiers, when Geddes' monster appeared with an ear-splitting roar. In the bucket seat and apparently enjoying the ride was Suzy, whose prompt two-week grounding by mum severely upset 'Swede's' social life.

Native car-thieves became bolder as life returned to normal. Once I had the car stolen but recovered, later some technically-trained Arabs removed the engine, which was replaced and bonnet-locks fitted. Then one night, as I was leaving Eddie's apartment, an attempt was being made to remove a bumper, with one rogue, apparently a lookout, asleep in the back seat. It wasn't so much what they stole, but the foul smell they left behind. Like that of the skunk, it persisted for days.

With the surrender of the remaining *Afrika Korps* at Cape Bon on 12

May 1943, preparations for the next step, obviously Sicily, went ahead. Shortly Algiers would become a backwater, so I began to elbow John Roe for my return to carriers. Just about this time *Formidable* came in and disembarked aircraft to Blida, where I learned sadly that Peter Large and Eddie Pipe had crashed into the sea at night with depth charges on. Exploding, they had killed Peter outright and a very badly-wounded Eddie spent three days in a dinghy exposed to the North African sun before being picked up fortuitously by a French fishing trawler. Years later I tried to meet Eddie in Opotiki, his New Zealand home, but he didn't want to relive those days. We didn't meet, but his undergraduate daughter told me sadly that he was still suffering pain from wounds of 30 years ago.

A little good news (or so we thought at the time) was a radio announcement 'that the new high performance torpedo dive-bombing reconnainssance aircraft, the Barracuda, was fast coming off the production line, and the aircraft carriers would soon be re-equipped with this modern aircraft'. In those days we were looking forward to a change from biplanes. We were due for a lot of surprises!

Later in May, my younger brother, Tony, appeared on the scene, stationed at Fort de l'Eau, just outside the city and on the way to Maison Blanche. He had joined the Army under age, and even now, a lance-corporal, was only a month over 18 years of age, which made me feel very protective. In the event, I need not have lost any sleep, since he had learned rapidly and knew all the ways of 'dodging the column'. As he was currently enjoyed a few days' leave, he stayed at my apartment and was able to see a few of the sights and sounds of Algiers which as a 'squaddy' he might not otherwise have experienced. For the next couple of months he stayed with me whenever he had leave, and I think we saw more of each other than in the previous ten years.

So we came to the month of July, with lots of huddles and conferences going on all over the place, and especially at AFHQ in the Hotel St George. Three days later came the invasion of Sicily.

A surprise visitor about this time was Bobby Bradshaw, who was going home on leave, and taking passage in a cruiser. He had been in the Eastern Mediterranean rather longer than normal and was due for relief. Bobby himself professed to dislike leave, and usually spent such periods flying with the RAF or USAAF, much to the annoyance of his seniors. It was a sensible step, squadron COs of his experience and ability were rare and to be prized. Though not exactly under supervision, for it was known that he might slip off to Maison Blanche, Algiers, to fly some new type of aircraft, he had to give his word to be back on board by 1700, as the ship was leaving at 1900 for home. Since it was likely that we would not see each other again for some time, we decided to make a day of it, and I took off, leaving Staff Sergeant Lewis in charge.

Regrettably, I never again met Bobby during the war, though I followed his career with considerable interest. One of his later and more renowned exploits occurred in August 1944 when the Canadian escort carrier *Nabob* was torpedoed by *U-354* in the Arctic. Bobby insisted on being catapulted off the damaged and listing ship to search for, and attack the U-boat, despite repeated warnings from the flightdeck engineer that he could not guarantee that the catapult would operate properly, and could well just simply slide the Avenger aircraft over the bows and into the sea.

But all went well, and after searching unsuccessfully for several hours, though preventing the enemy from administering the coup de grâce, he finally crash landed back on the steeply-listing flightdeck, *Nabob* eventually making it successfully into port. For this courageous and voluntary episode, Bobby was awarded a second bar to his DSC. His successive senior officers would, I am sure, have echoed the words of a popular song of that time – 'You might have been a headache but you never were a bore'.

At the end of July 1943 Flying Officer Davies became my assistant, and I began to train him with a view to his taking over when I returned to the Royal Navy. Though relatively inexperienced and a 'Penguin' or non-aviator, he learned quickly what we had to achieve, and within a few weeks had met all my contacts, so that he would have recourse to hands which would steer him in the right direction and enable him to check for accuracy before bursting into print. Master Sergeants Winston Potter and Bert Z Lewis had come along splendidly, and given a few fundamental details could be relied upon to produce sketches and layout often needing no more than approval.

Accuracy in detail was most important as I discovered now and again to my embarrassment. The American Forces always identified their aircraft by type and number rather than by a name. Thus, when we spoke of Flying Fortresses, they referred to B17s, whilst the Lightning fighter was to them a P38, B stood for Bomber, P for Pursuit or fighter, the figures for the acceptance number by the Air Force. One day an urgent request came for us to do a quick job on the B26 Marauder, a twin-engined medium bomber, since several squadrons were arriving shortly in North Africa. Apart from the silhouette, dimensions and equipment detail, we knew little about it, except that someone who should have known better vouchsafed that this was the aircraft which had attacked Tokyo from the carrier *Hornet*, so I instructed Sergeant Potter to make this the theme of his cartoon.

Some days later, Major General James Doolittle, when making an informal visit to his intelligence HQ, came into our planning room to tell me personally that he was under the impression that it was a B25 Mitchell squadron which he'd led from 'Shangri-La' to the Japanese capital – similar, but quite a different silhouette and tail assembly. So I'd better withdraw all the posters before he changed his mind and had me hanged from the nearest yardarm. My apologies were profuse, and the posters had all been withdrawn anyway, as minor explosions had occurred nearby when they were delivered. He left my office in a fairly good temper but on his way out, almost bumped into Eddie Bradford, who had mislaid his very powerful spectacles, without which his sight was poor. However, spotting two silver 'things' on the departing officer's shoulders, Eddie did manage 'Hi, Captain, pardon me' quite politely. But the General was not amused.

On the first Monday in August, while enjoying a quiet lunchtime aperitif outside a café in one of the tree-lined squares, I saluted Ralph Orcutt, an American friend in CIC. Ralph was escorting two extremely attractive WAAF officers, one slim and blonde, the other dark and of slightly fuller figure. Obviously he was in need of help, added to which both young ladies were far too young for him, so I wandered over to be introduced. The ladies were from AFHQ Codes and Cypher section, the blonde's name being Joyce Reynolds, the brunette Maureen Sidney-Smith, but usually addressed as 'Squeak'. After lunch together, I drove the ladies back to AFHQ, and managed to extract an appointment for dinner the following evening. Though both very charming, I was more attracted to the blonde, and happily, it was she who was off duty the following evening.

It so happened that our former combat school mess at La Senia had broken up with the various moves. With most of the former officers waiting orders to rejoin their units ready for the impending Italian invasion, it had been arranged to dispose of the surplus mess funds at a dinner party just up the coast at Ain Taiya. Joyce accompanied me there, where she was immediately waltzed around by all my alleged friends in turn, claiming that since they shared with Woodie, he must share with them. Once more it seemed my fortune to accompany the lady to and from the party, but not to be allowed to play. However, since Joyce was due back on duty at midnight, Cinderella-like she had to depart to take her night-watch.

And there the romance might have ended, as we shook hands and said our goodnights, save for the fact that either by design or accident – and she always swore it was the latter – her writing case was left in the car, so that I had to return it next day and so our romance began. She was from Cheshire, liked swimming, sunbathing, music, people and especially it seemed, mature aviators. We spent a lot of time at Guyotville, eating at the Normandie, and one evening our dinner was spoilt by some boorish behaviour by some young submariners, causing me to speak to them. When we came to leave, they had removed the rotor arm from the distributor, but fortunately I kept a supply of these, it being a favourite trick. Fitting this in the dark made us rather late back to Algiers, but we enjoyed the moonlit drive back, and I realised that here was a girl in a million. My friends liked her and she liked them, so three weeks later I asked her to marry me as soon as circumstances permitted. Happily for me she accepted my somewhat unpolished proposal, and a party followed on 25 August at the Oasis Restaurant on Boulevard Carnot, to which almost every aviator in Algiers seemed to have been invited, plus all the WAAF and Wrens we could muster. It was a good party, finally breaking up at dawn.

Chapter 16
The Salerno Invasion

Next day, I reported to 'Cloaks and Daggers' Division at Bouzarea, where operational planning was done under tight security. I was briefed by Tony Yeoman, a former CO of 820 Squadron, whom I now met in person for the first time. My next job was to rejoin the Royal Navy and take part in the impending landings in Italy at Salerno on 9 September, just two weeks ahead. There was much to do in the intervening 14 days.

I would first go to Bizerta, picking up on the way from Bône a petty officer telegraphist, three telegraphists and one coder. With our equipment in a small Hillman van, we would board a landing craft and land at Salerno just behind the Commandos whose duty it was to capture Montecorvino airfield. We would then take over airfield control, and look after all flying operations, as well as assisting any pilots who were in trouble, refuelling and re-arming if possible.

The reason Salerno had been chosen was that a major port was needed for the next and major phase of the invasion, and Naples was the obvious choice. Salerno was suitable for Army landings, but just too far from Sicily for RAF fighters to give proper cover over the beaches. So we had a support force of 4 escort carriers – *Attacker, Battler, Hunter, Stalker*, plus the light fleet carrier *Unicorn*, each full of Seafire fighters, which were RAF Spitfires adapted for decklanding with arrestor hook and flotation equipment. In turn, they would be protected from interference by the fleet carriers *Formidable* and *Illustrious*, equipped with both bombers and fighters. As soon as the beaches had been secured, estimated to take four days, and the airfield organised, all the carriers would withdraw from their vulnerable location and RAF Spitfires would take over, flying in from Sicily. Simple. In the event it was a near disaster, a real Catch 22 situation.

Commander Gerry Butler RN would be i/c signals at Salerno in the HQ ship USS *Ancon*. Our Hillman Utilicon van would be equipped in Algiers with radio sets to work on all frequencies – ships, aircraft and Admiralty. A small generator would be included to recharge batteries, but no one seemed to have worked out how we would carry all this equipment plus one petty officer and four ratings in the limited space the Hillman provided. No time for messing about, and Bert Lewis, though on the strength of the USAAF wanted to come to share the excitement. I said to myself 'what would Nelson have done?' and got into the Hillman, Bert following in the Peugeot, a car we had swapped for the Hotchkiss, which was becoming slightly unreliable. When I think today of the lack of preparation and the unjustified optimism of our planners, there is no wonder the war took six years out of our lives. Had it not been for the youngsters up in the sharp end, it would have taken longer.

Having said fond farewells to my affianced the previous night, the two cars left Algiers for Bizerta at 0830 on 28 August, driving through beautiful country to Bougie. There I collected PO Telegraphist Smith, Telegraphists Lussey, Mountford and Coder Thurston, packed them tightly into the two small vehicles and decided to spend the night there, when they could all reduce their gear by half – there just wasn't room. We left next morning at dawn for Setif through Constantine and finally into Bône, where I billetted the boys in the old FAA barracks and apparently lightened the lives of a couple of barrack-stanchion sub-lieutenants who were caretakers of the airfield. I managed to find oil and petrol next morning – this wasn't as easy as we had been led to believe, then crossed the old battlefields at Mateur, arriving at the RN Barracks, Bizerta, at nightfall. Unfortunately Bert had managed to sustain a flat tyre some miles back, and had not been missed immediately. Guessing that it was either a flat or engine trouble detaining him, I sought the base engineer, to find it was none other than 'Swede' Hansen, who brought out his breakdown truck, and everything was fine in no time, a good dinner, some good conversation, and a day or two to rest. Or so we thought on 30 August.

Telegraphist Cawthorne joined us next day, bringing our party to to six, which would have been seven if Bert Lewis had been allowed to come, but the local top Yank was adamant, and said he would get the stockade for being AWOL. So a farewell to a very faithful aide. In Bizerta we drew our armament, one tommy-gun, one rifle, plus a Webley .45 revolver. In addition I had 'liberated' a Colt .45 from the USAAF, complete with shoulder-holster. We then started to enquire as to where we should get our orders. The Army didn't know anything about us, the RAF knew nothing about themselves. SNAFU. Eventually we found an LST (Landing Ship Tank) full of Sherwood Foresters which was short of a party, but they thought bigger than this one. Another LST was looking for a 10-ton lorryload of radio equipment with troops. Eventually we found the Hampshires, with whom we were supposed to land, but their LST was full of everyone it should have. Back to the Sherwood Foresters who welcomed us aboard, but no one was allowed yet to embark, trucks only. The Foresters' officers, Major Dick Ward, Captain Lord Lytton and

'Goofy' Salmon had not eaten sitting down for days, and had nowhere to wash and change, so I took them up to the naval mess, where they showered, shaved, changed their clothes and ate sitting down, which they enjoyed tremendously. They came again several times before we left. Lord Lytton was killed at Salerno a few days later, but Dick Ward became a great friend in Leicester after the war.

It was discovered next morning that our truck hadn't been waterproofed. It was news to me that this was necessary, and we sweated like June brides to do this and re-embark the truck and ourselves. On 6 September we moved out into Ferryville Lake and the troops went over the side swimming all afternoon. As I sunbathed, the date reminded me that it was four years to the day since I had joined the Fleet Air Arm. My course officer, Lieutenant-Commander Richard Phillimore, had told me at the passing-out interviews that I was 'reliable, resourceful and resilient'. How he found that out in a few months escapes me, but he would have been proud of me that day. It also occurred to me that the Air Arm encouraged flexibility in its members, for where else would you find the combination of sailor, airman, and today a soldier too? Just as we left the jetty some mail arrived, Unbelievably, a pair of shoulder-straps from Gieves'. Perhaps I should have asked them for the invasion plans.

Now that we were committed and embarked, I began to worry about the Hampshires whom we were scheduled to join, but didn't want us. Major Ward of the Foresters assured me that things were now so fouled up that everything was bound to turn out all right. That evening the *Luftwaffe* bombed shipping in the Lake, and on the morning of 7 September we sailed in convoy for Salerno, hundreds of landing craft of all shapes and sizes. One of the Landing Craft Tanks (LCT) had a Piper Cub aircraft on deck in the flying position. It seems the Army were flexible too. A pipe sounded calling for 'last letters for home' which the LST would post on her return to North Africa. It seemed slightly macabre, but to be honest, I had a feeling that this could well be my last adventure. Previously the dangers were known and calculated, this time they weren't. My small party knew nothing of beach landings, were practically unarmed and lacked infantry training, which looked like being necessary. In addition, they didn't know too much about aircraft, which deficiency I sought immediately to remedy.

A large formation of B26 Marauders heading for Italy flew over our convoy, followed shortly by B17 Fortresses. Major Salmon asked if I would give a chat to the Sherwood Foresters on ship and aircraft recognition, which I did in the limited circumstances with only a blackboard and chalk. Maybe it helped. It certainly took their minds off thinking about the imminent landing. So passed 8 September, and I prepared for next morning by changing my underwear and donning khaki instead of navy blue battledress, which was almost a fatal mistake.

The late radio news announced Italy's capitulation. At least we reasoned quite wrongly, we wouldn't meet much opposition. In the event, the landings almost ended in another Dunkirk, partly through it being so obvious and partly because it was undertaken without a lengthy preliminary naval bombardment.

At 0135 on 9 September enemy coastal guns opened up on us, and landings began at 0320 under cover of a 15-minute barrage from the Royal Navy. Then all hell broke loose as we moved into the Gulf of Salerno and started to disembark, covered by Seafires from the carriers. Also covering us were P38 Lightnings from Sicily, but these were only able to stay in the combat zone for about 20 minutes, even with a 90 gallon drop-tank, before returning to base to refuel and rearm. There were, however, abundant Seafires, but just one small problem – there was practically no wind in the Gulf, and the maximum speed of the escort carriers was about 18 knots; insufficient for take-off and landing. However, *Unicorn*, with a longer deck and more powerful engines, did keep patrols going over the beach-head. The entire operation was based on the premise that naval fighters would provide cover for four days, but, with no wind, take-offs were dicey and landings near-suicidal on the smaller carriers. Additionally those who did try to land on had a tendency to tip on the nose after the arrestor hook caught, shattering the propeller blades. As a result, five inches was hacksawed off every blade of every propeller, which seemed to solve the problem without reducing performance. So it was vitally necessary that Montecorvino airfield be secured as early as possible.

Up until this point I had not thought too much about being the last vehicle to embark, but suddenly it was brought home to me that we would also be the first vehicle off. The Foresters pushed our 'Bread van' ashore, the sides decorated with graffiti such as 'Two sliced and a small brown' and 'Join the Navy for a loaf'. But there the humour stopped. We hadn't enough weight to get up the slope which had been torn up by heavy trucks into deep ruts. An officer with what looked like two pips on his shoulders began to shout at me 'Get that bloody thing up here of I'll have you thrown into the minefield'. Now no two-pipper speaks to Woods like that, so I told him to shut his cake-hole and give us a push, which he did, revealing a crown and crossed swords on his shoulder-straps. Christ, I thought, a General of some sort. And so we slowly made our way from the noisy beach and in the general direction of the airfied. Unfortunately, the Germans had been expecting us, since it didn't take a genius with a protractor and a pair of dividers to surmise that if a landing was to be made on the European mainland, a large port would be necessary, and the nearest was Naples with the Gulf of Salerno, ideal for large-scale invasion 30 miles southeast. Trucks jammed solidly on the road to the airfield.

As the day wore on and my impatience grew, I decided to send one of our number ahead to find out if the Commandos had yet taken the airfield. If so, we had the choice of lugging our equipment by hand or parking the truck and 'liberating' a land-line from the army signallers, since we had to report the airfield's condition to the HQ ship USS *Ancon* as quickly as possible. It was at this point that I discovered that nobody else in the party could drive a car. Hells bells, now we were in a mess. So Lussey and Mountford went ahead, shortly reporting back that the airfield was still in enemy hands, leaving no alternative but to advise *Ancon* accordingly and keep listening watch during the night. Additional information indicated that the enemy troops occupying the airfield were the Herman Goering Panzer Grenadiers, equipped with Tiger tanks, 88mm guns and flamethrowers. We looked somewhat ruefully at our weapons and slept fitfully, artillery barrages crashing round us all night.

PO Smith had the middle watch. At about 0100 he shook me 'Sir, I think we're surrounded!' Nerves sticking out like piano wires, we crept out and listened to soldiers all round us conversing in a language neither of us knew. What an ignominious end to our venture. What should we do, escape one by one, or make a concerted rush? Suddenly one of the soldiers began to sing 'Blaydon Races'. No wonder we couldn't understand them, they were Geordies!

Though the airfield never really fell completely into our hands until the fighting had moved northwards, we were able next day to set up on the perimeter, protected by the RAF Regiment. Droves of Italian prisoners moved south to the cages, ragged, dishevelled, without arms, unshaven, and with their baggy breeches hanging round their ankles. Revolting, but at least for them the war was over. The Germans had their mobile 88mm guns well hidden in the hills surrounding the airfield, and rained shells on the beach, dropping a few onto the airfield just to remind us that they had everything ranged and plotted. It would have been stupid to set up in the control tower for this reason, but also we knew that everything inside was booby-trapped. So we simply maintained contact, giving what news we could, including our ability to take emergency landings with certain provisos. The German gunners' fire was accurate, and anything that moved was shelled. So, we advised *Ancon* that any emergency landing would necessitate the pilot getting out immediately he touched down and running for the dry ditch that surrounded the airfield.

The first to land was Sub-Lieutenant 'Cappy' Masters, RNZNVR who obeyed our instructions and dived for the ditch. I went round to bring him in. [Many years later, when we met again in New Zealand, he told my wife and I that he had me in the sights of his .45 Webley for some seconds, believing me to be a German because of my khaki battledress. When just about to fire, he saw my cap-badge!] He brought us up-to-date with the news and requirements from the carriers, and during that day and ensuing days, we took about 30 aircraft in, losing only a few to gunfire and prangs. Among the pilots of the Seafires rescued were Al Wright of the Royal Marines, whom I should have flown with to Malta in 1940, David Ogle and 'Hooky' Walker. Where the aircraft were serviceable, but couldn't land back on board, the best we could do was to advise the ship that the pilots were safe and the state of the aircraft. Later, when the firing had died down, we could refuel the Seafires, so that they could return to their ship if the weather conditions had improved, or fly south and land at one of the airfields liberated by the 8th Army moving north (and now only 70 miles away from us) or to fly slowly to Malta. Most of them seemed to opt for Malta. Meantime the marauding German 88s in the hills had not been winkled out completely, and were playing cat and mouse with the emergency landings, picking them off desultorily so as to keep us in a state of permanent twitch. Eventually the 2/6th Queens' Regiment made a night attack and sorted them out.

On 12 September an Italian general arrived in a motorcycle combination sidecar, the driver being his ADC, a captain. Both were quite beautifully dressed, covered in gold leaf, medals, aiguillettes, and looking more like commissionaires from the Odeon than fighting men. They had come to surrender, having apparently first offered to do so to an army patrol just up the road, but had been referred to us, who did not want them either. 'Cappy' took them down the road to the nearest army post, returning later with their .22 calibre Beretta pistols and the motorcycle combination. Since I already had a Webley and a Colt automatic, I didn't really want the Beretta, and shortly afterwards a British Army major arrived, demanding the return of all the prizes, since the Italian officers were in grave danger of being killed by their own troops. 'Cappy' protested loud, long and lewdly, but in the end had to give in, though we kept the combination. It would be ideal for messenger duty once I'd taught the troops to ride it.

That evening Major Randolph Churchill came to us, demanding priority for his newspaper dispatches by air to Malta. Although eminently recognisable, he still insisted on telling us several times who he was, just in case the barrage had deafened us. 'Cappy' knew only one Churchill, and this wasn't him, so he told our visitor in Maori to go away. We really were too busy talking to the ships and answering queries. Our batteries too were beginning to fail until we could charge them that night on the Stuart generator. Churchill strode off, intent, he said, on reporting our non-cooperation to our CO, whom he expected to find in the control tower, still booby-trapped with 'red devils', a fiendish Italian hand-grenade which, when detonated, shot out very lethal sharp steel wire. Even though we didn't like our visitor's manner, we didn't want to upset dad, so one of the telegraphists headed him off.

At midnight that same evening, we had just finished listening to the

BBC news, which had informed us how well everything was going, when the German Panzer Grenadiers counter-attacked the airfield in strength, and at the worst possible moment. Our radio batteries had been run down flat, and we were using the truck 12-volt as a temporary measure, so even if we'd wanted to run for it, we couldn't. Throwing all the confidential books into a weighted sack, I gave them to Coder Thurston, telling him to head for the beach, find a safe hole and stay there until we came along and the situation clarified. Meantime, we dismantled the radio sets without damaging them. At this time, there were rumours flying in all directions that an evacuation was about to be ordered, and certainly we had taken nothing like the ground we anticipated. Thurston grabbed the sack, and by mistake or in the bad light put a German helmet on his head – one of many the boys had liberated for souvenirs – and started off down the road. Clad in navy blue, with this novel headgear, he wondered why troops had begun firing at him, and realising, flung the helmet away. We started down the road soon afterwards, accompanied by a few pilots, found an abandoned truck, staying therein all night, but not sleeping as this was impossible with barrages going over us from both sides.

The Grenadier and Coldstream Guards straightened the line out during the night, and we returned to our truck for breakfast, finding nothing touched, but inspecting very carefully first for booby-traps. As we were enjoying our early morning tea, 4 Focke Wulf 190 fighters screamed out of the sky, dropped some very large bombs a few hundred yards away, beating it fast as Seafires got amongst them. At noon I decided that the present situation was far from satisfactory, and with the airfield still untenable, we should find an alternative airstrip where we could operate with less noise, confusion and opposition. Down by the beach we found an American bulldozer with a driver who would do anything for a couple of bottles of Scotch, which I hadn't, but could get. He would level us a surface hard enough to take Seafires. These would not be shot at by the German 88mm guns, and provided we could get a few spares, a petrol bowser and some starter cartridges, we could do a much better job. In the midst of this brilliant thinking, who should appear but Commander Charles Coke, formerly in *Ark Royal*, and now on Admiral Sir Philip Vian's staff, accompanied by John Cockburn, Commander Flying in one of the carriers. Though admiring our initiative, they told us that the Seafires would be staying only another 24 to 36 hours and the RAF were already bulldozing some strips on the beach until Montecorvino was fully operational. Charles went on to say that our signals, even if mainly negative reports, had been invaluable.

The bulldozer driver got one bottle only for being co-operative. That evening, when talking to the intelligence officer of 128th Infantry Brigade, of which the Hampshires were part during the landings, we learned that they had landed on the wrong beach and the three battalions had been savagely mauled. The one we should have been with – the 5th Battalion – had been practically wiped out to a man by a tank attack. Dick Ward was right, I should have stopped worrying at Bizerta.

A further shudder ran through us just before dark when an Italian Army engineer came to show us where he had mined the airfield on German instructions. With typical Italian thoroughness he had forgotten to prime them, but, we asked, suppose an 88mm shell had hit one of them? A shrug of the latin shoulders – maybe, maybe not. Since the evening seemed so much quieter, and the control tower had been defused, we took our first shower and shave for four days. It had been a damned close-run thing, and certainly at one time, evacuation had been seriously discussed by the American Army commanders, but was ruled out somewhat contemptuously by General Alexander.

Our job seemed to be almost over as the 8th Army approached, and shortly it would be possible for the RAF Spitfires from Sicily to land and give fighter cover. I therefore made a signal to AFHQ Algiers, starting that we had completed what we had to do, and indicating that in default of other instructions, proposed to return after 48 hours to North Africa. Such impertinence usually brings a snappy reply, but not this time. That night Captain 'Scupper' Geyer of 51st Troop Carrier Wing turned up in a jeep, had supper and stayed with us in the candlelit control tower. He had taken a couple of days' leave, and wanted to see something of the Sorrento peninsula before it got too regimental, so would I join him? He had money, side-arms, transport and several cases of 'C' rations, rather more tasty than British Army 'Compo'. It seemed a good idea. I left 'Cappy' Masters in charge, with the ratings taking 4 hours on and 8 off until my return. Before leaving, I took 'Scupper' on a tour of the airfield to see the pranged Seafires, and he estimated that his C47s could haul out the engines and other spares worth recovering, sending them on to Malta. His eyes lit up at the heap of Axis aircraft at the mountain end of the field. The swastika tailplanes and panels alone would fetch very high prices from the chairborne troops. Even German steel helmets fetched $5 each, $10 if one were smart enough to put a few bullets through them first. Geyer had a good commercial brain.

So we set off at dawn for Salerno, hoping to get through to Maiori and perhaps Amalfi to see the Emerald Grotto. Stopping at the first village, we were trying with our limited Italian to trade 'C' rations for wine. A 'Moustache Pete' forced his way through the villagers, and in best Brooklyn demanded 'Waddya want General? – vino – no food – plenty vino, plenty pretty gals too, Say, how's da Dodgers doin'?' So for a box of rations, we had 4 litres of musky smelling wine. In the next village, near to Maiori, we met Sam, formerly of Detroit, with similar history and services available. His cottage was white, with a view across the bay. He gave us a meal of spaghetti, and for the first time I saw how

Italians eat it, with mouth horizontal to the plate, reeling it in. Fascinating. Before we left, having traded more rations for more wine, Sam asked 'Scupper' to give him a recommendation to the next mayor, to say that Sam had helped the US Army, and should be given a good post in the administration. 'Scupper' obliged. As we drove up the road, I said, 'Scupper, was that wise? You only met the chap an hour ago.' 'It's OK', said 'Scupper', 'I wrote on the paper "This SOB is commended to your attention, and should be watched very carefully. Very carefully".'

'Scupper' had a great deal to tell of his adventures since we had last met at Maison Blanche in Algiers. The 51st Troop Carrier Wing had been one of the units towing gliders loaded with airborne troops and their equipment into Sicily for the landings. 'Jesus!' he commented, 'am I glad I am a hotos pilotos' (he would lapse into Spanish equivalent to Luke's French from time to time) 'them poor bastards in the Glider Pilot Regiments, they really got guts. No goddam engine after we cut 'em loose, and sometimes a ginormous tank or artillery piece on board. Man gets hit by flak, it sure is a one-way trip. As a matter of fact, Woody Boy, I composed an anthem to praise their courage. Like to hear it?' 'Certainly would, "Scupper", K for King' 'Howzat K business?' 'Oh, that means proceed, friend.'

And so, bowling along the Italian road, 'Scupper' proceeded to sing his song. Tune it hadn't, and 'Scupper' couldn't carry a tune anyway. I couldn't help but be reminded of some part of *Alice Through the Looking Glass*, where the doleful White Knight sings his inconsequential song regarding the search for Haddocks' eyes among the heather bright ....

'Scupper' began his madrigal:

'ODE TO A GLIDER PILOT'
(His singing implied capital letters)

Do you see spots before your eyes?
Does your arsehole snap at flies?
Are you a Glider Guider?

CHORUS, one line only:

Brother you've had it.

Does your head spin round and round?
Are your bowels tightly bound?
Does your arsehole drag the ground?

CHORUS, one line only:

Brother, you've had it.

There were more verses, but these are all I can remember. Somehow one feels that it wouldn't have made the Top Ten, but at least the message was understandable.

As we drove north the sky was blue and cloudless, the sea magnificent. We had enjoyed our first home-cooked meal for months. Not a care in the world. Approaching a small but sturdy wooden bridge, a GI saluted and said we should look out for pockets of Germans still known to be in the area. We thanked him and drove slowly over the bridge. A few hundred yards further along, we saw a number of soldiers on a hillside who appeared to wave to us. We waved back, then suddenly 'Scupper' said 'Those guys saluted funny – Oh Christ, Woody, down quick!' as a burst of machine gun fire hit the road just behind us. Side-arms at the ready, we rounded the next band to find a platoon of US Rangers whom we directed back to the bridge. Soon a burst of fire and the Germans surrendered. Fortunate, as we had to go back over the bridge, deciding that a trip to Amalfi was probably tempting Providence.

Arriving back at Montecorvino, a signal requested my presence onboard *Ancon* next morning early to see Gerry Butler. Going over in an MTB, I enjoyed my first gin for two weeks, though 0900 is a bit on the early side. Aboard *Ancon*, the Combined Operations HQ ship, I was shown to Gerry Butler's cabin, where shortly the door opened, and in walked a very tall lieutenant-commander USN with a wide smile and wall-to-wall teeth. I knew his face, but couldn't think of the name. He came over, hand outstretched. I did know him, my mind must be going. He said, 'I'm Douglas Fairbanks.' Gerry shortly arrived, and advised me to stay another week until the RAF were properly installed, then repair in leisurely fashion to Algiers. It made sense.

Hardly had we clutched our valedictory gin before all hell was let loose up top. Up we went, to find that *Ancon* and *Biscayne* were under attack from glider bombs, radio-controlled from German Dornier 217 aircraft standing well back out of our range. So the bombs had to be hit, and were, but not before they had scored a hit on the heavy cruiser USS *Savannah*, killing 100 men, later hitting and damaging the cruiser *Uganda* and a tanker with some loss of life. They were the forerunners of later and larger 'buzz bombs' that caused such panic in London.

After staying another week to see the airfield and the motorcycle combination properly handed over (I have the receipt for the latter still), I tried to get my small party back to Algiers the official way. No dice. So 'Scupper' reappeared and said, 'The 51st don't forget its friends', led us to Capaccio airfield nearby, and flew us back by a personal C47 to Licata in Sicily, where 'Red' Harrison offered to fly us to Algiers. We went next day to Tunis, with Big 'Swede' Anderson at the controls.

And there I said farewell to my loyal helpers, wishing them luck as we went our separate ways, they back to their barracks, hoping for a draft chit home, I to Algiers.

John Roe asked me to write a report on the operation, which I did, stressing the inefficiencies in planning, instructions, equipment and armament. Next day he read it and said, 'If I send that in, you will be court-martialled.' I replied that quite a lot of the planners should have seen what I had seen, the completely unnecessary slaughter of hundreds, if not thousands, of young and brave men who had walked into a trap that could so easily have been avoided. John then agreed on a compromise – that I would write another report as if for a newspaper, but my original report would be passed on direct to Tony Yeoman, who in Planning at Bouzarea would be in a better position to amend the ground rules for next time and the next poor sod who got a job like this for which he had little or no specific training or even clear instructions.

Tony saw me at AFHQ instead, and assured me that he would see that my critical report would be given to the right people. He also told me that I would be going home very soon and that a recommendation had gone in for me to have a squadron command, probably departing within four weeks.

Joyce and I decided to get married as soon as possible, since it seemed that I was unlikely to stay in the Mediterranean. Scapa or Colombo seemed much more likely at this stage of the war, which then looked like going on for ever. Once more we ran into the Rule Book, her CO taking a poor view of his WAAF officers getting married before they'd served a dogwatch, and the various chaplains saying it couldn't be done in less than two months. There were, of course, perfectly valid reasons for this 'cooling period' as it was known. It was instituted to prevent British troops from marrying local ladies and thoughtlessly setting themselves killed, so leaving a British subject and possibly offspring to be brought back to England, pensioned, housed etc, in a foreign land. After seeing Major Woolley VC, the senior Army padre, our own Chaplain of the Fleet and sundry others, the task seemed impossible. Then one evening, I met an old friend, Leroy Benoit, a lawyer on the staff of the Judge Avocate General of 12th USAAF. Roy said the British Law recognised any marriage as legal provided it is legal in the country in which it is contracted. Thus, if we were married under the law of Algeria, it would be recognised by the Navy and RAF. Not only did he spring that welcome advice, he also had the papers authenticated so that we could be married five days later on 14 October 1943.

For several days I tried to obtain some recognition for PO Smith, who had done a remarkable job at Salerno, both as a petty officer and as a telegraphist. Without him, we would have had practically no success. Unfortunately, according to Captain Ritchie of Honours and Awards section, a Distinguished Service Medal was out of the question because we were not under enemy fire. Now I'm not as clever as paymaster captains on such fine points of the King's Regulations, but if sitting in that Hillman truck packed with humanity and radio sets, and positioned almost equidistant from a Royal Artillery barrage at one end of the airfield and a barrage from the Herman Goering Panzer Grenadiers at the other, with 88mms in the hills also dropping a few on the airfield isn't 'under enemy fire', then I'd like to know what is? Also, if a pilot shoots down 5 enemy aircraft in four or five days, he will probably get a decoration. My little party saved 25 of our own aircraft from destruction and quite a few lives in five days, which should have received some recognition for the senior NCO. For a career man of Smith's calibre it would have been a just reward, but my reasoning was all to no avail.

Anyway, about six months later, on the recommendation of either Charles Coke or John Roe, I was awarded a Distinguished Service Cross. Fortunately I never met PO Smith again. I'm glad, I could never have faced him.

The night before our wedding, I had taken Joyce to l'Ours Blanc for dinner, and we were walking to the car when an inebriated American captain of engineers walked into us waving a Luger pistol. Not wishing my lady to become a widow before her time, I did not attempt to reason with the man, but was happy to see a British MP bring the 'Snowdrops' to deal with the situation, the Americans requesting our presence as witnesses. After explaining that we had urgent business on the morrow, we were allowed to make depositions in which we did attempt to assist the accused as much as possible, since obviously he had spent the evening in company of charitable friends.

So next day we were married, and all our colourful friends were witnesses. First we were joined in holy matrimony by the Mayor of Algiers, top-hatted and tricolour-sashed and an hour later by the Chaplain of the Fleet, the Wedding March from *Lohengrin* being bashed out on the NAAFI piano. Then away to the reception, chez Harry and Eddie, Hamilton Darby having already left for Saipan in the Pacific. The drinks and food were laid on by the Régence mess, and a splendid time was had by all. We had a week's honeymoon at Chréa in the Atlas Mountains – where Tartarin slew the mountain lion, according to legend. Just above Blida, we were seldom alone by day, since relays from Algiers and Blida came to lunch, dine, drink or just chat. It was a happy time.

A week later I took passage back to Britain in the battleship *Nelson*, arriving at Rosyth on 6 December, my new wife being left at the Front, as it were. The passage home was pleasant enough, *Nelson* and *Rodney* in company, with a small destroyer screen. For company, also taking passage were one or two old shipmates, 'Tarzan' Fisher, the former Captain's Secretary from *Formidable*, Jack Geater, a course-mate and Bill Fairchild, a pilot-turned-FDO; all of whom brought me up-to-date with the whereabouts of old mates. Two of *Nelson's* engineer officers were old shipmates – Len Wills and Bryant – so altogether one had a choice of companions. Also a passenger was Desmond Tighe, war correspondent, then working for Reuter's Agency, who had some amusing reminiscences.

When relating the aftermath of the Salerno episode one evening, and my inability to obtain well-deserved recognition for PO Smith, someone pointed out that the two captains on the AFHQ Staff, Dorling and Ritchie, representing press liaison and honours and awards respectively, were both well-established authors of naval history, Dorling was 'Taffrail' and Ritchie 'Bartimeus'. Perhaps their ideas of heroism had become romanticised by their many books, and nothing short of leaping ashore, cutlass in hand, or volunteering for underwater swims to cut anchor cables, would earn a decoration for Smith.

With no ship's duties whatsoever, it was also a time for reflection and self-analysis long overdue. Why was I so anxious to get home, get flying again and off to the war? I was no Bobby Bradshaw, who had to be physically restrained at times from flying and sent on leave. One evening I think it all finally jelled. First there was some guilt experienced at having done a minimum of operational flying with the 12th Air Force while contemporaries had been getting themselves shot at and sometimes killed. It wasn't that I was anxious for promotion, though obviously with the increased responsibilities of marriage, it was sensible to get ahead as far as was possible. So it wasn't entirely ambition, but possibly partly conceit, in that I wanted my wife, my parents, my friends and contemporaries to be impressed and proud of me. But above all, it seemed that the sooner I got down to some hard work, preferably new stuff which kept me 101 per cent busy, the sooner I would stop brooding about my new bride left behind. After all, this was hardly a unique situation, even though the roles were usually reversed.

At Rosyth, I had my first experience of being interviewed by the press, who appeared to have Captain Dorling's press release for comment. Though sorely tempted to try again for Smith, our conversation was monitored by the Admiralty's local lieutenant-commander who let very little pass him in the way of 'Extras'.

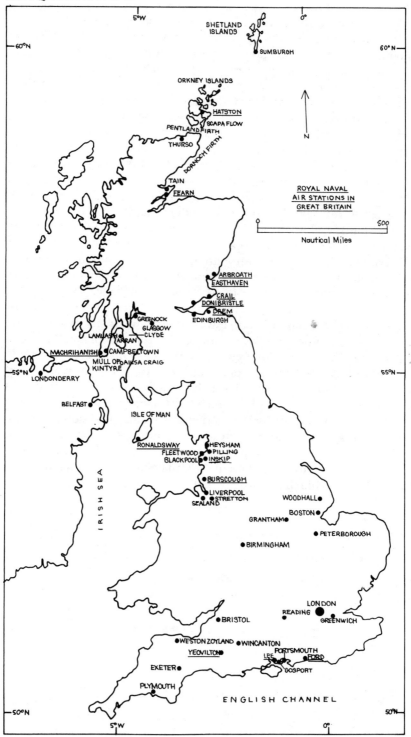

ROYAL NAVAL
AIR STATIONS IN
GREAT BRITAIN

Nautical Miles

Chapter 17
The Dreaded Barracuda or 'Any Old Iron'

In these circumstances, leave was even more of an anti-climax, despite national and local newspapers lauding the performance of the Fleet Air Arm at Salerno. We who had seen it all knew how near it had been to another Dunkirk. My new appointment, to command 822 TBR squadron complete with promotion to Lieutenant-commander (acting) arrived fortuitously on my 25th birthday, with instructions to report to RAF Tain, Ross, forthwith. This entailed a very long and cold railway journey ·via Grantham, being part of the way accompanied by a Job's comforter in the shape of a warrant engineer officer from RNAS Donibristle who related horror stories of all the bad habits of Barracuda aircraft, on which I had thoughtlessly sought his advice, never having seen one before.

The officer temporarily in charge of 822 was Lieutenant Tom Bassett, a solid and dependable New Zealander, formerly senior pilot under 'Bing' Boulding, who had recently completed an unrehearsed inverted spin over the sea, and was lucky to escape with his life. 'Bing' was convalescing and unlikely to return in the time available before we joined our ship. This was to be either *Indefatigable* or *Implacable*, both newly-commissioned, and the squadrons would work up in the Home Fleet. The atmosphere in the officers' mess was far from encouraging, and after a couple of days, I could cheerfully have thrown in my hand, reverted to perhaps senior observer in a·worked-up and operational squadron and gone back to sea. But it seemed such a challenge that I decided to stick it out if only as an academic exercise.

In the year I'd been absent from the flying side of the Navy, enormous expansion had taken place. The training schools in Canada and Trinidad had been churning out pilots and observers like giant sausage machines, anticipating as almost everyone did then that the war was going on for many years ahead. Aircraft production had been stepped up not only in Britain, but also in Canada and Australia, so that for once we began to have enough of everything statistically. Due to this expansion there were insufficient officers with even a few years' experience as senior pilots and observers so that squadron commanders were being appointed, as in my case, with just over a year as lieutenants. This may have been perfectly sound in the RAF, with whom we were competing for recruits of the right calibre, they had adequate 'penguins' in the supply, secretariat and administration branches to deal with almost everything outside flying. It may be an oversimplification, but all that the RAF needed was a few more Nissen huts at each airfield, whereas in the Fleet Air Arm we were packing our carriers with aircraft and stores, living quarters being a secondary consideration in the new ships. Thus, squadron commanders had to deal with all the 'bumph' as well as leading their squadrons. Some of the new COs had this ability, some didn't, and as a result, or so it seemed to me, discipline suffered in the squadrons, many of which were now entirely RNVR-officered with ratings who were engaged 'for hostilities only'.

Their Lordships began to realise this problem, and began to recruit RN officers especially as pilots, some as observers, to give a leavening of regulars in command. This raised other problems, since some regulars became squadron commanders after limited first-line experience. The 'Wing' was also introduced, formed of two or more TBR or fighter squadrons, and commanded by a Wing Leader in both training and operations, leaving squadron commanders more time for administration and welfare of their officers and men. Humans, being what they are, this sometimes caused friction, since most squadron commanders believed that they should also lead when airborne.

In my own case, matters were exacerbated by two ineradicable facts. First, 822 had been commanded by no fewer than 8 COs in the four years of war, so that none had sufficient time to generate any esprit or folklore, so dear to a squadron's self-image. Second, through no fault of its own, 822 had taken part in very few operational missions. Shortly after my arrival, Vernon Crane, then No 2 pilot and No 1 humourist, said to me one evening 'Would you like to hear about our operation?' Paradoxically, their main battle-honour, the dive-bombing of La Senia airfield during the North African landings, led to the loss of half the squadron's Albacores, though only the CO and his crew were killed. Lieutenant J G A (Jimmy) Nares RN, an observer, his pilot and former *Ark Royal* shipmate, Lieutenant (A) J V (Jock) Hartley RN and the TAG, Leading Airman George Dixon, were killed during 822 Squadron's attack from *Furious*, resulting in the destruction of 47 aircraft on the ground, so that the Allied invasion in the Oran section suffered minimal losses; 5 of the 8 attacking Albacores were hit either by the heavy AA batteries' fire, or by French Dewoitine 520 fighters. Jimmy Nares' aircraft was seen to be on fire, and although the crew could have baled out, their attack was pressed home with gallantry and selfless determination. At the time it was rumoured that Their Lordships were considering the award of a Victoria Cross, though in the event, the alternatives – posthumous Mentions in Dispatches – were actually granted.

In addition to this lack of 822 Squadron heroes and legends, several of the observers were of my own vintage, and felt, with some reason, that Tom Bassett should have become CO on 'Bing's' leaving. As I got to know Tom better, I was inclined to agree with them, since he had both the experience and requisite toughness. However, we had not yet come to that type of democracy in the Royal Navy. The job had been given to me, and resentment or not, we'd give it a try. It was, I learned later, not uncommon. Perhaps I am an unduly sensitive person.

Fortunately the other squadron commanders – 'Buster' May of 817; Bobby Lawson of 815 and Leslie Watson of 823 were pleasant and helpful. 'Buster' and Bobby had been on the same original pilots' course with me, so my changeover in seats had been no handicap. Leslie – or 'Dago', as I christened him, on account of his dark complexion – has been a good friend ever since. 'Buster' is a South African, and Bobby has spent most of his postwar career in Turkey, so we have not met since 1945. These three being pilots gave them easier control through their ability and experience. Though probably the most experienced aviator in 822 Squadron, I was rather out of practice, and faced the twin problems of improving my own performance as an individual, while simultaneously attempting to realise every young aviator's dream of commanding his own squadron with distinction.

But above all these reigned one insoluble – the Barracuda had a name as an unpredictable aircraft, with a number of serious faults yet to be ironed out. To begin with, it wasn't a pretty aircraft, and was once described as 'looking like a chunk of the Forth Bridge airborne'. It was a high-wing monoplane with a high tailplane. In flight, with its undercarriage stowed, to me it always looked like a glider, especially as it had a slightly nose-down position. Coming in to land, with the wide undercarriage slowly unfolding, it resembled a pterodactyl. Not a pretty sight at all, especially when one considered that the fighter side of the Air Arm had Seafires, Sea Hurricanes, Wildcats, Hellcats and Corsairs, all both attractive and efficient. It seemed that the Navy was unable to design a decent TBR aircraft.

Whether the story is true or not doesn't matter, but it was rumoured that the Barracuda was designed around the very successful Sabre engine, which was instantly 'stolen' by the Air Ministry for the Typhoon, Merlin 32s, which powered the Spitfires, being given the Admiralty in exchange. Thus we had a single-seat fighter engine to power a three-seat torpedo/dive-bomber of considerably greater weight and drag. So, with all these disadvantages, small wonder that an aura of suspicion surrounded this aircraft. The US Navy was free to place its contracts where it would, and so had a cornucopia to go at, with suppliers fighting each other for approval.

A few days and many chats with officers and NCOs confirmed my thoughts, so I called a meeting of all the officers one evening, and asked them all to speak their minds freely, taking off my reefer jacket to signal that rank meant nothing, only opinions would be remembered. Almost to a man, they underlined my own feelings, and I let the discussion run without hindrance except for the refilling of beer glasses. Finally the time had come to speak, so I thanked them for their very valuable contributions, summarising that their views were appreciated and would be passed forward when the right opportunity presented itself. In the meantime, we had the Barracuda, and we had to make the best of it, there was no alternative, since Swordfish and Albacore production had ceased, and though the Avenger was spoken of as an excellent aircraft, it was believed that the American torpedo was not as good as ours, and Avengers were being used more as dive-bombers nowadays, with high losses. However, within a year, the Barracuda was being replaced by the Avenger in operational squadrons, but we were not to know that at the time. Finally I warned them that although in my hearing, some officers had spoken about transfers, none would be forwarded if requested. In fact, only one transfer was requested, and since this was one of the trouble-making observers I did send it on with a recommendation it be implemented.

Tain, on the Dornoch Firth, may not be the coldest place on earth, but it's damned near to it. Facing bleak winds from the Arctic and North Sea, it was probably an ideal place to site a torpedo-training unit. If crews survived training there, they could fly anywhere, but our stay there, though invaluable, was not always enjoyable. The naval air station at Fearn, eight miles away, housed the other wing, and it was, I believe an excellent place for exercising several squadrons together in wing and group exercises. We had no naval fighters to exercise with, but a squadron of Typhoons lived at a nearby RAF station, and was always glad to co-operate. Also, in this area were strong combined operations forces assembling for pre-D-Day training in beach landings and equally anxious to exercise with us. We had our own target vessel, the old American four-stacker destroyer *Reading*, an able and efficient bunch of WAAF torpedo assessors, and around us the extraordinary scenery (when it could be seen) plus the hospitality of the Scots, which as always, far exceeded our expectations.

My first flight in a Barracuda on 5 December 1943 impressed me, if only on account of the equipment, which was infinitely better than in 'Stringbag' or Albacore days. The aircraft was equipped with ASV radar, excellent blister-windows for observation, some cockpit heating, pee-tubes – a real luxury – and stowages for everything from thermos to Bigsworth Board. The radio was excellent, and incorporated R/T intercommunication with a fair range for squadron work, crystal-tuned radio and a twin-gun mounting for the TAG. For some strange reason, the Barracuda must have been the only aircraft of its type NOT to have at least one front gun, a matter deprecated by most pilots, especially in song:

Any old iron, any old iron, any, any, any old iron?
Talk about a treat, spotter for the Fleet
A match for any Messerschmitt that you may meet.
When you meet the Hun, you've no front gun
And an engine you can't rely on.
So you know what to do with your Barracuda Two –
Old iron, old iron!

The problem was, they really meant it, and there was little to be done, except to wait for the moment to give opinions to the right people.

Maintaining a strategic deafness as a guard against complaints, we flew as much as possible in all weathers. There were birth-pangs in the new Wing organisation, the weather varied between terrible and unbelievable, with snow, sleet, hail and sometimes if we were lucky – rain. I flew with eight different pilots in December 1943, and clocked 27 hours' flying time, all in the name of trying to build up squadron esprit. I chased the sports officer, and we played every possible game on every possible occasion, which wasn't too often owing to the weather. We gave Christmas leave in two watches, dear to the hearts of matelots everywhere, all the Scots opting for the New Year rather than Christmas. Having had leave only recently, I stayed on, probably enjoying the celebrations more than I would have, wifeless at home. Never having taken part in 'First-Footing' before, our New Year's·Eve stretched from Friday night until Tuesday morning – as Paddy Devine, a South African RAF pilot put it – two days for 'First-Footing' and two days for apologising. The WAAF torpedo assessors at Tain were a fine bunch – Mac, Jane, Jessie, Rosemary and Maggie Brown – all of whom dressed in their civilian finery by special permission. Lots of local lovelies also came to the mess party. One particularly beautiful girl was squired by a pilot who shall be nameless. I commented to him 'Doesn't she dress beautifully?' To which he replied, 'Yes, and quickly too!' It was a time to remember.

Then back to work, conferences at Fearn, introductions to Commanders Buchanan-Dunlop and Humphreys, who would be our new Commander Ops and Flying respectively in *Implacable*, and flying whenever we were able to do so, and often when we shouldn't have been. Fighter evasion was one of the things we practiced incessantly. Unfortunately the monoplane didn't manoeuvre anything like as well as the biplane, and great care had to be taken to avoid the inverted spin to which the Barracuda was prone, and from which it was difficult to extricate oneself. Squadron morale suffered a setback on 15 January 1944, over some latch pins, which lock the wings in position after they have been unfolded. It was said that a batch had come through without being hardened properly, and all aircraft were grounded until checked by Fairey's test engineer, who gave all of ours the OK. The following day one of 829 Squadron's aircraft lost a wing on a steep turn during a

A Barracuda II from one of the RNAS Easthaven training squadrons in flight over Carnoustie Golf Course with Barry Camp and the Tay estuary astern, 12 July 1944. *Conway Picture Library*

dummy torpedo attack, and all aircraft were re-inspected. Next day Admiral Lumley Lyster and Vice-Admiral Boyd visited us at Tain, probably routine, but during conversation I managed to voice some of my pilots' opinions, which appeared to be duly registered by Admiral Lyster, but I am not too sure about Vice-Admiral Boyd's reception, he being known as a staunch admirer of the Barracuda, if not one of the founders of it.

Several old shipmates came in from time to time, the ubiquitous Pat 'Prune' Chambers, Alan Swanton and John Hoare, who was in charge of the night fighter school at Drem. Good to see them all, and we brought each other up-to-date with the whereabouts of our various mutual friends. A replacement observer arrived, James Burbidge, known as 'Hiram' on account of his having spent some time in carrier USS *Wasp*, where he had learned, and brought with him, many US Navy expressions with which he would amuse us.

On 1 February we moved to RNAS Crail to carry out a series of runner attacks, these being part of the final stages of working-up, though in my opinion we were not by a long stretch yet ready for sea. I voiced this opinion to Captain H G Stokes at Crail, who assured me that any rough spots would be ironed out in our work-up aboard *Implacable*. Captain Stokes was a remarkable man. Previously a destroyer commander, who won the DSO he was given command at Crail, and promptly learned to fly at an age – even being charitable – of about 40. Not content with just flying training aircraft, he took a conversion course on the Barracuda, and spent a lot of time overseeing what his temporary charges were doing on the torpedo and bombing ranges.

Commander Flying was Mervyn Johnson, an old *Ark Royal*

squadron commander, who proved both efficient and most helpful. Among the instructors there were Nigel Gardner, Pat Chambers, Peter Grant, all from 820, and no less than 'Lucky' Sutton, an old course-mate, met again for the first time since *St Vincent*. 'Lucky' had flown on about 200 night operations in the Western Desert, dropping flares for night attacks on enemy tanks by the 8th Army. On returning to Crail as an instructor, he was given the flying medical examination, mandatory every six months, and failed of all things, the night vision test. Knowing that his two DSCs were for night operations, one had to wonder about the practicality of flying medicals!

Tom Bassett was promoted, and happily took command of a training squadron at Ronaldsway, Isle of Man, an excellent appointment. His relief was 'Flossie' Howell who had recently been instructing on night fighters at Drem, under John Hoare. It was a clear case of taking a man from a job where he was both happy and efficient, and placing him where he would be unhappy, and not so efficient as we would like him to be. I pulled a few strings, and he went smiling back to night fighters, so that it was possible to keep the promotion in the squadron, Vernon ('Killer') Crane being the incumbent. The sobriquet came to him, not because of any special aggressive history on his part,

The observer's window in the Fairey Barracuda Mark II, under the wing on the port side. Internal stowage for a compass is on the left. The entire aerodynamic concept of the Barracuda (Fairey Type 100 Albacore replacement) was changed to a shoulder (high) wing because of Admiralty insistence that a gunner be carried. This prevented the observer/navigator's rear position from remaining aft. Once moved forward the wing had to be raised so that large downward vision panels like this could be provided. *Ian Huntley Collection*

but because most of the observer COs in 822 had flown with him and hadn't lasted so long as he had. Thinking his performance too much of a mere coincidence, and using the excuse that two such senior people shouldn't fly together (which was in fact an Admiralty directive after losing both in the earlier 822 operation at Oran) I changed my pilot, and now flew with Patrick 'Dizzy' Whatmore, the No 2 pilot. 'Dizzy' was a delightful person to fly with, serious in the air, and quite irrepressible on the ground, a good mixture. Our airgunner was PO Boddy who had won a DSM in the Desert, and was also a Navy cap at hockey (field, not deck).

Our next visitor from the staff of Flag Officer Flying Training was Clancy O'Neill, to give us a mild pep-talk. Since my last encounter with Clancy had been in *Illustrious*, where he had pranged an Albacore rather badly, I was kind enough not to mention the fact, and found him most helpful in obtaining for us various items of stores which official channels had been unable to produce.

After all this accent on carrier training, it was hardly surprising that a week later, in February 1944, our remaining programme was cancelled, and we flew to RNAS Burscough for a pier-head jump to India, though I was not able to divulge this to the squadron at the time. In the murk we flew down under visual flying rules, formation being both impossible and dangerous. Like the animals into the Ark, we arrived two by two. The air for days was rife with buzzes, and no CO could open his lips.

Chapter 18
In Defence of India

There was little to recommend Burscough, lying as it did in the shadow of Liverpool, unless it was the fact that it was an airfield boasting a public house within the perimeter. The 'Bull and Dog' had, in fact, been barbed-wired outside the airfield boundary, but this did not seen to affect the landlord's loyal patrons from inside. We arrived on 17 February, went on leave on the 21st, and were recalled on 24th, par for the course. Most unfortunately, the night before I received the recall I walked in my sleep after a nightmare, climbed out of a bedroom window and jumped, probably out of an imaginary aircraft. The fall was not too severe, but cracked my ankle and scaphoid and fractured my right arm. Returning by train across England, there were servicemen and civilians assisting this poor wounded hero with his kit, never guessing how it happened. It was important that I got back to the squadron, joined the ship, reporting sick once on board, having no desire whatever to stay behind. 'Killer' gave me one of his 'I told you so' looks, which made me even more determined. In the event, we sent our aircraft to Speke airport, Liverpool, where they were loaded on board the escort carrier *Searcher*, and we never saw them again until we reached Madras, except in the distance, usually the ship taking it green and we all wondering how the corrosion would affect the engines, since the aircraft were lashed on deck. Once on board, my right arm and left leg were put into plaster.

The first part of the voyage was quite delightful, since we had mixed service personnel on board, WAAFs for Egypt and Italy, Wrens for various places, and miscellaneous NCOs and ratings, but mainly the groundcrews of the four squadrons. The food was excellent, the troops enjoyed themselves, despite their parochial officers' attitudes who tried to keep the sexes separate. It's difficult in the Mediterranean at night, in reasonable March weather, especially on the boat deck and how pleasant to go through the Skerki Bank and Sicilian Narrows without wearing tin hats and anti-flash gear. We floated past Algiers and Tunis, me hoping to get lightly torpedoed so that I could spend a few weeks in hospital ashore with daily visits from my ever-loving. Alas, no such luck, and a selfish thought anyway, as we disembarked passengers in Alexandria, Port Said and Port Tewfik. Somewhere we changed ships, the trooper being required urgently elsewhere. I think it was Bombay, where we embarked in a smaller ship, picked up Freddie Arnold and 845 Squadron's Avengers, Freddie telling me that they were coming out to relieve a Barracuda squadron in *Illustrious*. Since the Barracudas had only been out a few months in this theatre, maybe the news was better than we thought.

Somewhere too, Bill Sears and Tom Jamieson joined us, our new Captain and Operations Commander respectively. I had crossed Bill's bows in Algiers some months earlier, and he remembered, letting his glance rest slightly longer than on the other COs. A large and experienced pilot, his disciplinary attitudes were decidedly old-fashioned and often inappropriate in a Group where 95 per cent were non-career reserve officers.

Our ultimate destination was Madras, where we disembarked on 10 April, all wondering how the hell we were going to get our aircraft ashore. We need not have worried, it was all to be done in the Admiralty way – the hard way. *Searcher* docked and the Barracudas were craned out and deposited on the wharf. Each pilot then taxied his aircraft with wings folded (contrary to regulations), through the streets of Madras to St Thomas' Mount airfield. Three 'Barras' each preceded by a matelot with a red flag got through all right, but the fourth, turning a corner with a boost from the engine, unwound an Indian woman's sari and left her considerably *déshabillé*. Madras will never be the same again. Fortunately no sacred cows were encountered, and the operation was completed in a day, with heaven knows what effect upon the population, the airframes, the engines and of course, the pilots, whose nerves must have been shattered. This vignette will always stand out in my memory. As dusk began to fall, it was obvious that one or two aircraft would have to make the trip in the dark, or wait until dawn, which would interfere with the maintenance programme next day. Bill Sears fumed at delays, but what could he expect? The 48 Barracudas had travelled 6000 miles on heaving decks with no maintenance for six weeks, and from wintry England to tropical India. Leslie Watson, i/c unloading, endured the mounting wrath in dignified silence.

The groundcrews worked like beavers on the aircraft next day, most anxious to get somewhere where they could remain settled for a short while and get themselves and their kit sorted out. Bill meantime summoned all crews to the conference room at St Thomas' Mount, to give us the glad tidings. The big push was starting up north under Earl Mountbatten, and all available RAF aircraft were moving into Burma. Our unit, the four Barracuda and four Hellcat squadrons – which we hadn't yet seen – would come under 225 Group RAF Bangalore for the defence of India. Initially we would be based on Ulunderpet, some 80 miles from the sea, where naturally, we would be responsible for coastal defence.

Ulunderpet was a brand new airfield, and we were the first operational aircraft to land on its runways. Welcomed by Group Captain Whittington, who was obviously glad to have some people to use his station, we parked our aircraft on the perimeter and took a look at the living quarters. These were bungalow type, two officers to a hut, airy, cool, extremely spacious and made of kajan, or palm fronds with wooden frames. Mosquitoes abounded and the thatched roofs were alive with tree rats, a type of Indian squirrel whose curiosity and thieving characteristics made sleep a little difficult. Snakes also abounded, especially after rains, which washed them out of their holes, and the RAF doctor very soon gave us lectures on snakes, snake-bites, and how to treat them. It was encouraging to learn that most of the local varieties, cobra, kraits and vipers carried poisons which would kill in a matter of minutes, and struck usually at night or at dawn. A few days after our arrival we began cautiously to look ahead at eye-level, prior to which we always walked looking at the ground about two yards ahead.

A great hullabaloo arose one day shortly after our arrival, outside my hut. Emerging cautiously, I saw Manoel, our Goanese cook, clad only in a sari, holding a stick and pursuing something moving quite fast over the ground. Behind him tagged most of the 822 officers, all wielding Webley .45 revolvers. The quarry was a cobra, which can attain 30 mph it is said, and was currently heading for a hut that we all hoped was empty. Fortunately it was, and the young gentlemen now surrounded the hut which Manoel made to go inside, his 5ft forked stick at the ready. Realising that if anything emerged that was not Manoel – and there were many possible exits – it would get a volley of rather large slugs, most of which would hit fellow officers, I called them to put their guns away and stand clear, since Manoel obviously was the only person present who knew what he was doing. Inside he went, fearlessly, and we heard him shout and deliver tremendous whacks with his stick, eventually emerging with a very long and very dead cobra, which he skinned, selling the skin to Jamie Robertson who was going to cure it and make a belt.

The krait is probably the most deadly of all Indian snakes, About, two and a half to three feet long, it is in a sort of tiger-striped skin and emerges around dawn. One morning, the driver of the truck taking the crews to the airfield for a dawn mission ran over a krait, but wasn't certain if he had killed it. Ordering the crews to stay in the truck, he took his flashlight and searched underneath the truck chassis, eventually discovering the reptile wrapped around the front axle, whence it could easily have struck at one of the crews, since they usually had to unload their flying kit from the truck. Again, it was smartly despatched by a guard with knowledge of how to deal with the local fauna. A story I heard, which may be true, was that one wag put a dead viper into the bed of his cabinmate. When the cabinmate went to bed later, he was bitten by the mate of the dead viper which had come to find its fellow.

The tree rats were a real pest, chattering for 24 hours a day, and descending to eat or steal anything left lying around. They had a great partiality for trouser fly-buttons, which they chewed off and bore away to feast on later. For some reason they preferred Gieves' buttons, perhaps working on commission for the Bond Street tailors. One of our more senior observers, whom we shall call 'Ferdie' to save embarrass-ment, was particularly sensitive to the tree rats, and one or two of the younger gentry would tease him by rattling a stick across the kajan as they passed his hut. 'Ferdie' announced in the mess one evening that he was fed up with this and that in future he was sleeping with a .45 under his pillow and would shoot at anything disturbing the peace. Two of our perpetual comedians were 'Hiram' Burbidge and Tom 'Fingers' Esen-court – so nicknamed because he once brought back his torpedo from an operational mission, having failed to drop it because 'his finger stuck in the firing button'. On another occasion he waved to a Junkers 88 on parallel patrol in the Mediterranean because he thought it was a Beaufighter. Both were charming fellows and always cheerful.

One day they went into Madras, and after a somewhat liquid dinner, strolled round the market, where they purchased a magnificent-ly life-like stuffed reproduction of a combat between a mongoose and a cobra. This was too good to miss, so bringing it back, they tip-toed into 'Ferdie's' cabin and placed it on the end of his bed, intending to rattle on the walls of the hut by remote control. Unfortunately one or the other got an acute fit of the giggles when tip-toeing out, waking 'Ferdie', who reached under his pillow, seized a powerful electric torch therefrom, switched on and saw this fight to the death going on at the end of his bed. Whipping out his .45 revolver, he fired again and again at the struggling beasts, and effectively blew them to smithereens. Despite the sawdust on the floor, nothing would ever convince 'Ferdie' that this wasn't the real thing – 'Boy if you'd seen their eyes', he recounted next morning, 'you would have known they were real!'.

After being checked out by the RAF doctor, I went up to Trichinopoly Army General Hospital to have my limbs X-rayed with a view to removing the plaster. Though it was comfortable in more temperate climes, it was agony in India, especially as small bugs were apt to nest inside the plaster during the night, making sleep impossible. The army hospital was enormous and well-staffed, but they didn't have any X-ray equipment! Heavens knows how they dealt with cases such as mine. They sent me downtown to a small surgery run by an Indian doctor, who had all the latest GEC equipment, not only the large table machine, but also hand-held equipment, the like of which I had not seen before. He pronounced me OK, cut off the plaster and allowed me to watch him at work in his children's clinic, a heart-breaking sight.

Inside the portals of Trichinopoly Army General Hospital were two unforgettable posters. One depicted how to recognise poisonous from non-poisonous snakes. It appears that the poisonous variety have slightly different-coloured scales on the upper surface of the neck. The other poster was equally thought-provoking, depicting the method of differentiating Japanese from other Oriental soldiers. This was to do with the way their sandals are thonged. After reading these, one felt that some of the Admiralty-issued posters were almost normal.

We slowly got Ulunderpet into working order. The war started at dawn, but broke off at noon since the aircraft were too hot to touch, and certainly to stay in on the ground for more that a few minutes. There was also the grave danger of overheating the engine. Hostilities restarted at around 1600, concluding with a dusk patrol over Cuddalore, Vizagapatam and Pondicherry to a depth of about 50 miles, then northward to Madras and home. In between we flew many hours on dummy torpedo and dive-bombing attacks, navigation and other exercises.

Life became very boring, since it was almost impossible to play games of any description. The only relief was a weekly leave truck into Madras, Pondicherry or Cuddalore but even on the coast swimming was akin to bathing in warm cocoa, the only good part of a leave day was the sundowner followed by a good curry dinner.

Pondicherry was an interesting city. Prior to 1944, the Governor of this small French colony had followed the Vichy line, but whether through a crisis of conscience or a resurgence of French realism as the war began to go at last towards the Allies, the border guards and customs people were instructed to allow entry to visitors. Considerably smaller and cleaner than Madras, a great deal of European French-ness was everywhere apparent, not only in the abundant Catholic churches and schools, but also in the population, where a higher percentage of intermarriages could be seen than was normal in British India. Our hotel manager, himself the son of such a marriage, explained one of the major reasons. Pondicherry was a garrison city, and many French career soldiers found that their small pensions went a great deal further in such outposts, with the added possibility of a Government job on retirement from active duty. Also, a great number of Foreign Legionnaires, many of whom were not born in France, but had acquired French nationality through their army service, did not wish, on discharge from the Legion, to return to their native land. Here they could meet daily with the only friends they knew – other old soldiers. 'After all,' he concluded, 'to a man without a country, what could be better – a good climate, good food, good wine, good friends and plenty of girls?'. As we sipped our pernods and looked through his almost-European menu, we could not disagree.

As we took our coffee and cognac in the gathering dusk, we were assailed by several mothers with deformed and screaming babies gathered near the terrace. One of the minor industries in all Indian cities, and a major one in the larger cities of Bombay, Madras and especially Calcutta, is begging. Fortunate indeed is the parent of a deformed child, the more hideous its deformity the better, since it will bring more pity from visitors, especially Europeans, and so, more rupees. But to give money to beggers only invites a bigger crowd, and will also ensure that conversation with friends is quite impossible, as the babies are pinched to make them scream. 'Guilty money', said 'Killer', as we left an extra tip for distribution.

Our hearts leapt on 9 May when we flew two squadrons to China Bay, Trincomalee, to carry out 'runner' attacks, the nearest to the real thing. Our first attack was an ALT ie a smoke-float was dropped to simulate the torpedo's point of entry, and the target ship would calculate whether or not we had made a hit. Our target was a 'Flower' class corvette. I forget her name, there were so many, she may have been *Harebell*. We flew in loose formation to the target area searching for the corvette without result. Suddenly in the distance we saw a white ship, not in the area proper, but we knew the sort of navigators the RNVR produced from time to time. Happily there was a little cloud cover, so we climbed into this and shadowed the target, which didn't look at all like a 'Flower' class corvette. Straight out of the sun we went into attack, making perfect bow and quarter drops in four sub-flights. But there was something funny about the attack, the ship seemed to be flying the Italian ensign, and men were jumping overboard as we shot astern to open the range.

Back at the airfield on China Bay, I was requested to see the captain immediately. It appeared we had attacked the wrong ship – the Italian colonial sloop *Eritrea* – and we *had* seen some of the crew leap overboard. This ship, when Italy had surrendered in September 1943, was in the Red Sea, and wishing to carry on the war, her captain had taken her to Japan, an incredible journey when he had to navigate through the British and American fleets to get there. Arriving in Japan, he was made to understand that the Japanese did not want him or his ship, and put him on harbour patrol, a great loss of face after his navigational triumph in getting there at all. Although kept on low fuel supplies, the captain managed to save up enough to get away, and had escaped from Japan, quite sure that he would be welcomed by the British in Ceylon. A breakdown had necessitated a major engine overhaul at sea, but he finally made it to Trincomalee, where once again his pride was hurt by being placed on menial tasks there. Eventually, after much pleading he was given more responsible duties only a day or two before our ALT when his men imagined that, to crown all their misfortunes, the perfidious inglesi had decided to torpedo them at sea.

We visited *Eritrea*, profferred our apologies, stayed for lunch, and believe me or not, they became a target ship for China Bay, and enjoyed the task immensely.

The Fleet carriers had left to attack the Sabang oil refineries on Sumatra, leaving a trail of broken Barracudas at China Bay, and it was rumoured that Avengers would be taking over. We had not lost any crews, due probably to most 822 pilots having been trained on biplanes and therefore being less prone to take risks, other squadrons had. It was never a popular aircraft, despite the fact that in the hands of the conversion squadron COs, such as 'Vera' Thorpe or 'Ace' Wallace, the Barracuda could become a very potent aircraft. But certainly not an aircraft one takes liberties with.

The Supremo, Admiral Lord Louis Mountbatten, visited China Bay while we were there, and it is not impossible that he was instrumental in having Barracudas finally withdrawn, since he inspected all squadrons and talked very frankly and intimately with squadron commanders rather than Commanders Ops and Flying, trying to get the view of 'the boys in the sharp end' as he himself put it.

There was an amusing incident as he inspected us. Prior to leaving England, we had seen an American gangster film, probably an Edward G Robinson. At a tense moment in the story, the top 'hoods' are in quiet conference when the telephone rings. Edward G, cigar in mouth turns to one of his gorillas and says, 'Louie – da 'phone'. This became one of our squadron funnies, and everytime the 'phone rang out at flight, a voice would roar 'Louie – da 'phone'. So there we were at China Bay, lined up just outside the control tower, and immediately Lord Louis began his inspection of 822 Squadron, so the telephone rang loudly inside. A titter really did run through this audience, so much so that the Captain wanted to know later what the hell was so funny. He laughed too.

The Supremo was awe-inspiring. The troops all fallen in, hollow square fashion, and as he inspected, he spoke without rehearsal to many, being particularly interested in Dominion personnel, and knew most of the towns they came from, asking intelligent questions of each. One Kiwi, whose name I forget, told where he came from, and Lord Louis said, 'What's happened to Charlie Bloggs – or some such similar name – who used to be Mayor there?' 'He's my uncle, and still mayor', replied the astonished Kiwi. Then a pep talk, but not the usual 'flannel'. Instead he took the boys of all ranks into his confidence, so that every man stood ten feet tall. What a personality.

After a party with the torpedo-assessor Wrens led by Ruth Rose, who habitually rode a motorcycle and carried a .22 rifle, we journeyed back to Ulunderpet, literally the back end of civilisation compared with China Bay. We had finally got the Indian *Naiks* (corporals) and *chowkidars* (civilian watchmen) used to the 'Big Birds' which had at first frightened them. One day a fault in the electrical system in the noonday 120 degrees Fahrenheit had caused the yellow aircraft dinghies to inflate and burst out of their stowages aft of the airgunner's cockpit. The soldiers fled when the 'Big Birds' they had just become used to started laying eggs!. Sometimes they weren't so stupid. Several of our ratings must have been missing their bromide, and went one night with a local Indian villager to a place where they had been promised an amorous evening with some of the local beauties. One of our casanovas decided that his paramour wasn't quite reacting with the agility he had been led to expect, and flashing his pocket torch on this lady, he found she was certainly no chicken and most probably a great-grandmother. The ratings then smashed the village up as the broker had headed for the tall timber, as a result of which all local villages were put out of bounds to all personnel, which was a pity, since each had much history in an area where Clive and Hastings had founded the Indian Empire.

We had some thieving in the camp, hardly surprising when one saw the poverty around us, and the enormous disparity between their standards of living and ours. Eventually one miscreant was apprehended, and the local headman asked it they could be allowed to punish him, since the villagers were anxious to retain their employment with us. The district police superintendent finally took the matter over.

The corruption amongst Indian officials and merchants was unbelievable and shocking. Yet it was their way of life, and I understand even today that an independent India is still – if not even more – corrupt. One incident will serve to illustrate the racketeering. The food at our camp was provided by 'contractors' who did just that, contracting to supply our cooks. After a few days we became rather disenchanted with the monotony of the tough meat, which was known as 'camel's hump'. One day we asked if we could not, for a change have some bully beef, which must have been available to the British Army then in their tens of thousands in India, and, we believed, complaining of the monotony of bully beef. Our contractor regretted but it was not at all possible, bully beef was not available. Soon after this incident, 'Killer' and some friends went into Madras, where they had dinner at a restaurant, naturally a curry, but the meat tasted somehow familiar. It was unquestionably bully beef. 'Killer', never known for diplomacy, walked into the kitchen where he saw stacks of cases of Army corned beef, and went to see the local police. It transpired that these rations should have come to British units such as ourselves, but had been diverted by the contractors who had substituted 'camel's hump'. Eventually the contractor, an extremely wealthy man, was brought to trial, but avoided having his villainy publicly exposed by contributing the price of a Spitfire to the local War Weapons Week, as a result of which he was lauded as a public benefactor and patriot.

The outcome didn't satisfy 'Killer', who claimed that he would have sold him a Barracuda at a much more competitive price.

Our fighter cover was Grumman Hellcats, two squadrons of which were commanded by 'Tiny' Devonald and Dennis Jerram, old chums from 888 in *Formidable*. An extremely powerful aircraft, and a larger edition of the Wildcat, it was reputed to be the best fighter in the Pacific carrier forces. The main competitor was the Chance-Vought Corsair, a gull-winged aircraft of similar performance, but reputed to be much more difficult to handle – at least by our pilots – and a pig to land on a flightdeck. Corsairs had a long engine, which impeded the pilot's vision, so that he had to 'crab' or lurch sideways during the final approach to read the batman's signals. In spite of Hellcats having a somewhat delicate-looking undercarriage, their landings were far less noisy than those of Corsairs, but the bottom line would suggest that Hellcats had everything a Corsair had, and was better in terms of handling, manoeuvrability, comfort and decklanding. Everywhere, apparently, except speed, where the Corsair had an edge. The important point was that both aircraft could handle the fastest Japanese aircraft, the Navy 00 or 'Zero' with ease. Yet only two years earlier, the 'Zero' was reigning supreme in the East Indies and Pacific.

The Grumman Avenger was now seen at close quarters at Trincomalee, and appeared also to be built to a pilot's specification, rather than the near-Heath Robinson designs which seemed to be the basis for our British-built torpedo-bombers. Carrying a crew of three, it was better armed than the Barracuda, with 3 front- and 2 rearward-firing Brownings, with far greater destructive power than our twin Vickers' GO rear guns. The Avenger was faster, had greater range and was equally versatile. Given the choice, there was never any doubt which aircraft our TBR squadrons would choose – the Avenger by a large majority vote.

The prospect of 822 and 823 ever joining *Implacable* was now becoming more and more remote, even if she came to join Eastern Fleet eventually, being at the moment very involved in the Home Fleet's attempts to destroy *Tirpitz*. We began to wonder what would happen next, especially now that rumours were circulating that Barracuda squadrons were to be replaced by Avengers as quickly as possible, and an ironic buzz that Swordfish production was recommencing. The latter would have been ridiculous even if true. What was, in fact happening was that owing to changes to tactics in the anti-U-boat war, especially in the Atlantic, many Swordfish aircraft were being re-activated since A/S warfare methods had swung in favour of this old warhorse, as I was to discover quite soon. The news from the Atlantic was that hardly any convoy which had air protection had suffered any losses for several months, due at last to there being sufficient small carriers of the escort and MAC-ship categories available. On the Russian run, despite dreadful weather and mass aircraft and U-boat concentrations, we were also winning the battle.

So we continued our defence of India through May and June, though it was becoming obvious that our time out here was limited. The enemy was on the run on land and on the sea, and especially in the air. We did not recognise the detail at the time, but so long had the Japanese lines of supply become that they were vulnerable to the repeated attacks by Eastern Fleet's carriers (*Indomitable, Illustrious, Victorious* and *Indefatigable*) on their oil installations and storage – two on Palembang, and also Sabang and Sourabaya. It was all very encouraging, but we still knew that we had to fight every inch of the way back to Japan.

It had now become possible to give weekend leave to the squadron on a flight system so that a quarter were away at one time. The usual course was to take a train down to Madras and stay at the Connemara Hotel, where the weekend would be given over to drinking, dining and generally raising hell with like-minded souls from the other services. The British residents were not particularly noted for their hospitality in terms of invitations to their homes, though there were exceptions. On one of the train journeys one of our roving casanovas had seen a rather attractive young lady on the train. He learned her name – shall we say Baker-Dobson (which it wasn't) and was soon after asked to meet Mummy. Entering the compartment, Elspeth, the daughter said 'Lieutenant Crane, I'd like you to meet Mummy, Mrs Baker-Dobson'. To which Mummy, a real original memsahib said, 'Actually Mrs COLONEL Baker-Dobson. How do you do'. 'Killer's' sense of humour was so tickled by all this that he managed to finagle an invitation for a few of his brave colleagues to visit the Baker-Dobsons at their home. It transpired that the Colonelcy was in some militia battalion and the Colonel was far too old to do more than reminisce.

Their residence was in the compound of one of the large manufacturing companies of India, who seemed to produce everything from tea to boiled sweets. Just how Mrs COLONEL Baker-Dobson had got herself embroiled in trade, we never quite fathomed. So, two weekends later, six of the Wing turned up at the home, and were well entertained. Among the party was 'Oscar' Wilde, never happier than when tinkling the ivories, which he offered to do. The piano at the club (which was in the centre of the compound) was rather ancient and badly in need of tuning and after a few tries 'Oscar' asked if there wasn't perhaps another piano available so that he could better show his appreciation of the hosts' hospitality. There appeared to be another piano, not just another one, but a Bechstein Grand. Unfortunately it was owned by one of the technical managers, who, regrettably was Indian, and though he lived in the compound, he was not a member of the club, and it would be embarrassing to ask if his piano might be used. We didn't ask why, we knew the reason.

And so we said our goodbyes, thanking them especially for a very splendid weekend which in all respects but one it was – the food and drinks had been quite exceptional, and the service by the hired help fantastic. We were asked to come again in two weeks' time.

One company made a very potable gin in large ceramic containers, modern versions of the old ceramic barrels often seen on show on the shelves of public houses. They must have held about five gallons or more. Colombo at this time had a gin drought due to the tremendous influx of ships, and especially carriers, often four or five and as many escorts being in or around the port. Even Saccone and Speed could not cope with the rush. An SOS went out, and every aircraft which flew down from Ulunderpet or Madras to Colombo or China Bay had to carry its full payload of gin. I'm sure we were evading custom duties, which wasn't then the point. The fact was that the Air Arm just couldn't exist without its gin. On one occasion a Barracuda landed and taxied to the hangar, where the pilot emerged from his cockpit to observe a growing pool of liquid under his aircraft, 'My God!' he was heard to exclaim 'I hope it's glycol'.

On 10 June a Wing conference was held at Racecourse airfield, Colombo, where it was announced that each Wing comprising 2 Barracuda squadrons of 12 aircraft would be reduced to one squadron of 15 aircraft. It was obviously the beginning of the end for Barracudas in Eastern Fleet. In terms of number reduction, it presented no problem, since we had already left several of our original 12 on various scrap-heaps. A few days earlier, while moving an aircraft around the compass base, Air Mechanic 'Candy' Johnson and his team had actually pushed the tail right off one of the Barracudas. Another curious incident was when Jock Carruthers, a steady and reliable pilot, suddenly found his aircraft out of control when test-flying from Ceylon. The more he opened his throttle to gain height, the more the aircraft sank, finally burying itself in a swamp, from which we were able to raise it with airbags. Jock's explanation sounded so impossible that it was beginning to make him doubt his ability. We found in fact that some part of the boost mechanism had been fitted back to front, giving exactly that performance. And this was a new aircraft, so it was not a squadron maintenance fault.

On 19 June I led 822 Squadron in the air for the last time, from Ulunderpet to Katukurunda, where I handed over command to Leslie Watson, who, if he is to be believed, envied me in the fact that I would probably now have a choice of new jobs to undertake. Never having volunteered for anything, I'd take my chances. A great disbanding and reforming party followed. It was heartening to know that the new squadron would be 822 rather than 823, and though sad to leave my first command, I did so with the knowledge that it would be in Leslie Watson's capable hands, who knew them all. 'Killer' confided as the evening wore on and inhibitions wore off, that I had lasted much longer than he had anticipated. So, after several impromptu and alcoholic speeches, we went our separate ways, knowing that many of us would meet again.

Some years after the war, I met 'Killer' in Leicester. One always worries about one's ability, and I asked 'Killer' (who also had eventually commanded his own squadron) how he rated me as the ninth CO of 822. He thought a moment and then said, 'The boys would have followed you anywhere'. My chest swelled with pride, but then he added, 'Though mainly out of curiosity'.

Chapter 19
Injury Time

It transpired that a number of senior pilots and observers were needed back home to man the instructional and training squadrons and stations, so that in six months' time the final push on the Japanese mainland could begin. There was sound sense in this and at last the Admiralty were beginning to modernise their ideas about training. Instead of, as in the past, instruction being concentrated on the individual at each stage, the new idea was to form a series of Operational Training Units, or OTUs. There the aircrews would come together, form into crews and squadrons, so that their bonds would be formed early, under the CO, senior pilot and senior observer, and they would complete all their training together before going off to a ship. This would differ from the old system where a squadron moved along on an old-fashioned type production-line, with bits being added at each stage. It sounded interesting.

Finally, we who were about to go home became assembled at Ratmalana, 'Ceylon', and boarded a Dakota C47. The senior officer of the party was Captain Robert Cunliffe, formerly in command of the carrier *Illustrious*, going home to become Commodore Portsmouth. We knew of his excellent reputation, but didn't know him as a man. All we knew was that we would be going home in several hops – Ratmalana to Bombay – Karachi – Bahrain – Cairo – Tunis – Gibraltar – England, staying overnight in most places.

By this time my wife had moved up to Mediterranean Coastal Air Force HQ at the Royal Palace of Caserta, just outside Naples, and a dark plan was forming in my mind to get her posted home. The only way so far as I could see. So, quietly, I worked out the nearest airfield to make a detour to Naples, knowing as I did that once home, the appointments branch would send us all home for three weeks' leave, which I might just as well spend with my ever-loving. So, finally, when we arrived at Cairo West, I summoned up my courage, and told 'Bob' Cunliffe of my sad situation. He said nothing for a moment, then 'Woods, you look a trifle sick to me. I suggest you go to the sick bay in the morning and get the doctor to look at you.' Then, almost in an aside, 'And if you have any problems with NA2SL Appointments, refer him to me'.

A luxuriant lie-in next morning, though in the words of the gunner's mate 'Hassuming a haspect mournful but subdued' in case anyone came looking for me. Hardly surprisingly no one did, as most fellow passengers knew my plan. In fact, I didn't feel too good, having visited Cairo the previous night with several chums, including the hirsute Canadian, 'Moe' Dunfield. Although we were all short of clean raiment, 'Moe's' rig was startling by any standards, comprising a short-sleeved white shirt with RNVR lieutenant's shoulder-straps, rather soiled khaki shorts, white knee-length hose and black half-wellingtons badly in need of a shine. A few US Navy officers were in the bar, knife-edge smart as only Yanks can be with laundries in their ships. They eyed 'Moe' with great curiosity, trying to identify this bewhiskered and dishevelled apparition who was having such an enjoyable time. 'Moe' had a slight speech impediment, which, coupled with his Canadian accent and dress, had them puzzled. Eventually, one of them walked over to our side of the bar, and addressing 'Moe', said, 'Excuse me sir, but my friends and I are having an argument over which Navy you serve in. Would you be kind enough to settle it for us?'. I suppose Canadians have the same sort of love-hate for Americans which New Zealanders reserve for us Pommies. 'Moe' looked up, moustaches a-bristle and barked 'The ROYAL Navy. Is there another?'. We almost went to action stations in the bar of Shepheards' Hotel.

After the Dakota had left, for the sake of form and an alibi, I went to the sick bay and was passed fit for duty. By noon, 'Dinty' Moore, the RAF Transport Command duty pilot, had me on another Dakota bound for Naples.

A very surprised wife met me at the Royal Palace at Caserta, now the Mediterranean Allied Air Forces HQ and since no other accommodation was available in the city, we stayed overnight at the YWCA Naples, moving on next day to Sorrento, where for one shilling per head per day we could stay at the aircrew rest centre, the Hotel Coccmella. We encountered many strange looks from those who thought wrongly that this lone naval person was poaching without a licence, but all was soon explained. The great Austrian violinist Fritz Kreisler had once played in this hotel, but the Italian orchestra at this time had a repertoire limited, it seemed, to 'Lili Marlene' and 'Return to Sorrento'.

After ten glorious days of sunbathing, swimming, dancing and eating decent food once more, I redeemed my promise to Bob Cunliffe and returned to London via Tunis and Gibraltar, where 'Chalkie' was still frightening the transients. The leave in Italy could have been extended since NA2SL Appointments had nothing for me until 21 August, when I was bidden to report to the RNAS Inskip, Lancashire, as air staff officer, or in real terms, as chief instructor to observers and airgunners at an Operational Training Unit.

It seemed likely that for at least the next six months, and probably for a year, I would be non-operational, A couple of months would be necessary to understand and fit into Training Command disciplines, and further time would elapse before intelligent improvements could be made to the training schedules if and when they became necessary. The first essential was to find out how much the pupils had learned, as their syllabus must have changed considerably since my training days of 1939/40. Then one had to find out how much they didn't know, and fill in the gap. Most important, at least for a while, was to keep ears open and mouth shut. Some first-line people joined OTUs believing that they knew it all and their new charges knew nothing, not realising that all the time enemy inventiveness was introducing new weapons and methods, calling for new and effective counter-measures.

Many young men who had accepted responsibility had come a long way in five years of war. Some had tasted that most satisfying situation which is the natural ambition of every young aviator – command of his own squadron. True, my own incumbency was less than a year, but even at that was longer than the average of 822's previous COs. The odds against achieving such an appointment were at least 8 to 1 against since only four of my original course of 33 did so, and as intakes became larger as the war progressed, so the odds-against increased, despite the growth of the Fleet Air Arm. In 1939 a course of 30 to 40 candidates began training every other month, but by 1942, courses of 100 and upwards were entering every month. A high percentage came from New Zealand, where a blockage had occurred in training aircrew volunteers for the RNZAF and eventually over 1000 impatient and patriotic young Kiwis gladly accepted the alternative of joining the Fleet Air Arm in Great Britain. We were very lucky to have them.

Thus it seemed that when I did return to first-line flying, it was more than likely to be in an administrative role such as air staff officer in an escort carrier. Very few observers were selected as wing leaders of torpedo-bomber squadrons, and now that Europe had been invaded and we had moved from defence to attack in the Far East, there would be a greater requirement for strike aircraft wings. I reasoned that it was likely that pilots would take over as strike wing leaders as the war was carried into the German and Japanese homelands. Though this had little bearing on my present appointment to Inskip, it was well to keep such probabilities in mind, the better to plan one's future career.

There were times when the past five years seemed an eternity and some moments when it seemed not very long at all. The former illusion applied when one considered technical innovations. Radar, especially the airborne types such as ASV, was a complete mystery to us until early in 1941 in Force H. True, we had heard of a mysterious electronic system, originally called 'RDF' during Signal School, Portsmouth in the winter of 1939 when two Canadian destroyers, *Assiniboine* and *Restigouche*, came to be equipped with this magic box, but all we managed to learn from the Canadian ratings who came for training was that it was an improved type of D/F apparatus. Damning it with faint praise kept the inquisitive away from the restricted area where training took place.

New types of aircraft, better-equipped, faster, and with longer range had also come along. Compared with the Swordfish of 1940, which had only the bare essentials such as radio, homing beacon and IFF to ensure our returning to base without being shot at by friendly ships or aircraft, the difference was almost like comparing the 1914-18 Sopwith Pup with the Hurricane. Yet amazingly, the Swordfish was one of the few Allied aircraft to serve operationally right through the war, sinking more tonnage of enemy shipping than any other aircraft. Increasingly, large task forces of carriers were being used in the East Indies and Pacific theatres, frequently capable of operating 300 fighter and bomber aircraft from six carriers. In the final stages of the war against Japan, 100 carriers were in the Pacific, 17 of which were British. Compared with the one-carrier forces of 1940-42, the new strategy called for a different type of naval aviator. It was our job to help provide them.

In 1940 my course had gone operational practically straight from the party to celebrate our passing-out. Casualties were high – Busby, Marais and Lane were all killed in their first month of operations. While the desperate days of 1940 called for desperate measures, there is little doubt that if those young men and the hundreds after them who were listed as casualties could have undergone operational training before joining squadrons, they would have been better prepared, and could have inflicted more damage on the enemy. Even better, many might still be alive today. Clearly, my first priority in this new appointment was to pass on the experience I had gained in the previous four years.

RNAS Inskip, HMS *Nightjar*, situated between Preston and Blackpool, introduced me to Fleet Air Arm training for the graduate. My immediate colleague, the Chief Flying Instructor, or CFI was Lieutenant-Commander Johnny Ievers, a very experienced regular with an elfin-type humour, later to become a rear-admiral. One of the most charming captains ever met, J B Heath, ran the Station by persuasion and example, scarcely ever raising his voice. 'Wings' was Commander Kit Nicholson RNVR, a famous architect by profession, regrettably killed in the 1948 Olympics as a member of the British Gliding team in Switzerland. The training squadron COs were the Australian Bernard 'Digger' Morgan with 766 Swordfish and N G 'Bob' Haigh with 763 Avengers, and 'Pansy' Kelsall with 760, a small Hurricane squadron not quite big enough for him to qualify for an acting half-stripe, his daily song of woe. 'Pansy', the nickname happily referring ironically to his usually scruffy sartorial appearance, had our sympathy, and also that of Captain Heath but nothing could be done. Among the instructors were several old shipmates in 'Davy' James and Clifford Wearden of 766, Philip Ford the chief decklanding instructor, and the many other new friends who soon made me feel at home. The outgoing air staff officer, Mallett, was apparently surprisingly happy to be returning to sea in the escort carrier *Campania*, which seemed to spend most of her time on the North Atlantic and Russian run.

Almost as soon as I arrived, probably my initial reporting to Captain Heath, he proceeded to give me in the presence of 'Kit' Nicholson a well-intentioned homily on the value of we experienced officers to a training establishment. 'So many who come here', he said, 'want to turn round immediately and go back to operations. I do trust that you will not be like that. We need your sort here'. In fact, having been overseas for the previous four years, nothing was further from my thoughts, a spell at home was needed, but not in the Home Fleet, which usually meant Hatston/Iceland/Bear Island. On the other hand one didn't want to give the impression that the old spark of aggression had gone, so I mumbled some suitable reply.

What did later begin to cause a few nagging fears was the legend that so many senior aviators who were given their spell of instructional duties seemed to get written off in some stupid accident through the aberration of a pupil. This had happened to Hughie Hunter, 'Feather' Fausset and others. There was also another factor silently surfacing from time to time in my thoughts, that even the best of aviators have temporary lapses which can be fatal. The great Dicky Cork, Corsair wing leader and winner of DSO and DSC (and if legend speaks true, almost a DFC too, from the Battle of Britain) had been killed during my recent stay in Ceylon. Whether this was over-confidence on his part or a mental lapse as he landed his aircraft on top of one taking off at Trincomalee will never now be known, since both pilots died instantly. Ransford Slater OBE, DSC, one of the most experienced Swordfish pilots who ever donned a Mae West, was killed low-flying near Londonderry, at a time, it was said, when he'd no need to be flying at all. They were all infinitely better than most of us normal average aviators, so did this mean we were more, or less vulnerable? Someone once said during a discussion on psychology that the stupid ones among us would survive, as those with imagination would either do very brave deeds or let their fears get on top of them. I began to hope fervently that he was right, and then began to wonder if, by even thinking about this, my own imagination wasn't beginning to work overtime.

As Paddy McGrath, who always spoke in shorthand would have said – Psalms 5:11 ('Let them perish through their own imaginations'). These macabre speculations probably sprang from the realisation that after four years' flying and various other strange and unscheduled adventures without adequate preparation, it would be prudent not to take many risks. So, no ambition to be best, just the oldest naval aviator.

With the landings in France successfully made, and progress maintained, the war against Germany in all probability would end within six months. There was then the Japanese theatre, and even though their army was in retreat through much of Asia, physical subjugation of Japan was not only essential, it would also be bloody with no holds barred. One could expect no mercy, friends had been shot down, captured and beheaded. How long could individual luck hold out? It seemed odds-on that in six months' time I would be heading for Japan in some fairly vulnerable capacity anyway.

There was much to do at Inskip, as the station changed its role for the nth time. Although it had always concentrated on anti-submarine warfare, tactics and strategy had changed for the U-boats, and ours must keep pace. A recent innovation was the invention of the schnorkel, a device which enabled a submerged submarine to breathe and thus remain submerged for very long periods as well as presenting a much smaller target for airborne radar detection. The Battle of the Atlantic was still proceeding though increased use of aircraft had reduced shipping losses to a fraction of those sustained in 1940 to 1942, which, if they had continued, would have starved Britain into surrender. The ships from which aircraft flew on convoy protection duties were either fleet carriers such as *Victorious, Furious*; escort carriers which were smaller, such as *Nairana, Campania, Activity*; and MAC ships, which were tankers or grain carriers with a superimposed flight deck. MAC ships – short for merchant aircraft carrying – were usually of 8000-9000 tons. Converted tankers carried their three or four Swordfish permanently on deck, while the grain ships, which discharged their cargo by suction, had a small hangar between decks that could take all four aircraft.

The escort carriers' complement of aircraft was much larger, and included fighters as well as Swordfish. There were good reasons for this. Much of the reconnaissance work of the Germans was made by aircraft, either the Focke-Wulf four-engined Kondor of exceptional range, or by Junkers 88s and Heinkel 111s. If they sighted a convoy, they would home-in the U-boat pack, ergo, if they could be shot down quickly, preferably before making their reports, the U-boats could be dealt with more easily, if not kept completely at bay. Mention must be made of Catapult Aircraft Merchant ships (Camships) which carried a single Hurricane fighter on a catapult in the bows. These extraordinarily courageous pilots, who had little chance of anything better than a bale-out and pick-up by the convoy at the end of their action against enemy aircraft, and frequently against U-boats, did an invaluable job until the first MAC ships were built and sufficient escort carriers were available to take on the duty of protecting convoys aggressively and efficiently. The United States' shipyards became very efficient in building escort carriers on the 'Liberty Ship' principle. These ships, known as 'Woolworth carriers', though somewhat stark and functional were both adequate and efficient. The Salerno landings in September 1943 were covered by fighters from such ships. Though never quite so comfortable as the British-built *Vindex, Nairana* and *Campania*, their numbers grew quickly, so that our merchant ship losses fell as dramatically as U-boat sinkings increased from 1943 on. Side-effects were also important in that CAM ships could be dispensed with, releasing experienced fighter pilots back to the RAF, and as escort carriers took on greater and more aggressive roles, fleet carriers could be spared to go where the carrier war was beginning – in the Pacific and East Indies.

My wife returned from Italy in November 1944, proving that my leave there, by courtesy of Captain Cunliffe, had been fruitful. Inskip was a station where living-out was not only permitted, it was actively encouraged to provide more accommodation for pupils who were passing through at an alarming rate. We set up home first in Lytham St Annes', and after my son was born the following April, in Churchtown, near Garstang. It wasn't like peacetime living-out, since I was flying or working seven days a week, at least we saw each other most days, and could spend evenings at home when there was no night-flying. The impact of civilian life upon us was rather startling, since both of us had been used to the comparative luxuries of service messes. Even though the Fylde is a rich farming area, and eggs, butter, chickens and other edibles were available if one knew the right people, our visits to homes of relatives and friends where such items were luxuries, brought home the realities of wartime rationing. The average civilians' meals seemed to consist of bread and margarine, with occasionally something to put on it, and meat only once a week. Even the mainstay of the British kitchen, a cup of tea, was reserved for close friends. We just didn't know how well-off we were in the services. As for gathering together furniture for our small flat, it was almost impossible. True, there were 'Utility' styles, like escort carriers, functional and adequate, but even with the necessary dockets, items weren't always available. Secondhand furniture of average quality fetched very high prices, and this continued for several years after the war ended. But we managed, viewing the whole thing as a bit of a lark, and got together quite a respectable little home.

There was something about the instructors at Inskip who were experienced in practical anti-submarine warfare. Probably because the job called for instant decisions, it seemed to breed nonconformists. It was not that they were undisciplined, but more that they were disciplined in an undisciplined way. There were more than average numbers of eccentrics – Johnnie Winstanley, a cleanshaven Groucho Marx, with a new, hilarious dialect story every day. Mike Wargent, a smiling Rudolf Hess who couldn't ever remember a punch-line but had a bar-clearing guffaw for Winstanley's classics. To have Mike and Harry Kenworthy laughing in unison was hard on the eardrums, though others, like David Glassborough, Cyril Davidson and Pat Calcutt, of more studious natures, made a very agreeable balance in Wharles Mess, where 766 Swordfish Squadron HQ officers lived. The other mess, at the far end of the airfield, known as Inskip Mess was the home of 763 Avengers and the 760 Squadron Hurricane pilots, plus most of the station maintenance officers. I have commented before on the differences between atmospheres in ships and squadrons. Here, on the same station, the wardrooms differed. Of course Inskip was where the Captain lived, and though no martinet by any stretch of the imagination, his presence had a somewhat restraining effect. At Wharles, our highest rank was Commander Flying, which might account for the occasional outbursts.

Each camp had a First Lieutenant, and one at Wharles when I first arrived was straight from P G Wodehouse. Monocled, and with a 1914-1918 DSC, one could not at first believe that his name really was Lieutenant-Commander Paddy Carruthers. A most delightful and helpful character, always ready for a party, but at the same time running a taut ship, he taught the young pupils wardroom manners often without their knowing it. His war – the First – had seen a Paddy much of the stamp of these youngsters of 1944. Doubtless it brought back his youth, but he had some sparkling tales to tell. How well I remember his face when we went to the wardroom piggery on St Patrick's Day to find his charges painted Killarney green. He loved it, probably because a young Paddy would have done the same thing.

Our bombing ranges were at Pilling and Fleetwood, target and recovery vessels at Heysham, farther north up the coast. In both places were outposts with personnel who must, in the frequent autumn mists and winter snows, have felt that civilisation had forgotten them. Captain Heath recognised this and ensured that they were invited to RNAS Inskip as frequently as possible. Their work was hard – recovering runner torpedoes in the ex-drifters *Netsuke* and *Sunny Bird* or in the two motor launches towing a target for rocket-firing Swordfish calls for steady nerves, especially in some of the ever-changing weather conditions.

The bomb-range Wrens spent much of their time either closed-up in reinforced concrete marking shelters or up to their wellington-clad knees in mud. The captains of our motor-launches, George Sykes, a former policeman, and Hamish, a Channel Islander, were visited or invited back to camp as frequently as possible for discussions and hospitality, and the Wrens given every opportunity to attend dances and other social functions at the air station, if only to reprove the pupils for their unseemly language after a poor bombing exercise.

Petticoats were much in evidence at Inskip. The senior lady was one Olivia Nepean, possessed of twin senses of duty and humour, in just the right proportions. She was a first officer, the equivalent of a lieutenant-commander, having achieved this rank from her initial one of officers' steward. A slight and splendid lady, she was referred to by her Wren officers as 'She who must be obeyed', but did a fine job. We had Wren air mechanics, dealing with airframes, engines, armament, photography, clerical, medical, drivers, parachute packers, bomb range markers, torpedo assessors, radar mechanics – you name it the Wrens did it, and did it very well. Our staff officers, Kilminster, a second officer, and Baxter, a delightful and very humorous third officer looked after the control tower's problems very efficiently, where pupils and their instruction were concerned. In the aircraft control, up in Annie's Room , was yet another set of very efficient aircraft controllers, who were also very beautiful. Although officers and ratings – even if female – were not officially allowed to drink and date together, there was a great number of genuine, as distinct from transient, romances. Inskip was a happy station, and again, it is my belief that this spread from the top down.

Our main exercises were anti-submarine, and a rather fine modus operandi had been built up for the MAC ships, who were now using Swordfish and Hurricanes in team attacks. When a submarine was detected, two 'Stringbags' and one Hurricane would go off together. The first Swordfish was equipped with depth charges, the second with armour-piercing rockets, while the Hurricane was armed with cannon. The scheme was that the first Swordfish would drop depth charges on the submerged U-boat, forcing it to the surface. Seconds later, with the U-boat on the surface, the second one would come in on the beam of the enemy craft and fire its rockets, either all eight at once, but more likely in two sets of four, or four sets of two in separate attacks, depending on the state of the U-boat. The Hurricane would strafe the U-boat fore and aft or as required, keeping heads down in the conning tower, and especially keeping the crew away from the gun positions.

Although I never saw this operation in action, reports indicated that it was highly successful if the crew of the aircraft were well drilled and co-ordinated. Obviously they must know each other's idiosyncracies, and their R/T intercommunication must be first class. To quote one trio of crews I met – the depth charges brought up the U-boat as if it were trying to take off, the rockets opened up the casing like a sardine can while the Hurricane's strafing must have had them farting like racing camels. Imaginative, but probably quite true. Strangely, at this late stage of the war I began to understand why aviators and submariners had a few punchups ashore. At Inskip we had this whole operation with three aircraft all over and completed in under 30 seconds. It became a showpiece we put on for VIP visitors, most of whom were glad they hadn't joined the submarine service, but were also not too sure they'd been any happier in the air arm.

Other exercises with Swordfish, Avengers and Hurricanes were fairly standard – navigation and radar, ALTs, ADTs, ARTs, though by this time we tended to cut the torpedo work to a minimum since it was considered that this was highly unlikely to be used against submarines at this stage of the war, especially now that we seemed to have the upper hand. Or thought we did until one day we had reports of U-boats operating in the Irish Sea. Naturally everyone wanted to get at 'em, but the flap passed quickly. It was probably our tame submarines practising diving and surfacing which had caused the excitement. The Avengers, too, reduced their torpedo exercises carrying out dive-bombing instead, since although the Avenger was an excellent aircraft, competently replacing the Barracudas in the East Indies and Pacific, but not yet the Home Fleet, the American torpedo had a habit of thinking it was a porpoise, surfacing and diving before its run was complete. In any case, dive-bombing, which the Japanese had brought to a fine art, was now considered to be just as effective as a tinfish, cheaper and probably less lethal on the aircrew.

Our 'chummy station' was RNAS Ronaldsway in the Isle of Man. The vagaries of weather in the Irish Sea were such that if we were in the clear, Ronaldsway was likely to be fogged in and vice-versa. There were, of course, other airfields on the mainland, Salmesbury, Ringway, Stretton, Speke and even Blackpool at a pinch, but most of them would be enduring our weather in time of need. Moreover, our pilots liked landing in the Isle of Man since there were a few goodies there which were not always available our side – mostly edibles, but the hardstuff always seemed to be more plentiful there and if my memory serves me right, somewhat cheaper too, thanks to the Tynwald or something similar. However, landing at Ronaldsway was not all fun. One night an Avenger squadron torpedo attack was under way when heavy fog came down. The aircraft were recalled to Inskip in the hope that they would reach home before the fog. Regrettably they did not, and were instructed to return to Ronaldsway, where it was reported that the mist was lifting, and landings would be possible. Most unfortunately two of the pupils hit the cliffs on which Ronaldsway stands – not high, but high enough if you don't expect them. It was a macabre affair, since the aircraft both caught fire, and when the coffins were returned to us for the funerals, we were advised that under no consideration whatsoever should the caskets be opened for relatives.

There were many amusing incidents with the pupils. At one time we had a complete squadron of Royal Netherlands Navy aircrews who were carrying out their forming up with us prior to commissioning their own carrier. They were so happy to be doing their own thing, instead of being lodgers in Royal Naval Air Squadrons. Their chatter over the R/T had to be disciplined early, since they became so exuberant when their bombing or rocket firing practices were getting good scores. One young man, who should have been giving the executive signal 'Attack, attack,

attack', suddenly forgot his English and screamed 'Attick, attack, attock'.

On another occasion, in an Avenger, a young observer pupil pressed the wrong tit on his Bendix radio – a good set anyway, but if the continuous wave button is used, it blasts everyone else off the air, and is intended to be used only in emergency, such as an enemy report, or when ditching. It is an easy mistake to make, I've done it myself, but on this occasion, the pupil was causing us to miss messages. When he returned, he was sent to report to me in the control tower, where I was loftily arrogant, mainly because it was night flying, it was late and I was missing drinking time. The pupil was instructed to report to me in the morning, when I gave him the requisite dressing-down, and as he mumbled his apologies and assurance that he wouldn't do it again, I said 'And how many hours flying have you logged so far?'. The sub-lieutenant replied 'Just over a thousand, sir'. After a sharp intake of breath, I enquired 'How did you log so many?' 'I was loaned to a Catalina squadron, Sir'. The best I could muster after this, having just over a thousand hours myself in five years of flying was a not very convincing 'Which is another good reason why you should have know better'. Life is full of surprises.

'Pansy' Kelsall was becoming a Notifiable Disease, Johnny Ievers decided one morning. He had started to come up to the control tower, stopping at our door on the first floor, opening it without knocking, making some facetious remark about his lack of promotion, wagging his beard at us, then going up to the top deck, his pause with us taking not more than half a minute. We decided he needed to be taught a lesson, and borrowed a boxing glove from the gym, which we padded well and then attached to a clothes prop. The drill was that we would see when 'Pansy' arrived on his motorcycle, since he had to park it just underneath the window where the deck landing controllers had their office, and they would give us the high-sign. 'Pansy' duly arrived, and we were warned. He would look in, see Johnny Ievers hard at work, but not see me, behind the door, and since only his head entered the room, a short sharp punch with the boxing glove would probably stop this caper for ever. It all went according to plan except that the glove caught in the door handle, and the door slammed on 'Pansy's' neck. He had gone through red in the face and was slowly going purple before we could release him. One good thing – he never did it again.

Those of us who lived in villages were sometimes called out for extra-mural duties since most of the menfolk were away in the services. As 5 November 1944 was going to be a bit miserable in Churchtown because there weren't many fireworks for the kids and they'd have to make do with a bonfire, I mentioned to John Heath that quite a number of Very cartridges were over-age and should be disposed of – what better than to combine a duty with a little kindness and fire them on Guy

Fawkes' night. Provided we informed all local interested parties, such as the airfields, fire brigades, coastguard etc, all was well. Ably assisted by Mike Wargent, we gave the kids of Churchtown a party they will probably still remember. Christmas, too was unusual in this village, since they had two Santa Clauses, again Mike and me, hoping it wouldn't shatter all their childish illusions. Not that wartime children were allowed many of those.

So we passed our days at Inskip, into 1945 and the realisation that soon we would be getting ready for the Pacific, since in the spring Avenger squadrons began to come through, together with the new Firefly from Fairey Aviation, a beautiful-looking thoroughbred, neater than the Fulmar, and equipped with cannon, but still no rear gun for the observer. It was able to carry a small bombload or rockets, all in all a very flexible machine. We loved them, and flew a lot of hours in them. Alas, at this time Johnny Ievers went to a promotion, Davy James and Cliff Wearden to new squadrons as senior pilots. My time would soon be up – probably just after Easter by my calculations. But now there were conferences we had to attend, at Arbroath, Crail and Lee-on-Solent, piloted by John Heath; the new CFI Tony Kennard or by Kiwi Blackburn. We were making recommendations for improvements in the training schedules, and we'd better learn the new moves ourselves, for quite soon we'd be out there using them.

My son, named by unanimous vote 'Roger', was born on 17 April 1945 and a short time after this came VE Day, truly a day to remember. I can hardly recollect anyone dead-stone-cold-sober. 'Chiefy' Walker, a grizzled World War I Engineer, scarcely ever known to take more than the odd beer in the mess took a few more than usual aboard and was seen trying to ride his motorcycle combination – know as 'La Composita' down the main runway. Fortunately there was unlikely to be anything flying that day. Mr East, the warrant telegraphist, who was known to take more than one beer in the mess, had in anticipation of the announcement brought a bottle of 'neaters' rum down to the wireless office to celebrate with his 'sparkers'. Their ideas had coincided, and eventually Mr East decided it was time for lunch. Neat rum can have an almost hypnotic effect on some people, which is probably why it is administered to encourage men before, during, and after some heroic or traumatic action. Mr East, despite almost 40 years in the Navy was certainly hypnotised that day. Mounting his motorcycle, he rode from the W/T office to the exit gate but for some strange reason omitted to turn left to go to Inskip Mess. He went straight ahead across a 'B' road, fortunately devoid of traffic, through a five-barred gate from which he emerged looking like one of the star turns at the Royal Tournament, ploughing on literally through a field, whence he was smartly retrieved by the W/T department battery truck. It appeared later that he suffered from nothing worse than a fractured bottle of 'neaters'.

It must have been about this time that I had occasion to go to Lee-on-Solent for a conference, and decided to visit some of the hostelries in Old Portsmouth. Crossing on the Gosport to Portsmouth Harbour Station Ferry, who should I meet but CPO George Oliver, Gunner's Mate, formerly my instructor at *St Vincent* in September and October 1939. 'Good evening, Chief Petty Officer Oliver' I greeted him. Oliver saluted and said 'I'm afraid you have the advantage of me, sir'. 'Woods,' I replied, 'No 8 Pilot's course, September 1939'. We shook hands. He eyed me up and down. 'Blimey', he said 'a bleedin' two-and-a-half. Reckon I should be a bloody admiral – SIR'. How fitting that Chief and Petty Officers are referred to as 'the backbone of the Royal Navy'.

As the lights slowly came on all over Europe, so the social life improved. As is said, improvement from nought to ten percent is a thousandfold increase. Many of our older officers and men could be released on compassionate grounds for family reasons or under Class 'B' if required for a vital industry. .This began to affect another social item, our weekend shooting parties.

Inskip was built on part of Lord Derby's estate and abounded in game. As part of the training equipment, we had a skeet shooting range, intended to improve the marksmanship of aircrew, and hence had a good allocation of cartridges for the 12-bore guns. It was not used as much as it might have been, consequently there were surplus cartridges and guns. Lieutenant-Commander Dukinfield ran a sports store in Liverpool in peacetime, and was a shooting enthusiast. Another First War veteran, he found two good beaters from Inskip camp and trained two more as reserves, so that every available Saturday afternoon in season, a party would venture forth, headed by Captain Heath, to knock down a few for the pot – hares, pheasant, partridge, snipe and rabbits, sometimes in sufficient quantity to offer a few to the wardroom galleys after our own needs had been met. One inexperienced and nameless gun, claiming more than a passing knowledge of the sport, got over-excited one day and shot a swan. Perhaps 'shot down' would be a more apt description as he gave it both barrels from about 20 yards. We buried the big bird hastily, swearing each other to secrecy as well as to never inviting Wyatt Earp again. Shortly after this incident, 'Duk' and his senior beater were released and demobbed, which left us somewhat bereft of experienced men to prepare for the shoot.

Many of the Dominion aviators were going home on long leave, presumably preparatory to the Last Act in Japanese waters. The Dominion navies were either talking about or actually forming their own air branches, and retrieving their own experienced nationals. Since pay and prospects generally were better in these new air arms, many whom one had always assumed to be British-born suddenly remembered and revealed their birth in the Dominions. 'Dizzy' Whatmore became an

Instant South African and John Hoare reverted to his Canadian status. Small blame to them, they were all capable of greater responsibility and higher rank. Simultaneously invitation came round for applications for permanent commissions in the Royal Navy. I thought about it, but in my opinion it was no sort of a life for a married man with a family, and really only postponed the eventual decision of making a fresh start as a civilian.

Assuming also that one survived the war, which despite the continuing good news from the East, looked like going on for up to another four years, that would have meant more than nine years' flying, and I began to feel that I'd had enough. At first it seemed to be a sort of mild apathy, but apathy is mental indolence, and my brain wasn't indolent, it was anti-flying. Maybe, I reasoned, it's anti-backseat flying and to rationalise this feeling, organised trips in our various dual-control aircraft. Charles ('Daddy') Gibb, who had replaced 'Kit' Nicholson as Wings, took me up in the station flight Tiger Moth, Tony Kennard, the CFI and Keith Haskins of Communications in the Stinson Reliant. But airborne musical chairs wasn't the answer, it was a feeling that I'd had enough. Mild, but still there, and I knew from experience that an aviator with that feeling is eventually going to kill not only himself but also possibly one or two of his squadron mates as well.

In the RAF there were set limits for aircrew on operations, usually 25 operational missions before a rest period. In some Commands, such as Bomber, these were extremely difficult to attain, possibly Fighter Command too. The Navy didn't do it that way, so aircrew went on until they got what is known as 'The Twitch', ie the nerves become distinctly ragged. The only solution was to report sick and undergo a medical board. This was not unreasonable, but an insensitive Admiralty could well approve an aviator being taken off flying, but mark his record 'LMF' which stood for 'Lack of Moral Fibre'; and so perpetuate what they sought to avoid, since few red-blooded aviators were likely to want that comment on their record.

Lately a new approach had been made, with doctors trained to detect the changes in their charges and to understand the fears and phobias of those who flew. We had such a doctor at Inskip, but I didn't go to him because I was Gerry Woods, the chap who had taken on all the weird jobs Their Lordships had thought up, and had made a fair fist of them all. Sometimes it had seemed a bit of a game, testing each others' breaking point. I began to wear two faces, one at home, another on duty, becoming snappy and short-tempered at home, always the laughing boy at Inskip. One day we had a tearful scene at home, eventually analysing the situation into the fact that it wasn't really being scared for myself, but worrying about what would happen to those I left behind should the Old Grim Reaper beckon me. We agreed that I should carry on, limiting my flying to the necessary, and re-examine the situation when my new appointment came along.

Strangely enough, it all passed when we received the first batch of ex-prisoners of war for retraining. Among those coming to Inskip were several old chums – Eric Margetts, Idwald 'Taff' Evans, 'Clog' Taylor, all of whom had been 'in the bag' with my brother-in-law, Earle White of the RCAF. A delightful addition too was Johnny Olsen, shot down at Petsamo who had been four long and boring years looking at the barbed wire from the inside, which seemed to have increased rather than decreased his sense of humour. He told of the ways the 'Kriegies' had outwitted the camp guards and security (known as 'Goons') assembling their escape equipment right under their noses. Pullovers were sent in, saturated with dark dye that could be washed out, collected, and used to re-dye blankets, which were then cut into facsimile *Wehrmacht* uniforms. Unfortunately John was wearing one at an unscheduled 'Appel' or muster, and stood in the rain with the dye pouring out of the garment, yet the 'Goons' didn't notice. Gardening equipment came in through the Red Cross, and was easily adapted to tunnelling tools. Even the powdered milk tins when empty were used to construct primitive air-conditioning for the escape tunnels.

He was so uninhibited that we recruited him as a guest lecturer in our training programme, advising the 'sprogs' in the squadrons forming up – and the seniors too – on how to escape, survive and be a general bloody nuisance to one's captors. I began to think very seriously that if these people could live through four years of unremitting gloom in a PoW camp, underfed, ill-clothed, with little or no social life, yet come back for re-training, then by God, so could I get through this black period. It should be said that, unhappily, Johnnie Olsen was killed a few months later carrying out his deck-landings on an escort carrier, but at that time, he brought me down to earth.

Many changes occurred over the next few months. John Heath departed to command another air station, and was relieved by Captain H G Scott, in whose appointment Inskip was again fortunate, despite his being a non-aviator. Newly-formed squadrons, both Firefly and Avenger, passed through at an increasing rate, some led by old shipmates such as Bob Woolston and Alan Swanton. So the time for my decision came nearer, at which point we'd give it a try, and if it didn't work, no fooling around, straight to the doctor. There'd be no fear of Fear itself for me.

But suddenly it didn't matter any more. I don't remember the exact occasion, but we had a dining-in night, unusual, but not unknown. It isn't impossible that it was sheer coincidence, nor equally that the Captain knew something we juniors didn't, but the latter is unlikely. During dinner he received a signal, and waiting decently for the end of the course, stood and announced that the first atomic bomb (as they were known in those days) had been dropped on Hiroshima, and an ultimatum had been delivered to the Japanese with the promise of a second bomb on Nagasaki in three days' time. We stood and cheered, not having the faintest idea what an atomic bomb was, but so long as it would end the war quickly, who cared about technical detail? How our education has progressed since that day!

So I did continue flying right up to my demobilisation in January 1946, when my personal war ended. In all, it was 6½ years, and that was over 40 years ago. I am still trying to fathom what it is that makes me keep in touch with friends of those days, meeting them on regrettably too few occasions, and talking as if it were all only yesterday.

Psychologists and other clever people will tell us that it's something to do with the formation of 'bonds', the sharing of experiences, both good and bad. Others suggest that it comes of a retarded adolescence, but to me it goes much deeper. I spent more than this 6½ years at school, yet when I do – rarely – meet old school friends, I am groping for conversation after five to ten minutes. One enormous international company employed me for 24 years, 18 of them in the same city but with few exceptions I can meet with former colleagues and maybe chat for half an hour, after which it's all over. We have exhausted our personal reminiscences. With old flying mates I can go on for hours, sometimes days, never seeming to exhaust the vein of remembrance, and boring the pants off everyone else present.

The fact defies analysis, and when brought to task for 'swinging the lamp', I may politely desist, but my unspoken reply will never vary.

Those who for various reasons – youth being the most likely – have not experienced the camaraderie which we enjoyed, have missed a way of life that probably will never recur. To feel the chilling cleanliness of a desert dawn or a Mediterranean sunset – certainly a Cook's tour will give you these same things, but they can never give you the same emotional reactions they gave us unless you are fortunate enough to have as companions the splendid people I have known. People who would have risked their lives for me, as I would risk mine for them. So it is not possible to savour these treasured memories, which are said to be boring and old-fashioned, but in fact are nothing of the sort. They are reaffirmation of the affection and trust we had for each other, and still have. Not one of my old flying mates ever let me down.

Never again shall we know the thrill of standing in the open cockpit of a Swordfish, high over the Atlantic, straining back to the ship in a 40 knot headwind, or off China Bay as the sun is setting, chilled to the marrow, but loving the job and the people with whom we share it. Knowing as we stand there, with one-sixteenth of an inch of fabric under that lightweight aluminium floor between us and the freezing ocean 5000ft below that this is just about as insecure as a man can possibly be. At any minute the engine may stop, the radio won't work when it is needed, but we know that if everything goes wrong, they'll come looking for us, and in all probability find us.

You'll never enjoy the small things the way we did: the smell of the dewy grass on a summer morning in Hampshire; the golden beauty of a Scottish autumn dusk or that elysian feeling as the flightdeck party takes the wire out of the arrestor hook and relaxation begins to warm the spirit after five hours' patrolling and searching.

You'll never be lucky enough to experience these emotions, and above all, you will never have the friends whom I have still, 'Jock', 'Prune', 'Dusty', 'Klondyke', 'Tony', 'Davy' and 'Pussy' and 'Scruffy', with many others, most of whom I haven't seen for years, but hear of from time to time, knowing that if we meet tomorrow it will be just as if we'd spoken only yesterday, except that yesterday was over 40 years ago

And you could never know friends like the ones I'll never see again – Paddy, Swede, Hughie, Murray, Bobbie, Eddie and Harry. Because their sort isn't made any more, and that's why I always have an unmanly weep whenever their tune is played – that beautiful sailors' hymn – 'Eternal Father, strong to save'.

The HQ Staff of RNAS Inskip (HMS *Nightjar*) on 9 January 1945. Back row: Lieutenants (A) RNVR J D Kelsall (CO 760 Hurricane Squadron); W Gill and Kenny Nicholson (Fighter Direction Officers); Lindsay Polwin (Decklanding Control Officer). Front row: Lieutenant-Commanders (A) G A Woods DSC RNVR (Air Staff Officer); J A Ievers OBE, RN (Chief Flying Instructor); Commander (A) Kit Nicholson RNVR ('Wings') Lieutenant-Commanderr E B ('Digger') Morgan RANVR (CO 766 Swordfish Squadron); and Second Officer Kilminster (WRNS Staff Officer). *Author's collection*

Glossary

ADT Here a dummy torpedo is carried, to accustom the pilot and crew to the weight and effect of a warload. Drill otherwise as for ALT.

AFHQ Allied Forces Headquarters.

AIO Air Information Office.

ALT Aerial Light Torpedo attack. In this exercise a marker is dropped to simulate the point of entry of the torpedo. A synchronised camera in the aircraft photographs the target simultaneously, so that skilled assessors can estimate the height, range, and probability of a hit.

AOR Air Operations Room, where Commander (Operations) who is normally an observer, plans all flying operations, and keeps track of all shipping and aircraft in the area. Situated adjacent to the bridge.

ART Nearest to the real thing, except that the torpedo contains a buoyancy chamber instead of explosives. After running normally, the torpedo surfaces, floats, and is recovered to be used again.

A/S Anti-submarine.

ASKARI Arabic word for African native soldier or policeman, specifically in the King's African Rifles.

ASV Air to Surface Vessel radar. The first airborne equipment.

BANDIT R/T code for enemy aircraft. 'Bogey' or 'Rats' also used.

BARRACK STANCHION One who is not drafted to seagoing ships, usually for compassionate reasons, eg permanently sick wife etc, but more usually applied to those who use various subterfuges to avoid being drafted to sea.

BATSMAN Officially 'Deck Landing Control Officer' or DLCO responsible for bringing aircraft down on to the flightdeck. So called because his signals are made with paddles resembling large ping-pong bats.

BIGSWORTH BOARD The observer's chartboard (designed in World War I), about 2ft 6in square, with built-in 360-degree protractor and parallel rule.

CFI Chief Flying Instructor.

CO Commanding Officer.

COMB TRACKS To turn towards torpedoes in the hope of avoiding their hitting the ship while she is broadside on, ie presenting a smaller target.

CPO Chief Petty Officer.

CRABFAT The Navy's pet-name for RAF personnel. Derived from sailors' slang for regulation grey paint, which crustaceans are said to feast upon.

D/F Direction Finding. Equipment used to trace origin of radio transmissions. If two stations some distance apart can both obtain a 'cut' the exact position of the originator can be found.

ETA Estimated Time of Arrival.

FDO Fighter Direction Office or Officer. Duties of the latter in the former are to direct carrier aircraft, usually fighters, to targets detected by radar equipment. Used also to home lost aircraft.

DSB Originally 'Duty Steam Boat', but in World War II a motor-boat kept standing by for messages and routine work.

DSC Distinguished Service Cross, instituted in 1914 for RN officers below the rank of captain and for Warrant Officers.

DSM Distinguished Service Medal, instituted in 1914 for all petty officers and ·ratings of the RN, NCOs and men of the Royal Marines and since 1942 for the Merchant Navy.

DSO Distinguished Service Order, instituted in 1886 for conspicuous service in action by commissioned officers of HM services (and since 1942 for the Merchant Navy).

FAA Fleet Air Arm, successor of the 1914-18 Royal Naval Air Service, actually so-named in 1924. Its aircraft remained under RAF control from 1 April 1918 until May 1937. At the outbreak of war it had only 250 aircraft to operate from 7 carriers and another 90 land-based. There were only 700 aircrew (300 pilots) in 20 squadrons. By late 1944 these were 3300 pilots plus 2500 observers. In mid-1945 all personnel totalled over 70,000, operational carriers 49, shore establishments 56 and aircraft 3700 (1336 front line).

FLIGHTDECK OFFICER Responsible to Commander Flying for all flightdeck matters, ranging, spotting, aircraft handling, catapulting off, flying off, batting on. Next to the Captain and Departmental Heads, a most critical job.

GONG A decoration, usually for bravery, eg DSO, DSC, DSM etc.

GOON Generally, someone not too bright. Specifically, guards in PoW camps.

GOOFERS Strictly speaking any coin de vantage in an aircraft carrier, where those not flying can watch those who are. Later in the war, with faster and more dangerous aircraft, 'goofing' became forbidden, and kamikazes finally ended the sport.

IFF An electronic device fitted to aircraft which on the radar screen 'indicates friend or foe' to those below.

ISLAND The whole of the carrier's bridge superstructure.

KG5 Naval shorthand for the battleship *King George V.*

Kriegie Kriegsgefangener – German for Prisoner-of-War.

LADDER A gunnery term. 'Up ladder' would order that the guns' range should be lengthened, 'Down ladder' that it should be reduced.

MAKEE-LEARN As the name implies, a junior under instruction.

MP Military Police.

NA2SL Naval Assistant to the Second Sea Lord. This officer – usually a Captain RN is responsible for all officers' appointments.

OBSERVER I can only hope that after reading this book you realise the numerous duties officers (and petty officers) of this persuasion are called upon to perform. No wonder they are acknowledged to be the Brains of the Fleet Air Arm.

OERLIKON A multi-purpose, quick-firing short-range 20mm weapon, manufactured in several sizes and magazine-fed. Operated by one man.

OWNER Affectionate name for the ship's captain.

PO Petty Officer.

PONGO The dictionary says 'a large anthropoid African ape', but here a pet-name for our friends in the Army, and sometimes for our own soldiers, the Royal Marines. Probably derived because of the soldier's known lack of ability when waterborne.

POMPOM Multi-barrelled, short-range anti-aircraft weapon firing a 2lb shell. Nicknamed the 'Chicago Piano'.

POM/POMMIE Pet-name for Britons used by New Zealanders and Australians.

RN 'A' Fleet Air Arm officers on short-service commissions. Some entered as pupil pilots and observers, others were pilots transferred from the RAF.

RNC The Royal Naval College at Greenwich.

RNAS Royal Naval Air Station.

RNR Royal Naval Reserve. Mainly Merchant Navy officers. Also know as 'Rockies' because of their double-wavy interlaced stripes of rank. Formed in 1859 and absorbed the RNVR in 1958.

RNVR Royal Naval Volunteer Reserve. The 'Wavy Navy' of 1903-1958.

RNZNVR Royal New Zealand Naval Volunteer Reserve.

R/T Radio-telephone, used for short-range communication air to air, air to ship and ship to ship.

ROUND-DOWN The after-end of the flightdeck, angled slightly to aid landing-on.

RPO Regulating Petty Officer. Usually from the Seaman Branch, and in ships and squadrons responsible for disciplinary and welfare matters.

SHAEF Supreme Headquarters Allied Expeditionary Force, established 8 August 1942 by General Dwight D Eisenhower at Norfolk House, St James's Square, London and dissolved 14 July 1945.

SHAGBAT Affectionate name for the Supermarine 'Walrus' amphibian aircraft (see Appendix I). Widely used in cruisers and battleships for reconnaissance and spotting for gunfire. Also employed ashore as air/sea rescue aircraft.

SNOTTIE A midshipman. So called because the original uniform included brass buttons on the sleeve, said to prevent midshipmen from wiping their noses thereon.

SQUIRTED Catapulted off.

STEP-ASIDE SEARCH A reconnaissance aircraft would fly on a course, searching both sides to visibility or radar distance. At the turning-point, the pilot would steer 90 degrees to port or starboard as ordered, for double the visibility distance, then turning on to a course reciprocal to the original outward course, effectively covering a wide area economically.

STRINGBAG Affectionate name for the Fairey Swordfish, derived, it is said, from the old ladies' string shopping bag which could be expanded and expanded to hold more and more.

SUB-FLIGHT Formation of two or three aircraft.

TAG Telegraphist Airgunner. Duties as the name implies.

TANNOY Ship's broadcasting system.

TBR Torpedo-bomber-reconnaissance aircraft. Originally they were called TSR, ie torpedo-spotter-reconnaissance, but spotting for ships' guns, though envisaged by the battleship lobby before World War II was in fact carried out very rarely.

VERY LIGHT A pyrotechnic cartridge fired from a wide-mouthed pistol and named after its 1877 inventor. Various colours would indicate the recognition signal, reds and greens wre used to indicate various stages of emergency in decklanding. White was not infrequently used to illuminate a target at night.

VICKERS GO A light air-cooled 0.303in machine gun fitted in single or twin mountings in the rear of aircraft. GO indicates gas-operated, ie the gas released on firing each round activates the mechanism to fire the next.

'WINGS' Commander Flying. The most senior pilot on board, who, with Commander Operations, advises the Captain on all flying matters.

WOP/AG RAF equivalent of TAG. Wireless Operator/Air Gunner.

W/T Wireless-telegraphy. Transmission of signals by Morse key.

YARPIE Affectionate name for a South African in the Royal Navy. Believed to emanate from the fact that so many of them are of Dutch extraction and bore the baptismal name 'Jaap', pronounced 'Yarp'.

Appendix I

FAIREY SWORDFISH

Role Torpedo-bomber-reconnaissance
First flew 17 April 1934

In service July 1936 – July 1945 (first embarked with 825 and 811 Squadrons in *Glorious* and *Furious*, 13 squadrons equipped by 1939 rising to 25 front line and 22 second line with 11 catapult flights)

Dimensions 45ft 5in span (17ft 3in with wings folded), 36ft 3in long, 12ft 10in high (12ft 4in with wings folded), 607 sq ft wing area

Maximum weight 9250lb (4.1 tons)

Powerplant Bristol Pegasus III M3 engine, 690 hp at 4750ft, Pegasus XXX (750hp) in late Mark II and Mark III

Maximum speed 100kts (115 mph) at 4750ft

Range 450nm at 91kts (104mph), 896nm at 91kts with 93 gallon additional 'marathon' tank

Fuel capacity 143 gallons

Rate of climb 10 minutes to 5000ft, 565ft per minute at sea level

Service ceiling 12,400ft

Crew 2 or 3

Deck distance for take off 540ft with 20kt wind over deck, 345ft with 30kt wind

Take off stall speed 64kts (73mph)

Landing stall speed 54kts (62mph)

Landing weight 8120lb (3.6 tons)

Armament 2 x 0.303in Vickers GO MG; 1 x 18in Mark XIIB 1610lb torpedo or 3 x 500lb or 6 x 250lb bombs or 8 x 60lb rockets or 1 x 1610lb mine 'A' or 4 x 250lb depth charges .

Total built 2392 (692 by early 1940, 1080 Mark II in 1942-44 with strengthened bottom mainplane to fire rockets, 320 Mark III which had ASV Mk XI radar between the undercarriage legs)

FAIREY ALBACORE

Role Torpedo-bomber-reconnaissance

First flew 12 December 1938

In service March 1940 – December 1943 (embarked with 826, the first unit, and 829 Squadrons in *Formidable*, November 1940, a maximum of 15 FAA squadrons plus 1 RAF and 1 RCAF in 1942)

Dimensions 50ft span (17ft 9in with wings folded), 39 ft 10in long, 15ft 3in high (12ft 6in with wings folded), 607sq ft wing area

Maximum weight 11,186lb (4.99 tons)

Powerplant Bristol Taurus II or XII, 1085hp at take off, 1130hp dash

Maximum speed 150kts (172mph) at 5000ft

Range 550nm at 130kts (149.5mph), 900nm at 100kts (115mph) with 120 gallon additional tank

Fuel capacity 193 gallons

Combat radius 180nm

Rate of climb 8 minutes to 6000ft

Service ceiling 20,700ft

Crew 3

Armament 2 x 0.303in Vickers GO MG; 1 x 18in Mark XII torpedo or 4 x 500lb or 6 x 250lb or 12 x 100lb or 4 Mark VII or 6 Mk XI depth charges

Total built 800

FAIREY BARRACUDA

Role Torpedo-bomber-reconnaissance

First flew 7 December 1940

In service January 1943 – 1953 (first with 827 Squadron, 12 squadrons by 1944)

Dimensions 49ft 2in span (17ft 7½in with wings folded), 39ft 9in long, 15ft 1in high (12ft 3in with wings folded), 414 sq ft wing area

Maximum weight 18,200lb (8.1 tons)

Powerplant Rolls Royce Merlin XXXII, 1640hp normal at 1750ft (Mark II)

Maximum speed 150kts (172mph)

Range 596nm at 150kts, 1000nm at 145kts (166mph) with 116 gallon additional tank

Fuel capacity 226 gallons

Rate of climb 6 minutes to 5000ft, 850ft per minute at 1350ft (minimum combat height)

Service ceiling 18,200ft

Deck distance for take off 805ft with 20kt wind over deck, 600ft with 30kt wind

Take off stall speed 71kts (81mph)

Landing stall speed 65kts (74mph)

Landing weight 12,321lb (5.5 tons)

Armament 2 x 0.303in Vickers K MG; 1 x 18in Mark XII 1610lb torpedo or 3 x 500lb or 6 x 250lb bombs or 4 x 450lb depth charges

Total built 2572 (Marks I-III, only 25 Mk I with 1260hp Merlin XXX engine, mostly Mark II)

BLACKBURN SKUA

Role Fighter/dive-bomber-reconnaissance

First flew February 1937

In service late 1938 – August 1941 (first with 800 and 803 Squadrons)

Dimensions 46ft 2in span (16ft 2in with folded wings), 35 ft 7in long, 14ft 2in (with wings folded), 312 sq ft wing area

Maximum weight 8320lb (3.7 tons)

Powerplant Bristol Perseus XII, 620hp normal, 830hp take off, 905hp dash

Maximum speed 196 kts (225mph) at 6700ft, 177kts (203 mph) at sea level

Range 760nm

Endurance 4½ hours at 125-143kts (143-164mph) at 15,000ft

Fuel capacity 163 gallons

Rate of climb 43 minutes to 20,000ft, 740ft per minute at sea level

Service ceiling 19,100ft

Crew 2

Armament 5 x 0.303in MG (4 Vickers, 1 Lewis), 1 x 500lb bomb

Total built 192

FAIREY FULMAR

Role Fighter

First flew 13 January 1937 (Mark II in January 1941)

In service June 1940 – March 1945 (first with 808 Squadron at Worthy Down, peak of 14 squadrons in 1942, few night fighters by 1945)

Dimensions 46ft span, 40ft 2in long, 11ft 6in, 377 sq ft wing area

Weight 10,350lb (4.6 tons)

Powerplant Rolls Royce Merlin XXX engine, 1260hp at 7250ft (Mark I Merlin VIII, 1080hp)

Maximum speed 231.3kts (265mph) at 9600ft

Range 691nm at 152kts (174mph)

Fuel capacity 155 gallons

Service ceiling 23,900ft

Crew 2

Deck distance for take off 420ft with 20kt wind over deck, 260ft with 30kt wind

Armament 8 x 0.303in Browning MG, 2 x 250lb bombs

Total built 600 (350 Mark II, last delivered February 1943)

HAWKER SEA HURRICANE

Role Fighter

In service July 1941 aboard *Furious* (19 squadrons equipped at one time or another)

Dimensions 40ft span, 31ft 4in long, 10ft 5in high, 258 sq ft wing area

Maximum weight 7015lb (3.1 tons)

Powerplant Rolls Royce Merlin III, 1030hp (840hp at 16,250ft), Mark IC and IIC Merlin XX

Maximum speed 267.8kts (307 mph) at 9600ft

Range 482.6nm at 180.9kts (208mph), 957nm at 181kts with 90-gallon drop tanks

Combat radius 200nm

Fuel capacity 97 gallons

Rate of climb 10 minutes to 20,000ft

Service ceiling 32,700ft

Crew 1

Deck distance for take off 400ft with 20kt wind over deck, 270ft with 30kt wind

Landing stall speed about 75kts (86 mph)

Landing weight 6100lb (2.7 tons)

Armament 8 x 0.303in Browning MG (Mark IB), 4 x 20mm cannon (Mark IC and IIC), 2 x 250lb bombs

Total built about 800 conversions (last delivery August 1943)

GRUMMAN MARTLET (US WILDCAT F4F)

Role Fighter

First flew September 1937

In service September 1940 (first with 804 Squadron at Hatston, Mark II first in carriers from September 1941, used by 13 squadrons, by mid-1944 Mark IV and V being flown by 15 squadrons)

Dimensions 38ft span (14ft 4in with wings folded), 29ft long, 10ft high (9ft 2½in with wings folded), 260 sq ft wing area (all data for Mark IV)

Maximum weight 7975lb (3.5 tons)

Powerplant Pratt & Whitney Twin Wasp R-1830-86, 1100hp normal, 1200hp at take-off

Maximum speed 278.3kts (320mph) at 18,800ft, 238.3kts (274mph) at sea level

Range 722nm at 140kts (161mph), 1109nm at 133kts (153mph) with 2 x 58 gallon (US) drop tanks

Combat radius 91nm

Fuel capacity 120 gallons

Rate of climb 5.6 minutes to 10,000ft, 12.4 minutes to 20,000ft, 3650ft per minute at sea level

Service ceiling 34,000ft

Crew 1

Deck distance for take off 640ft with no wind over deck, 278ft with 25kt wind

Take off stall speed 70.6kts (81mph)

Landing stall speed 66.7kts (76mph)

Armament 6 x 0.50in MG (4 in Marks I-III), 2 x 100lb bombs

Total delivered over 863 (91 Mark I in 1940-1, 220 Mark IV from 1942, 312 Mark V from 1943, 340 Mark VI from late 1944)

SUPERMARINE SEAFIRE

Role Fighter

In service June 1942 – 1954 (equipped 12 squadrons by August 1945)

Dimensions 32ft 7in span, 30ft long, 13ft high, 232 sq ft wing area (all data for the LIIC low-altitude version of the Seafire IIC)

Maximum weight 7006lb (3.1 tons)

Powerplant Rolls Royce Merlin XLVI, 1415hp at 14,000ft

Maximum speed 295kts (340mph) at 6000ft, 275kts (316mph) at sea level

Range 440nm at 192kts (220mph), 600nm at 190kts with 1 x 45-gallon drop tank

Combat radius 140nm

Fuel capacity 85 gallons

Rate of climb 5 minutes to 15,000ft, 8 minutes to 20,000ft, 4380ft per minute at sea level

Service ceiling 24,000ft

Crew 1

Deck distance for take off 225ft with 30kt wind

Armament 2 x 20mm cannon, 2 x 0.303in Browning MG, up to 1500lb (3 x 500lb) of bombs etc

Total built over 1666 (156 Mark IB in 1941-42, 400 Mark IIC from September 1942, 1100+ Mark III from April 1943, some Mark XV with Griffin engine by VJ-Day)

FAIREY FIREFLY

Role Fighter-reconnaissance

First flew 22 December 1941

In service 1943-1956

Dimensions 44ft 5in span (13ft 5in with wings folded), 37ft long, 13ft 7in high (12ft 3in with wings folded), 328 sq ft wing area (data for Mark I)

Maximum weight 12,131lb (5.4 tons)

Powerplant Rolls Royce Griffon II, 1735hp at take off, 1495hp supercharged

Maximum speed 277.4kts (319mph) at 17,000ft, 257.4kts (296mph) at 3500ft

Range 671.3nm at 187.8kts (216mph), 1186nm at 188kts with 2 x 50 gallon drop tanks

Fuel capacity 192 gallons

Rate of climb 9.6 minutes to 15,000ft, 2260ft per minute at sea level for combat

Service ceiling 29,700ft

Crew 2

Deck distance for take off 490ft with 20kt wind, 330ft with 30kt wind

Take off stall speed 71kts (81mph)

Landing stall speed 62kts (71mph)

Landing weight 10,290lb (4.6 tons)

Armament 4 x 20mm cannon, 2 x 500lb bombs, 8 x 60lb rocket projectiles

Total built 1515 (870 Mark I by 1946, 160 Mark IV, 485 Mark V and VI till 1951)

GRUMMAN HELLCAT (US F6F)

Role Fighter/dive-bomber

First flew 26 June 1942

In service July 1943 – August 1945 (first with 800 Squadron, replacing its Sea Hurricanes and embarked in escort carrier *Emperor*, 12 squadrons by VJ-Day)

Dimensions 42ft 10in span (16ft 2in with wings folded), 33ft 7in long, 14ft 5in high (12ft 6in with wings folded), 334 sq ft wing area (all data for Mark II)

Maximum weight 13,797lb (6.1 tons)

Powerplant Pratt & Whitney P-2800-10W, 1675hp normal, 1000hp take off, 2135hp dash

Maximum speed 330kts (379mph) at 23,400ft, 276kts (317mph) at sea level

Range 950nm, 1339nm at 148.7kts (171mph) with 1 x 125 gallon drop tank

Combat radius 375nm

Fuel capacity 208 gallons

Rate of climb 5.2 minutes to 10,000ft, 7.9 minutes at combat rating to 20,000ft

Service ceiling 35,100ft

Crew 1

Deck distance for take off 799ft with no wind, 384ft with 25kt wind

Take off stall speed 79.2kts (91mph)

Landing stall speed 72.2kts (83mph)

Armament 4 x 0.50in MG (400rpg), 2 x 20mm cannon, 2 x 1000lb bombs or 1 x 18in torpedo or 6 x 60lb rockets

Total delivered 1182 (252 Mark I, 930 Mark II)

CHANCE VOUGHT CORSAIR (US F4U)

Role Fighter-bomber

First flew 29 May 1940

In service June 1943 – August 1946 (first with 1830 Squadron in USA, 19 squadrons by early 1945)

Dimensions 41ft span (17ft 1in with wings folded), 33ft 8in long, 15ft 1in high (16ft 4in with wings folded), 314 sq ft wing area (all data for Corsair I)

Maximum weight 13,597lb (6 tons)

Powerplant Pratt & Whitney R-2800-18W, 1700hp normal, 2100hp take off

Maximum speed 393kts (451mph) at 20,500ft, 325kts (373mph) at sea level

Range 1005nm at 185kts (212mph), 1300nm at 180kts with 2 x 125 gallon drop tanks

Combat radius 525nm

Fuel capacity 194 gallons

Rate of climb 4.2 minutes to 10,000ft, 8.8 minutes to 20,000ft, 4770ft per minute dash at sea level

Service ceiling 38,400ft

Crew 1

Deck distance for take off 790ft with no wind, 377ft with 25kt wind

Take off stall speed 81kts (93mph)

Landing stall speed 66.9kts (77mph)

Armament 6 x 0.50in MG (400rpg), 2 x 500lb or 2 x 1000lb bombs or 2 x 11.75in AR plus 8 HVAR

Total delivered 2012

GRUMMAN AVENGER (US TBF1, TBM1, TBM3)

Role Torpedo-bomber-reconnaissance

First flew 1 August 1941

In service April 1943 – June 1946 (first with 832 Squadron, embarked in USS *Saratoga*, then HMS *Victorious*)

Dimensions 54ft 2in span, (19ft with wings folded), 41ft long, 15ft 8in high (13ft 9in with wings folded), 490 sq ft wing area (all data Mark III)

Maximum weight 16,761lb (7.4 tons)

Powerplant Wright Cyclone GR-2600-8, 1600hp normal, 1800hp take off, 1750hp dash

Maximum speed 232kts (266mph) at 15,000ft, 219.1kts (251mph) at sea level

Range 983nm at 131kts (150mph), 2200nm at 125kts (143mph) with a 228 gallon tank in the bomb bay and 2 x 83 gallon wing tanks

Combat radius 183nm

Fuel capacity 278 gallons

Rate of climb 10.7 minutes to 10,000ft, 30 minutes to 20,000ft, 1170ft per minute at sea level

Service ceiling 22,600ft

Crew 3

Deck distance for take off 1106ft with no wind, 455ft with 25kts wind

Take off stall speed 67.7kts (77mph)

Landing stall speed 63.4kts (73mph)

Armament 5 x 0.5in in Browning MG, 1 x 22in torpedo or 2000lb bomb or 2 x 1000lb or 4 x 500lb or 8 x 60lb rockets

Total delivered 958 (402 Mark I, 334 Mark II, 222 Mark III)

VICKERS-SUPERMARINE WALRUS

Role Spotter-reconnaissance-air sea rescue

First flew 21 June 1933

In service Summer 1936 – June 1946 (216 ordered in 1935-36 for battleships and cruisers, all catapult flights part of 700 Squadron)

Dimensions 45ft 11in span, 37ft 3in long, 15ft 3in high, 610 sq ft wing area

Maximum weight 7610lb (4900lb empty)

Powerplant Bristol Pegasus, 775hp

Maximum speed 135mph at 4750ft, 95mph cruising

Range 600nm

Service ceiling 18,500ft

Crew 3

Armament 2 or 3 x 0.303in Vickers K MG, bombs or depth charges

Total built 740 (287 Mark I by Supermarine in wood, 453 Mark II by Saunders-Roe in metal by January 1944)

Appendix II

HMS *ARK ROYAL*

Built by Cammell Laird of Birkenhead

Laid down 16 September 1935

Launched 13 April 1937

Commissioned 16 November 1938

Displacement 22,000 tons standard, 27,720 tons deep load

Dimensions 800ft long overall, 685ft at waterline, 106ft 9in maximum beam, 94ft 9in at waterline, 27ft 9in draught at deep load, 22ft 9in mean

Machinery 3-shaft Parsons geared turbines, 6 Admiralty 3-drum boilers, 102,000 shaft horsepower = 31 kts

Oil fuel 4443 tons

Range 7600nm at 12kts, 4300nm at 20kts.

Armour 2½-3½in armour deck, 4½in belt

Gun armament 8 twin 4.5in/45 calibre QF Mark I high angle, 48 x 2pdr (6 x8) pompom, 8 quadruple 0.5in machine guns, 4 x 3pdr saluting

Flightdeck dimensions 797ft x 96ft

Catapults 2 forward able to launch a 12,000lb aircraft

Hangar dimensions 568ft (upper), 452ft (lower) x 60ft

Hangar height 16ft

Cross-deck arrestor wires 11

Lifts 3 (2 of 45ft x 22ft to starboard at each end of the hangar, 1 of 45ft x 25ft to port amidships)

Aircraft 12 fighters and 48 torpedo bombers (full establishment, originally 72), Began the war with 40 aircraft, had 54 with Force H August 1940 – April 1941, ie 30 Swordfish, 12 Skuas and 12 Fulmars. From April it was 30 Swordfish and 24 Fulmars

Aviation fuel 100,000 gallons

Complement 858 ship, 742 air group. Total 1600

Weight breakdown Hull (including personnel weight and stores) 13,651 tons, equipment 1382 tons, armour 2854 tons, machinery 2468 tons, armament 1042 tons, aeronautics (aircraft, their fuel and weapon loads plus support equipment) 1629 tons. Total 23,026 tons

Fate Torpedoed by *U-81* (one hit) 50nm east of Gibraltar on the afternoon of 13 November 1941 and sank at dawn on the 14th in sight of the Rock. The torpedo hit was deep on the starboard side and bottom abreast the starboard boiler room making a hole 130ft x 30ft and causing violent vertical oscillations with an immediate 10° list. Flooding spread and eventually reached the middle and then the port boiler room via the smoke ducts which had no baffles and were taken across the ship too low down. Electric power failed as there were no diesel dynamos, and after 14 hours the ship capsized.

APPENDICES

ILLUSTRIOUS CLASS

HMS *VICTORIOUS*	HMS *FORMIDABLE*
Built by Vickers-Armstrong, Tyne	Harland & Wolff, Belfast
Laid down 14 May 1937	17 June 1937
Launched 14 September 1939	17 August 1939
Commissioned 15 May 1941	24 November 1940

Displacement 23,207 tons standard, 28,619 tons

Dimensions 753ft 3in long overall, 673ft at waterline, 106ft 9in maximum beam, 95ft 9in at waterline, 28ft 2in draught at deep load

Machinery as *Ark Royal*, 111,000 shaft horsepower = 30.5kts

Oil fuel 4854 tons

Range 11,000nm at 14kts

Armour 4½in belt, 4½in hangar side, 3in flightdeck, 2½in-3in hangar deck (to be proof against 500lb bombs and 6in shells)

Gun armament 8 twin 4.5in/45 calibre QF Mark III high angle, 48 x 2pdr (6 x 8) pompom. *Illustrious* finished the war with 40 x 2pdr, 3 x 40mm Bofors and 52 x 20mm Oerlikon. *Formidable* added 12 Bofors and 34 Oerlikons

Flightdeck dimensions 740ft x 95ft 9in

Catapult 1 forward and to port, able to launch a 14,000lb aircraft

Hangar dimensions 458ft x 62ft

Hangar height 16ft

Cross-deck arrestor wires 6

Lifts 2 (each 45ft x 22ft bow and stern amidships)

Aircraft 12 fighters and 18 torpedo bombers (nominal). *Victorious* had 6 Fulmars and 9 Swordfish for the *Bismarck* pursuit, 12 Fulmars and 21 Albacores for the Kirkenes strike. *Formidable* began operations with the same air group. *Victorious* had 38 aircraft (18 Fulmars, 6 Hurricanes, 14 Albacores) for Operation 'Pedestal' in August 1942. *Formidable* had 44 in the Indian Ocean that year (16 Martlets, 21 Albacores, 1 Swordfish, 6 Seafires). Both ships had 42 planes for Operation 'Torch', each having 6 Seafires, *Formidable* carried 24 Martlets to *Victorious*' 12 with 6 Fulmars and 12 Albacores to her sister's 18. *Formidable* operated 49 planes (5 Seafires, 32 Martlets and 12 Albacores) at Salerno. *Victorious* flew 39 Corsairs off Sabang on 25 July 1944, then 28 with 21 Barracudas of 822 Squadron for two subsequent Indian Ocean strikes. Her early 1945 air group numbered 32-34 Corsairs and 21 Avengers plus 2 Walruses. Off Japan she carried the latter, 16 Avengers and 37 Corsairs. *Formidable* carried 54 aircraft in the Pacific Fleet (36 Corsairs and 18 Avengers reduced to 12 when 6 Hellcats were embarked)

Aviation fuel 51,000 gallons

Complement 842 ship, 434 air group. Total 1276 (about 2000 by 1945)

Weight breakdown Hull 12,724 tons, equipment 1264 tons, armour 4941 tons, machinery 2464 tons, armament 997 tons, aeronautics (see *Ark Royal*) 1186 tons. Total 24,576 tons

Fates Both ships survived 2 kamikaze hits in May 1945, operating normally within a few hours. *Victorious* sold in July 1969 to be broken up at Faslane, *Formidable* likewise in November 1953 (Inverkeithing).

271

INDEX